Promises to Keep

Originally published in the series:

ORGANIZATION OF
AMERICAN HISTORIANS BICENTENNIAL
ESSAYS ON THE BILL OF RIGHTS

By General Editor
Kermit L. Hall

With Editorial Board
Michal R. Belknap

Harold M. Hyman

R. Kent Newmeyer

William M. Wiecek

Promises to Keep

*African Americans
and the Constitutional Order,
1776 to the Present*

Second Edition

DONALD G. NIEMAN

OXFORD

UNIVERSITY PRESS

OXFORD
UNIVERSITY PRESS

Oxford University Press is a department of the University of Oxford. It furthers the University's objective of excellence in research, scholarship, and education by publishing worldwide. Oxford is a registered trade mark of Oxford University Press in the UK and certain other countries.

Published in the United States of America by Oxford University Press
198 Madison Avenue, New York, NY 10016, United States of America.

© Oxford University Press 2020

Library of Congress Cataloging-in-Publication Data
Names: Nieman, Donald G., author.
Title: Promises to keep : African Americans and the constitutional order,
1776 to the present / Donald G Nieman.
Description: Second edition. | New York, NY : Oxford University Press, [2020] |
Series: Organization of American Historians bicentennial essays on the Bill of Rights |
Includes bibliographical references and index.
Identifiers: LCCN 2019031629 (print) | LCCN 2019031630 (ebook) |
ISBN 9780190071639 (hardback) | ISBN 9780190071646 (paperback) |
ISBN 9780190071660 (epub) | ISBN 9780190071653 (updf) | ISBN 9780190071677 (online)
Subjects: LCSH: African Americans—Civil rights. |
Civil rights movements—United States—History. | Civil rights—United States—History.
Classification: LCC E185.61 .N5 2020 (print) | LCC E185.61 (ebook) | DDC 323.1196/073—dc23
LC record available at https://lccn.loc.gov/2019031629
LC ebook record available at https://lccn.loc.gov/2019031630

1 3 5 7 9 8 6 4 2

Paperback printed by LSC Communications, United States of America
Hardback printed by Bridgeport National Bindery, Inc., United States of America

Cover image: Jacob Lawrence (American, 1917–2000). *The 1920's . . . The Migrants Cast Their Ballots* from Kent Bicentennial Portfolio: Spirit of Independence, 1974. Serigraph in seven colors plus white on Domestic Etching paper, edition 83 of 125 plus 10 artist's proofs; 32 × 24 7/8 inches (81.28 × 63.18 cm). Collection Albright-Knox Art Gallery, Buffalo, New York; Gift of Lorillard Company, 1975 (1975:9.8).

For Leigh Ann & Brady
Who bring love, joy, and meaning to my life

Contents

Preface

I wrote *Promises to Keep* almost thirty years ago. Since then a lot has changed. The internet put a wealth of sources at my fingertips, making trips to the library far less frequent. When I needed the text of a statute, an obscure court case, a *New York Times* story from 1981, or polling data on public support for affirmative action in 1995, a Google or Lexis search quickly retrieved the information. Changes in politics and public policy have also been remarkable. The United States elected an African American president in 2008, something few would have predicted in 1991, when some Democrats doubted they would see a member of their party in the White House in their lifetimes. In 2015, the US Supreme Court ruled that the Fourteenth Amendment guaranteed same-sex couples the right to marry. And in 2016, Hillary Clinton became the first woman to win the presidential nomination of a major party and secured a 3 million vote popular majority, only to lose the electoral vote to a reality TV star who bragged about groping women.

While much has changed, some things have not. Race—especially African American identity and experience—remains central to public discourse, political debates, and constitutional interpretation. Barrack Obama's election in 2008 and reelection in 2012 were historic events that showed how far Americans have come, but they did not herald a post-racial era. Segregation remains a reality; African Americans suffer disproportionately from poverty, are imprisoned in shockingly high numbers, and die at the hands of police far too frequently; Neo-Nazis march by torchlight; a successful presidential candidate used more openly racist language in 2016 than George Wallace did in his 1968 and 1972 campaigns; and states adopt voter ID laws that deny many persons of color the right to vote. Central to American politics, public policy, culture, everyday life, and law since the seventeenth century, race—and racism—remain hotly debated as the nation enters the third decade of the twenty-first century.

History is central to this debate. Those who believe that institutionalized racism perpetuates racial hierarchy and that race-conscious remedies for it—legal, political, and economic—remain necessary to achieve substantive equality take the long view. They point out that the vestiges of a racial caste system rooted in four centuries of slavery, segregation, and racist violence remain. These continue to burden African Americans even though "whites only" signs have disappeared, blacks vote at about the same rate as whites, racist language brings swift rebukes, and an African American has held the nation's highest office. From this perspective, racism remains woven into of the fabric of American life and strong, purposeful action is necessary to reduce and ultimately remove it. Conservatives, on the other hand, focus on the recent past. They tout the undeniable progress achieved in the past half century. Drawing on the language of the early civil rights movement, whose target was de jure segregation, they often cite Martin Luther King's dream that "my four little children one day will live in a nation where they will not be judged by the color of their skin but by the content of their character." In their view, race-conscious policies, even when designed to remedy the effects of past discrimination, violate the values of the civil rights movement, the Civil Rights Act of 1964, and the Fourteenth Amendment's equal protection clause and are unconstitutional.

Because race remains a hotly contested issue and history figures prominently in the debate, a second edition of *Promises to Keep* seemed in order. My goal was twofold. First, I wanted to incorporate some of the most important insights from scholarship published since 1991 into the original narrative and analysis. This has allowed me to read many truly fascinating books and articles, some written by a new generation of scholars, others by old friends who continue to contribute to our understanding of law and race in the United States. Not only has my reading been enjoyable, but it has also underscored how vibrant the fields of African American, legal, and civil rights history remain. My second objective was to analyze and make sense of developments of the past three decades and place them in the context of more than two centuries of African American engagement with the Constitution.

No one should be surprised that race and civil rights continue to occupy a prominent place in constitutional as well as political discourse. Since the nation's founding, race has been a dominant force in American life and, therefore, central to its constitutional order. During the Revolutionary era, as they drafted new constitutions, Americans fiercely debated the place of slavery in a republican society that was founded on the "self-evident" truth that "all men are created equal" and "are endowed by their Creator with certain unalienable rights," including the right to "Life, Liberty, and the pursuit of Happiness." Debate over slavery not only figured prominently at the Constitutional Convention in 1787, but played a crucial role in the evolution of constitutional doctrine during the next six decades. Fundamental matters—the scope of national power, the nature of the federal system, the definition of citizenship, the rights of US citizens—were shaped by the debate over slavery and racial subordination. Ultimately, slavery proved the nemesis of the Union, shattering the constitutional order and plunging the country into a bloody Civil War.

Slavery was a casualty of the war, but its death did not end the pivotal role of race in American politics and law. In attempting to root out slavery and its vestiges, Reconstruction-era Republicans adopted the Thirteenth, Fourteenth, and Fifteenth Amendments and the nation's first civil rights laws. In the process, they created a new Constitution, extending to African Americans full rights of citizenship, establishing a constitutional guarantee to equal rights, and empowering the national government to protect the fundamental rights of its citizens. Although by 1900 white violence, narrow, formalistic judicial interpretations of the Reconstruction Amendments, and congressional neglect had destroyed the promise of Reconstruction, African Americans never gave up their faith in the promise of equality or their willingness to challenge the caste system. Beginning in the 1910s, black plaintiffs prodded the US Supreme Court to begin the long process of resuscitating the Reconstruction Amendments. That process gained momentum in the 1930s and 1940s and triumphed in the decades following World War II, as litigation, activism, presidential leadership, and legislation toppled the twin pillars of the southern caste system—Jim Crow and disfranchisement. Despite the nation's conservative turn in the 1970s and 1980s, civil rights advocates found new allies in the women's movement and built on the victories they had won in the 1960s to attack the vestiges of the caste system. As the twentieth century ended and the twenty-first began, however, victories were harder to come by, defeats more common, and solutions to the problem of inequality elusive.

African Americans have been important agents in this process. From the Republic's earliest days, black leaders embraced principles of equality and constitutional rights, using them to attack slavery and racial subordination. They were well aware of the American paradox: that the land of the free was the home of the slave; that, in practice, equality was circumscribed by race, gender, and economic status; and that constitutional liberty was guaranteed only to white men. Yet African American leaders understood that the general language of the Constitution made it a malleable document whose meaning was subject to redefinition through the political and legal process, that the polity was, in a sense, an ongoing constitutional convention. Appealing to principles embodied in the Declaration of Independence and the Constitution, African Americans and their white allies forged an equalitarian constitutionalism and skillfully used it to reshape the Constitution and American society. From the antebellum conventions held by free blacks to the constitutional conventions and legislatures of the Reconstruction South and the National Association for the Advancement of Colored People's monumental campaign against segregated education, African Americans effectively wielded constitutional principles to extend justice to all Americans irrespective of race.

Equalitarian political and constitutional principles have been embraced not only by the black elite, but also by the black masses, who have seen in them an affirmation of their dignity and a tool to break the caste system. During Reconstruction, former slaves imbibed equalitarian constitutional ideas from black veterans, northern teachers, the press, and the Union League and invoked them to assert rights. Although the promise of Reconstruction was cut short, the demand for equal rights among the black rank and file remained alive. It inspired boycotts of segregated streetcars that swept southern cities in the first decade of the twentieth century; popular support for A. Philip Randolph's March on Washington Movement in the 1940s; Oliver Brown's 1951 challenge to segregated schools in Topeka, Kansas; and countless other individual and collective acts against discrimination.

African Americans have not acted alone in their quest for freedom and equal rights. Since the late eighteenth century, white men and women have joined them in the struggle. From the abolitionists and Radical Republicans to the founders of the National Association for the Advancement of Colored People and hundreds of college students who participated in Mississippi Freedom Summer in 1964, some whites have taken a stand for equality. Indeed, given African Americans' minority status and their historical exclusion from the ballot box, most black leaders have recognized the importance of white support and worked to build interracial coalitions. Nevertheless, African Americans have been at the center of the struggle and have played an essential role in transforming the Constitution from a document principally concerned with property rights and federal relations into a charter of equality. Together with their white allies, blacks have used the constitutional process to push a nation built on slavery and racial subordination closer to its self-proclaimed ideals. In the words of Langston Hughes, they "let America be America again/The land that never has been yet."

In *Promises to Keep*, I have attempted a brief history of the complicated relationship between African Americans and the nation's constitutional order from the late eighteenth century to the present. In telling this story, I have sought to show how law, society, race, and politics interact. Emphasizing the malleability of the US Constitution, I have stressed the powerful role of politics, ideology, culture, and social forces in producing constitutional change. I have attempted to show as well that legal institutions and principles have played an equally important role in shaping social relations and politics. Treating such a broad topic in a brief book inevitably requires cursory treatment of many individuals, issues, and episodes that deserve fuller coverage. Nevertheless, I hope this brief survey of constitutional law and race in America will reveal the broad contours of constitutional change, highlight the pivotal role that race has played in American law, call attention to the important contributions African Americans have made to the nation's constitutional order, and offer a historical perspective that will inform contemporary discussions of civil rights and the law.

The nation's promise of equality has far exceeded its performance. For most of the nation's history, law has served as a tool of white supremacy, and constitutional principles have too frequently been mobilized to legitimize racial oppression or explain why it could not be rooted out. In the recent past, much of the legal structure of white supremacy has been dismantled by legislation, court decisions, and direct action. As a result, some now believe that we have wiped the slate clean. Indeed, during the past forty years many have invoked the idea of a color-blind Constitution to argue that taking race into account in crafting remedies to end the continuing vestiges of the nation's racial caste system is unconstitutional. This perspective underestimates the weight of history. Two decades into the twenty-first century, Americans live in a racially segregated society in which race shapes opportunity. Only by understanding that the accomplishments of the recent past are a beginning rather than an end, and that they are threatened if we forget how deeply rooted racism is, will we take the steps necessary to fulfill the long-deferred promise of equality.

Vestal, New York   DGN
May 2019

Acknowledgments

Writing the second edition of *Promises to Keep* has been a joy. Since 2000, I have served as a dean or a provost. I have found the work challenging and interesting, the relationships I have developed rich, and what I have learned about the inner workings of higher education fascinating. During this time, I have taught on a regular basis and found that interactions with students and thinking about history as I prepared for class provided balance to my professional life and kept me grounded. Until about two years ago, I did not believe I had time to pursue research and writing. However, ongoing discussions of race, especially during and in the wake of the 2016 election, drew me back to thinking about civil rights, the nation's dark history of racism, and efforts to embrace our better angels and overcome that history. Encouraged by my wife, Leigh Ann Wheeler, I contacted my publisher, suggested a second edition, and was delighted (and a little scared) when David McBride responded positively. Writing a new final chapter that places developments of the past thirty years in the context of African Americans' long struggle for equality, catching up on recent scholarship, and revising the chapters that appeared in 1991 have reminded me that the decision I made many years ago to become a historian was the right one.

I owe a huge debt to scholars of legal history, African American history, and the history of race relations and civil rights. When I published *Promises to Keep* in 1991, the literature in these fields was as rich as it was extensive. In the past three decades, scholarship has continued to grow in volume, range, quality, and insights. Because of an editorial decision to keep notes to a minimum, I have cited in the endnotes only material I have quoted or mentioned directly in the text. As a result, the notes do not fully acknowledge my intellectual debt. The bibliographical essay discusses the works on which I have relied and offers readers an overview of the rich scholarship that illuminates the troubled history of race in United States history.

In completing the first edition of *Promises to Keep* thirty years ago, I benefited from a remarkable group of friends and colleagues who provided encouragement, read and commented on the manuscript, and helped sharpen my prose, strengthen my arguments, and tighten the book's organization. The late Kermit Hall, a prolific scholar, master organizer, shrewd critic, and good friend, offered sage advice and knew when to encourage and when to prod. I have been blessed to have two wise, supportive, generous mentors, Harold Hyman and the late La Wanda Cox. Harold and La Wanda not only inspired my scholarly work but provided models for how to live a purposeful, satisfying life. Both gave encouragement, read portions of the original manuscript, offered valuable advice, and were always there when I needed them. For twenty-five years, I spoke by phone with La Wanda almost every Saturday morning, sharing personal news, talking about politics, and discussing history. Michal Belknap, Kent Newmeyer, and Bill Wiecek read the entire manuscript of the first edition, provided important suggestions, and saved me from a number of errors.

In preparing the second edition, I have once again benefited from the generosity of colleagues—and this time, students. I presented the final chapter, freshly written for this edition, at Binghamton University's Modern US History Workshop, which includes a remarkable group of faculty colleagues and graduate students who read carefully, offer thoughtful suggestions, have a great sense of humor, and stimulate thoughtful discussions of works-in-progress that are as smart as they are enjoyable. It represents the academy at its best. I would especially like to thank Nancy Appelbaum, Jessica Derleth, Julia Haager, Chelsea Gibson, Yong Hyeon Kim, Sarah King, Josh Kluever, Colin Kohlhaas, Jean Quataert, Katie Stankiewicz, Wendy Wall, Leigh Ann Wheeler, and the commentator for the session, Evan Faulkenbury of SUNY Cortland.

My greatest debt is to my family. My son, Brady, provided many a welcome diversion from my "day job" as provost. Thanks to Brady, I was able to help with science fair projects or short stories, spend many memorable weekends at Yankee Stadium cheering on our favorite team, keep the scoring book for his Teener baseball team, listen to him play cello at Binghamton Youth Symphony concerts as well as daily practice sessions, and play whiffle ball in the back yard or at the beach. Brady makes life so much richer and more fun than I could ever have imagined when he entered the world sixteen years ago. Leigh Ann Wheeler fills my life with wit, a razor-sharp intellect, an irreverent sense of humor, provocative ideas, beauty, and a passion for justice, history, and much more. She inspired me to write a second edition of *Promises to Keep* by her gentle insistence that it was worth doing and also by the example of outstanding scholarship that she sets for her students and me. She also read the entire manuscript, using her grace as a writer, highly refined editorial skills, and deep knowledge of civil rights and women's history to make the book better. No one I have ever known is more devoted to the craft of history, as a teacher and scholar. She inspires everyone around her to be better, including Brady and me. But I am especially lucky because she loves me even when I'm not particularly loveable, takes the time to understand me even when I make little sense, and is the best partner anyone could ever hope for.

1

With Liberty for Some

The Old Constitution and African American Rights, 1776–1846

Like thousands of African Americans, Jupiter Nicholson tasted the fruit of freedom that ripened during the age of the American Revolution. Born into slavery in North Carolina, Nicholson, his wife, and his parents were freed by their owners sometime in the 1780s. Taking advantage of his liberty, Nicholson went to work as a sailor, trying to scrape together enough money to buy a farm and acquire the economic independence that would give substance to his freedom. He soon found, however, that freedom's fruit had a bitter aftertaste. As a growing number of slaveowners—prompted by a combination of religious zeal and revolutionary principle—freed their slaves, many prominent North Carolinians feared that slavery was being undermined from within. In response, the legislature reiterated its restrictions on manumission: slaves could be freed only as a reward for meritorious service and all manumissions must be approved by a county court. Moreover, it authorized citizens to seize blacks who had been freed illegally and to sell them into slavery. Attracted by the prospect of a quick dollar, many white men began to seize illegally freed blacks, quickly turning the dream of freedom into a nightmare for Nicholson and other free blacks. Coming ashore one day about two years after he had been freed, Nicholson was set upon by armed whites who chased him with dogs. Although he eluded the slavecatchers and fled with his wife to Portsmouth, Virginia, his parents and his brother were not so fortunate; they fell into the hands of whites who returned them to bondage.

Nicholson and his wife found refuge in Portsmouth, where they established a home and lived in relative safety as free persons of color, for four years. Yet they could not escape the reign of terror unleashed by the North Carolina legislature; any day slavecatchers from North Carolina might cross the Virginia border, track them down, and carry them back to slavery. Seeking greater security, they left Virginia in the early 1790s and settled in Philadelphia,

Promises to Keep. Donald G. Nieman, Oxford University Press (2020). © Oxford University Press.
DOI: 10.1093/oso/9780190071639.001.0001

which had a reputation among blacks as a "city of refuge."[1] A bustling sea-port situated in a state that had adopted a program of gradual emancipation during the preceding decade, Philadelphia offered African Americans a live-lihood and the pure air of freedom. Yet even in Philadelphia, black emigres found security elusive. In 1793—about the time Nicholson and his wife arrived there—the US Congress bowed to the demands of southerners and passed the Fugitive Slave Act. The law authorized slaveowners to seize run-away slaves who had fled to free soil and take them before federal or state judges, who were to issue warrants authorizing them to return fugitives to bondage. Because it did not afford alleged fugitives an opportunity to prove that they were free, the act made free blacks like Jupiter Nicholson vulner-able, even in a haven of freedom like Philadelphia. Indeed, their vulnerability was underscored in late 1796, when a North Carolina slavecatcher came to Philadelphia and arrested a black man who had been illegally freed by his owner.

Alarmed by the arrest, Nicholson and three other blacks who had sought refuge in Philadelphia immediately turned to Absalom Jones, founder of the city's Free Africa Society and its African Church. Jones had helped to forge a sense of identity and community among Philadelphia blacks and was an ob-vious source of assistance. He alerted members of the community, warning them to be on the lookout for slavecatchers and to be ready to hide neighbors who were in danger. Jones also used the occasion as an opportunity to call Congress's attention to the evils of the Fugitive Slave Act. In the first peti-tion to Congress by African Americans, Jones described the terror of men and women threatened with reenslavement after having once had their "human right to freedom . . . restored" and called on lawmakers to honor the nation's commitment to liberty and natural rights. "May we not be allowed to consider this stretch of power, morally and politically, a Governmental de-fect . . . ," he asked, "and . . . is not some remedy for an evil of such magni-tude highly worthy of the deep inquiry and unfeigned zeal of the supreme Legislative body of a free and enlightened people?"[2]

Jones's eloquent appeal to revolutionary principles failed to persuade members of the House of Representatives. Although George Thatcher of Massachusetts moved to instruct the committee on commerce to study the matter and suggest amendments to the Fugitive Slave Act, southerners ad-amantly resisted any action that might weaken the law. William L. Smith of South Carolina led the offensive against Thatcher's motion, arguing that the petitioners were "not entitled to the attention of this House" and demanding that their petition be dismissed.[3] In the face of southern opposition, northern congressmen broke ranks and Thatcher's motion went down to defeat, 50–33.

Congress's action exemplified the retreat from the equalitarian possibilities of the American Revolution that was already underway. Revolutionary principles had fueled a potent attack on slavery and racial subordination during the 1770s and 1780s. Yet slavery and racism were deeply rooted in the new Republic, proving more than a match for revolutionary principles. By the late 1780s the practical exigencies of nation building had led to a compromise of revolutionary principle that soon transformed the American constitutional-legal order into a bulwark of slavery and white supremacy. As a result, the chains of bondage were tightened on slaves in the plantation South, and free blacks like Jupiter Nicholson lived, even in the North, under the shadow of slavery in a land of liberty.

Revolutionary Ideals and Political Realities

The dream of freedom, security, and opportunity, which Jupiter Nicholson found so elusive, had its genesis in the momentous changes that transpired during the age of the American Revolution. In the heat of revolution, Americans forged doctrines of liberty and equality that quickly became an integral part of American political culture and sparked widespread criticism of slavery. The intellectual currents of the Enlightenment deeply influenced the attitudes and assumptions of educated Americans as well as Europeans during the second half of the eighteenth century. Enlightenment thinkers asserted that in the mythical state of nature—before the formation of society and government—all individuals were born free and equal and had enormous capacity for improvement. They believed that human beings were malleable and contended that differences among individuals and cultures were the result of environment and circumstance. This helped them explain the gap between human capacity for improvement and the reality of an imperfect world. The evil and misery experienced by humanity was not a result of defects in human nature but a product of superstition, bigotry, and flawed social and political institutions inherited from the past. Reason and institutional reform, however, could remove these barriers to progress and secure human happiness. For European intellectuals and many of the Americans whom they influenced, slavery was a perfect example of an institution that upset the natural order and stifled progress: it rejected the natural equality of all persons, produced incalculable suffering, and denied slaves the opportunity for mental and moral improvement. Once removed from the debasing effects of slavery, they maintained, blacks had the potential to become the equals of whites.

Powerful religious currents also encouraged antislavery sentiment. During the Revolutionary era the Quakers and the two most rapidly growing denominations in America, the Baptists and Methodists, subjected slavery to withering criticism. These groups emphasized the importance of humility, the equality of all persons in the eyes of God, and the imperative for Christians to treat others in the spirit of Christian love. This led them to criticize slavery as an embodiment of hierarchy and coercion that flew in the face of Christ's great commandment: that Christians should love their neighbors. Because they believed that slavery was a sin, they often attacked it with a sense of urgency, pressing members of their congregations to free their slaves and organizing antislavery societies.

Ideas unleashed by the Revolution interacted with these beliefs to strengthen antislavery sentiment. Between 1763 and 1776, patriot leaders charged that Parliament repeatedly denied the colonists rights guaranteed by the British Constitution. Parliamentary legislation, they argued, limited their right to jury trial and peaceable assembly, eroded constitutional restrictions on a standing army, and, most important, deprived them of liberty and property without their consent. These acts were ominous because they suggested that Parliament suffered no restraints in dealing with the colonists and could govern them arbitrarily. Without rights, subject to arbitrary power, merely enjoying such privileges as their parliamentary masters chose to give them, Americans repeatedly asserted, they were reduced to slavery. Parliament's program was clearly "a system formed to enslave America," the Continental Congress declared in 1774. A year later, in the Declaration of the Causes and Necessity of Taking Up Arms, Congress asserted that Americans were "resolved to die freemen rather than to live Slaves."[4]

Patriots did not refer to the chattel slavery that blacks suffered, but, instead, invoked a political concept ubiquitous in eighteenth-century polemical writing on both sides of the Atlantic. As the historian John Phillip Reid has noted, "To warn against slavery was the way Britons raised questions about constitutionality."[5] Nevertheless, many Americans realized that as long as they held half a million blacks in bondage their defense of liberty rang hollow and argued that fidelity to revolutionary principles demanded abolition. Combined with Enlightenment notions of the natural equality of all persons and evangelical warnings that British tyranny was divine punishment for the sin of slavery, the rhetoric of rights and liberty convinced many Americans to join the attack. A Virginia conference of Methodists, acting in the wake of the Revolution to bar slaveholders from communion, suggested this melding of secular and religious ideas when it noted that slavery was "contrary to the Golden Law of God . . . and the inalienable Rights of Mankind, as well as every Principle of the Revolution."[6]

Revolutionary thought contained an equalitarian emphasis that reinforced antislavery arguments. As Americans rejected monarchy in 1776, they embraced republicanism, a set of ideas with far-reaching implications. Republican government, according to American writers, was more than government purged of monarchy and resting on popular will. Its survival required a virtuous people willing to sacrifice for the common good. Virtue, they claimed, could only exist in a society that did not suffer great extremes of wealth. The lure of opulence would make the very rich self-indulgent and reluctant to sacrifice, while the misery of the poor would provide pliable material for self-serving demagogues. Although republicanism did not lead to leveling programs designed to redistribute wealth, it did suggest that some degree of material equality was necessary for the survival of republican government. Republicanism also demanded that government promote the common good and refuse to serve the special interests of the privileged few, a principle asserted in the revolutionary state constitutions. Hostility to privilege carried with it the implication that all men—few extended the principle to women—were entitled to equal rights.

During the decades following the Revolution, ideals of liberty and equality came squarely into conflict with the realities of slavery and racial subordination, systems supported by powerful economic interests and entrenched social mores. When the Revolution began, slavery existed in all of the American colonies. Slaves were most numerous in the South, where they made up substantial minorities (30–42 percent) in Virginia, North Carolina, and Maryland and a majority (60 percent) in South Carolina. Slave agricultural laborers and craftsmen were essential to the plantation economies of these states. Even in the North, where they ranged from less than 2 percent of the population in Massachusetts to more than 10 percent in New York, slaves played an important economic role because of the shortage of labor. Moreover, white attitudes toward blacks, which had taken root during the previous century, reinforced slavery and the system of racial hierarchy it created. The vast majority of African Americans were slaves who occupied a degraded and subordinate position, and most whites viewed them as ignorant, shiftless, and lazy. Such attitudes legitimized existing social arrangements and provided ready arguments against emancipation: once freed from white control, blacks would become paupers and criminals and threaten social stability.

Although they faced formidable obstacles, antislavery advocates made great strides toward implementing the truths proclaimed self-evident by the Declaration of Independence. They achieved their greatest success in the North where few owned slaves and African Americans were not numerous. Vermont, with a slave population of fifty, quickly abolished slavery in its 1777 constitution. In Massachusetts, the Supreme Court of Judicature used the equalitarian language of the state's 1780 constitution ("all men are born free and equal") to end slavery in the early 1780s. Northern opposition to abolition was not always so completely or quickly overcome, however. Most northern states passed laws providing that slaves born prior to enactment of the legislation would remain in slavery while those born thereafter would be freed when they reached adulthood. Pennsylvania (1780), Connecticut (1784), and Rhode Island (1784) quickly passed similar legislation, but New York (1799) and New Jersey (1804) acted only after twenty years of pressure from well-organized antislavery groups. The hard-earned victory over slavery in the North was significant because it transformed slavery from a national to a sectional institution.

Southerners also subjected slavery to criticism. Baptists, Methodists, and Quakers—groups that drew members primarily from non-slaveholders—led the way. Although slaveholders refrained from calling for abolition, some acknowledged that slavery violated the ideals of the Revolution, supported legislation permitting individual owners to free their slaves, and manumitted some or all of their own slaves. In Virginia, where private manumission was common, the free black population grew from 2,000 in 1782 to 20,000 in 1800. Nevertheless, the private acts of well-intentioned slaveholders did not imperil the institution; 345,000 Virginia blacks remained in bondage in 1800. Indeed, slavery was the social and economic foundation of the planter class, the most influential group in Virginia and the rest of the South, and it was economically important to tens of thousands of farmers who owned one or two slaves. Moreover, because African Americans constituted between 30 and 60 percent of the population of the southern states, even non-slaveholders—conditioned by racism to believe that blacks were incapable of freedom—equated abolition with social chaos. As a result, no southern legislature seriously considered even a gradual emancipation law during the late eighteenth century.

Antislavery reformers also encountered formidable obstacles to their effort to guarantee the rights of free blacks. Most whites viewed free blacks as pariahs, generally excluding them from their churches, theaters, and inns and relegating them to unskilled, low-paying jobs. Indeed, marking all blacks as inferiors elevated the status of the poorest white. In the South, antiblack feeling prompted lawmakers to consign free blacks to an inferior legal status; throughout the region they were prohibited from testifying against whites or having sexual relations with them—a stricture often ignored by white slaveholders. In addition, most southern states barred African Americans from voting and serving in the militia, and South Carolina and Georgia explicitly denied them citizenship.

Although they suffered from social and economic discrimination, northern free blacks escaped systematic legal discrimination during the late eighteenth century. While routinely excluded from the militia, free blacks enjoyed the same right to vote and testify as whites, were eligible for citizenship on the same terms as whites, and generally had the same legal rights and obligations as whites. In 1785, when the New York legislature passed a bill denying free blacks the right to vote and testify against whites and prohibiting interracial marriages, the state's Council of Revision vetoed it. According to the council, the measure created "an aristocracy of the most dangerous and malignant kind, rendering power permanent and hereditary in the hands of those persons who deduce their origin through white ancestors only."[7] In the North, at least, revolutionary principles occasionally prevailed over racial prejudice and class interest.

The Constitutional Convention, however, was not one of those occasions. The delegates who met in Philadelphia during the summer of 1787 believed that the weakness of the existing national government had created an economic and political crisis that threatened America's republican experiment. Most blamed the Articles of Confederation and called for a new Constitution to create a strong national government that would achieve economic recovery, promote prosperity, cope with threats from abroad, reestablish the public credit, and restrain the states from interfering with property rights. Although many delegates expressed reservations about slavery and a few denounced it, political realities foreclosed meaningful antislavery action. Constitutional reform and continued union required southern support, and southern delegates would not accept constitutional provisions that threatened the economic well-being of the South and its powerful planter class. Consequently, the price of constitutional reform was northern concession on the slavery issue.

Southerners won a significant victory in debates on representation in Congress. Although they failed to have slaves counted fully for purposes of determining representation, they secured a provision that apportioned representatives among the states "according to their respective Numbers, which shall be determined by adding the whole Number of free Persons . . . and . . . three fifths of all other Persons."[8] Because these "other persons" were slaves, northerners objected to the three-fifths clause, charging that it allowed southerners to use property to increase their clout in the national government. Southerners, however, insisted on the extra political security that the three-fifths clause conferred. North Carolina's William Davie, for example, explained that he "was sure that N. Carola. would never confederate on any terms that did not rate them [slaves] at least 3/5. If the Eastern [i.e., northern] States meant . . . to exclude them altogether the business was at an end."[9] Ultimately, northern delegates accepted the three-fifths clause as the price of a strengthened national government that they deemed vital to their interests.

The three-fifths clause rested solely on considerations of sectional power and had nothing to do with whether slaves—who could not vote—would be represented in the national government or whether they were considered persons in the eyes of the law. The South's share of population and therefore seats in the House of Representatives increased from 41 percent when only free persons were counted to more than 46 percent under the three-fifths formula. This increased the region's strength in the House and also in presidential politics because a state's presidential electors equaled the number of its senators and representatives. Consequently, it became an important tool that southerners would use during the next seventy years to bend national policy to their will.

The convention proved less willing to bow to the South on the slave trade. In early August, after the convention had been in session for more than two months, delegates considered a controversial proposal denying Congress authority to enact "prohibitions on ye Importations of such inhabitants or people as the sevl. States think proper to admit" or "duties by way of such prohibition."[10] Representatives from South Carolina and Georgia, eager to protect the flow of slaves from Africa, were the principal supporters of this measure. A number of northern delegates, however, objected because it protected the most brutal aspects of slavery: tearing Africans away from their homeland; crowding them into the hot, foul holds of ships where they suffered unspeakably and many died; and selling them like cattle at auctions in America. Gouverneur Morris, the voluble Pennsylvania delegate, charged that it protected "the inhabitant of Georgia and S.C. who goes to the Coast of Africa, and in defiance of the most sacred laws of humanity tears away his fellow creatures from their dearest connections & damns them to the most cruel bondages."[11] These northerners were joined by delegates from Maryland and Virginia who not only regarded the slave trade as immoral, but represented states that had a surplus of slaves and stood to benefit from the higher prices that would result from closing the African trade.

After acrimonious debate, delegates ultimately accepted a compromise. New Englanders agreed to support an obliquely worded provision that prohibited Congress from interfering with the slave trade for twenty years: "The Migration or Importation of such Persons as any of the States now existing shall think proper to admit, shall not be prohibited by the Congress" prior to 1808.[12] In return, the South Carolinians supported deletion of a provision requiring two-thirds majorities for Congress to pass commercial regulations. The New Englanders thus sacrificed their scruples against the slave trade in order to win a concession vital to northern commercial interests. Connecticut's Oliver Ellsworth captured the spirit of pragmatism that paved the way for the compromise: "let every State import what it pleases. The morality or wisdom of slavery are considerations belonging to the States themselves—What enriches a part enriches the whole, and the States are the best judges of their particular interest."[13] The compromise meant that the slave trade would continue for at least twenty years and an additional 100,000 Africans would be forced into bondage in the United States. It resulted in shattered families, subjected its victims to brutality and exploitation, and strengthened the institution in the United States. But the compromise also gave the federal government authority to outlaw the trade, authority Congress exercised in 1808.

On the heels of the slave trade compromise, the convention quickly agreed to another southern demand. Slaveholding delegates in the convention knew that their slaves, far from being docile, frequently ran away. Fearing that if they reached states that had abolished slavery, their human property would win freedom, they sought a constitutional remedy. Pierce Butler and Charles Cotesworth Pinckney of South Carolina proposed a clause requiring "fugitive slaves and servants to be delivered up like criminals."[14] The following day, delegates accepted the Constitution's fugitive slave clause with little debate. As finally approved, it was an indirect and obscurely worded guarantee: "No Person held to Service or Labour in one State, under the Laws thereof, escaping to another, shall, in consequence of any Law or Regulation therein, be discharged from such Service or Labour, but shall be delivered up on Claim of the Party to whom such Service or Labour may be due."[15] The clause clearly created a personal right slave owners might claim. But how would they enforce it? Did it give Congress authority to legislate? Would Congress exercise that authority? Answers were left for another day.

Delegates conferred perhaps the greatest constitutional protection on slavery when they granted Congress enumerated powers rather than giving it plenary legislative authority. They did not intend to limit Congress to exercise of those powers expressly listed in the Constitution. Indeed, the framers gave it authority "to make all laws which shall be necessary and proper" for carrying out any of the enumerated powers. This broadened national authority and gave Congress considerable flexibility without threatening slavery. The nature of Congress's enumerated powers precluded it from outlawing slavery or from interfering with its day-to-day operation in any state that chose to make it lawful. The framers, concerned more with union than with liberty, thus made freedom a matter of local option.

When the final gavel fell at Philadelphia, delegates had created a framework of government that tacitly recognized slavery without naming it, offered protection to it, and, most important, strengthened the hand of its advocates in the national government. Yet it would be wrong to view the Constitution as uniformly and consistently proslavery; the framers created an open-ended document that, while favorable to slavery in many respects, contained a reservoir of antislavery potential. Because many of the framers believed, with James Madison, that it would be "wrong to admit in the Constitution the idea that there could be property in men,"[16] they refrained from including the words "slave" or "slavery" and thus refused to give explicit recognition to the institution. Moreover, the Constitution did not require the national government to promote slavery or, as southerners would subsequently argue, refrain from action hostile to it. For example, the slave trade clause prohibited Congress from interfering with the importation of slaves into the original states until 1808. This suggested that after that date Congress could use its power to regulate commerce (a power denied it in

the Articles) to end the trade. Indeed, it did so at the earliest possible moment. Moreover, the fugitive slave clause did not require or explicitly authorize Congress to help slaveowners recapture runaways. The wording of
the clause and its placement in Article IV, Section 2 (which deals with interstate relations) suggested merely that states ought not prevent slaveowners
from reclaiming fugitives.

Several other features of the Constitution mitigated the concessions to
slaveholders. Because Americans had begun by the late eighteenth century
to migrate to the Trans-Appalachian West, the future of slavery depended on
whether it moved with the settlers. The Northwest Ordinance of 1787, passed
by the Confederation Congress as the Constitutional Convention met, prohibited slavery in the territories north of the Ohio River. Coupled with the
postrevolutionary emancipation acts of the northern state legislatures, the
Ordinance made slavery a local institution rather than the national institution it had been in 1776. The Constitution gave Congress authority to carry
out the spirit of the Northwest Ordinance and further circumscribe slavery.
It empowered Congress "to make all needful Rules and Regulations respecting the Territories," thus conferring authority to exclude slavery from
the western territories, and contain it in the southeast. Moreover, the Bill of
Rights, the ten amendments that became part of the Constitution in 1791,
proclaimed a host of fundamental liberties—freedom of speech, the right to
jury trial, protection against unreasonable search and seizure, the guarantee
of due process of law—which were hostile to the arbitrary power essential to
maintain slavery.

This is not to suggest—as abolitionists and Republicans would do later—
that the framers were closet abolitionists who created a thoroughly antislavery Constitution. They made important concessions to slavery that
proslavery advocates later effectively exploited. Nevertheless, the antislavery sensibilities of many delegates placed limits on how far they would go
to protect slavery. Northern delegates made concessions to slaveholders'
demands, but they did not seek to create a document that would promote
slavery. Moreover, the framers did not carve the Constitution in stone.
They wrote it in general language that was susceptible to a variety of interpretations. And they created a document that was inherently political because it defined governmental authority. Of necessity, such a document
would evolve as rival political forces mustered their strength to shape the
general language of the Constitution to their ends, whether proslavery or
antislavery.

Toward a Proslavery Constitution

Between ratification of the Constitution and the Mexican War (1846–1848), the American political system worked against realization of the Constitution's antislavery potential. As they had at the Philadelphia Convention, southern political leaders doggedly insisted that the national government show solicitude for slavery and challenged measures that threatened the institution. Although northern politicians sometimes resisted these demands, more often they backed down or broke ranks in the face of southern initiatives. Confronted with southern assertiveness, many northern leaders believed that preservation of the Union required them to make concessions to southerners on an issue so vital to their interests. Moreover, the growth of a two-party system served to mute criticism of slavery within the national government. Between 1795 and 1815, as Federalists and Republicans vied for power, and, again, from 1832 until 1854, as Democrats and Whigs dominated the political scene, both major parties sought support in the North and the South. Consequently, party leaders generally avoided action that would alienate southerners and splinter their party organizations.

The breakdown of the two-party system in the 1810s demonstrated its value to intersectional harmony—and southern interests. After the War of 1812, the demise of the Federalist opposition encouraged factionalism in Republican ranks and quickly led to a breakdown of party unity. This was a blow to southerners because it undermined the bisectional political alliance that had served to protect slavery. Indeed, in 1819, when Missouri sought admission to the Union as a slave state, northerners in the House of Representatives closed ranks in an effort to block the spread of slavery. The Missouri crisis precipitated bitter sectional conflict, arrayed northern politicians against slavery, and resulted in legislation (the Missouri Compromise of 1820) excluding slavery from the northern portion of the vast Louisiana Purchase Territory.

Southern leaders quickly recovered. In the late 1820s and early 1830s, supporters of Andrew Jackson—most notably New York's Martin Van Buren—forged a powerful new coalition, the Democratic Party. Resting on a strong southern base, it also attracted considerable support in the North and the rapidly growing Midwest. Despite competition from a formidable Whig opposition, it became the dominant force in antebellum politics, controlling the White House for all but eight years between 1829 and 1861. Because southerners played a prominent role in party councils and northern

Democrats with aspirations for the presidency realized that they needed southern support, Democratic hegemony guaranteed that national policy was favorable to slavery.

Northern politicians were able to make concessions to southerners because of the attitudes of their constituents. A small minority of northerners worked actively against slavery among an indifferent, ambivalent majority. Some were proslavery, others tolerated slavery, and still others opposed slavery in the abstract but placed antislavery low on their list of priorities. A variety of factors explain this state of affairs. Many settlers in Ohio, Indiana, Illinois, and Iowa had been born in the South, and they and their descendants shared southern mores. Apart from southern immigrants, racism was strong throughout the North and led many to have little sympathy with enslaved blacks. In fact, many northerners feared that emancipation in the South would lead to a northward migration of freed slaves. Still other northerners believed that acceptance of slavery was the cornerstone of the Union and were willing to make concessions necessary to preserve national unity.

The national government began its support for slavery shortly after George Washington assumed the presidency in 1789. Presidents and Congresses allowed slavery to take root in the Old Southwest (the area south of the Ohio River stretching from the Appalachian Mountains to the Mississippi River). In 1789, Congress accepted North Carolina's cession of its western lands to the United States, even though the grant stipulated that "no regulation made or to be made shall tend to emancipate slaves."[17] Lawmakers organized territories in the region without reference to slavery, fully aware that immigrants from the older southern states would bring slaves with them. Subsequently, they admitted these territories to the Union as slave states. In 1801, shortly after the government moved to Washington, DC, Congress decreed that the laws of Virginia and Maryland, which recognized slavery, should remain in force in the District of Columbia. The nation's capital thus became a slave city, replete with slave markets where human beings were bought and sold, and city officials, acting under congressional authority, enforced laws supporting the institution.

Federal officials also worked to insulate slavery from attack. During the 1830s radical abolitionists in the North subjected slavery and slaveholders to withering criticism in hundreds of pamphlets and thousands of petitions to Congress. Southerners were offended by this criticism and feared that it would incite slave insurrection. Although Congress refused to enact legislation excluding abolitionist pamphlets from the mail, it did not object when

President Andrew Jackson's postmaster general authorized local postmasters to destroy antislavery tracts. Though a violation of the postal laws and the First Amendment's guarantee of freedom of the press, postal officials continued to enforce the policy until the Civil War. Faced with abolitionist petitions, Congress also acted with flagrant disrespect for the Constitution. In 1836, the House of Representatives adopted a resolution, popularly known as the "gag rule," that stopped members from reading petitions concerning slavery. Although abolitionists charged that the rule abridged the right "to petition the Government for a redress of grievances" guaranteed by the First Amendment, it remained in force until 1844.

Congress also bolstered slavery by helping slaveowners secure the return of runaway slaves. In 1793, after little debate, Congress passed "an Act respecting fugitives from justice, and persons escaping from the service of their masters." The first part of the law implemented the constitutional provision requiring states to extradite fugitives from justice. Without providing any federal enforcement machinery, it simply admonished state officials to return fugitives from justice when requested to do so by the governor of another state. The fugitive slave clause, like the extradition clause, was a directive to the states and did not expressly authorize congressional action. At the insistence of southerners, however, the second part of the 1793 act went beyond directing state officials to fulfill their obligation to return runaway slaves. It authorized slaveholders (or their agents) to seize runaways and take them before a US district judge or any state justice of the peace. After presenting evidence of ownership—either an oral statement or a written affidavit made before a justice of the peace in the owner's home state—the claimant was to be given a warrant authorizing him or her to take the fugitive back to slavery. Alleged fugitives were denied due process of law: they had no right to testify, to command witnesses to appear, or to counsel. By establishing this procedure, Congress not only commanded state and federal officials to aid in the return of runaways but stipulated that they employ the assumptions and procedures of slave state law in doing so. Northern state law presumed all persons to be free and required slaveowners to establish their claims beyond a reasonable doubt. Under the Fugitive Slave Act, however, African Americans were presumed to be slaves, and claimants had to provide only minimal evidence that they owned the alleged fugitive. Thus to protect slaveowners, Congress gave extraterritorial application to southern state law.

Because of the summary procedure it authorized, the act threatened free blacks as well as runaway slaves. Free blacks who were kidnapped or mistaken for fugitive slaves were denied the procedural means necessary to establish their freedom. This undoubtedly violated the Fifth Amendment's guarantee that no person shall "be deprived of life, liberty, or property without due process of law." As commonly understood by contemporaries, due process obligated the government to follow traditional common law procedures when it deprived persons of life, liberty, or property. Because the Fugitive Slave Act allowed blacks to be denied liberty through ex parte testimony (the testimony of only one party to the case) and without the right to counsel or to trial by jury, it clearly violated due process.

Despite criticism of the procedure employed by the law, during the five decades following its enactment northern states generally cooperated with slaveowners who sought the return of runaways. Nevertheless, many northern legislatures took action to protect free blacks. Some merely passed statutes imposing fines and imprisonment on persons convicted of kidnapping free blacks with the intention of selling them into slavery. Several legislatures went further, however, stipulating that state judicial officers who heard fugitive slave cases must afford blacks greater procedural protection than required under the Fugitive Slave Act. An 1826 Pennsylvania law, for example, stipulated that slaveowners could take runaways out of the state only if they obtained a certificate of rendition from a state or federal judge, thus denying them the right to return fugitives without judicial intervention. The law also provided that in hearings before justices of the peace, slaveowners and other interested parties could not testify and that alleged fugitives were to be given sufficient time to obtain evidence that they were free. Thus Pennsylvania attempted to balance its obligation under the fugitive slave clause with its interest in protecting free black citizens from kidnapping or being condemned to slavery in a kangaroo-court proceeding.

A complicated series of events brought questions concerning the meaning of the fugitive slave clause and the constitutionality of the Pennsylvania statute before the US Supreme Court in 1842. Margaret Morgan was the daughter of Maryland slaves who had been permitted by their owner to live as free persons. Like her parents, she was not claimed by her owner, married a free black man, and in 1832 moved to Pennsylvania, where at least one of her daughters was born. When Morgan's owner died in 1837, his niece and heiress hired Edward Prigg to go to Pennsylvania and claim Morgan and her children as fugitive slaves. Although Pennsylvania law recognized as free persons all children born in the state, Maryland law provided that slave status passed through the mother, thus making Margaret Morgan and all of her children slaves. Prigg obtained a warrant for the arrest of Morgan and her children, but the justice of the peace before whom they were brought refused to hear the case. Prigg then took matters into his own hands, seizing his prey and carrying them across the Maryland line to slavery.

Subsequently, Prigg was convicted of kidnapping by a Pennsylvania court, and the state supreme court upheld his conviction. In the 1842 case *Prigg v. Pennsylvania*, he appealed to the US Supreme Court, contending that the Pennsylvania law under which he was convicted violated the Constitution's fugitive slave clause and the Fugitive Slave Act of 1793. Justice Joseph Story, the distinguished Massachusetts jurist, wrote the opinion for the Court. Although Story personally disliked slavery, he feared that northern impediments to the return of fugitives would produce sectional animosity that might ultimately destroy the Union. Therefore, he offered a strongly proslavery interpretation of the fugitive slave clause, sacrificing black rights to the interest of sectional harmony and national unity.[18]

The decision upheld the constitutionality of the Fugitive Slave Act. Even though the fugitive slave clause did not expressly authorize congressional action, Story argued that it recognized the right of slaveowners to recover runaways and therefore implicitly empowered Congress to adopt legislation to enforce the right. He also struck down the Pennsylvania law under which Prigg had been convicted, asserting that the fugitive slave clause gave Congress exclusive authority to regulate the return of fugitive slaves (even though it did not give Congress express, much less exclusive, authority to legislate). Therefore, he reasoned, any state legislation on the subject was unconstitutional. Three of the nine justices disagreed on this point, arguing that state legislatures could or must pass laws to help slaveholders regain their property; however, even these justices agreed that the procedure mandated by the 1826 Pennsylvania law created barriers to the return of fugitives and was therefore unconstitutional. Despite this disagreement, the Court clearly suggested that the summary procedure authorized by the 1793 Fugitive Slave Act was constitutional and that state legislation seeking to add procedural safeguards to allow blacks to prove their freedom was unacceptable. When African Americans were involved, whether slave or free, the Court did not consider it necessary to require Congress to honor the procedural guarantees of the Bill of Rights or to permit state legislatures to compensate for Congress's omission.

A final aspect of the opinion, which went unchallenged, bears mention. Story held that the fugitive slave clause recognized a property right that extended throughout the Union. Therefore, he reasoned, slaveowners and their agents had the right to enter free states, seize fugitives, and carry them back to the South without obtaining judicial authorization. The definition of personal status contained in the law of the southern states thus had extraterritorial force in the free states, regardless of the policy of those states. Moreover, Story's interpretation left free blacks at the mercy of those who had the audacity to claim them as slaves and the power to seize them and carry them out of the state. Any legislation enacted by the states establishing mandatory procedures that gave alleged fugitives the opportunity to prove their freedom and protect themselves from enslavement was impermissible.

Ironically, *Prigg* offered blacks some hope. Story's opinion asserted that since justices of the peace were state officers, Congress could not compel them to enforce the Fugitive Slave Act. States might accept Congress's invitation to have their officials execute the law, but they were not required to do so. Many northern states responded by ordering state functionaries—sheriffs and jailers as well as justices of the peace—to refuse to arrest, hold, and return fugitives. Since there were few federal district judges to enforce the act (generally only two in each state), this aspect of the ruling made it difficult for slaveholders to obtain official assistance in securing runaways. Despite this bright spot, the *Prigg* decision gave explicit constitutional sanction to slavery, eroded the rights of free blacks, and made their liberty precarious. Moreover, the benefit that blacks received from *Prigg* was short-lived; in 1850, Congress gave in to southern demands, passed an even harsher fugitive law, and provided a small army of federal officials to enforce it.

Although fugitive slave legislation posed a special threat, other congressional measures eroded the rights of free blacks. In 1790, when Congress established regulations for immigrants to become naturalized citizens, it excluded blacks. Two years later it limited service in the militia (one of the responsibilities of citizenship in a republic) to whites, and in 1810 denied African Americans the right to carry the mail. In 1820, lawmakers authorized white citizens of the District of Columbia to establish a municipal government and to create a legal code for slaves and free blacks. In 1848, when Congress created the Oregon Territory, and again in 1850, when it established the New Mexico Territory, it denied African Americans the right to claim federal land there.

Because the national government exercised limited functions during the nineteenth century, state and local governments were far more significant in determining the rights that African Americans enjoyed. Moreover, in defining these rights, states operated virtually without restraint by the national government. The Constitution contained no guarantee of equal rights (except to states, which were guaranteed equal representation in the Senate) and few provisions protecting individual rights from infringement by state and local governments. It forbade states to enact ex-post-facto laws, bills of attainder, and laws impairing the obligation of contracts, but these restrictions offered slender protection to blacks. The Bill of Rights contained a long list of fundamental rights such as freedom of speech, press, and religion; the right to counsel and jury trial; and protection from self-incrimination and unreasonable search and seizure. In *Barron v. Baltimore* (1833), however, the US Supreme Court ruled that the Bill of Rights had been added to the Constitution to assuage fears of a powerful national government and served as a restriction on the national government but not on the states.[19] Although state constitutions generally contained provisions similar to those in the national Bill of Rights, state legislatures and courts determined the scope and applicability of such guarantees.

The privileges and immunities clause of Article IV, Section 2 ("the Citizens of Each State shall be entitled to all Privileges and Immunities of Citizens in the Several States") held out the possibility of national protection of individual rights. During the early nineteenth century, however, politicians, judges, and constitutional commentators disagreed over what the clause meant, and the US Supreme Court did not resolve the dispute. Some, including James Kent of New York, one of the nation's most influential judges and legal writers, believed that it did not create a body of fundamental rights that were protected against violation by the states. Rather, Kent contended, it merely guaranteed that a citizen of one state who entered a second state was entitled to whatever rights that state accorded its own citizens. In Kent's words, the clause "means only that citizens of other states shall have equal rights with our own citizens."[20] This reading of the clause neither shielded free blacks from denial of basic rights by the state in which they resided, nor protected them if they ventured into states that imposed discriminatory laws on their own black citizens.

Other judges and legal commentators argued that the clause was designed to protect the fundamental rights of United States citizens. US Supreme Court justice Bushrod Washington gave the most thorough statement of this position in his opinion in *Corfield v. Coryell* (1823), a case he decided while sitting as a US circuit court judge. Equating the rights guaranteed by the privileges and immunities clause with natural rights, he argued that they included those rights which "are, in their nature, fundamental; which belong, of right, to the citizens of all free governments." Noting that these were "more tedious than difficult to enumerate," Washington explained that they included "Protection by the government; the enjoyment of life and liberty, with the right to acquire and possess property of every kind, and to pursue and obtain happiness and safety; subject nevertheless to such restraints as the government may justly prescribe for the general good of the whole." Because these rights were fundamental and existed throughout the nation, citizens were entitled to enjoy them at home as well as in other states.[21]

Even when judges and legislators accepted this approach, it did not offer blacks unassailable protection. Washington himself noted that the fundamental rights he sketched were "subject . . . to such restraints as the government may justly prescribe for the general good of the whole." This had important implications in light of the expansion of state police power during the 1830s and 1840s. Most judges and legal experts agreed that the Constitution divided power into federal and state spheres, and that the police power—the authority to promote the public health, safety, and welfare—resided with the states. Thus states might justify special restrictions on free blacks on the grounds that they were necessary to prevent slave insurrection or to control individuals who were incapable of responsibly exercising rights enjoyed by whites.

A more fundamental problem stood in the way of using the privileges and immunities clause to protect blacks from discriminatory state action: there was no consensus that free blacks were citizens entitled to constitutional rights. The Constitution did not define national citizenship. Some legal writers pointed out that under traditional legal norms birth conferred citizenship and contended that all free persons born in this country were US citizens. Others argued that state citizenship was controlling and that all state citizens were citizens of the United States. The fact that the Constitution conferred important rights on state citizens seemed to support this view. For example, Article III provided that federal judicial authority extended to cases "between Citizens of different States," suggesting a federal right (to bring suit in federal court) that rested on one's status as a state citizen. Similarly, the privileges and immunities clause, read literally, conferred rights on state citizens. Because most free blacks were born in the United States and many were state citizens, either of these definitions entitled a significant number of free blacks to United States citizenship.

Most white southerners, however, denied that free blacks were United States citizens. Their position stemmed from self-interest. White southerners feared that as citizens, free blacks would be entitled by the privileges and immunities clause to travel freely throughout the South, perhaps encouraging slave rebellion. As Philip Barbour, who later served on the US Supreme Court, remarked in 1820, free blacks were "the most dangerous [class] to the community that can possibly be conceived. They are just enough elevated to have some sense of liberty, and yet not the capacity to estimate or enjoy all its rights . . . and being between two societies, above one and below the other, they are in a most dissatisfied state . . . firebrands to the other class of their own color."[22] To protect themselves, southerners argued that the framers had not considered blacks eligible for citizenship and that, consequently, they were not entitled to any rights created by the federal Constitution, including the rights conferred by the privileges and immunities clause. In 1820, for example, Charles Pinckney, who had been a delegate to the Constitutional Convention, asserted, "There did not then [1787] exist such a thing in the Union as a black or colored citizen, nor could I have conceived it possible such a thing could ever have existed in it."[23]

During the antebellum period, there was no authoritative resolution of the debate over African American citizenship. In the winter of 1820–1821, Congress discussed the issue when Missouri sought admission to the Union under a constitution that barred immigration by free blacks. Northern congressmen argued that this provision was unconstitutional because it denied free blacks the right, guaranteed by the privileges and immunities clause, to enter any state in the Union. Southerners responded that blacks were not US citizens and therefore were not entitled to rights created by the Constitution. Congress failed to resolve the issue, ending the debate by adopting an ambiguous compromise. Shortly after the Missouri debate, Attorney General William Wirt, a southerner, issued an opinion that lent support to the southern position.[24] Nevertheless, it had no legal authority and left the question unresolved.

In the 1820s and again in the 1840s, passage of state laws requiring incarceration of black sailors who entered southern ports renewed the debate. Because the laws affected African Americans who were citizens of northern states and who claimed to be US citizens, they raised the question of whether blacks were citizens protected by the privileges and immunities clause. As in the Missouri debates, however, there was no resolution. In 1823, Justice William Johnson of the US Supreme Court, while sitting as circuit judge for

South Carolina, struck down the South Carolina law, and Attorney General William Wirt issued an official opinion declaring the law unconstitutional. However, both did so on the grounds that it interfered with Congress's power to regulate interstate and foreign commerce and violated the treaty rights of foreign shippers. Neither held that the law violated rights enjoyed by African American sailors as state or US citizens under the Constitution's privileges and immunities clause.

In the early 1840s, when a congressional committee examined the constitutionality of the Negro seaman laws, a majority of its members supported a resolution declaring that the laws violated the rights of free blacks. However, a minority report asserted that African Americans were not US citizens and therefore not entitled to protection by the privileges and immunities clause. The full House of Representatives rejected the majority's resolution, implicitly endorsing the minority report. Dissatisfied by the House's action, the Massachusetts legislature dispatched lawyers to Charleston and New Orleans to file suits challenging the constitutionality of the laws. This tactic also failed to produce a ruling because mobs in both cities ran the Massachusetts emissaries out of town.

Slaves, Free Blacks, and the Law

Although the issue of African American citizenship remained unresolved, one thing was clear. Few Constitutional limitations governed how states might treat persons residing within their borders and even fewer if they were black. States, in the North as well as in the South, used this discretion to enact laws denying African Americans equal rights.

The slave codes of the southern states were the most egregious examples. They included statutes enacted by state legislatures and rules established by state courts as they interpreted and applied existing law to individual cases. Although this body of law varied among states and changed over time, there are enough similarities between states and sufficient continuity during the antebellum years to permit generalization. Southern law stipulated that a person born of a slave mother was the property of his or her mother's owner, who had an absolute legal right (in the words of the Louisiana code) to "sell him, dispose of his person, his industry, and his labor."[25] Regarded as things rather than persons, slaves did not enjoy a legal right to own property. In practice, some slaves were allowed to work for others during their spare time or to sell produce raised in their gardens, and many used the proceeds to acquire property. However, they had no legal title to this property and held it at the sufferance of their masters, not as a matter of legal right.

Slaves could not enter legally binding contracts and, because marriage was a civil contract, could not legally marry. Most slaves established long-term monogamous relationships, expected fidelity from their spouses, and established families and complex kinship networks. Because slave marriages were not recognized by the law, however, masters could separate husbands from wives and parents from children. "The relationship between slaves is essentially different from that of man and wife joined in lawful wedlock," noted the North Carolina Supreme Court, for "with slaves it may be dissolved . . . by the sale of one or both, depending upon the caprice or necessity of the owners."[26] Indeed, the sale of slaves—whether to obtain needed capital, get rid of a recalcitrant slave, settle an estate, or satisfy the judgment of a court—was common. And sales frequently ended marriages and separated family members.

Southern law also stripped slaves of other personal rights. Concerned about the problem of runaways, legislatures required slaves to carry passes when they left their owners' plantations and established slave patrols whose members had authority to beat slaves found traveling without passes. In order to prevent slaves from reading abolitionist tracts and forging passes, statutes barred anyone from teaching a slave to read or write. Southern legislatures attempted to prevent slave insurrections by prohibiting slaves from possessing firearms or other weapons and by making it illegal for slaves to gather in groups of five or more outside the presence of a white person. To encourage deference, southern law made it a crime for a slave to strike a white person and authorized whites to chastise insolent slaves. According to a North Carolina judge, insolence could manifest as "a look, the pointing of a finger, a refusal or neglect to step out of the way when a white person is seen to approach. . . . such acts violate the rules of propriety, and, if tolerated, would destroy that subordination, upon which our social system rests."[27]

To protect slaveowners' property and bring the law into line with southerners' claim that theirs was a mild, paternalistic form of slavery, the slave codes afforded slaves protection against abuse by their owners and other whites. Statutes defined the willful and malicious killing of a slave by an owner or other white person as murder and provided that whites might be fined for undue cruelty to slaves even if it did not result in death. Thus the Louisiana code provided that an owner or overseer might be fined for punishing a slave with "unusual rigor . . . so as to maim or mutilate him."[28] As might be expected, such laws afforded slaves little protection. Masters and overseers had the right to whip or use other forms of "moderate correction" on slaves who disobeyed, worked poorly, stole, or ran away. And if a slave resisted, a master, overseer, or patrol member might employ sufficient force to quell the resistance, even if it led to the slave's death. Because whites had such broad authority to use force and only whites sat on juries, whites were rarely indicted or convicted of murdering or abusing a slave.

Policy as well as prejudice led southern whites to subordinate free blacks as well as slaves. "If all blacks see all of their color slaves, it will seem to them a disposition of Providence, and they will be content," observed one Virginia legislator in 1806. "But if they see others like themselves free, and enjoying rights they are deprived of they will repine."[29] Lawmakers throughout the South did their best to guarantee that free blacks enjoyed few rights. In the early years of the nineteenth century most southern states regarded free blacks as citizens, albeit citizens who did not enjoy all the rights of white persons, and several permitted free blacks to vote if they met existing property-holding requirements. By the 1820s and 1830s, however, the rapid growth of the free black population in the Upper South, combined with growing fear of slave insurrection and the insistence of proslavery writers that all blacks were naturally suited to slavery, led to steady erosion of the rights of free blacks. As the century progressed, the few states that had permitted free blacks to vote disfranchised them, judges handed down decisions declaring that they were not citizens, and legislators enacted a remarkable array of restrictions on their freedom. Joseph Lumpkin of the Georgia Supreme Court perhaps best summarized the position of the South's 250,000 free blacks on the eve of the Civil War:

> The *status* of the African in Georgia, whether bond or free, is such that he has no civil, social or political rights or capacity, whatever, except such as are bestowed upon him by statute; . . . the act of manumission confers no other right but . . . freedom from the dominion of the master, and the limited liberty of locomotion. . . .[30]

As Lumpkin's statement suggests, the law frequently equated free blacks with slaves, in the process diminishing their status as free persons. In most states free blacks accused of noncapital crimes were tried by the same panels of justices of the peace and citizens that meted out summary justice to slaves. When convicted, they were not only liable to imprisonment but, like slaves, might receive thirty-nine lashes at the public whipping post. The law also demanded that free blacks as well as slaves be submissive to whites. Mississippi and Florida provided that any black who "shall at any time use abusive and provoking language to, or raise his hand" against a white person might be whipped. Other states authorized whites to chastise "insolent" free blacks. "Free negroes . . . ought by law to be compelled to demean themselves as inferiors," noted John B. O'Neall of the South Carolina Court of Appeals. "I have always thought [this] and while on the circuit ruled that words of impertinence and insolence addressed by a free negro to a white man, would justify an assault and battery."[31] In addition, every slave state except Delaware and Louisiana denied free blacks as well as slaves the right to testify in cases involving whites, making it difficult to prosecute whites who committed crimes against them.

Free blacks also suffered significant restrictions of their personal liberty. Because southern state law assumed that African Americans were slaves, free blacks were required to carry papers proving their freedom and could be seized as fugitive slaves if they were unable to produce them. They also had to register periodically with local authorities, thus subjecting themselves to questioning and scrutiny by whites. Southern state and local officials used laws prohibiting free blacks from meeting without white supervision to deter them from establishing independent churches, and several states went so far as to make it illegal for free blacks to learn to read and write. Highly subjective vagrancy laws provided that free blacks who lived in idleness or who lacked industrious habits could be bound to labor for whites. State laws and municipal ordinances prohibited free blacks from practicing many occupations.

Worst of all, the legal system left free blacks at the mercy of whites. Those who were suspected of criminal activity or impropriety, offended the sensibilities of whites, or aroused the jealousy or enmity of whites were likely to be victims of mob violence. "Who does not know that when a free Negro . . . has rendered himself obnoxious to a neighborhood," noted a Virginian in 1832, "how easy it is for a party to visit him one night, take him from his bed and his family, and apply to him the gentle admonition of a severe flagellation, to induce him to go away."[32] Indeed, African Americans could be induced to go away because there was little chance that white sheriffs and juries would afford them redress against their assailants. Moreover, given the complex web of laws that entwined them and the fact that many of these gave considerable discretion to local officials, whites could snatch away the limited liberty that free blacks enjoyed. If they failed to register with local authorities at the prescribed time, lacked adequate documentation to prove their freedom, practiced a forbidden occupation, or appeared to local whites to be indolent, they could be dragged to the whipping post, hired out to white farmers, or (in some states) sold into slavery.

Between 1800 and the mid-1840s, African Americans who lived north of slavery also witnessed a steady erosion of their rights. Most northern states banned interracial marriages, and many either permitted or required school boards to establish segregated schools. Six northern states denied African Americans an essential tool of self-protection by prohibiting them from testifying in cases in which a white person was a party. Ohio (1804), Indiana (1831), Illinois (1813), Iowa (1839), and Michigan (1827) attempted to prohibit blacks from entering their borders by enacting measures requiring black immigrants to post bonds guaranteeing their good behavior or by imposing fines or imprisonment on black immigrants.

Northern states also restricted blacks' political rights. In 1800, most permitted black men to vote, provided they met the property requirements that applied to white men; however, as states expanded whites' access to the ballot box by abolishing property requirements, they generally excluded blacks from the polls. With the exception of Maine, none of the states that entered the Union after 1800 permitted blacks to vote in general elections. Among the older states, New Jersey (1807), Connecticut (1818), and Pennsylvania (1838) stripped blacks of political rights as they established universal white manhood suffrage. By 1860, only Massachusetts, Maine, New Hampshire, Vermont, and Rhode Island allowed blacks to vote on the same terms as whites, and New York permitted black men to vote if they owned $250 worth of property, a requirement that did not apply to white men.

Still there were significant differences between the plight of northern and southern free blacks. Southern laws governing free blacks were much more restrictive and repressive than those on northern statute books, making southern free blacks little better than slaves without masters. Moreover, because it was absolutely unthinkable for them to demand equal rights and they had no allies in the white community, the plight of southern free blacks could only worsen. In the North, proponents of racial equality were not popular and were sometimes mobbed or even murdered. There was sufficient tolerance, however, that blacks could organize and protest against discrimination and find white allies to help them press their demands. Therefore, while the position of southern free blacks steadily deteriorated, northern free blacks made important gains during the late 1840s and the 1850s.

That was in the future, however. As the nation annexed Texas in 1845 and went to war with Mexico in 1846, it had moved far away from the antislavery and equalitarian promise of the Revolution. Delegates to the Constitutional Convention had made important concessions to slavery, and during the succeeding decades politicians and judges had used these to create a constitutional order that promoted slavery and permitted racial subordination. As a result, free blacks in the North as well as the South had seen their rights steadily erode. Slavery, which had appeared to be receding in the Revolution's aftermath, had marched triumphantly westward, establishing beachheads across the Mississippi River in Louisiana, Arkansas, Missouri, and Texas. As the United States went to war with Mexico in 1846, many predicted that it would move to the Pacific. Yet not everyone was willing to concede that the Constitution was a proslavery document; northern blacks and white abolitionists were already busy creating an antislavery constitutionalism. The war with Mexico would prove to be a watershed, polarizing American politics along sectional lines, reviving a broad-based northern antislavery sentiment, and reestablishing the allure of the Revolution's commitment to the "rights of man" among northerners.

2

Law and Liberty, 1830–1860

Thirty-seven African American delegates assembled in the Second Baptist Church of Columbus, Ohio, on a cold January day in 1851 to open the annual Convention of the Colored Citizens of Ohio. Representing 26,000 black Ohioans, the delegation included artisans, barbers, teachers, and ministers. Although delegates discussed strategies for repealing discriminatory state laws and building a united, self-conscious black community, they were especially concerned about the Fugitive Slave Act of 1850, which Congress had passed the previous fall to replace the venerable 1793 law. Like the old law, the 1850 statute allowed masters to reclaim runaway slaves merely on the basis of sworn testimony and denied alleged fugitives basic procedural rights. The new law went further, however, creating a formidable enforcement apparatus. It authorized appointment of hundreds of US commissioners to conduct hearings and to authorize the return of runaways, making it much easier for slaveowners to recover their human property. It also provided commissioners a $10 fee if they ruled in favor of masters and only half that amount if they found in favor of an alleged fugitive. The law not only posed a serious threat to fugitive slaves but placed northern free blacks in danger of legally sanctioned kidnapping. Indeed, thousands of northern blacks— including some of the delegates' friends and neighbors—had fled to Canada in the wake of its passage, and as the convention met, delegates learned that a black man had been seized as a fugitive slave in southwest Ohio.

Emotions ran high as delegates denounced the new law and demanded its repeal. In leading the attack, John Mercer Langston—who would later join the bar, establish the Law Department at Howard University, and become Howard's president—invoked the Constitution. Citing its guarantee of trial by jury, due process of law, and habeas corpus, he contended that the fugitive law was not only unjust but flagrantly unconstitutional. "This enactment," Langston charged, "possesses neither the form nor the essence of true law . . . [and] is a hideous deformity in the *garb* of law. It kills alike, the true spirit of the Declaration of Independence, the Constitution, and the palladium of our liberties."[1]

Promises to Keep. Donald G. Nieman, Oxford University Press (2020). © Oxford University Press. DOI: 10.1093/oso/9780190071639.001.0001

That Langston's speech invoked constitutional principles to attack slavery and discrimination was hardly surprising. The Constitution was a vital part of antebellum popular consciousness, and nineteenth-century Americans—not just lawyers—commonly spoke in constitutional terms when debating political and social issues. Indeed, Langston's constitutional analysis was quickly challenged by H. Ford Douglas, a nineteen-year-old barber from Cleveland. Although he had escaped from a Virginia plantation only four years earlier, Douglas was a formidable opponent, on the rise as one of the most forceful abolitionist orators in the state. He argued that the Constitution protected slavery and stood as an obstacle to black liberation:

> I hold, sir, that the Constitution of the United States is pro-slavery, considered so by those who framed it. . . . It is well known that . . . in the Convention that framed the Constitution, there was considerable discussion on the subject of slavery. South Carolina and Georgia refused to come into the Union [unless] the Convention would allow the continuation of the Slave Trade for twenty years . . . the Convention submitted to that guilty contract. . . . Here we see them engrafting on the Constitution a clause legalizing and protecting one of the vilest systems of wrong ever invented by the cupidity and avarice of man. . . . That instrument also provides for the return of fugitive slaves. And, sir, . . . the "Fugitive Law" is in accordance with that stipulation;—a law unequaled in the worst days of Roman despotism, and unparalleled in the annals of heathen jurisprudence. . . .

Douglas concluded that African Americans must reject such a document and refuse to participate in a constitutional order that held millions of African Americans in chains. Consequently, he urged African Americans to remain aloof from a system that originated in a corrupt bargain and proposed a resolution declaring that "no colored man can consistently vote under the United States Constitution."[2]

Douglas's characterization of the Constitution did not meet a sympathetic response. William Howard Day charged that Douglas failed to distinguish between the Constitution and the interpretation given it by proslavery judges and politicians. The Constitution was a malleable document, he contended. Correctly understood, it was a force for black liberty and equality. Day explained:

Sir, coming up as I do, in the midst of three millions of men in chains, and five hundred thousand only half-free, I consider every instrument precious which guarantees to me liberty. I consider the Constitution the foundation of American liberties, and wrapping myself in the flag of the nation, I would plant myself upon that Constitution, and using the weapons they have given me, I would appeal to the American people for the rights thus guaranteed.[3]

In the end, Langston and Day easily prevailed, and Douglas's motion went down to defeat, 28–2.

The debate at Columbus suggested that northern blacks had kept the dream of freedom, citizenship, and equality alive. In the face of six decades of steady defeats, they continued to cling to the equalitarian principles of the Revolution. Indeed, between 1830 and 1860, northern blacks and their white abolitionist allies skillfully used these principles to develop a powerful constitutional attack on slavery and racial subordination. Initially rejected as the work of a lunatic fringe, by the late 1840s and the 1850s their views gained wider currency among mainstream northern politicians who subjected proslavery constitutionalism to its severest challenge and the Union to its supreme test.

African Americans, Abolitionists, and the Emergence of Antislavery Constitutionalism

Northern blacks took the lead in challenging proslavery constitutionalism. Beginning in 1830, northern black leaders organized a series of national conventions that met sporadically throughout the antebellum years. Given the state-centered nature of the pre–Civil War constitutional system, however, many of the problems confronting free blacks were local rather than national. Therefore, black leaders increasingly turned their efforts to state conventions; the first state convention met in New York in 1837 and was followed by a proliferation of local meetings during the 1840s and 1850s. These national and state conclaves—like the 1851 Columbus meeting—not only helped beleaguered free black communities develop the institutions and solidarity necessary to survive in an increasingly hostile world, they also served as the whetstone on which African Americans honed their attack on slavery and racial discrimination.

The genesis of the convention movement paralleled the emergence of a small but imaginative cadre of radical abolitionists. Rising to prominence in the North during the early 1830s, this diverse group—which included blacks and whites, women and men—denounced slavery in harsh, uncompromising terms. While abolitionists charged that slavery made a mockery of the republican principle of equality, they rested their attack primarily on religious principles and passions. Slavery was a sin, they contended, because it "debased the physical, and defiled the moral workmanship of the great God" and ignored the Gospel's admonition to "love your neighbor as yourself." Claiming that "there is no such thing as holding on to sin with safety," abolitionists eschewed gradualism and called for immediate emancipation.[4] They also challenged racism, the foundation of the proslavery argument, by asserting that it violated the Christian belief that all were equal in God's eyes. Consequently, abolitionists created a powerful argument for black equality.

Not content to wage a campaign of conversion, many abolitionists turned to political action. Shortly after its inception in 1833, the American Anti-Slavery Society sponsored a massive petition campaign designed to prod Congress to abolish slavery in the nation's capital. Throughout the 1830s abolitionists also attempted to influence the political process by questioning candidates about their views on slavery and throwing their support to those who best approximated the antislavery standard. By the late 1830s, however, many were disenchanted with the effectiveness of this strategy and moved toward formation of a third party. Although some prominent leaders (most notably William Lloyd Garrison) opposed them, such antislavery radicals as Henry Stanton, Alvan Stewart, James Birney, Joshua Leavitt, William Goodell, and Gerrit Smith eagerly embraced independent political action and formed the Liberty Party in 1839.

The debate over political action led abolitionists into the realm of constitutional theory, as they, like other Americans, looked to the Constitution for justification of their political agenda. Garrison and his supporters, eager to prevent northerners from smugly assuming that they had nothing to do with slavery, argued that the Constitution supported slavery. Exploiting James Madison's notes on the Constitutional Convention, which first appeared in 1840, Garrisonians gleefully debunked the framers' reputation as opponents of slavery. They charged that southern delegates had demanded protection for slavery and that northerners had cravenly abandoned their principles and acquiesced in provisions that protected, even promoted, slavery. According to Garrison, who dramatized his position by publicly burning a copy of the

Constitution, the document was "a covenant with death, and an agreement with Hell."[5] Northerners should annul it and withdraw from the Union because it protected slavery and slaveholders.

Other abolitionists categorically rejected Garrison's analysis. Frederick Douglass, a onetime ally of Garrison who rejected Garrisonian constitutional ideas in the late 1840s, most eloquently and persuasively articulated their position. Douglass argued that a close reading of the Constitution demonstrated that it did not expressly mention slavery, much less guarantee its existence. On the contrary, it contained provisions that were incompatible with slavery. He also brushed aside the contention that Madison's notes proved that the framers had acceded to southerners' demands for provisions that would protect and promote slavery. Douglass suggested that such an argument was preposterous: it "disregarded the plain and common sense reading of the instrument itself" and assumed that "the Constitution does not mean what it says and says what it does not mean." He also chided his opponents for confusing the Constitution with the way in which it had been interpreted by proslavery politicians and judges. "The Constitution is one thing, its administration is another," he noted, "and, in this instance, a very different and opposite thing." Finally, Douglass recognized that the Constitution, because it was written in general language, was an open-ended document capable of serving the cause of freedom and equality. "The Constitution, as well as the Declaration of Independence, and the sentiments of the founders of the Republic," he explained, "give us a platform broad enough, and strong enough, to support the most comprehensive plans for the freedom and elevation of all the people of this country, without regard to color, class, or clime."[6]

Rejection of the Garrisonian position led to an outpouring of abolitionist books and pamphlets that found in the Constitution a powerful weapon against slavery and discrimination. Although abolitionist constitutional theory did not win acceptance by the courts, Congress, or the president in the decades preceding the Civil War, it was not without effect. It gave birth to constitutional principles that would become influential during the 1860s, helping to transform the Constitution into a document that promoted equality and individual rights and empowered the national government to protect them.

The dominant group in the Liberty Party developed a moderate antislavery constitutionalism. Led by Salmon P. Chase, a future US senator and chief justice of the United States, it attempted to deflect charges that they were irresponsible radicals whose policies would drive southerners to secession.

Figure 2.1. Antislavery meeting, Cazenovia, New York, 1850, to protest
the Fugitive Slave Act. Frederick Douglass is seated to the left of the table,
Theodosia Gilbert is on his right, and Gerrit Smith is standing behind them.
The Edmundson sisters, whose freedom had been purchased by members of
Henry Ward Beecher's congregation in Brooklyn after their celebrated but failed
attempt to escape, are on either side of Smith. *Madison County Historical Society,
Oneida, New York.*

Moderates conceded that in order to bring the South into the Union, the
framers had agreed to deny the national government authority to interfere with slavery in states where it already existed. Nevertheless, moderates
argued that the framers, hostile to slavery, had attempted to put it on the road
to extinction. They insisted that the Declaration of Independence stated the

fundamental values that the framers of the Constitution attempted to implement and argued that its powerful assertion of equality and natural rights clearly established the framers' antipathy to slavery. They reinforced this argument by referencing the Northwest Ordinance of 1787. In attempting to keep slavery from spreading into new territory, moderates claimed, the Confederation Congress, which included a number of delegates to the Philadelphia Convention, reasserted its hostility to slavery and its commitment to the Declaration of Independence.

Moderates also identified specific provisions in the Constitution as hostile to slavery. The clause recognizing congressional power to end the importation of slaves after 1808, they argued, was designed to restrict the growth of slavery. They contended that the commerce clause, by giving Congress plenary authority over interstate commerce, empowered it to prohibit the interstate slave trade. This would prevent slaveowners in Virginia and Maryland, where the soil was depleted and plantation agriculture unprofitable, from shipping their slaves to the West and, instead, would encourage manumission. Moderates even interpreted the fugitive slave clause as restricting federal support for the return of runaways, arguing that it did not permit federal action to return fugitives but was merely an admonition to the states. Constitutional provisions giving Congress full authority over the District of Columbia and the territories, antislavery moderates asserted, also enabled it to strike at slavery by abolishing it in the District and, following the example of the Northwest Ordinance, forbidding it to enter the territories.

The most innovative aspect of the moderate position was its use of the Fifth Amendment's due process clause. Traditionally, lawyers understood due process to guarantee persons accused of crimes certain procedural rights such as the right to be informed of the charges against them, the right to counsel, the right to trial by jury, and protection against self-incrimination. Abolitionists, however, gave the clause a substantive interpretation, suggesting that there were certain fundamental rights—such as liberty of movement, freedom to pursue the occupation of one's choosing, and the absolute right of self-ownership—that government could not abridge. Consequently, they argued that slavery violated the due process clause and that the federal government could not tolerate it anywhere within its jurisdiction, whether in the District of Columbia or the territories.

Moderates asserted that the framers had intended to make slavery a local institution, confined to the southeastern states, where it would gradually wither and die. This far-sighted policy, they contended, had been subverted by proslavery domination of the national government, which had resulted in federal action to protect slavery and, worst of all, to promote its expansion. Moderates thus called for a return to the original principles of the founders: the federal government must divorce itself from slavery, abolishing it in the District of Columbia and the territories, repealing the Fugitive Slave Act, and prohibiting the transport of slaves in interstate commerce. Because moderate abolitionists, like most other Americans, believed that slavery had to expand to remain economically viable, they assumed that this would strangle slavery, as the founders had intended.

Radical abolitionist legal theorists—Alvan Stewart, William Goodell, Lysander Spooner, and Joel Tiffany—took this argument further. They argued that all persons possessed certain natural rights, including freedom, personal security, and a right to the fruits of their labor, and that government existed to guarantee these rights. Drawing on a natural rights tradition that had deep roots in popular political culture and constitutional theory, they took the radical position that Congress had an obligation to extirpate slavery. Indeed, they cited US Supreme Court justices Samuel Chase, John Marshall, and Joseph Story, who had suggested that statutes violating principles of natural law lacked legitimacy. Radicals also used the Declaration of Independence to attack slavery, appealing to deeply rooted values with broad popular appeal. They argued that the Declaration contained the principles on which the nation had been founded and asserted that the framers had intended to implement these principles when they drafted the Constitution. To accept the Constitution as a substitute for the Declaration, they insisted, "would be to accept the shell, and throw the kernel away."[7] Radicals contended, therefore, that principles of natural rights and equality suffused the Constitution, empowering—indeed, requiring—Congress to abolish slavery throughout the nation.

Radicals also found grounds for emancipation in the text of the Constitution. They argued that the Fifth Amendment's due process clause applied not only to the federal government but to the states and that it prohibited them from enforcing laws that maintained slavery. Although the Supreme Court had held that the Bill of Rights restricted only the federal government, the radical position was not without merit. As agitators for constitutional change, radicals could hope to convince the Court to reverse itself, as it had done on more than one occasion. Indeed, unlike the First Amendment which explicitly restricts Congress, the wording of the Fifth Amendment ("No person shall be . . . deprived") could be easily construed to apply to state governments, giving the Court an opening to reverse itself. Radicals also exploited the guarantee clause (Article IV, section 4), which provided that "the United States shall guarantee to each State in this Union a Republican form of Government." Because slavery created a privileged caste and stripped African Americans of the most fundamental rights, they argued, no state that tolerated slavery could be truly republican. Radicals therefore concluded that Congress could only fulfill its obligation under the guarantee clause by abolishing slavery.

Abolitionists also devoted considerable attention to the plight of free blacks. Black abolitionists were especially sensitive to this issue because they understood the social consequences of discrimination. They realized that discriminatory law was not merely an effect of racism, but that it marked African Americans as inferiors and thus deepened the racism that constrained black economic opportunity. "The colored people of this State are, from the non-possession of the right of suffrage, the proscribed class," representatives of New York's black community explained. "This proscription is the fountain Marah, from whence proceed those bitter waters that run through all the various ramifications of society, connecting themselves with all our relations." African American leaders also understood that only by asserting their right to equal treatment could blacks achieve self-respect. As Michigan blacks noted in demanding political rights, "the enjoyment of those rights in a free country, is a stimulant to enterprise, a means of influence, and a source of respect; they send life, vigor and energy through the entire heart of a people."[8]

African American abolitionists built their case for equal rights on the foundation of citizenship. As historian Martha Jones has demonstrated, African Americans "claimed an unassailable belonging, one grounded in birthright citizenship."[9] Black abolitionists pointed out that European, English, and American authorities agreed that "the strongest claim to citizenship is birthplace" and that "in whatever country or place you may be born, you are in the first and highest sense a citizen." "The claims are . . . founded in the fact that they [blacks] are citizens by birth and blood," noted Hosea Easton, a black minister, in 1837. "Complexion has never been made the legal test of citizenship in any age in the world. It has been established generally by birth and blood."[10] Because the framers did not explicitly define citizenship, abolitionists contended, they accepted this common understanding. The most potent argument on behalf of African American citizenship, however, grew out of the historical memory of the black community. Black abolitionists reminded Americans that in 1787 free blacks had been citizens with access to the ballot box in many states and that they had shouldered the responsibilities of citizens, serving with distinction in the Revolution and the War of 1812. "We are Americans. We were born in no foreign clime," explained the report of the 1840 New York State Convention of Colored People. "We have not been brought up under the influence of other strange, aristocratic, and uncongenial political relations. In this respect, we profess to be American and republican."[11]

Abolitionists argued that if they were to be true to the principles of republicanism and the ideas expressed in the Declaration of Independence, states must grant all citizens equal rights, regardless of race. "That Declaration, and that Constitution . . . may be considered as more fully developing the ideas of American republicanism, than any other documents," delegates to the 1840 New York Convention of Colored Men asserted in a petition calling for an end to discriminatory voting requirements. "In these, individuals are regarded distinctly and respectively—each and every one as men, fully capacitated by the Creator for government and progressive advancement." Members of the Liberty Party agreed. The party's 1844 platform urged "the friends of Liberty in all those free States where any inequality of rights and privileges exists on account of color, to employ their utmost energies to remove all such remnants and effects of the slave system."[12]

Some abolitionists went beyond this, urging that the national government had authority to protect individual rights against infringement by the states. Radical constitutional theorists, most notably Joel Tiffany and Lysander Spooner, argued that the national government, by its very nature, had the authority, indeed, the obligation to protect the fundamental rights of its citizens. Such rights included "full and ample protection . . . of . . . personal security, personal liberty, and private property, . . . protection against the oppression of individuals, communities and nations, foreign nations and domestic states: against lawless violence exercised under the forms of governmental authority."[13] Moreover, Tiffany and Spooner insisted that the Constitution and Bill of Rights were designed to protect these fundamental rights from encroachment by national and state governments and private individuals.

In the antebellum federal system, states could define the rights of individuals with only minimal interference or supervision by the federal government. In this context, Tiffany's and Spooner's argument was truly radical. While it would enter political discourse and become influential in the 1860s, it had limited utility in the antebellum years. Not only did it go against the assumptions of most Americans, who saw local autonomy as essential to democracy and necessary to the continued existence of a nation as large and diverse as the United States. But with the federal courts, Congress, and the presidency in the hands of those sympathetic to slavery, it made little sense to press for federal action against state discrimination. Nevertheless, abolitionists' understanding of the Declaration of Independence, republicanism, and citizenship enabled them to develop strong arguments against discriminatory state law and policy.

Consider two examples. During the early nineteenth century the Boston School Committee established a separate elementary school for African American children and excluded blacks from the city's other elementary schools. In the 1840s, after a campaign of sit-ins and political action that compelled the state's railroads to end segregation, Boston blacks trained their sights on segregated schools. In 1849, when the committee rejected petitions calling for admission of African Americans to the white schools, Benjamin Roberts, a black activist whose six-year-old daughter Sarah had been denied admission to the school closest to her home, challenged school segregation in the Massachusetts courts.

Robert Morris, a black lawyer, and Charles Sumner, a white abolitionist who would go on to a distinguished career in the US Senate, represented Roberts. Building their case on the Declaration of Independence and the Massachusetts Constitution's assertion that "All men are created free and equal," they rejected the Boston School Committee's contention that it provided blacks with an equal, but separate, education. Morris and Sumner argued that segregation recognized distinctions among citizens on the basis of birth and therefore violated the principle of equality. "The equality declared by our fathers . . . was *Equality before the Law*," they explained. "Its object was to efface all political or civil distinctions, and to abolish all institutions founded upon *birth*." Morris and Sumner also charged that segregation hurt African Americans by marking them as a proscribed class and teaching white children to despise them. "Nursed in this sentiment of Caste . . . they [whites] are unable to eradicate it from their natures . . . and . . . continue to embody and perpetuate it in their institutions."[14] The Massachusetts Supreme Judicial Court rejected these arguments, holding that as long as African Americans enjoyed access to schools that provided an education equivalent to that enjoyed by whites, the Constitution's guarantee of equality was met, even if they were educated in segregated schools. Undaunted by their failure in

Figure 2.2.   Robert Morris. *Social Law Library, Boston, Massachusetts.*

court, African Americans turned their attention to the legislature, which recognized their claim by outlawing segregation in the state's schools in 1855.

African Americans in New York City also challenged segregation.
Manhattan's numerous street railroads, operated by private companies
under charters from the city, offered thoroughly segregated service. Black
customers might ride outside on the platforms of the cars reserved for whites
or wait for one of the few cars set aside for the exclusive use of blacks. Shortly
after the street railroads began their operations in the early 1850s, African
Americans engaged in direct action to challenge segregation, entering
whites-only cars, refusing to leave, and, usually, being assaulted and thrown
into the streets by drivers and conductors. In 1854, Elizabeth Jennings sued
the Third Avenue Railroad after being forcibly expelled from a whites-only
car, and a jury awarded her $225 in damages. African American leaders used
Jennings's victory to encourage black assertiveness. "Don't let them [rail-
road officials] frighten you with words," one urged, "the law is right, and so is
public sentiment."[15]

MRS. ELIZABETH GRAHAM.

Figure 2.3. Elizabeth Jennings. *Kansas State Historical, Topeka, Kansas.*

Most of the companies, however, continued to practice segregation. In 1855, the Reverend James Pennington, a black Presbyterian minister, was thrown out of a whites-only car on the Sixth Avenue Railroad. Pennington sued the company, arguing that, as a citizen, he was entitled to service without distinction or discrimination from a company that was chartered to serve the public. As the suit dragged on, Pennington and other black leaders encouraged continued resistance to segregation by forming the Legal Rights Association, an organization designed "to raise means to protect persons who are assaulted while standing up for their rights." The association did not win a ruling against segregation, however. When Pennington's case went to trial, the judge informed the jury that the companies might make reasonable rules and regulations to govern passengers. In deciding whether rules prescribing segregated service were reasonable, he added, jurors must consider "the probable effect upon the capital, business and interests of companies admitting blacks into their cars indiscriminately with whites." Not surprisingly, the jury decided against Pennington. Despite this setback, the city's blacks continued to enter whites-only cars, convincing some, but not all, of the companies to abandon segregation.[16] Thus in New York, as in Boston, equalitarian ideas served as a rallying point for African Americans, encouraging them to assert their rights and challenge the caste system.

Antislavery Constitutionalism Enters the Political Mainstream

The political crisis of the late 1840s and 1850s broadened the appeal of abolitionist constitutional ideas, giving them currency outside the ranks of northern blacks and white abolitionists. The annexation of Texas in 1845 and the Mexican War of 1846–1848 added the vast territories of the Southwest to the Republic. They also ignited a bitter debate over slavery and whether it should be permitted in the newly acquired territories. While Congress patched over the territorial question in the Compromise of 1850, a part of the compromise, the draconian Fugitive Slave Act of 1850, brought the grim reality of slavery to northern attention as slaveowners stepped up efforts to capture runaways, and blacks and abolitionists resisted. While this perceptibly increased northern antislavery sentiment, it was the Kansas-Nebraska Act of 1854 that irreversibly damaged sectional harmony. By accepting southern demands for repeal of the Missouri Compromise's exclusion of slavery from the two territories, Congress appeared to many northerners to be in the grip of proslavery forces intent on expanding slavery and, concomitantly, southern political power. Northerners flocked to the Republican Party, which emerged in the uproar over the Kansas-Nebraska Act, calling for an end to southern domination of the national government, denouncing the social system of the slave South, and demanding containment of slavery.

The new party made the Kansas-Nebraska Act and the issue of slavery extension matters of vital importance to northerners. Republicans denounced the Kansas-Nebraska bill as yet another example of slaveholders' domination of the national government. Embracing the abolitionist interpretation of the Constitution as an antislavery document, they contended that the Kansas-Nebraska Act subverted the design of the framers and further eroded the principles of equality and natural rights on which the nation had been founded. They also argued that the expansion of slavery had serious social consequences for whites; slavery destroyed the work ethic by associating labor with a despised caste, discouraged whites from diligent toil, and thereby deprived individuals of the means of advancement. If slavery took root in the West, Republicans warned, it would diminish opportunities for aspiring northerners and strengthen a decadent social system. Even though the party won virtually no support in the South, it spread triumphantly across the North, enjoyed substantial strength in Congress by 1855, and came remarkably close to winning the presidency in 1856.

Despite Republican denunciation of the South and slavery, it was not an abolitionist party and in fact sought to distance itself from the abolitionists. Republicans promised to stop the spread of slavery, which they asserted would lead to the gradual death of slavery where it already existed; however, they were eager to dispel the charge that they were irresponsible fanatics who threatened the Union and repeatedly said that the national government had no authority to interfere with slavery in those states that sanctioned it. Moreover, Republicans, themselves by no means free of prejudice, realized the depth of northern racism and trimmed their position accordingly. In the face of taunts by Democrats denouncing them as proponents of African American equality who condoned interracial marriage, most Republicans repeatedly proclaimed that they did not support black suffrage or social contacts between the races. In addition, many Republicans asserted that colonization was the best solution to the nation's racial problem and enthusiastically supported schemes to encourage free blacks to emigrate and establish colonies in the Caribbean, Central America, and Africa.

The party, nonetheless, took a position on African American rights that reflected the influence of abolitionist constitutional ideas. Republicans agreed with non-Garrisonian abolitionists that the framers of the Constitution had attempted to prevent the spread of slavery and had hoped to set it on the path to extinction. Like moderate abolitionists, they asserted that the Fifth Amendment's due process clause guaranteed all persons freedom and natural rights and of its own force abolished slavery in all areas—such as the territories—under the exclusive control of the national government. Many Republicans also contended that native-born free blacks were state citizens and thus entitled to rights guaranteed by the US Constitution. During the late 1850s, Republican conventions in several states affirmed that free blacks were citizens, as did Republican-controlled legislatures in New Hampshire, New York, Vermont, and Ohio, and the Republican justices on the Maine Supreme Court.

Perhaps even more remarkable, given widespread northern racism, Republicans argued that the principles of the Declaration of Independence established the foundation of republican government and applied to all persons, regardless of race. Granted, they hedged their position, explaining that this did not entitle African Americans to political rights or to social equality. What it did guarantee, they asserted, was equality of civil and natural rights. Thus, while most Republicans did not believe that free blacks were entitled to vote or to receive service in hotels and restaurants frequented by whites, they did insist that all free persons should enjoy the same rights to freedom of movement, to own and control property, to testify in courts, and to the protection of the laws. Abraham Lincoln best articulated this position in his 1858 debates with Stephen Douglas. He admitted that he had "no purpose to introduce political and social equality between the white and the black races," but asserted that "there is no reason in the world why the negro is not entitled to all the natural rights enumerated in the Declaration of Independence. . . . I hold that he is as much entitled to these as the white man."[17] Indeed, Republicans worked to guarantee blacks' civil rights: in Ohio they blocked efforts by Democrats to pass legislation barring black immigration (the state's old anti-immigration laws had been repealed in 1849); in Indiana and Illinois they unsuccessfully supported repeal of laws excluding black immigration; in New Hampshire they repealed the law excluding blacks from the militia; and in Iowa they repealed the statute prohibiting blacks from testifying against whites.

Not only did mainstream Republicans offer cautious support for freedom and black rights, a powerful minority of genuine radicals pressed the party to claim higher ground. Salmon Chase, Joshua Giddings, and Charles Sumner—all Republican radicals—played a role in developing abolitionist constitutional ideas. Their presence in party councils guaranteed a hearing for these ideas. Most radicals, for example, urged the party to support political as well as civil equality for blacks, and in several states—Iowa (1857), Wisconsin (1857), and New York (1860)—they had sufficient influence to persuade state legislatures to authorize referenda on black suffrage. Although black suffrage was rejected in all three states with many (and in Iowa most) Republicans voting against it, radicals' success in forcing the party to bring the issue before the electorate suggested that they were capable of moving the party.

The Climax of Proslavery Constitutionalism

Although Republicans offered a genuine challenge to proslavery constitutionalism, opponents of slavery were not optimistic as the 1850s drew to a close. A solidly proslavery administration controlled the presidency, and southerners in Congress pressed their demand for a federal code establishing and protecting slavery in the territories. Even more distressing, the Supreme Court, in its 1857 ruling in *Dred Scott v. Sandford*, offered a stinging rejection of antislavery constitutionalism and a resounding affirmation of the South's views on African American citizenship and slavery in the territories.

Dred Scott began his long, tortuous road to the Supreme Court when he accompanied his owner, an army surgeon named John Emerson, on a long tour of duty in Illinois and the Wisconsin Territory during the 1830s. In 1846, after he had returned to St. Louis and Dr. Emerson had died, Scott obtained the services of several local lawyers and sued Irene Emerson, the doctor's wife, for his freedom. He argued that during his travels with Dr. Emerson, he had lived for two years in the free state of Illinois and for three years in Wisconsin Territory, where the Missouri Compromise of 1820 prohibited slavery. Since slavery was illegal in both places, Scott claimed, he had become a free man and was illegally held in bondage. The proceedings in state circuit court ended with a verdict for Scott, but Mrs. Emerson appealed. In 1852 the Missouri Supreme Court overturned the decision of the lower court, holding that under principles of comity[18] Missouri courts were not bound to enforce the law of another state or territory that was against its policies. In a departure from its earlier decisions, the court ruled that Missouri did not accept and would not give effect to the laws of states that freed slaves who were temporarily taken there by their owners. Whatever Scott's status had been in Illinois or Wisconsin, he was still a slave in Missouri.

Scott, however, refused to give up. In 1850, Irene Emerson had remarried and left Missouri, and her brother, John Sanford (the Supreme Court's reporter spelled his name incorrectly, making him Sandford in the title of the case), had gained control of Scott. Because Sanford was a citizen of New York, Scott was able to begin his freedom suit anew in federal court. Under Article III of the Constitution and the Judiciary Act of 1789, US circuit courts had jurisdiction over cases between citizens of different states, and Scott claimed that this allowed him, as a citizen of Missouri suing a New Yorker, to have a hearing in the US circuit court in St. Louis. Yet Scott fared no better in the new forum; the trial in federal court ended in 1854 with a jury verdict against him.

Scott appealed to the US Supreme Court, but he had little reason to expect victory. Chief Justice Roger B. Taney and four of his colleagues were southerners, and two northern justices were Democrats sympathetic to the South and slavery. Moreover, Taney's opinion for the Court in *Strader v. Graham* (1851) boded ill for Scott. The chief justice had asserted that when slaves returned to a slave state after having traveled or resided in a free state, the courts of the slave state could decide whether they had become free or remained in bondage. Because Missouri's highest court had already ruled against Scott on this very point, the *Strader* precedent seemed to doom his chance for victory. There was little surprise, therefore, in early 1857 when the Court ruled against Scott by a 7–2 majority. Nonetheless, few observers could have predicted that the Court would issue such a sweeping proslavery polemic. But the chief justice and his southern brethren, alarmed by the rising tide of northern antislavery sentiment, were determined to slay the twin dragons of abolitionist equalitarianism and Republican anti-extensionism.

Each justice wrote a separate opinion, and historians have endlessly debated what (beyond the fact that Scott was still a slave) the Court actually decided. The chief justice's opinion, however, was authoritative. Not only did a majority authorize Taney to write "the opinion of the Court," but as Don Fehrenbacher notes in his Pulitzer Prize–winning study of the case, "Taney's opinion was accepted as the opinion of the Court by its critics as well as its defenders."[19] Taney held that the circuit court should have dismissed the case for want of jurisdiction. Because Scott was a African American, he explained, he could not be a citizen, even if free, and therefore he had no right to sue in federal court on the basis of diversity of citizenship. He reinforced this position by arguing that Scott could not be a citizen because he was a slave. The Missouri Compromise, which Scott claimed had made him free, was unconstitutional because Congress lacked authority to exclude slavery from the territories.

Taney's holding that free blacks were not US citizens was a shot at antislavery constitutionalism. The chief justice asserted that at the time of the Revolution and the Constitutional Convention, Americans regarded blacks as inferiors who had "no rights which the white man was bound to respect."[20] Consequently, the framers of the Constitution had not regarded African Americans as citizens of the United States. Because US citizenship gave persons certain rights that were enforceable throughout the United States, Taney argued that no state could confer US citizenship on African Americans merely by making them state citizens. To do so would enable a single state to confer national citizenship on a group that the states had collectively excluded when the Constitution was adopted. Thus, even if Scott were a citizen under Missouri law, he could not be a US citizen entitled to rights (such as bringing suit in federal court on the basis of diversity of citizenship) created by the US Constitution.

Taney's analysis rested on bad history and a careless reading of the Constitution. The Constitution did not define national citizenship and crucial provisions guaranteed rights, not to US citizens, but to state citizens. The chief justice's poorly reasoned argument was, nevertheless, purposeful. By denying that free blacks were entitled to rights under the Constitution (including those conferred by the privileges and immunities clause) he enabled southern states to prevent the entry of free blacks from other states and thus to protect themselves from outside agitators bent on fomenting slave insurrections. Moreover, by excluding free blacks from citizenship, he reinforced the principles of white supremacy which undergirded the South's slave system.

The second part of Taney's ruling—that Scott's residence on free soil had not made him free—was equally polemical and unpersuasive. Here the question of Scott's freedom involved residence in a free state and in a territory where Congress had prohibited slavery. Taney realized that his agenda would be ill-served by first addressing himself to the effect of Scott's residence in Illinois. If he ruled (as he subsequently did) that it did not affect Scott's status once he returned to Missouri because Missouri law denied that temporary residence on free soil freed slaves, he would also dispose of the effect of Scott's residence in Wisconsin Territory. Consequently, Taney turned first to Scott's sojourn in Wisconsin Territory, arguing that residence there did not free Scott because Congress did not have the authority to exclude slavery from the territories. Therefore, the prohibition on slavery contained in the Missouri Compromise, which Scott claimed made him free, was unconstitutional. Only after he had disposed of Scott's claim to freedom on the basis of living in Wisconsin Territory did Taney turn to Scott's Illinois sojourn, ruling that it did not affect Scott's status once he returned to Missouri.

The chief justice's attack on the Missouri Compromise was as poorly argued as his polemic on citizenship. Despite the clear language of Article IV, section 3, authorizing Congress to "make all needful Rules and Regulations respecting the Territory and other property belonging to the United States," Taney flirted with the implausible argument that Congress did not have authority to govern the territories; however, he ultimately retreated from this position. While it would have denied Congress the power to prohibit slavery in the territories, it would also have taken away Congress's authority to enact a slave code for the territories, which was rapidly becoming a crucial southern demand.

This led Taney to focus on the rights of the residents of the territories. Turning abolitionist constitutionalism on its head, he suggested that the Fifth Amendment's due process clause prohibited Congress from excluding slavery from the territories because to do so would interfere with the property rights of slaveowners who migrated there, by depriving them of their slave property. This remained a suggestion; however, as Fehrenbacher notes, Taney did not explicitly declare the Missouri Compromise unconstitutional on due process grounds. He also flirted with the notion, popularized by the proslavery theorist John C. Calhoun, that the territories were the common property of the states, held in trust for them by the national government. Congress, Taney hinted, could not prejudice the rights of the southern states by preventing their citizens from migrating to the territories with their property. Yet he failed to develop this argument fully or use it to strike down the Compromise's ban on slavery. He also asserted that the Constitution "distinctly and expressly affirmed" the right to slave property and, in the fugitive slave clause, pledged the national government to protect it. While this assertion accurately stated the proslavery reading of the Constitution, it was a distorted reading of the Constitution itself. Nevertheless, Taney contended that Congress did not have "greater power over slave property . . . than property of any other description" and that "the only power conferred is the power coupled with the duty of guarding and protecting the owner in his rights."[21] Yet he did not explicitly conclude from these assertions that Congress lacked authority to exclude slavery from the territories. Indeed, while Taney clearly declared the antislavery provision of the Missouri Compromise unconstitutional, he did not explain precisely his grounds for doing so.

Despite the manifest weaknesses of Taney's argument, it dealt a devastating blow to antislavery constitutionalism and the Republican Party. In declaring that African Americans, whether free or slave, were not citizens and were not entitled to constitutional rights, he undermined one of the strongest arguments for black rights. In asserting that Congress did not have the power to exclude slavery from the territories and hinting that it had an obligation to protect it there, he also repudiated important abolitionist constitutional ideas. According to Taney, the Constitution, far from being intended to promote freedom in all areas save the states in which slavery had already been established, demanded that slavery be allowed and perhaps promoted except in those states that explicitly excluded it. Turning the abolitionist argument on its head, Taney asserted that slavery was national and freedom local. The chief justice also repudiated the Republican program, saying, in effect, that the key element in the party's platform was unconstitutional.

Abolitionists and Republicans subjected Taney's opinion to withering criticism. Lincoln, for example, refused to accept the *Dred Scott* case as the final word on the subject, noting that the Supreme Court did not have exclusive authority to interpret the Constitution and that courts sometimes reversed themselves. Nevertheless, the Court's ruling, when coupled with memories of the annexation of Texas, the Fugitive Slave Act of 1850, and the Kansas-Nebraska Act, did little to encourage faith in the triumph of antislavery constitutionalism. Indeed, Lincoln and many Republicans predicted that the Court would soon hand down an opinion prohibiting the northern states from excluding slavery, thus completing the process of nationalizing the institution. Among northern blacks, the decision was the latest blow to the dream that one day they would enjoy true freedom and equality in their native land. Consequently, it gave impetus to the black emigration movement that already had the support of such prominent leaders as Henry Highland Garnet, Martin Delany, Robert Campbell, and H. Ford Douglas.

Despair was not uniform, however. Frederick Douglass argued that antislavery forces had "nothing to fear" from the *Dred Scott* decision. "The whole history of the antislavery movement," he explained, "is studded with proof that all measures devised and executed . . . to . . . diminish the antislavery agitation, have only served to increase, intensify, and embolden that agitation." Douglass argued that the true principles embodied in the Constitution would ultimately triumph and allay the possibility that "it might be necessary for my people to look for a home in some other country."[22] Events of the 1860s would at least partially vindicate Douglass's faith. Taney's proslavery Constitution would be swept away and a new Constitution, informed by the antislavery ideas that emerged in the dark days of the 1840s and 1850s, would emerge. This new Constitution and a more perfect Union would be forged, not solely through political and constitutional processes, but on the fields of Antietam, Gettysburg, Cold Harbor, and Petersburg.

3

The National Commitment to Civil
Equality, 1861–1870

On August 21, 1872, seven years after the Civil War had ended, Emma Coger, a teacher from Quincy, Illinois, prepared to return home after visiting friends in Keokuk, Iowa. Although her complexion was fair, Coger had one black grandparent, making her a Negro in the eyes of race-conscious nineteenth-century American whites. When she went to the office of the North West Union Packet Company to purchase a ticket for passage aboard the Mississippi River steamer SS *Merrill*, the agent suspected that she had African ancestry and refused to sell her a first-class ticket. Following company policy, he offered her passage without a private sleeping berth or access to the dining room. Coger demanded first-class passage and initially declined to purchase a ticket when the agent refused. She finally relented, accepting a ticket entitling her inferior accommodations.

Aboard the steamer, Coger continued to encounter demeaning treatment. When she sent the ship's chambermaid to purchase a dinner ticket for her, she received a pass marked "colored girl," not "lady," the term of respect universally applied to middle-class white women, and was informed that she would be served in the pantry. Refusing to accept such treatment, she persuaded a white traveler to purchase a first-class dining ticket for her. When dinner was announced, she entered the cabin, took a seat at a table reserved for ladies traveling without male escort, and refused to move when a waiter ordered her to the pantry. The dining room abuzz over the confrontation, the captain appeared, demanded that Coger leave the ladies' table, and attempted to remove her. Coger resisted, "so that considerable violence was necessary to drag her out of the cabin, and, in the struggle, the covering of the table was torn off and dishes broken, and the officer received a slight injury."[1]

Determined to challenge such degrading treatment, Coger filed suit in state district court, seeking damages from the company for the assault on her by its employees. She alleged that the Iowa constitution, which declared that "All men are, by nature, free and equal," entitled her to equal treatment

Promises to Keep. Donald G. Nieman, Oxford University Press (2020). © Oxford University Press.
DOI: 10.1093/oso/9780190071639.001.0001

on the *Merrill*, which had a common law obligation to serve the public. She also claimed that changes in federal law and the US Constitution growing out of the abolition of slavery and the postwar effort to protect the rights of the former slaves reinforced this right. The Fourteenth Amendment, ratified in 1868, not only conferred national and state citizenship on blacks, but prohibited discrimination, stipulating that no state "shall deny . . . any person . . . equal protection of the laws." Moreover, Coger pointed out that Congress's Civil Rights Act of 1866 provided that all citizens were entitled to "the same right . . . to make and enforce contracts . . . as is enjoyed by white persons." Because a steamboat ticket was a contract, she contended, the company was obligated to offer her the same ticket and service that it offered white women.[2]

The Iowa courts sustained Coger's position. In his charge to the jury, the trial court judge explained that, while the company might make reasonable rules and regulations, it could not make distinctions among passengers on the basis of race. When the jury returned a verdict for Coger, the company appealed to the Iowa Supreme Court, which upheld the lower court. Chief Justice Joseph M. Beck's opinion revealed his own racial stereotypes, noting that Coger's "spirited resistance . . . exhibited evidence of the Anglo-Saxon blood that flows in her veins." He nonetheless rejected the company's claim that it was free to practice racial segregation. Dismissing as irrelevant arguments concerning Coger's race, Beck paid tribute to the radical transformation brought about by emancipation and postwar constitutional change. "However pertinent to such a case the discussion may have been, not many years ago . . . the doctrines and authorities involved in the argument are obsolete, and have no longer existence or authority, anywhere within the jurisdiction of the federal constitution, and most certainly not in Iowa," Beck explained. Equality before the law, "the very foundation principle of our government," had been expressly extended to African Americans by the Fourteenth Amendment and the Civil Rights Act of 1866. "If the negro must submit to different treatment, to accommodations inferior to those given to the white man, when transported by public carriers," Beck concluded, "he is deprived of the benefits of this very principle of equality."[3]

Although it had authority only within Iowa, Beck's opinion suggested how far the revolutionary upheaval of the Civil War and Reconstruction had moved the nation. Only a dozen years before, the US Supreme Court's holding that African Americans were not citizens had stood as the supreme law of the land, and Republican critics of slavery had been tentative in their support for black rights. Under the pressure of Civil War, however, Lincoln and the Republican leadership in Congress embraced emancipation as a war goal and recruited 180,000 black troops to help subdue the Confederacy. In the war's aftermath, Republican leaders, determined to secure the fruits of victory, were pulled inexorably toward abolitionist constitutionalism. They not only removed the incubus of *Dred Scott* and admitted African Americans to citizenship, but expanded federal responsibility for protecting individual rights from violation by states and individuals, thereby significantly altering the antebellum federal system. Furthermore, they moved beyond antebellum distinctions between civil (or legal) rights and political rights, extending to black men the full rights of citizenship, including the right to vote. Well might Daniel Corbin, a white South Carolina Republican, remark in 1871, "we have lived over a century in the last ten years."[4]

War, Emancipation, and Equal Rights

In the spring and summer of 1861, few predicted the revolutionary consequences of the Civil War for American constitutionalism and the rights of blacks. Lincoln and Republican leaders in Congress made it clear that they prosecuted the war in order to preserve the Union, not to extirpate slavery. Although hostile to slavery, they entered the war clinging to the time-honored notion that slavery was a local institution and that the national government lacked constitutional authority to interfere with it in any state that chose to sanction it. More to the point, expediency militated against antislavery action. Republicans needed support from northern Democrats if they were to unite the nation behind the war effort, and many northern Democrats were willing to support a war to preserve the Union but not an antislavery crusade. Then, too, four border slave states—Delaware, Maryland, Kentucky, and Missouri—remained in the Union despite pressure from secessionists. Embracing emancipation as a war aim might drive these states and their considerable resources into the Confederacy. In a message to Congress on July 4, 1861, Lincoln explained that his administration had "no purpose, directly or indirectly, to interfere with the institution of slavery in the States where it exists." Several weeks later Congress, with little dissent, passed a joint resolution declaring that the US government had no intention of "overthrowing or interfering with the rights or established institutions" of the rebel states, but sought only "to defend and maintain the supremacy of the Constitution and to preserve the Union."[5]

Although impatient with such timidity, abolitionists rallied to support the war effort, perceiving that, for the first time in the nation's history, the exigencies of preserving the Union would promote black liberty. From the outset, northern blacks, abolitionists, and Republican radicals argued that the Union could be saved only by abolishing slavery. Because slavery had pushed the nation to war, restoration of the Union without abolition, they claimed, would prove illusory. "Slavery is the disease, and its abolition in every part of the land is essential to the future quiet and security of the country," argued Frederick Douglass in early 1861. Abolitionists also pointed out that, as an integral part of the southern economy, slavery supported the rebellion. Slave laborers in southern fields and factories— not to mention the tens of thousands of African Americans who built fortifications and roads for the Confederate army—provided crucial support to the rebellion and freed white men for combat service. A forthright policy of emancipation would not only weaken the Confederacy's ability to fight, but, coupled with an aggressive program of recruiting African American troops, would strengthen Union forces. "More effective remedies ought now to be *thoroughly* tried, in the shape of warm lead and cold steel," a meeting of New York blacks urged, "duly administered by two hundred thousand black doctors."[6]

Prodded by abolitionists, Republican leaders soon began to reassess the government's policy with respect to slavery. Aware that victory would not be achieved quickly or easily and that slavery supported the Confederacy, Republicans began to find antislavery action more attractive. Expediency alone did not drive Republicans to act, however. Democrats like Horatio Seymour and George B. McClellan were no less committed to preserving the Union than Republicans, but their proslavery attitudes led them to balk at antislavery measures as a means to that end. Because most Republicans had entered the war opposed to slavery on moral grounds, they were more inclined to equate antislavery action with military necessity. Indeed, the expediency of antislavery measures complemented Republican antislavery inclinations. By linking antislavery policies with preservation of the Union, Republicans were able to deflect the charge that they were fanatics willing to sacrifice white soldiers for black liberty. The military necessity argument also permitted Republicans to invoke the Constitution's war powers to attack slavery, helping them transcend concerns about the constitutionality of antislavery action. As LaWanda Cox has explained in her analysis of the Republican president, "Lincoln was alert to the expanding potential created by war. Military needs . . . did not force him upon an alien course but helped clear a path toward a long-desired but intractable objective."[7]

During the first half of 1862, Republicans invoked the concept of military necessity and the war powers to justify radical antislavery action. After abolishing slavery in the District of Columbia and the territories, areas clearly within Congress's jurisdiction, Republicans turned on slavery in the states, something that even moderate abolitionists had admitted to be unconstitutional fifteen months before. The war had changed things, Republicans argued. By giving Congress the power to declare war, to raise and make regulations for armies and navies, and to provide for calling out the militia to suppress insurrection, the Constitution conferred on it broad war powers that it might use to enact legislation, even antislavery legislation, necessary to prosecute the war. In July 1862, Congress invoked this theory to pass a Confiscation Act that authorized seizure of property owned by persons who aided or abetted the rebellion.[8] With respect to human property, it stipulated that slaves owned by rebels "shall be forever free of their servitude" on entering Union lines, thus providing a legal claim to freedom for tens of thousands of slaves who had fled to Union forces by the summer of 1862.[9]

At the time Congress passed the Confiscation Act, Lincoln initiated sweeping action against slavery. On July 21, 1862, he informed members of his Cabinet that, under his constitutional authority as commander-in-chief, he would issue a proclamation freeing all slaves in areas that were in rebellion against the United States. Heeding the advice of Secretary of State William H. Seward, who argued that recent Union military defeats would make the proclamation look like a desperate appeal for European support, Lincoln agreed to await a Union victory. On September 22, after Union troops turned back a Confederate invasion of Maryland, he promptly issued a preliminary proclamation, promising that if the rebellion continued on January 1, he would free all slaves in states and parts of states under rebel control. On New Year's Day, 1863, as northern blacks and abolitionists crowded churches and public halls throughout the North in celebration, Lincoln proclaimed the Jubilee.

Many historians have characterized the Proclamation as an act of expediency or even a meaningless sham. Because it applied only to slaves within rebel lines and not to those in the border states or parts of the Confederacy occupied by Union troops on January 1, 1863, they argue that it actually freed no slaves. Critics have also claimed that the text appealed to military necessity, not moral principle, and had "all the moral grandeur of a bill of lading."[10] These charges distort the Proclamation by taking it out of its political and constitutional context. While Lincoln hoped to cripple the Confederacy, he equally welcomed the opportunity to act on antislavery principles he had espoused for years. He couched the document in terms of military necessity because his constitutional authority as commander-in-chief permitted him to free slaves as an act of war, but not to strike at slavery as a moral evil. This also helps explain why Lincoln did not free slaves within Union lines. To have done so could not have been justified as an act of war aimed at weakening the enemy, and it would have opened Lincoln to charges of usurpation and provided critics ammunition to attack the Proclamation's constitutionality. Moreover, Lincoln used the military necessity argument to assuage conservatives who supported the war effort but opposed black liberty. By tying emancipation to preservation of the Union, he created a broader base of popular support for black freedom, transforming the war into a struggle tor liberty *and* Union.

While the Proclamation may have freed no slaves at the moment it was promulgated, it would bring freedom to hundreds of thousands in the coming months, as the Union army pushed deeper into the Confederacy. "By making the army the agent of emancipation and wedding the goals of Union and abolition, it assured that northern victory would produce a social transformation in the South and a redefinition of the place of blacks in American life," according to Eric Foner.[11] Because of political and constitutional considerations, Lincoln understated the importance of the Proclamation, issuing a document whose "prose was legalistic" and that "supposedly did not free anyone." Yet according to historian Louis P. Masur, it made a statement as important as the Declaration of Independence. "The Declaration . . . envisioned a new country; the Proclamation remade one."[12]

The Proclamation left many slaves—including most of those in the border states—in bondage and was almost certain to be challenged in the courts. Consequently, Republicans employed the amendment process to make emancipation universal and irreversible. Senate Republicans mustered enough votes to pass an antislavery amendment in early 1864, but despite solid Republican support, the House fell several votes shy of the two-thirds majority necessary to pass it. On January 31, 1865, however, with Lincoln promising patronage to gain votes from the opposition, Congress passed an amendment prohibiting slavery and involuntary servitude in the United States and giving Congress authority to enforce the prohibition. Before the year was out, three-fourths of the state legislatures had given their assent, and the Thirteenth Amendment became part of the Constitution.

The amendment significantly altered the American constitutional order. Prior to its adoption, most judges, lawyers, and politicians had agreed that slavery was beyond the reach of the national government and that states possessed almost unlimited authority to define and protect individual rights. By banning slavery and giving Congress enforcement power, the new amendment expanded national power and limited the authority of the states, although the extent to which it did so depended on how slavery was defined. If it merely meant chattel slavery—ownership of one person by another— Congress's newly won authority was quite narrow. But if slavery extended to the web of discriminatory laws and customs designed to support the institution—what some Republicans called the vestiges of slavery—the amendment gave Congress broader authority.

Debating the amendment, supporters in Congress did not argue expressly that it went beyond elimination of chattel slavery. Perhaps they feared that articulating a broader interpretation of the amendment would alienate conservative Republicans and Democrats whose votes were needed for passage. Or perhaps with chattel slavery still alive, they focused on the immediate problem. Congressional silence, however, did not necessitate a narrow reading of the amendment. During the Civil War, Republicans had developed what the historian Harold Hyman has described as "adequacy constitutionalism."[13] They did not view the Constitution as a list of restrictions on government, but as an instrument that empowered it to pursue broad objectives and gave it discretion to choose the means most suitable to achieve those ends. To Republicans, the Constitution was organic, a document capable of meeting new exigencies. Viewed through this prism, the Thirteenth Amendment offered Congress authority to root out slavery and its vestiges and to guarantee former slaves the rights essential to freedom.

Republicans' understanding of those rights sharpened considerably as the war progressed. During the 1850s, Republicans had invoked the Declaration of Independence to criticize slavery, charging that it violated the principle of equality on which the Republic had been founded. As Union war aims expanded to include emancipation, and 180,000 black men shouldered the obligations of citizenship by serving in the Union army, Republicans became more vigorous in their support for equality. Indeed, by 1865, the war to preserve the Union had become for most Republicans a war to create a more perfect Union, one that guaranteed the equality of all citizens.

Republicans' commitment to equality was reflected in policy as well as rhetoric. By 1865, California and Illinois Republicans had repealed

Figure 3.1. "Shall I Trust These Men, and Not This Man?" *Harper's Weekly*, August 5, 1865 https://www.loc.gov/item/2010644408/. This drawing by Thomas Nast suggests the way that African American military service fostered northern white support for equal rights during Reconstruction. *Library of Congress.*

all discriminatory state statutes except those denying blacks the ballot. In Massachusetts, Republicans pushed further, enacting a public accommodations law that prohibited racial discrimination by operators of inns, places of public amusement, common carriers, and public meeting places. Congressional Republicans likewise demonstrated a clear commitment to civil equality for blacks. In 1862 they repealed the ban on African American mail carriers. Two years later, they permitted African Americans to testify against whites in federal courts and granted black soldiers equal pay and benefits. Congressional Republicans underscored their growing commitment to equality when they created the Freedmen's Bureau in March 1865. Aware of the myriad problems faced by newly emancipated African Americans, Republicans saw the necessity of a federal agency to assist them in their transition from slavery to freedom. Carefully avoiding any suggestion that the former slaves were a separate class incapable of full freedom and subject to restraints not applicable to other free persons, they marked the bureau as a temporary agency, locating it in the War Department and limiting its existence to one year after the war. They also carefully pruned language giving the bureau authority to make special regulations for blacks and provided that the agency was to assist white refugees as well as emancipated slaves. As Representative Robert Schenck of Ohio explained, the law made "no discrimination according to color—a favorite phrase . . . in these days among us all."[14]

Reconstruction and National Protection for Civil Rights

Although the pace of constitutional change during the war years was dramatic, it accelerated during the years after Appomattox. Conflict between black and white southerners over the meaning of freedom drove this change, spurring Republicans to translate their support for equality into bold measures that dramatically expanded national protection for individual rights. Although hundreds of thousands of African Americans had won their freedom during the war, most slaves first tasted liberty in the weeks and months after Confederate forces surrendered and Union troops occupied the Confederacy. African Americans viewed emancipation as a providential act of deliverance, "the work of Almighty God," one former slave later recalled. Indeed, it was such a pivotal event that seventy years later, many former slaves vividly recalled the day they learned they were free. "I won't never forget dat day," recalled Lydia Jefferson in 1937. "Yes suh, de freedom sun shine, and de black times all gone." For men and women whose family life, work, religion, and physical well-being had been subject to white control, emancipation offered a new beginning free of white domination. "Glory, halleluyer, dere ain't no marster and dere ain't no slave!" a black minister informed a meeting of Florida blacks. "From now on my brudders an' my sisters, old things have passed away an' all things is bekum new."[15]

African Americans had clear expectations of the new order. They placed a premium on freedom of movement, not only because it allowed them to break the master-slave relationship by leaving their former owners, but also because it enabled them to search for husbands, wives, and children from whom they had been separated forcibly as slaves. Indeed, African Americans' greatest expectation of freedom was that it would permit them to reunite families and protect them from interference by whites. In the predominantly agricultural society of the South, landownership was also a high priority. Land would enable former slaves to become independent farmers and permit them to escape supervision by plantation owners and overseers, affording heads of household greater control over their own work and also removing wives and children from white authority. African Americans' hopes for land were raised as word spread across the South that wartime legislation authorized confiscation of land owned by rebels and distribution of it to former slaves.

There was also a nascent demand for equality among African Americans. During 1865, southern blacks organized state conventions that, like the antebellum conventions of northern blacks, demanded that the nation live up to the promise of the Declaration of Independence. These conventions reflected the views of the literate urban free men who dominated them. Yet former slaves also became politically conscious, as black army veterans, black teachers from the North, and agents dispatched by the conventions spread the gospel of republicanism among them.

African Americans' aspirations clashed with southern whites' determination to maintain control over their former slaves. Planters and farmers feared that emancipation would destroy their operations unless they could impose on black workers restrictions that would enable them to maintain a cheap, tractable labor force. But whites' concerns rested on far more than economic considerations. Products of a deeply racist culture that viewed African Americans as incapable of living in a civilized society without white control, they assumed that freed blacks would refuse to labor and would turn to crime, transforming southern society into a hell for whites. Fear of retribution by former slaves was also widespread among whites, sparking rumors of a bloody uprising that swept the white South like a wildfire during the last months of 1865.

Given the stakes, southern whites quickly mounted an informal campaign to minimize the consequences of emancipation. Although the threat of confiscation hung over them, whites nevertheless controlled the land. In a predominantly agricultural society, this conferred considerable economic leverage against African Americans. Whites refused to rent land to blacks, fearing that to do so would encourage black independence. Instead, they used their control over the land to compel African Americans to work as plantation laborers under white supervision. Planters frequently colluded to hold wages down and—in order to restrict blacks' movement—sometimes refused to hire those who could not produce references from their former owners. In many areas whites formed vigilante groups to shore up their control.

Occasionally vigilantes beat or murdered those who attempted to leave their former owners and, more commonly, compelled African Americans to work on terms favorable to planters. They also frequently visited African Americans' cabins, seizing firearms and beating and driving away those perceived as encouraging black assertiveness—especially African American veterans and teachers. Moreover, in day-to-day encounters between whites and blacks, white men frequently beat or even murdered blacks who were insufficiently deferential. As an Arkansas Freedmen's Bureau agent noted in informing his superiors of the appalling number of assaults on African Americans, "in nine cases out of ten" whites attacked blacks simply because they "dared to refute a charge prejudicial to their character as false; and have been impudent enough to take a stand for their rights as men."[16]

Southern whites also used the power of the state to reassert control over blacks, a benefit made possible by President Andrew Johnson's program of Reconstruction. Johnson was a Unionist Democrat from Tennessee who had been selected as Lincoln's running mate in 1864 to strengthen the Republican ticket's appeal among Democrats. When he came to the White House in April 1865 after Lincoln's murder, Johnson turned his attention to Reconstruction. A states' rights advocate who shared white southerners' views on race, Johnson quickly adopted policies that speedily restored self-government to southern whites and gave them authority to define the legal status of African Americans. He freely offered amnesty and pardon to former rebels, thereby restoring their political rights. He also recognized the white Unionist governments Lincoln had established during the war in Louisiana, Arkansas, Tennessee, and Virginia and appointed provisional governors for the other seven rebel states. These men were to conduct elections (in which only whites could vote) for delegates to state constitutional conventions. After these conventions drafted new constitutions, the governors would hold another round of elections to choose state officials and members of Congress. When this process was complete, Johnson expected Congress to seat southern senators and representatives, completing the process of Reconstruction.

Johnson's program seriously threatened the newly won rights of the freedmen. By the summer of 1865, the Freedmen's Bureau—which was authorized to take possession of land seized under the confiscation laws and to lease it to the freedmen—held 800,000 acres of land taken from Confederate supporters during the war. But Johnson ruled that his pardons entitled the recipients to restoration of their property rights, and ordered bureau officials to surrender this land to pardoned owners. Furthermore, the president prevented additional seizure of land by forbidding US attorneys to institute new cases under the confiscation laws. These directives protected southern planters, dashed African Americans' hopes of obtaining land, and reinforced whites' economic leverage against their former slaves.

As state legislatures elected under Johnson's program met during the winter of 1865–1866, they passed repressive measures known as *black codes*. Designed to reinforce white power, these laws attempted to guarantee whites a cheap and tractable labor force and to compel African Americans to re-main on plantations and farms where they would live and work under close supervision by whites. In some states, African Americans who wished to live in towns and cities were required to obtain permits from local officials, and in all southern states blacks were subjected to harsh vagrancy laws. These measures authorized local officials to fine persons who were not gainfully employed. Those who could not pay the fines, which combined with court costs, typically totaled $100 or more (an amount far beyond the means of impoverished blacks), were sentenced to labor without compensation for as much as one year. This not only subjected African Americans to forced labor, but undermined their bargaining power as well. If African Americans withheld their labor in an effort to force planters to offer better wages and working conditions, local officials could use threats of prosecution for va-grancy to break blacks' resistance and compel them to work on terms favor-able to planters.

Other provisions of the black codes further extended white control over blacks. Apprenticeship laws authorized state judges to apprentice orphans and children whose parents failed to support them adequately, thereby making African American families vulnerable to white interference. Judges used the discretionary authority conferred by these laws to order thousands of African American children removed from their families and apprenticed to labor-starved white planters, ostensibly to learn agricultural and domestic service trades. Criminal law undercut blacks' chances of securing justice. Although they did allow them to testify in cases in which at least one party was black, this was of little practical benefit because all-white juries—which were notoriously hostile to African American witnesses, plaintiffs, and defendants—decided the cases. The black codes also enabled judges to im-pose harsher criminal punishments on African Americans than on whites, virtually guaranteeing that black convicts would be executed more fre-quently and receive longer prison terms than whites found guilty of compa-rable crimes.

Republicans, firmly in control of both houses of Congress, were appalled by the results of Johnson's program. Clearly, white southerners had demonstrated their determination to preserve the essence of slavery even as they surrendered formal claims to ownership of African Americans. Congressional acceptance of Johnson's program, Republicans believed, would permit white southerners to restore through politics what they had lost on the battlefield. In the eyes of Republicans and a majority of northerners this would deny the nation the fruits of victory and mean that 400,000 Union soldiers had died in vain. If Congress recognized the Johnson governments, senators and representatives from the South would join forces with northern Democrats, who were strident foes of African American rights. Together they would not only threaten Republican hegemony, but would block legislation necessary to ensure African American liberty. Consequently, when Congress met in December 1865, Republican leaders quickly agreed that they would not seat representatives from the rebel states until Congress devised measures to protect black freedom.

Radicals, most notably Pennsylvania's Thaddeus Stevens, advocated new confiscation legislation to reverse the effect of Johnson's pardon policy and provide land to the freedmen. Former slaves, they argued, would remain vulnerable to control by whites as long as they remained propertyless laborers. The vast majority of Republicans, however, rejected confiscation, viewing legal equality, not grants of land, as the best means to protect black freedom. In part, this perspective was a legacy of the antislavery movement. Because slavery had rested on the systematic denial of rights to slaves and free blacks, its critics had attacked legal restrictions on African Americans and had invoked Christian principles and the Declaration of Independence in arguing that African Americans were entitled to equal rights. The fixation on equal rights that grew out of antislavery agitation was reinforced by the widespread appeal of what the historian Eric Foner has called *the free labor ideology*.[17] As products of a rapidly expanding, highly competitive capitalist economy that was dominated by small-scale producers, most nineteenth-century Americans believed that theirs was an open society in which individuals could advance by hard work and careful planning. Accepting this belief, Republican leaders assumed that if African Americans were not restrained by artificial legal barriers and enjoyed the same rights as whites, they would rise according to their merits. Indeed, they argued that by giving African Americans land, the government would discourage self-reliance, undercutting blacks' chances of success in a competitive society. Although these ideas were naive and ill-suited to the needs of impoverished former slaves, they were accepted as conventional wisdom by most nineteenth-century Americans and exerted a powerful influence on Republican policy.

Republican leaders also rejected radicals' call for black suffrage. They realized that by extending the franchise to African Americans, Congress would repudiate the presidentially reconstructed governments (which had been elected by white voters) and necessitate beginning the reconstruction process anew. This not only guaranteed conflict between Congress and the president, but risked alienating conservative Republican senators and representatives as well as many northern voters. Unwilling to accept the political risks inherent in supporting black suffrage, Republican leaders settled for a program that permitted presidentially reconstructed governments to stand but compelled them to grant African Americans equality before the law.

Lyman Trumbull of the Senate Judiciary Committee introduced two pieces of legislation designed to provide national protection for the rights of African Americans. The first offered temporary protection by extending the life and expanding the power of the Freedmen's Bureau. Trumbull argued that Congress's war powers "do not cease with the dispersion of the rebel armies," but "are to be continued and exercised until the civil authority of the Government can be established firmly."[18] With the war power still in force, Congress could provide summary protection for black rights in the rebel states. Thus the bureau bill stipulated that African Americans were entitled to equal rights in state law and authorized bureau officials to establish tribunals to enforce these rights when state authorities failed to do so. Persons accused of enforcing discriminatory laws and regulations were subject to prosecution in bureau courts and fines of as much as $1,000 and imprisonment for up to one year. Moreover, bureau courts might try cases involving African Americans—cases involving contract disputes, property rights, violations of criminal law, and the like—who were denied or unable to enforce their rights because of any "State or local law, ordinance, police, or other regulation, or custom or prejudice."[19]

Because the Freedmen's Bureau's judicial authority rested on the war power, it extended only to the rebel states and would cease there as soon as Congress seated their representatives and senators. To provide long-term protection throughout the nation, Trumbull introduced the Civil Rights Act of 1866. Resting on the Thirteenth Amendment, which Republicans viewed as authorizing Congress to eradicate the vestiges of slavery, the Civil Rights Act declared that African Americans were citizens and guaranteed them legal equality throughout the nation. Carefully excluding political rights, the bill provided that African Americans "shall have the same right in every State . . . to make and enforce contracts, to sue, be parties, give evidence, to inherit, purchase, lease, hold, and convey real and personal property . . . as is enjoyed by white citizens." They were also entitled to "full and equal benefit of all laws and proceedings for the security of person and property" and liable to the same criminal laws as whites. Persons denied these rights might seek redress in the federal courts. Anyone acting "under color of any law, statute, ordinance, regulation, or custom" to deny a citizen's civil rights was subject to prosecution in federal court and, on conviction, a fine of $1,000 and imprisonment for one year. Persons who were "denied or cannot enforce" their rights in state courts might have their cases tried in federal courts, giving them impartial forums in which to obtain justice.[20]

The Freedmen's Bureau and civil rights legislation represented a radical departure. By declaring that all persons born in the United States were citizens regardless of race, the Civil Rights Act ended decades of uncertainty over the definition of national citizenship and repudiated the Supreme Court's *Dred Scott* ruling. Both measures asserted broad national authority to define the rights essential to freedom and, if necessary, to protect them through federal courts, matters over which the states had enjoyed almost exclusive authority in the antebellum era. Thus they embraced ideas of color-blind citizenship and national protection of individual rights that only abolitionists had dared assert a few years earlier. Speaker of the House Schuyler Colfax, a Republican moderate, reflected this in his assessment of the Civil Rights Act. "Wasn't yesterday a glorious day," he inquired the day after the bill was enacted. "Our birthright being born on American soil means something now for everyone." Democrats made the point more directly, denouncing the bill as a revolutionary measure "designed to take away the essential rights of the States."[21]

Nevertheless, as the historian Michael Les Benedict has demonstrated, Republicans did not break completely with antebellum constitutionalism.[22] They valued the decentralized federal system because it permitted local self-government and obviated the need for a vast national bureaucracy. Therefore, they wanted states, not the national government, to continue to exercise primary responsibility for defining individual rights. The bureau and civil rights bills compelled states to grant African Americans the same legal rights they conferred on whites, but left them free to define these rights. The bills also left with state courts the primary authority to protect civil rights; only if states failed to guarantee equal rights would national courts have authority to act.

As Trumbull pushed his bills through the legislative process, Congress's Joint Committee on Reconstruction hammered out a constitutional amendment designed to settle a variety of problems arising from the war. Although committee members were primarily concerned about political matters, they could not escape the issue of civil rights. A few Republicans, believing that the Thirteenth Amendment did not authorize the Civil Rights Act, demanded that the new amendment provide clear constitutional support for it. Others, aware that Democrats would repeal the act if they regained control of Congress, wanted to write civil rights guarantees into the Constitution, putting them beyond the reach of transient congressional majorities. Section 1 of the Fourteenth Amendment reflected these concerns. It declared that all persons born or naturalized in the United States were citizens of the United States and the state in which they resided. This offered a clear definition of US citizenship and prevented states from excluding blacks from the benefits of state citizenship. Section 1 also established constitutional guarantees for individual rights reminiscent of those championed by abolitionists. It forbade states to "make or enforce any law which shall abridge the privileges and immunities of citizens of the United States," to "deprive any person of life, liberty, or property without due process of law," or to deny persons "equal protection of the laws." Section 5 of the amendment authorized Congress to enact "appropriate legislation" to enforce these guarantees.

The language of section 1 was sweeping and majestic, but what did it mean? What were the privileges and immunities of citizens of the United States? What guarantees did the due process clause encompass? When Congress debated the amendment, senators and representatives offered different interpretations of the amendment's meaning. John A. Bingham of Ohio, the author of section 1, asserted that the privileges and immunities and due process clauses must be read broadly to "protect . . . the inborn rights of every person . . . whenever the same shall be . . . denied by the unconstitutional acts of any State."[23] But what precisely were these "inborn rights?" Senator Jacob Howard of Michigan, another member of the Joint Committee, was more specific, asserting that whatever these provisions meant, they clearly included the rights enumerated in the Bill of Rights. Other influential Republicans, however, denied that the amendment reached as far as Bingham and Howard suggested, and most did not comment on the issue, leaving the meaning of these phrases ambiguous.

The framers of the Fourteenth Amendment also created uncertainty by wording section 1 as a series of restrictions on the states. If state officials themselves did not deny persons the rights guaranteed by section 1, but were unable or unwilling to punish private citizens who assaulted, robbed, murdered, or discriminated against blacks, did the amendment authorize congressional action? If one read the amendment narrowly, it did not. It authorized Congress to provide remedies against state action, not against the acts of private citizens. A broader reading was not only possible, but truer to Republican principles. By failing to bring wrongdoers to justice, state officials as effectively denied persons equal protection as if they enforced blatantly discriminatory laws. Because the amendment authorized Congress to provide appropriate remedies when states denied persons equal protection, it might therefore be construed to authorize federal law enforcement officials and federal courts to provide the protection that state officials were unwilling or unable to offer. Indeed, such an interpretation was consistent with Republicans' oft-repeated determination to guarantee former slaves genuine freedom and legal equality, not merely their forms. Nevertheless, in debates on the Fourteenth Amendment, Republicans did not define precisely the extent of congressional power to provide remedies against private acts. Like the meaning of the privileges and immunities clause, therefore, it would be determined in the future by Congress and the courts.

Many Republicans wanted to extend the right to vote to African Americans but feared the political fallout given broad opposition to black suffrage among northern whites. If they failed to act, however, white southerners would benefit. The Constitution's infamous three-fifths clause permitted states to count 60 percent of their slave population in determining their representation in Congress. With slavery abolished, the South enjoyed a political windfall: all African Americans now counted in determining representation, even though they were barred from voting. Ironically, white southerners' political power would increase, more effectively allowing former rebels to control national policy and block measures to protect former slaves. Too timid to grant the vote to blacks, Republicans included language in section 2 of the amendment that penalized states that excluded black men from voting. Any state that "denied to any male inhabitant of such state, being twenty-one years of age, and citizens of the United States" the right to vote would have its representation in Congress reduced "in the proportion which the number of such male citizens shall bear to the whole number of male citizens twenty-one years of age in such State." South Carolina, where blacks constituted 60 percent of the adult male population, would lose more than half its seats in the House of Representatives and also see its weight in the Electoral

College reduced unless it allowed black men to vote. White southerners cried foul, but so did abolitionists, Radical Republicans, and women's rights advocates, who saw Reconstruction as a golden opportunity to achieve equal citizenship for African Americans and women. Supporters of black rights felt cheated because section 2 suggested that the right to vote was not a prerogative of citizenship. Women's rights advocates, who applauded the gender-neutral language of section 1, were also appalled by how section 2 privileged men. For the first time, they pointed out, the word "male" was included in the Constitution. And it was used in a manner that assumed voting was men's business.

Regardless of these conflicts and uncertainties, Republican leaders believed that the Freedmen's Bureau and civil rights bills, along with the Fourteenth Amendment, would guarantee black freedom. Most assumed that if the southern states signaled their acceptance of the war's outcome by ratifying the amendment, Congress would complete restoration. Indeed, when Tennessee ratified in June 1866, Republicans voted to seat the state's senators and representatives. Republican expectations, however, were quickly dashed. Before the Joint Committee completed work on the amendment, President Johnson announced his unqualified opposition to Congress's program, vetoing both the Freedmen's Bureau and civil rights bills. Anticipating the strategy opponents of civil rights would employ a century later, he appealed to whites' fear that black progress would come at their expense. Both measures, he charged, not only usurped states' rights but gave preferential treatment to African Americans. Republicans had sufficient strength to override the vetoes. In April they mustered the two-thirds majority necessary to enact the civil rights bill, and after an initial failure to override the Freedmen's Bureau veto, they passed an almost identical bill over Johnson's veto in July. Nevertheless, Johnson's opposition was not without effect. By encouraging southern legislatures to reject the Fourteenth Amendment, he helped delay ratification until 1868.

Despite conflict between the president and Congress, former slaves eagerly attempted to avail themselves of the remedies offered by recently enacted congressional legislation. Aware of the Civil Rights Act's guarantee of equality, they pressed federal officials to prosecute whites who discriminated against them. When the trustees of a Catholic church in Louisiana denied African Americans the right to rent church pews, for example, black parishioners demanded that the trustees be tried for violation of the act. Under threat of prosecution, the trustees relented and reserved one

Figure 3.2. "The Lobby of the House of Representatives at Washington, DC, during the Passage of the Civil Rights Bill," *Harper's Weekly*, April 28, 1866 https://www.loc.gov/item/2010652197/. Note the African American lobbyist in the right center of the picture. *Library of Congress.*

side of the sanctuary for blacks. Most frequently, blacks sought justice in informal hearings before local Freedmen's Bureau agents. "My office is so crowded . . . with freedmen coming to complain of not being settled with [by their employers] that . . . it takes four of us from 9 o'clock in the morning to 5 o'clock in the evening doing scarcely anything else but trying to adjust cases of cheating and stealing," noted a bureau agent in early 1867.[24]

African Americans' experience in seeking redress from federal officials had important consequences. As slaves, they had lived under the personal authority of their owners, whose arbitrary decisions had affected every aspect of their lives. Through contact with bureau agents and northern teachers, however, former slaves learned that law—a body of impersonal rules defining individual rights and obligations—could restrict arbitrary authority. Granted, these men and women, fearful that former slaves might confuse liberty with license, emphasized the obligations imposed as well as the rights conferred by law. Nonetheless, they stressed that law was a restraint on personal will. Although it was alien to their experience, former slaves quickly grasped the concept, finding in it a means of curbing arbitrary white authority. A group of Newberry, South Carolina, blacks reflected this understanding when, in asking the Freedmen's Bureau to afford them protection from "a reign of terror" established by local whites, they complained, "We have no law."[25]

Congressional civil rights legislation had other important consequences as well. The Civil Rights Act and debates surrounding its adoption had a powerful influence on black consciousness, convincing the former slaves that they were citizens entitled to equal rights and impartial justice. In October 1866, for example, a Freedmen's Bureau agent stationed in Staunton, Virginia, noted that blacks in his district were well informed on the civil rights question, adding that "news of that kind spreads through the country very quickly." "I am acquainted with one colored man who takes the 'Washington Chronicle,' " he explained, "and regularly imparts the news to his color."[26] The presence of federal officials encouraged former slaves to demand their rights and to challenge arbitrary white authority. Indeed, the records of bureau agents, which contain tens of thousands of complaints that African Americans brought against whites during the three years after the war, demonstrate that black men and women understood their rights and were not reluctant to assert them. The informal process that bureau agents used in adjudicating these complaints—calling parties before them, asking questions, collecting evidence, and making decisions—was also important. It enabled African Americans, most of whom were illiterate and had no experience with judicial proceedings, to become familiar with the legal process.

Nevertheless, the bureau's authority was fragile. Because it was an agency of the War Department, its officials fell under the authority of the president. Convinced that the rebel states had legitimate governments and were entitled to restoration, Johnson used his authority to limit the bureau's power to try cases involving blacks. In 1865, he had restricted the bureau's judicial authority, preventing it from adjudicating cases unless state officials persisted in denying African Americans the right to testify. As state governors and legislatures relaxed restrictions on black testimony during late 1865 and early 1866, Johnson pressed the bureau to surrender to state courts jurisdiction over African Americans. By mid-1866, bureau officials in most states had complied.

The Freedmen's Bureau Act of 1866, which became law in July, offered some hope, giving the bureau authority to intervene when state officials denied blacks their rights. The act provided that the bureau should exercise this authority under regulations approved by the president. When Bureau officials drew up such regulations, however, Johnson refused to approve them. Their hands tied by Johnson, bureau agents resorted to bluff. They cajoled local officials, demanding that they attend to complaints made by blacks, and threatened to intervene if they refused to guarantee justice. When African Americans complained that employers had cheated them, agents investigated, conducted hearings, and frequently ordered offending employers to pay their workers. Without legal authority to try cases and impose penalties, however, most were reluctant to enforce their decisions when local officials or private citizens refused to comply.

The Civil Rights Act also offered African Americans limited protection. Bureau officials initiated several successful prosecutions against state officials who enforced laws that expressly discriminated against blacks. Although few in number, these prosecutions deterred most state functionaries from enforcing discriminatory statutes. Where officials continued to enforce discriminatory laws, bureau officials succeeded in removing cases involving African Americans from state to federal courts. In Kentucky, for example, most judges persisted in enforcing the state law that prohibited blacks from testifying against whites, clearly denying African Americans one of the rights guaranteed by the Civil Rights Act. Invoking its authority under the act to try cases involving persons who were denied equal rights in state law, the US District Court in Louisville assumed jurisdiction over hundreds of cases in which whites were accused of murdering, assaulting, robbing, and otherwise maltreating blacks.

In most states, however, antebellum statutes had been modified to permit black testimony, and most officials refrained from enforcing blatantly discriminatory provisions of the black codes. Throughout the South, state law made it a crime to murder, assault, or rob any person, regardless of race, and permitted all persons to recover damages for breach of contract, trespass, personal injury, and the like. By law, therefore, African Americans "enjoyed full and equal benefit of all laws and proceedings for the security of persons and property," as demanded by the Civil Rights Act. They were denied justice, not by enforcement of discriminatory laws, but rather by discriminatory law enforcement. Prejudiced local officials refused to prosecute whites who beat, murdered, raped, robbed, or cheated blacks, or, if they did, all-white juries refused to convict white defendants. Nevertheless, many conservative US district judges and district attorneys—men who had been appointed by Johnson—read the act narrowly. They refused to take jurisdiction over cases involving blacks unless they were denied justice by enforcement of a blatantly discriminatory law.

Other problems hampered enforcement. Because the federal courts had previously possessed limited jurisdiction, there were few of them; in fact, no southern state had more than two US district judges assigned to it. For most people, therefore, federal courts were remote and difficult to access. The Civil Rights Act anticipated this problem, authorizing federal judges to appoint a US commissioner for each county in their district. Although commissioners were not authorized to try cases, they could hold preliminary hearings and order offenders to appear before district courts, making it easier to initiate proceedings under the act. Yet this offered no panacea. Commissioners were usually white southerners who had little sympathy for African Americans and were reluctant to risk their neighbors' wrath by initiating cases against whites. None of these problems was irremediable. A president sympathetic to the act would have directed his attorney general to press district attorneys to interpret the act more broadly. A Supreme Court decision sustaining a broad interpretation of the act would have brought conservative district judges into line. But as things stood throughout 1866, justice remained elusive for African Americans.

The consequences were disastrous for African Americans. Realizing that blacks had little chance of winning redress, planters took advantage. Their widespread cheating of workers, combined with a poor harvest in 1866, meant that most black agricultural workers remained impoverished and economically dependent on white landowners. It was not uncommon for a black family to end the year's labor breaking even or owing the planter for food and supplies advanced over the course of the year. Moreover, throughout the southern countryside, whites terrorized African Americans without fear of punishment by local officials. "Murders and all sorts of depredations are committed by the wholesale," noted a Freedmen's Bureau agent from Arkansas. "You cannot imagine how terrified the [black] people are. They are aware in case . . . murderers are arrested the criminal laws are so defective that in most cases they get clear, revenging themselves on those who have testified against them."[27]

From Legal Rights to Political Equality

In early 1867, Republican leaders agreed to extend to southern blacks the right to vote, embracing a policy that they had rejected as too radical a year earlier. The events of 1866 had convinced Republicans that whatever rights states might formally extend to African Americans, state officials could easily nullify in practice. But if African Americans possessed the ballot, Republicans believed that they could elect state and local officials who would be more responsive, enforce the law impartially, and, equally important, allow the party to grow roots in the South. Republican leaders also aimed to minimize the need for intrusive federal involvement in state affairs by giving the freedmen the ability to protect themselves through state political and legal institutions. In many ways this Republican position was naive. As radicals pointed out, it offered an impoverished people recently freed from slavery a paper shield to protect themselves from former masters who controlled the region's economic resources, rejected blacks' claim to civil equality, and remained committed to white supremacy. Republican support for black suffrage was, nevertheless, a radical step. In no other slave society in the world did former slaves win the ballot so quickly. In addition, African Americans would use political power effectively, to alter the political and social landscape of the South and challenge white hegemony.

Republicans embodied their new program in the Reconstruction Act, which they passed over a presidential veto in March 1867. Resting on the war power, which Republicans claimed Congress might exercise within the rebel states until they were restored, the act divided the ten unrestored states into five military districts and directed the president to appoint a major general to oversee each. District commanders might permit existing state officials to maintain law and order, but, if necessary, might use military personnel to make arrests and try offenders in military courts. Military authority would be short-lived, however. States were to hold elections for delegates to constitutional conventions, and black adult males would be permitted to vote in these contests. After the conventions had met and drafted new constitutions enfranchising black men, voters had ratified these documents, and state legislatures elected under the new constitutions ratified the Fourteenth Amendment, Congress would seat southern senators and representatives, thereby restoring the rebel states to the Union and ending military authority.

A political revolution swept the South during 1867, as military officials registered voters in preparation for election of convention delegates. African Americans viewed the ballot as both an emblem of citizenship and a means of breaking the chains that officials of the presidentially reconstructed governments had forged to limit their freedom. Consequently, they joined political clubs like the Union League, where they learned about the political process, debated political issues, and registered to vote at a rate that alarmed white southerners. With the political mobilization of the black community, a powerful Republican Party emerged across the Confederate South. Although African Americans made up the overwhelming majority of the party's rank and file, Republican organizers, aware that black majorities existed in only three states, also wooed white voters. They attracted northerners who had settled in the South after the war (so-called *carpetbaggers*), as well as a significant number of southern whites (derisively known as *scalawags*), most of whom had been wartime Unionists. Native whites constituted perhaps 20 percent of the party's supporters, making them crucial to Republican success.

Because they denied the legitimacy of black suffrage, most southern whites not only spurned the Republican Party but refused to vote in elections for constitutional conventions held in the late summer and fall of 1867. Consequently, Republicans won overwhelming majorities in the conventions, gained control over the process of constitution-making, wrote provisions asserting the equality of all men into state constitutions, established universal male suffrage, and repealed property-holding requirements for jury service and office holding. They also mandated establishment of public schools, a step viewed as essential to black advancement. Except in the South Carolina and Louisiana conventions, radicals failed to win acceptance of provisions prohibiting segregation in schools or public accommodations. Nevertheless, none of the new constitutions imposed racial segregation. Only the South Carolina convention took meaningful action to help blacks become landowners, establishing a state land commission to purchase land and to sell it on liberal terms to the landless. Elsewhere, Republican constitution makers clung to free labor orthodoxy, empowering state government to promote economic growth, thereby hoping to attract more white supporters and to expand economic opportunity for blacks and whites alike. Like the party's congressional leaders, southern Republican leaders defined equality in civil and political rather than economic terms.

During the first half of 1868, southern voters went to the polls to ratify the new constitutions and to elect state officials and congressional representatives. In seven of the ten unrestored states, the constitutions received a majority of the votes cast, and newly elected Republican legislatures ratified the Fourteenth Amendment. In June 1868, with a presidential election at hand, congressional Republicans voted to restore all seven states. Only Mississippi (where a provision calling for widespread disfranchisement of former rebels led voters to reject the new constitution) and Virginia and Texas (where intraparty divisions slowed constitution-making) remained unrestored by summer's end. Within eighteen months, these three had also ratified new constitutions and gained restoration.

When white Republicans won the lion's share of the offices in most states, most white southerners viewed the new regimes as revolutionary and illegitimate. As leaders of a party that relied on black votes, white officeholders supported civil and political equality for the freedmen, drawing the wrath of most of their white neighbors. While black Republicans did not win a share of offices equal to their strength in the party, some were elected to serve as US senators and representatives, state legislators, sheriffs, county commissioners, and justices of the peace. Thus for the first time, African Americans gained positions of prestige and power, a phenomenon most whites viewed as intolerable. And as African Americans' assertiveness and political sophistication increased, they gained a stronger voice in party affairs and won a greater share of offices. By the end of Reconstruction, two African Americans had served in the US Senate, 14 in the US House of Representatives, and over 1,500 as state and local officeholders.

The Republican revolution also produced a significant shift in public policy that affected the ongoing struggle between the races over the meaning of emancipation. During the early years of Reconstruction, southern whites had mobilized the power of the state to reassert their dominance over the former slaves and to guarantee white planters and farmers a continued tractable labor supply. But Republican legislatures denied whites this weapon, repealing the remnants of the black codes and giving African Americans a voice in the legal process by allowing them to serve on juries. They also attempted to strengthen the position of the vast majority of African Americans who worked as agricultural laborers, sharecroppers, and tenant farmers. Republicans gave agricultural laborers and sharecroppers more effective legal means to secure payment of their wages and also afforded

tenants greater protection against landlords. In addition, Republican home-
stead laws exempted small amounts of personal property (farming tools
and livestock, for example) from seizure by creditors. This afforded at least
some protection to poor sharecroppers and tenants who relied on planters
and merchants for credit and were thus in danger of losing everything in the
event of a poor harvest.

Practice changed as well as policy, a fact that was brought home to blacks
and whites by their day-to-day experiences. When they attended trials in the
county courthouse—a recreation popular among persons of both races—they
were struck by the presence of black jurors. Because jury service was a mark
of respect in rural communities in the nineteenth century and jurors made
decisions that directly affected the well-being of the community, nothing
conveyed more graphically the revolutionary nature of Reconstruction. But
the presence of blacks on juries was not merely symbolic. By giving blacks
a voice in matters that directly affected their lives, jury participation broke
another of the bonds of white authority that had circumscribed their lives.
With African Americans present, juries were more likely to consider seriously black testimony and cases initiated by freedmen. And they were less
likely to indict or convict African Americans merely because whites accused
them of crimes. This made blacks less vulnerable to white authority, shielded

Figure 3.3. A racially mixed jury. *Harper's Weekly*, November 30, 1867 https://
digitalcollections.nypl.org/items/510d47e1-3fa6-a3d9-e040-e00a18064a99.
Schomburg Center for Research in Black Culture, New York Public Library.

them from capricious prosecutions that threatened their liberty, and afforded them greater personal security.

Planters had to deal with local officials—sheriffs, district attorneys, judges, and justices of the peace—who were responsive to African Americans. Under Republican rule, arrests and prosecutions of blacks for vagrancy were almost unheard of, and planters and farmers lost an effective tool for compelling African Americans to enter contracts on their terms. They also found that local officials no longer automatically prosecuted black workers at the behest of their employers. When a group of planters in Greenwood, South Carolina, brought charges against blacks who took discarded fence rails to use for firewood, for example, a Republican justice of the peace dismissed the case, noting that the rails "are of no use to any but to assist the poor in the way of fuel." "I believe in justice," he explained, "and if they [the planters] do not like it they can lump it."[28] For planters accustomed to relying on law to reinforce their control over workers, the presence of such officials was a devastating blow.

Planters were also outraged when local officials proved responsive to African Americans' complaints against them. Republican justices of the peace frequently fined employers who assaulted their employees, and they offered African American workers redress against planters and farmers who attempted to defraud them of the fruits of their labor. Whites expected deference from blacks and bitterly resented being called to account by their former slaves. Unwilling to admit that freedpeople had a right to redress, they denounced Republican officials as troublemakers who needlessly encouraged African Americans to challenge their employers. "If a negro [sic] should sustain any ill feelings against a white man and can muster the slightest shadow of a case against him," seethed one wealthy South Carolinian, "he rushes off immediately to Beaufort [the county seat] and there he finds a ready and willing mill to grind the respectable portion of the community to ashes." Local officials' responsiveness to former slaves, complained another planter, led to loss of control over workers and "the disorganization of labor."[29]

Their world turned upside down by growing African American assertiveness, the vast majority of southern whites denied the legitimacy of the new order. They contended that black suffrage—on which the Republican state constitutions and governments rested—had been imposed unconstitutionally on the South by Congress and had given political power to "ignorant, stupid, demi-savage paupers." The natural result, they charged, was that scheming Republican politicians—the *Daily Arkansas Gazette* called them men whose "putridity stinks in the nostrils of all decency"—won office through demagogic appeals to ignorant black voters. This, they argued, guaranteed corrupt, rapacious governments that rode roughshod over the rights of upstanding citizens like themselves. Indeed, when Republican legislators raised taxes significantly to fund public education and economic development projects, white Democrats claimed that white property holders, who paid most of the taxes, were being "robbed by the no-property herd." And when evidence of corruption surfaced, their rage became white-hot. "This is the rule of the proletariat," Mississippi Democrats shrieked, "it is naked communism—and negro communism at that."[30]

Because most southern whites considered the Republican regimes illegitimate and viewed black political power as a threat to their social order, many justified violence as a legitimate means to throw off the Republican yoke. Between 1867 and 1870, paramilitary groups, most notably the Ku Klux Klan, surfaced in virtually every southern state. Directed from the grass roots rather than by national or state leaders, these organizations unleashed a campaign of terror designed to deter African Americans from voting, to destroy the Republican Party, and to reestablish white dominance. Aware that leadership was necessary to mobilize black voters, the Klan singled out local Republican leaders for special attention, beating and killing them, assaulting members of their families, and burning their homes. But they did not stop there. Klan members brutalized thousands of rank-and-file Republicans and beat and raped their wives and daughters, hoping to convince them to sever their ties with the party.

Klan violence convinced Republican leaders that a constitutional amendment was needed to protect the voting rights of African Americans. Because the Reconstruction Act applied only to the states of the former Confederacy, it left blacks in the border states and in most of the North without the franchise. Abolitionists, northern blacks, and Radical Republicans, having long argued that suffrage was an inherent right of citizenship, repeatedly called attention to the inconsistency of conferring suffrage on southern blacks while denying it to their northern counterparts. Mainstream Republicans were sensitive to such charges, finding it increasingly difficult to reconcile tolerance of discriminatory voting laws with their commitment to equal rights. In the four years following the war, Republicans in eight northern states had placed before the voters state constitutional amendments establishing equal suffrage. Although these amendments were approved by voters in only two states (Minnesota and Iowa), the vast majority of Republican voters in the other six states supported them. Yet party leaders, unwilling to jeopardize their chances of winning the White House, failed to include a plank supporting a suffrage amendment in the party's 1868 platform. But events in the South during the campaign made the demand for an amendment urgent. Klan terror decimated the Republican turnout in most of the South, putting Georgia and Louisiana in the Democratic column. If this trend continued, Republicans feared, southern Democrats would regain dominance and repeal state constitutional provisions guaranteeing African American suffrage.

By early 1869, congressional Republicans agreed that a suffrage amendment was necessary. But as they proceeded, they disagreed sharply over how to word the amendment. Many supported a narrow amendment barring the United States or the states from denying any person the right to vote on the basis of race. Radicals and many moderates sharply criticized this formulation, arguing that states could easily circumvent it by adopting property and literacy requirements that would effectively disfranchise most former slaves, who were poor and illiterate. Women's rights advocates, long allied with radical abolitionists, also dissented. The narrowly drawn amendment undercut their cause by allowing states to limit the vote to men. These critics championed a broader version that would prohibit state and national officials from denying persons the ballot on the basis of sex, nativity, property, education, creed, or race.

Although broadening the amendment's language attracted support, many Republicans feared that it would prevent the amendment from winning ratification by three-quarters of the states, as the Constitution required. Massachusetts and Connecticut had enacted literacy requirements to prevent immigrants from voting, and Rhode Island had established a property requirement for naturalized (but not native-born) citizens. In the Far West, where anti-Chinese sentiment ran deep, the nativity provision would almost certainly have resulted in rejection. No state allowed women to vote, and barring states from restricting suffrage on account of sex would align the party with a position that few voters supported. In February 1869, after bitter debate, congressional Republicans finally adopted a conservative version of the amendment. It simply prohibited the states or the United States from denying anyone the right to vote on the basis of race and authorized Congress to enforce this guarantee. Although it shattered the alliance between feminists and Radical Republicans and invited subterfuges to limit black voting, it quickly won approval by three-fourths of the states and became the Fifteenth Amendment in 1870.

Adoption of the suffrage amendment brought to a fitting end a turbulent decade of revolutionary changes in the American Constitution. Because of a complex interplay of principle and expediency, Republicans had transformed a war for the Union into a war to create a more perfect Union. Identifying the war effort and their party with freedom, Republicans were pressed by events to explore the meaning of freedom. Radicals complained that the party moved too cautiously, yet they succeeded in convincing moderates that African Americans were entitled to civil and political equality. Although intent on preserving federalism, mainstream Republicans had supported a series of constitutional amendments and a Civil Rights Act that gave the national government broad authority to guarantee civil rights. In many respects, then, by 1870 the demands made by African Americans and abolitionists in the antebellum years had been incorporated into American constitutionalism, an achievement few had thought possible at the beginning of the decade. Nevertheless, bitter resistance to the new order continued, suggesting that even more sweeping changes were necessary to secure the fruits of the Reconstruction revolution.

4

Equality Deferred, 1870–1900

Located in the rich Brazos River Valley some eighty miles northwest of Houston, Washington County, Texas, was part of the nineteenth-century South's cotton kingdom. Although fall usually focused the attention of residents on the harvest and the price of the fleecy staple, the fall of 1886 was different. Politics displaced cotton as the prime subject of discussion at the Barrel House, a popular African American bar in Brenham, the county seat; at Routt's bustling cotton gin in nearby Chappell Hill; and at dozens of other gathering spots throughout the county. With the support of the county's slight black majority, Republicans had controlled local government from 1869 until 1884, when Democrats had reclaimed the county court-house in a closely contested election. For Democrats, the victory had been sweet, bringing to an end fifteen years in which black men and their white allies had governed the county. But Democrats were worried as the 1886 can-vass approached. Republican leaders were formidable opponents, and the county's African Americans remained politically active and determined to return the county to Republican control. Republicans were equally appre-hensive. They recalled that two years earlier their opponents had used vio-lence to reduce the black turnout and believed that local Democrats would resort to any means necessary to guarantee white rule.

Republicans' fears were not misplaced. In three heavily Republican precincts located in the predominantly black eastern portion of the county, masked men clad in yellow slickers seized ballot boxes from election officials at gunpoint. The raids accomplished their purpose, destroying enough Republican ballots to give Democrats a narrow victory in the closely contested canvass. Yet all did not go according to plan for the Democrats. Anticipating foul play, a group of African American Republicans in the Flewellen precinct remained at the polling station as election officials tallied the ballots. When masked intruders burst into the room to seize the ballot box, Polk Hill, one of the black observers, opened fire with his shotgun, killing one of the bandits, Dewees Bolton, the son of a Democratic candidate for county commissioner.

Promises to Keep. Donald G. Nieman, Oxford University Press (2020). © Oxford University Press.
DOI: 10.1093/oso/9780190071639.001.0001

Although Hill fled, local officials arrested eight black men who had been present at the shooting and charged them with murder. In jailing the African Americans, they did more than satisfy whites' demands that Bolton's killing be avenged. Democratic leaders, including the county judge, Lafayette Kirk, had orchestrated the election-day fraud and feared that Hill's companions had seen too much. By identifying young Bolton's comrades, they might provide evidence that would enable Republicans to contest the election and put the Democratic conspirators behind bars. On the night of December 1, after Republican lawyer F. D. Jodon had initiated habeas corpus proceedings on behalf of the imprisoned blacks, a band of disguised men broke into the county jail in Brenham. Easily overpowering the jailer, they went to the cells where the black men were being held and asked for Shad Felder, Alfred Jones, and Stewart Jones. After identifying the three, they dragged them out of jail, took them to the bank of nearby Sandy Creek, and hanged them. Two days after the lynching, as an angry mob of whites gathered in Brenham, prominent Democrats informed Stephen Hackworth, James Moore, and Carl Schutze, three of the county's leading white Republicans, that they must leave town. Fearing for their lives, all three quickly departed.

Hackworth and his comrades refused to accept exile, however, and turned to the national government for redress. They found ready allies among Senate Republicans, who had long advocated stronger federal criminal sanctions against election fraud and violence. In mid-February 1887, William Evarts of New York, a Republican member of the Senate Committee on Elections, initiated hearings on the Washington County affair. During the ensuing three weeks, several dozen Washington County citizens—black and white, Republican and Democrat—made the long trip to the nation's capital and gave committee members their versions of the 1886 election and its violent aftermath. Running to almost seven hundred pages of small print, the testimony vividly detailed the fraud and violence that plagued southern elections, offering strong support for advocates of federal regulation of elections. Democrats now controlled the House of Representatives and the White House, however, and Republicans themselves were divided over the wisdom of more vigorous protection of their southern allies. Consequently, Republican leaders were unable to translate indignation over the violence and fraud employed by Washington County whites into legislation providing more effective protection for beleaguered African American voters.

Washington County Republicans did not pin all their hopes on congressional intervention. As the Senate hearings got under way, US Attorney

Rudolph Kleberg won an indictment against Lafayette Kirk and eight other prominent Washington County Democrats in the US district court in Austin. Framed under federal election laws adopted during Reconstruction, the indictment charged the defendants with conspiring to interfere with election officials and to steal ballots in an election at which a congressional representative was elected. Despite his own affiliation as a Democrat, Kleberg threw himself into the prosecution, conducting a thorough investigation and vigorously presenting his case to the jury. Nevertheless, after a lengthy trial in August 1887, jurors were unable to agree on a verdict, and the judge declared a mistrial. Undaunted, Kleberg brought the case to trial again in April 1888, only to have the jury return a verdict of not guilty. In both trials, the government had produced strong circumstantial evidence that Washington County Democratic leaders had stolen the ballot boxes. Yet because three key Republican witnesses had been lynched and other potential black witnesses were reluctant to give testimony that might cost them their lives, the district attorney did not have a "smoking gun." Not surprisingly, therefore, he was unable to convince juries composed mainly of white Texans to return a guilty verdict against the respectable white defendants. Federal officials could prosecute Washington County Democrats, but they could not bring them to justice.

The April 1888 acquittal brought an end to the Washington County affair. Because murder was a state, not a federal offense, the Washington County sheriff was responsible for investigating the lynching of the three black men and bringing the guilty parties to justice. Although the identities of the lynch mob's leaders were common knowledge among local whites, community leaders showed no interest in prosecuting the guilty parties. "Most good citizens regret the hanging," the *Brenham Daily Banner* piously noted, "but in the present state of public feeling it is regarded as one of those occurrences that could not well be avoided."[1] Not surprisingly, Sheriff N. E. Dever, a white Democrat, made no effort to arrest the guilty parties. This forgive-and-forget attitude did not extend, however, to Polk Hill. Dever and his deputies conducted a manhunt that led to Hill's arrest in late 1886. Hill was transferred to the Milam County jail for safekeeping, a step that probably saved him from the fate of his friends. Subsequently, he was convicted of manslaughter by an all-white jury and sentenced to twenty-five years in prison.

Events in Washington County reflected developments elsewhere in the South during the last decades of the century. Despite an unparalleled extension of federal authority during the early 1870s, by 1877 southern Democrats had reclaimed control of state government from the Republicans throughout the South. While the new regimes steadily chipped away at the rights African Americans had won during Reconstruction, Democrats' counterrevolutionary designs met determined resistance. Blacks refused to abandon the dream of citizenship and equality and skillfully used the political and legal avenues opened to them during Reconstruction to defend their newly won rights. Moreover, while the national government's vigor in protecting civil rights waned after the mid-1870s, neither Congress, the Justice Department, nor the federal courts completely abandoned blacks during the late 1870s and 1880s. Yet as the demise of Washington County Republicanism suggests, southern blacks were only able to slow, not stop, the counterrevolution. By the end of the century, northern Republicans paid little more than lip service to protecting African American rights, the federal courts had transformed the Reconstruction amendments into platitudes, and conservative Democrats had successfully employed terror and economic reprisals to overcome black resistance and reestablish white supremacy. It took three decades to accomplish, but by 1900, southern Democrats had reversed the Reconstruction revolution.

Securing the Republican Revolution

Even as Republicans celebrated ratification of the Fifteenth Amendment in February 1870, they recognized the vulnerability of the dramatic civil rights gains they had achieved in the 1860s. Across the South, the Ku Klux Klan and kindred groups had launched a campaign of terror designed to destroy the fledgling Republican regimes and reverse the Republican commitment to equality. Most state and local officials proved either unable or unwilling to challenge the Klan. Confronting a large, well-armed terrorist group, Republican sheriffs were reluctant to risk igniting a race war by mobilizing their supporters (most of whom were black) into posses to arrest Klansmen. Furthermore, when fearless local officials made arrests and initiated prosecutions, they struggled to win convictions. Witnesses, fearing for their lives, frequently refused to testify against Klansmen, and many jurors were too intimidated by or (in the case of whites) too sympathetic to the Klan to return guilty verdicts.

In early 1870, with Klan violence spreading and state officials unable to check it, congressional Republicans considered bold new legislation to enforce the Fourteenth and Fifteenth Amendments. As they had done during the Civil War, Republicans viewed the Constitution as a source of power, arguing that it gave Congress discretion to choose the means necessary to protect the rights of citizens. "The people know that . . . the Constitution is created for the people, and not the people for the Constitution," argued Mississippi Republican George McKee, "and I would rather trust the clear, simple judgement of the people than that of any legal quibbler who ever split a constitutional hair on either side of this House."[2]

Some Republicans argued that the national government had authority to legislate to protect its citizens, whether they were threatened by state or private action. "I desire that so broad and liberal a construction be placed upon its provisions as will insure protection to the humblest citizen," explained Joseph Rainey, an African American congressman from South Carolina. "Tell me nothing of a constitution which fails to shelter beneath its rightful power the people of a country."[3]

Most Republicans, however, feared that giving Congress such open-ended authority threatened the federal system. Carried to its logical conclusion, they argued, it would empower the national government to enact a general code of laws governing crime, property, contracts, family relations, and other matters that properly lay within state jurisdiction. Consequently, theirs was a more restrictive view of federal power. They acknowledged that the Fourteenth and Fifteenth Amendments were designed to prevent states from denying individual rights rather than to give Congress primary responsibility for defining and protecting individual rights. Nevertheless, they pointed out that the amendments gave Congress authority to enact "appropriate legislation" to enforce their guarantees, thereby conferring broad discretion to choose the means best suited to that end. They also pointed out that states could, through inaction, deny the rights guaranteed by the amendments. In other words, states might just as effectively deny individuals equal protection of the laws by failing to punish murderers as by enforcing blatantly discriminatory statutes. Most Republicans concluded that when states, through inaction, denied black citizens rights guaranteed by the Fourteenth and Fifteenth Amendments, Congress could provide remedies against private action that the states failed to afford.

Acting on this theory, congressional Republicans passed the Enforcement Act in May 1870, dramatically expanding federal protection for individual rights. Designed primarily to enforce the Fifteenth Amendment, the act made it a federal crime for state officials to deny otherwise qualified voters the right to register or to vote. It also established criminal penalties for private citizens who used force, violence, intimidation, bribery, or economic coercion to deny any person the right to vote. At the behest of their African American and white southern colleagues, who were particularly sensitive to the problem of violence, congressional Republicans went beyond protecting voting rights. They established stiff criminal penalties (fines of $5,000 and imprisonment for ten years) for those who conspired to deny persons rights guaranteed by the Constitution or federal laws. The act thus broke new ground, affording individuals federal remedies against private acts of violence, something that previously had been the exclusive responsibility of the states.

Less than one year later, in April 1871, congressional Republicans took even firmer action, passing a measure popularly known as the Ku Klux Klan Act. The law made it a federal crime for two or more persons to conspire to deprive any person of equal protection of the laws. Invoking Congress's authority to regulate federal elections, it also established criminal penalties for persons who used force or intimidation to prevent citizens from supporting candidates of their choice in congressional elections. More to the point, it gave the government additional tools with which to combat terrorism. When terrorist groups prevented state authorities from guaranteeing persons equal protection of the laws, the president might use the army or the militia to arrest offenders. And when such organizations were "so numerous and powerful as to . . . set at defiance the constituted authorities," the chief executive might suspend habeas corpus, allowing the military to hold those whom it arrested without initiating formal charges.[4]

Between 1870 and 1873, federal officials used the new legislation to mount an impressive and effective campaign against the Klan. Consider the government's effort in western South Carolina, where a powerful Klan organization (in York County more than three-quarters of adult white males were members) declared war on African Americans during late 1870 and 1871, murdering several dozen black Republicans, severely beating hundreds of others, and raping African American women. Federal officials conducted a thorough investigation of Klan violence in the region and gathered a massive amount of evidence. At the urging of Attorney General Amos T. Akerman, who had gone to South Carolina to consult with federal investigators and prosecutors, President Ulysses Grant invoked his broad authority under the Klan Act. In October 1871, he suspended habeas corpus in nine South Carolina counties and authorized the army to assist federal marshals in making arrests. Although many Klan members fled, marshals made hundreds of arrests, and hundreds of other Klansmen surrendered. By year's end, 195 York County Klansmen resided in the county jail, popularly known as the "United States Hotel." After filling the Spartanburg County jail, federal officials had to rent two additional buildings to house men arrested in that county.

During late 1871 and 1872, trials began in federal courts in Columbia and Charleston. Because federal officials had carefully assembled evidence and the juries impaneled contained African American majorities, prosecutors won convictions. The trials, however, were time-consuming; the first five cases that went to trial took more than one month to complete. And the creaky federal judicial system was ill-equipped to deal with large numbers of lengthy trials. With only two federal judges assigned to the state and two attorneys responsible for all of the prosecutions, federal officials soon realized that they could bring to trial only a small portion of those whom they had arrested. Consequently, they concentrated on the worst offenders, hoping that the mass arrests and the few dozen convictions they were able to win would demonstrate federal resolve and deter further terrorism. Their strategy worked. Although the government won convictions in only about 150 cases (most of which resulted from guilty pleas rather than jury trials) and ultimately dismissed more than 1,000 cases, it effectively destroyed the Klan in South Carolina.

In no other state did the president suspend habeas corpus; nor did federal officials make as many arrests or win as many convictions elsewhere. Nevertheless, the government's law officers were active, winning indictments against more than 1,200 persons in North Carolina, more than 750 in Mississippi, and some 350 in Alabama. They did not bring most of these individuals to trial, but the mass arrests convinced Klansmen that the government meant business. In North Carolina and Alabama, government attorneys won 63 convictions. In Mississippi, where only one case went before a jury, federal officials obtained guilty pleas in almost 600 cases, trading promises of suspended sentences for confessions. While this meant that most Mississippi Klansmen avoided punishment, they knew that they would go to prison if they were implicated in further Klan activity. As in South Carolina, the government's strategy worked; Klan activity virtually ceased in these states. The Klan had taken its toll, helping to drive Republicans from power in North Carolina, Tennessee, and Georgia in 1869 and 1870; but the government's firm action restored at least temporary peace to most of the South and helped Republicans in other states to retain power.

Not only did the president and Congress act boldly against the Klan, but federal judges were also willing to interpret the Fourteenth and Fifteenth Amendments broadly. From North Carolina to Mississippi, they rejected claims by defendants that key provisions of the Enforcement and Klan Acts were unconstitutional. And several opinions strongly endorsed Congress's authority to punish private individuals who violated citizens' rights. In an 1871 case, *United States v. Hall,* Circuit Judge William B. Woods ruled that the Fourteenth Amendment empowered Congress to protect the funda- mental rights of American citizens, including those guaranteed by the Bill of Rights. He also brushed aside arguments that the Enforcement Act was unconstitutional because Congress could only provide remedies against violations of citizens' rights by state action. Echoing the views of congres- sional Republicans, he pointed out that state officials might just as effectively deny these rights by failing to protect them against wrongs committed by private individuals as if they acted themselves. When this occurred, he con- cluded, Congress might provide appropriate remedies, acting directly against offending individuals if necessary.[5]

Congressional Republicans also confronted segregation. Although legally imposed segregation was rare in the years immediately following the war, whites resisted integration of public places. In the South, most hotels and restaurants denied service to African Americans; public schools, asylums, and parks generally excluded African Americans; theaters, railroads, streetcars, and steamboats frequently segregated African Americans or excluded them altogether. In the North, where segregation had been common in the antebellum years, intense prejudice against blacks continued, but it was neither as broad nor as deep as that which existed in the South. The result was a more complex pattern of race relations: African Americans were denied service at most hotels and restaurants, while others accommodated the few well-to-do African Americans who sought admission; most public school systems insisted that African Americans attend separate schools that were generally inferior to those provided for whites, but schools were inte- grated in New England and some other places; railroads, steamboats, and streetcars frequently, but not always, segregated African Americans.

In the North, the postwar years witnessed a renewal of the antebellum campaign against segregation. Energized by the triumph over slavery, northern blacks intensified their demands for an end to discrimination in public accommodations. With memories of African Americans' wartime service still vivid and support for civil and political equality growing, many white northerners became more responsive to these demands. This shift in northern temperament was by no means universal, however. Most whites remained reluctant to mingle with African Americans, and many were violently opposed to permitting any breach in the color line. In postwar Philadelphia, for example, blacks mounted an impressive campaign against segregated streetcars, forcing themselves into whites-only cars where they were routinely assaulted by company employees and white customers and arrested by city police officers. It was not until 1867—after the streetcar companies, city officials, and state judges had resolutely resisted their demands for two years—that Philadelphia blacks secured legislation banning segregation in public transportation. Although white opposition was equally strong elsewhere and segregation remained customary in many parts of the North, blacks did win other notable victories in the late 1860s and early 1870s. Massachusetts (1865), New York (1873), and Kansas (1874) passed laws banning discrimination in public accommodations; Michigan, Connecticut, Rhode Island, Iowa, Minnesota, Kansas, Colorado, and Illinois prohibited school segregation; and school boards in Chicago, Cleveland, and Milwaukee operated integrated schools and even employed a few black teachers.

Southern blacks also challenged the color line. In Charleston, New Orleans, Louisville, and Savannah, they used sit-ins to compel streetcar companies to end discrimination. Although white Republicans feared that integrationist policies would alienate the party's white supporters, African American leaders demanded public accommodations laws protecting African Americans' right to nondiscriminatory service on railroads and steamboats as well as in hotels, theaters, and restaurants. Texas, South Carolina, Louisiana, Mississippi, and Florida enacted such legislation, but it had little effect. Some railroads permitted blacks who could afford the fare to ride in first-class cars with whites, but most continued to demand that all African Americans ride in second-class cars with poor whites and those who wished to smoke or chew tobacco. Hotels and restaurants continued to exclude African Americans, and theaters persisted in assigning them to balconies. A few blacks sought legal redress under state public accommodations laws, but most, fully aware of the depth of white prejudice, wished to avoid insult, and avoided places where they were not welcome.

Separation of the races also became the norm in state-operated facilities. Southern Republican regimes ended the policy of excluding blacks from public schools and from institutions for the blind, the deaf, and the insane. They also devoted roughly equal resources to the education of black and white children and created professional opportunities for blacks by hiring thousands of African American teachers. Yet with the exception of the New Orleans school board, southern Republicans operated separate schools for blacks and whites and segregated residents in institutions for the blind, the deaf, and the insane. Although some African American leaders criticized these policies, most welcomed the opportunity that public schools offered to black pupils and teachers and were more concerned that black schools receive adequate support than that black children attend integrated schools.

Dissatisfied with their slow progress, integrationists turned to the national government. In 1870, Charles Sumner, the radical senator from Massachusetts who had championed school desegregation in antebellum Boston, introduced new civil rights legislation that prohibited racial discrimination in public transportation, hotels, restaurants, schools, churches, cemeteries, and juries. Sumner and his allies argued that the measure would banish the last vestiges of caste. "Is it not strange," asked Republican Congressman Ellis Roberts, "that it should be a matter of debate whether there should be . . . legislation guaranteeing to a certain class of our citizens their common law rights?"[6] Having successfully used law to destroy slavery, radicals were confident that law could end discrimination.

Opponents charged that Sumner's bill was both unconstitutional and impractical. By attempting to regulate the practices of private businesses, they charged, it exceeded Congress's authority under the Fourteenth Amendment, which was limited to providing remedies against state action. Critics also argued that while government might legitimately guarantee legal and political equality, it had no business enforcing "social equality." Individuals had a right to associate with persons of their choice, they insisted, and to avoid contact with those whom they found objectionable. Indeed, nothing could be more futile than legislating "social equality." "Where local sentiment is hostile to a statute," the *Baltimore American* asserted, "it becomes inoperative and void."[7]

The bill's Republican supporters offered a thoughtful response. *Harper's Weekly* argued that by forcing whites to change their behavior, the bill would gradually moderate their attitudes. Other supporters challenged the notion that the law interfered with purely personal associations, pointing out that it merely sought to end discrimination in public places. "It is not social rights that we desire," explained John Lynch, an African American congressman from Mississippi. "What we ask is protection in the enjoyment of public rights. Rights which are or should be accorded to every citizen alike." Civil

rights advocates also contended that the Fourteenth Amendment sanctioned the law. "If an inn, having its right to exist by state authority, being
a creature of the state, in fact regulated by it, [engages in discrimination],"
explained African American abolitionist George Downing, "it may be said
that the *state* does the discriminating." Moreover, they reminded opponents
that the Thirteenth Amendment supported the legislation. Tolerating discrimination in public accommodations, explained Senator Frederick
Frelinghuysen, "would be perpetuating that lingering prejudice growing out
of a race having been slaves which it is as much our duty to remove as it was
to abolish slavery."[8]

Despite Republican majorities in Congress, Sumner's bill met stiff resistance. Although the Massachusetts senator introduced it during every
session until his death in 1874, he did not live to see his bill become law.
Some northern Republicans argued that the measure would be a political liability. White Republicans from the South contended that the provision mandating integrated schools would cripple the party by driving away
white supporters. It would also, they insisted, destroy the region's fledgling
public school system by undermining white support for it. It was not until
1875, when almost half of the Republicans in the House were lame ducks
and the provisions concerning schools, churches, and cemeteries had been
deleted, that the bill finally passed. The hesitation and trimming that marked
its long incubation revealed limits to the party's commitment to equality.
Nonetheless, passage of the Civil Rights Act of 1875, with its assertion that
the national government had a responsibility to assure all citizens equality
in public accommodations, marked the high tide of the Reconstruction revolution. "It is the capstone . . . of the reconstruction edifice," the *Springfield
Republican* proudly asserted.[9]

The Counterrevolution Gains Force

Even as Republican radicals struggled to complete the capstone, cracks
appeared in the foundation. During the mid-1870s, with federal judges
supportive and the Klan on the run, Republicans backed away from vigorous federal intervention in the South. In part this was a response to the
success of the campaign against the Klan and the concomitant decline in
terrorism. Other issues, however, explain the party's new posture. Most
Republicans viewed law enforcement as a state, not a federal, responsibility,

and considered the campaign against the Klan extraordinary. They were also concerned about the political consequences of further federal intervention. In a society skeptical of active government and suspicious of a strong national government, few whites supported a large-scale federal enforcement program. Furthermore, Democrats charged that tales of Klan terror were nothing more than Republican propaganda, denounced the enforcement program as a ruthless effort to prop up unpopular, incompetent governments with federal bayonets, and portrayed President Grant as a latter-day Caesar. Aware that these charges effectively appealed to American fears of military despotism, Republicans agreed that they must curb federal intervention in the South.

During 1873, Republican leaders began to distance themselves from the mailed-fist policies that had proved so effective in South Carolina. Under George Williams, who succeeded Akerman as attorney general in late 1871, the Justice Department became more cautious about initiating new civil rights cases. Williams did not stop new prosecutions under the Enforcement and Klan Acts, but he did not encourage them or provide the resources necessary for large-scale prosecutions. In fact, the administration became more conciliatory toward white southerners, hoping that this would moderate their opposition to the new order and bring to an end charges of bayonet rule. Beginning in 1873, President Grant pardoned many of the Klansmen who remained in prison, and Williams ordered federal attorneys in the South to dismiss prosecutions against thousands of Klansmen who had been indicted between 1870 and 1872.

Beset by political scandals and economic collapse, Republicans became even more cautious. Members of Grant's inner circle and prominent Republican congressmen implicated in financial scandals were the subjects of congressional investigations during 1873. With the scent of corruption trailing it, the party was also saddled with blame for the severe economic depression that struck in September 1873. Facing a hostile electorate as the 1874 congressional races approached, Republicans were reluctant to undertake unpopular action in the South. When the dust settled after the election, the party had been routed and a 110-vote Republican majority in the House had become a 60-vote margin for the Democrats. Fearing further losses in important state elections in 1875, party leaders became even more reluctant to renew large-scale intervention in the South.

Taking advantage of Republican cautiousness, southern Democrats launched a new offensive against their adversaries between 1874 and 1876.

By making active support for the Democratic Party a test of racial solidarity, they increased white voter participation significantly. They also developed new techniques of intimidation that effectively reduced Republican turnout without reviving northern support for federal intervention. Armed Democrats regularly disrupted Republican meetings, demanding equal time to expose Republican "lies" or shouting down Republican speakers. Seeking to impress on African Americans the perils of political involvement, armed bands rode through the countryside at night during the weeks preceding elections, firing small arms and sometimes even cannon, and patrolled polling places on election day. And when they did resort to beatings and murders, they usually defined their targets carefully and struck quickly rather than inaugurating an extended campaign of terror. Democrats also mastered the technique of the "race riot." They provoked altercations between their own supporters and Republicans. Then, under the pretext of self-defense, they launched punishing attacks against their opponents. At the beginning of the 1875 election campaign in Mississippi, for example, white Democrats in Clinton precipitated a fight at a Republican rally in which several blacks and whites were killed. Alleging that the Republicans had initiated a war of the races, Democrats swept the surrounding countryside during the next two days, killing between twenty and thirty African Americans and beating hundreds of others.

Despite his recent policy of conciliation and caution, Grant did not ignore the resurgence of violence. He authorized the War Department to station small squads of troops in areas where Democratic intimidation was most pronounced, hoping their presence would cow whites and reassure blacks. Under instructions from Washington, moreover, district attorneys, supported by troops, occasionally arrested persons charged with intimidating voters. The government's effort, however, ultimately proved inadequate. Too few troops were deployed (by October 1874 only 7,000 remained in the South) to make a show of force in more than a few spots. And because the overwhelming majority were infantry, they possessed limited mobility. Then, too, the number of prosecutions initiated under the Enforcement Act by federal attorneys was too small to serve as a deterrent. What was needed was a large-scale campaign of arrests and prosecutions patterned after the South Carolina effort of 1871–1872. Republican leaders, however, feared that they lacked popular support for such a campaign and did not meet the Democratic challenge. "The whole public are tired out with the autumnal outbreaks in the South," President Grant wrote in 1875, "[and] the great majority are ready now to condemn any interference on the part of the government."[10]

HARPER'S

How easily wicked and treasonable organizations may gain the control over the peaceable and the industrious members of society has always been signally apparent at the South. A | Tennessee, venture even to denounce the murderers or the violators of the laws; or if any Northern journal, roused to a proper indignation by the wrongs inflicted upon peaceable settlers

Figure 4.1. "The Union as It Was," *Harper's Weekly*, October 24, 1874 https://www.loc.gov/item/2001696840/. This Thomas Nast drawing depicts the White League, one of the terrorist groups that emerged after the federal government defeated the Ku Klux Klan. *Library of Congress.*

The results were disastrous for southern Republicans. Democrats regained control of state government in Texas (where only one-third of the population was African American) and Arkansas and Florida (where bitter factional disputes doomed Republicans) without resorting to widespread violence. In the rest of the unredeemed South, however, the new techniques of terror were crucial. In 1874, Alabama Democrats carried statewide elections, in part by employing violence and intimidation in key black belt counties, while Louisiana Democrats smashed Republican organizations in many rural parishes, winning control of the state assembly. The following year white Mississippians mounted a ferocious campaign of terror to carry the state legislature. With that accomplished, they swiftly impeached Republican governor Adelbert Ames. In 1876, Democrats in Louisiana and South Carolina used violence to carry state elections, completing the process of redemption. By 1877, the Democratic counterrevolution had recaptured the South and ended Republican control in every state in the region.

Even though African Americans continued to vote in large numbers and Republicans held office in some predominantly black counties after 1877, southern Democrats relied on fraud and intimidation to cling to power. A prominent Mississippi Democrat admitted in 1890, "we have been stuffing the ballot boxes, committing perjury, and . . . carrying the elections by *fraud* and violence" since 1875.[11] The consequences of Democratic hegemony were momentous. While blacks remained eligible to serve on juries, in most areas local officials manipulated jury selection procedures to exclude them. Consequently, African American plaintiffs and defendants once again found justice elusive as they confronted all-white juries. Blacks also felt the economic consequences of redemption: Democratic legislatures repealed measures that the Republicans had enacted to protect agricultural laborers; state supreme courts developed legal doctrines that reinforced the authority of landowners over sharecroppers; sheriffs again used vagrancy statutes to compel reluctant African American workers to accept unfavorable contracts with planters; and white justices of the peace turned a deaf ear to complaints that black workers lodged against their employers. Absence of effective protection, combined with a steady decline in cotton prices, left black sharecroppers and agricultural workers impoverished, reinforcing their economic dependence on whites. African American children also suffered as state legislatures cut support for public education and local officials reduced the share of school funds for black schools.

As southern Democrats moved ahead with the counterrevolution, the US Supreme Court restricted national authority to protect civil rights. Most members of the Court were conservative northern Republicans who did not share the radicals' passion for equality. Like most of their contemporaries, they were committed to preserving a decentralized federal system that limited national authority. Most Americans living in the twenty-first century find this commitment to state-centered federalism puzzling. We are the heirs of more than eighty years of growing federal authority and accept that national power is broad. Nineteenth-century

Americans had a much different outlook. The federal government played little role in their day-to-day lives, and, with the exception of the local postmaster, they rarely encountered a federal official. Moreover, as products of a political tradition that equated centralized authority with tyranny, they believed that self-government demanded substantial autonomy for local communities.

This arrangement was not set in stone, however, as the dramatic expansion of national power during the Civil War and Reconstruction demonstrated. Why, then, were a majority of Supreme Court justices unwilling to accept a significant expansion of federal authority over civil rights? Comfort with familiar legal arrangements played a role. The justices were experienced lawyers whose training and practice emphasized the importance of precedent and the danger of disruptive change. Equally important, they embraced received wisdom extolling decentralized authority as vital to a nation as vast and diverse as the United States. But race also influenced the justices' choices. Sharing racist assumptions common in the North and lacking the commitment to black equality shared by Republican radicals, most neither understood nor empathized with former slaves and were oblivious to the odds they faced in securing freedom and equal citizenship. Armed with the rights others possessed, most of the justices assumed that southern blacks should protect their rights in the same way other Americans did—principally through state legal and political processes. Failing to empathize with African Americans and lacking the passion of the radicals, they rejected broad, disruptive interpretations of the Reconstruction Amendments advanced by federal attorneys, some judges, African Americans, and most Republican leaders.

The first indication of the Supreme Court's position came when it decided the *Slaughter-House Cases* in 1873. They were brought, not by former slaves, but by white butchers in New Orleans who challenged a state law that restricted their freedom to practice their trade. The butchers charged that the liberty to pursue a lawful occupation was a fundamental right of citizenship and therefore one of the privileges and immunities of US citizenship protected by the Fourteenth Amendment. The implications for African Americans were quite clear. If the Court accepted the butchers' argument, Congress and the federal courts would enjoy authority to protect a wide range of individual rights, thus enhancing their authority to guarantee the rights of African Americans.

In a blow to civil rights advocates, a sharply divided Court rejected the butchers' position by a 5–4 margin. Writing for the majority, Justice Samuel

Miller argued that the Fourteenth Amendment recognized dual citizenship, stating that Americans were citizens of the United States *and* the state in which they resided. He inferred from this that they possessed two separate and distinct sets of rights, one deriving from national and the other from state citizenship. Defining the former as those "which owed their existence to the national government," Miller suggested that they were limited. They included the right to habeas corpus, to assemble to petition the government for redress of grievances, to come to the nation's capital, to unfettered use of the nation's ports and navigable rivers, and to protection by the government while abroad. More basic rights, such as the right to pursue a trade, were among the rights of state citizenship and thus not protected by the Fourteenth Amendment. Since Miller made no reference to them, presumably the guarantees of the Bill of Rights were not included among the privileges and immunities of US citizens and remained merely limitations on the authority of the national government.

Miller's opinion was greeted by sharp dissent, with Justice Noah Swayne charging that the majority had ignored the intent of the framers, transforming "what was meant for bread into a stone." Other dissenters argued that by making national citizenship primary, the Fourteenth Amendment had transformed the federal system, transferring responsibility for protecting fundamental rights to the national government. Although this analysis was persuasive, it threatened the federal system by transferring authority to define and protect individual rights from the states to the federal government. Indeed, Miller feared that a broad construction of the amendment would lead to a "great departure from the structure and spirit of our institutions," "fetter and degrade" the states, and "radically change the whole theory of the relations between the State and federal government to each other and of both . . . to the people."[12] The threat of such revolutionary consequences prompted the Court's majority to slow the juggernaut of constitutional change, even if it had to do so through a strained interpretation of the amendment.

By ruling that the privileges and immunities of US citizens included only a few rights of limited importance to most persons, the decision trivialized the provision that contemporaries viewed as the heart of the Fourteenth Amendment. Nevertheless, in dismissing the claims of the butchers, Miller emphasized that Congress had passed the postwar amendments to guarantee full freedom and genuine equality for African Americans. The "pervading purpose" of the amendments, he emphasized, was "the freedom of the slave race, the security and firm establishment of that freedom, and the protection of the newly-made freeman and citizen from the oppressions of those who had formerly exercised unlimited dominion over him."[13] Thus Miller suggested that the Court would look favorably on efforts to protect the rights of the former slaves.

Any hope sparked by Miller's comment was dashed when the Court decided *United States v. Cruikshank* in 1876. William Cruikshank was a member of a paramilitary group of more than a hundred whites who attacked African Americans who had gathered outside the courthouse in Colfax, Louisiana, in April 1873 to support local Republican officials whose claims to office had been challenged by Democrats. After their initial attack forced approximately 150 freedmen to take refuge in the courthouse, the whites torched the building, killed dozens of blacks as they fled the blaze, and subsequently shot in cold blood between 30 and 40 blacks who surrendered. In all, perhaps a hundred freedmen died in the massacre. In 1874, Cruikshank and two other participants were convicted in federal circuit court in New Orleans for violation of the Enforcement Act of 1870, which made it a crime to use force to deprive citizens of rights granted by the Constitution or laws of the United States. Specific charges in the indictment accused the defendants of using violence to deny their victims the right to bear arms (protected by the Second Amendment), the right of assembly (protected by the First Amendment), and the right to equal protection of the laws and due process of law (protected by the Fourteenth Amendment).

In a complicated ruling that focused on the indictment under which the defendants had been convicted rather than the constitutionality of the Enforcement Act, the Supreme Court reversed the convictions and dealt a severe blow to the government's authority to protect civil rights. Chief Justice Morrison Waite noted that the right to bear arms, freedom of assembly, and the other guarantees of the Bill of Rights were merely limitations on the national government, not rights enforceable against states and private individuals. Following the logic of *Slaughter-House*, he suggested that they were among the rights of state citizenship. Consequently, Waite concluded that they were not rights granted by the Constitution. Violation of them by private citizens, therefore, was not punishable under the Enforcement Act. The Court was now harvesting the bitter fruit of *Slaughter-House*. It had circumscribed the rights of US citizens, rights that could be said to be granted by the Constitution and therefore were within Congress's power to protect. As *Cruikshank* tragically demonstrated, this seriously compromised the government's civil rights authority.

The chief justice also rejected those parts of the indictment that accused the defendants of depriving citizens of equal protection and due process of law. This amounted to charging the defendants with murder, he concluded, a crime within the purview of state authority. The due process and equal protection clauses of the Fourteenth Amendment, according to Waite, added "nothing to the rights of one citizen . . . against another," but were merely restrictions on state action. They authorized Congress to provide remedies against denial of equal protection or due process by states and their officers, but did not empower it to punish private citizens who violated the rights of others. Thus the Court implicitly rejected the expansive reading of the equal protection clause offered by Judge Woods in *United States v. Hall,* making it more difficult for the national government to protect blacks against wrongs inflicted by private citizens. With southern state governments now in the hands of white Democrats, the Court left blacks at the mercy of their white neighbors.[14]

When it decided the *Civil Rights Cases* in 1883, the Court used the state action theory announced in *Cruikshank* to strike down the provisions of the Civil Rights Act of 1875, which banned discrimination by hotels, restaurants, theaters, and public transportation. Justice Bradley, who wrote the Court's opinion, denied that the Fourteenth Amendment's equal protection clause authorized the law. Ignoring the broad enforcement authority conferred on Congress by the Amendment, he held that it merely prohibited discrimination by state authorities, not by private individuals and businesses. Bradley also denied that the Thirteenth Amendment authorized the statute. He admitted that it abolished all "badges and incidents" of slavery and decreed "universal civil and political freedom throughout the United States." He also conceded that the Thirteenth Amendment, unlike the Fourteenth, was not directed exclusively at state action, and that Congress's power to enforce it included authority "to enact all necessary and proper laws for the obliteration and prevention of slavery with all its badges and incidents." Bradley denied, however, that discrimination against African Americans by proprietors of hotels and restaurants, which had been common in the free states during the antebellum years, was a badge of servitude. "It would be running the slavery argument into the ground," he concluded, "to make it apply to every act of discrimination which a person may see fit to make as to the guests he will entertain, or . . . take into his coach . . . or admit to his . . . theater."[15]

The nation had abolished slavery and taken unprecedented action to enforce civil rights, Bradley asserted. Enough was enough. It was time for African Americans to stop their demands for special treatment. "When a man has emerged from slavery, and by the aid of beneficent legislation has shaken off the inseparable concomitants of that state," Bradley concluded, "there must be some stage . . . when he takes the rank of a mere citizen, and ceases to be the special favorite of the law." Oblivious to the racial caste system created by slavery and continuing barriers to equal citizenship it created, the majority equated remedies against blatant, persistent, systemic discrimination with favored status.[16]

Bradley's opinion did not go unchallenged. The black press likened it to Taney's infamous *Dred Scott* opinion, and one week after it was announced, Frederick Douglass denounced the decision at a mass protest meeting in Washington, DC. On the Court itself, Justice John Marshall Harlan, a Kentucky Republican and former slaveowner, penned an eloquent dissent. Hearkening back to the idealism that had animated the Republican Party's civil rights program, he characterized Bradley's analysis as "entirely too narrow and artificial," charging that its "subtle and ingenious verbal criticism" sapped "the substance and spirit of the recent Amendments." "Constitutional provisions, adopted in the interest of liberty, and for the purpose of securing . . . rights inhering in a state of freedom, and belonging to American citizenship," he explained, "have been so construed as to defeat the ends . . . which they attempted to accomplish."[17]

Although the Court narrowed the scope of national power under the postwar amendments, it by no means abandoned the framers' commitment to equality. In *Strauder v. West Virginia* (1880), it struck down a state law that restricted jury service to white men in violation of the Fourteenth Amendment's equal protection clause. In the process, it reaffirmed that the amendment had been designed to protect former slaves from hostile state action and to guarantee that "all persons, whether colored or white, shall stand equal before the laws of the States." Moreover, the Court suggested that it would not tolerate laws establishing racial classifications. As Justice William Strong explained,

The words of the [Fourteenth] Amendment . . . are prohibitory, but they contain a necessary implication of a positive immunity, or right, most valuable to the colored race—the right to exemption from unfriendly legislation against them distinctively as colored; exemption from legal discriminations, implying inferiority in civil society . . . and discriminations which are steps towards reducing them to the condition of a subject race.[18]

The justices also proved willing to provide remedies against state officials who were guilty of enforcing nominally impartial laws in a discriminatory fashion. In Ex parte *Virginia*, decided at the same term as *Strauder*, the Court upheld the prosecution of a Virginia judge charged with systematic exclusion of African Americans from juries in his court. Justice Strong noted that the Fourteenth Amendment was designed "to take away all possibility of oppression by law because of race or color," and denied that its reach was limited to formal enactments by the legislature. "Whoever, by virtue of a public position under a state government, . . . takes away the equal protection of the laws, violates the constitutional inhibition; and as he acts in the name and for the State, . . . his act is that of the State," he explained. "This must be so or the constitutional provision has no meaning."[19] In *Neal v. Delaware*, also decided in 1880, the justices ruled that African Americans might prove discrimination without showing that officials intended to discriminate. In reversing the conviction of a black man indicted by an all-white grand jury and tried by an all-white petit jury, the Court held that the fact that no African American had served on a jury in a state with a substantial African American population constituted adequate proof of discrimination, even in the absence of evidence that local officials intended to keep African Americans off the juries.

The Court's clearest statement against discrimination came in 1886 when it decided *Yick Wo v. Hopkins*. The case was brought by a Chinese laundry operator who challenged a San Francisco ordinance that prohibited laundries in wooden buildings without a permit from city officials. Although ostensibly designed to prevent fires, Yick Wo charged that the law's real purpose was to exclude Chinese from the laundry business. Indeed, he demonstrated that all applications for permits by Chinese had been denied while only one non-Chinese had been refused a permit. The Court noted that the "actual operation" of the law was "directed . . . against a particular class" and declared it a violation of the equal protection clause. "Though the law itself be fair on its face and impartial in appearance, yet if it is applied . . . with an evil eye and an unequal hand . . . the denial of equal justice is still within the prohibition of the Constitution," concluded Justice Stanley Matthews.[20]

The justices constructed a labyrinth for prosecutors to navigate, but they nevertheless provided a narrow pathway for federal officials to protect African Americans' political rights. In *United States v. Reese*, decided in 1876, the Court struck down two provisions of the Enforcement Act of 1870, one punishing state officials and the other private individuals who denied any otherwise qualified person the right to vote. The problem, according to the Court, was that the Fifteenth Amendment prohibited racially motivated interference with the right to vote while the sections of the Enforcement Act under consideration were worded more broadly. They authorized prosecution of persons who denied any qualified voter the right to vote for any reason whatsoever, not merely on account of race. Significantly, however, Chief Justice Waite did not invoke the state action theory to strike down the provision that punished private individuals. And he asserted that the Fifteenth Amendment "has invested the citizens of the United States with a new constitutional right which is within the protecting power of Congress: . . . Exemption from discrimination in the exercise of the elective franchise on account of race."[21] Waite's analysis suggested that the government had authority to prosecute both private individuals and state officials who used force, violence, intimidation, or economic coercion to deny citizens the right to vote because of their race. Indeed, a year later, sitting as circuit justice in South Carolina, Waite sustained indictments against whites who were prosecuted for acts of violence against blacks during the 1876 campaign, underscoring federal authority to protect voting rights.

In Ex parte *Yarbrough*, decided in 1884, a unanimous Supreme Court endorsed Waite's position. Jasper and Dilmus Yarbrough and seven other white Georgians were members of the Pop and Go Club, a Democratic paramilitary organization. They were convicted for violation of the Enforcement and Klan Acts for their part in violence against African Americans who had voted in a hotly contested congressional election in 1882. The defendants appealed, contending that under the Court's rulings in *Cruikshank* and the *Civil Rights Cases*, the federal government did not have authority to punish private citizens for civil rights violations. Justice Miller unequivocally rejected their argument. He pointed out that Article I, section 4 of the Constitution gave Congress power to regulate the election of its members and justified legislation punishing individuals who attempted to control congressional elections by fraud and violence. According to Miller, Congress had ample authority to protect the Republic by guaranteeing that "the votes by which its members . . . are elected shall be the *free* votes of the electors, and the officers thus chosen the free and uncorrupted choice of those who have the right to take part in that choice."[22]

The Court's ruling in *Yarbrough* recognized the government's broad authority to protect African Americans against political violence. Although it merely upheld federal authority to punish violence at congressional elections, both federal and state elections were generally held at the same time. As a practical matter, therefore, the ruling enabled federal officials to police most state elections. In fact, Miller's opinion strongly suggested that the government had authority to use the Enforcement Act against persons who attempted to intimidate African American voters in any election, regardless of whether candidates for national representative were on the ballot. He held that individuals enjoyed a constitutional right to be free from racially motivated interference with the right to vote. Because he ruled that Congress possessed authority to protect this right from infringement by private individuals as well as by state officials, Miller strongly suggested that the national government could prosecute parties who sought in any election to prevent individuals from voting because of their race.

While hardly a champion of African Americans, the Court thus supported limited federal protection of voting rights. Sections of the Enforcement Act of 1870 and the Klan Act punishing infringement of the right to vote, intimidation of voters, and election fraud remained on the books and, in fact, had been reenacted by Congress in 1874 as part of the *Revised Statutes*. Encouraged by the Court's rulings in *Reese* and *Yarbrough*, the Justice Department vigorously enforced these measures throughout the 1880s and the early 1890s, framing indictments to specify that defendants were motivated by race. Indeed, for attorneys general and their subordinates, Reconstruction did not end in 1877; prosecuting voting rights cases and ensuring "a free ballot and a fair count" continued to be a high priority.[23] Federal attorneys and marshals in the South won indictments against thousands of election officials who refused to permit African Americans to register or vote, stuffed ballot boxes, and engaged in other types of skullduggery aimed at neutralizing the votes of blacks and their allies. They also prosecuted hundreds of individuals who resorted to violence to keep blacks away from the polls or to punish those who had dared to vote.

Despite this effort, the Justice Department won few convictions. Defendants were generally regarded by their white neighbors as heroes persecuted by meddling outsiders. Communities contributed generously to their defense funds, and when cases went to trial, federal attorneys often faced batteries of skilled defense lawyers. In order to put together cases that experienced defense counsel could not pick apart, harried federal attorneys needed the services of detectives to help them assemble evidence. They also required the assistance of experienced trial lawyers who could help them develop strategies for prosecution and present cases effectively in court. These hotly contested cases frequently involved large numbers of witnesses and lengthy trials, thus resulting in substantial expenses for summoning witnesses and jurors. In keeping with bipartisan commitment to limited federal authority, however, Congress consistently sought to contain spending. As a result, it denied the Justice Department adequate resources. While federal attorneys' overall caseloads quadrupled during the last quarter of the nineteenth century, Justice Department appropriations only doubled. Consequently, department officials frequently denied prosecutors' requests to hire detectives and additional attorneys. In fact, they occasionally ordered federal attorneys to dismiss cases because they did not have sufficient funds to cover the costs of prosecution.

Juries proved an even greater obstacle to success. Although federal juries continued to be racially mixed, they also included white Democrats who sympathized with defendants and denied the legitimacy of the prosecutions. Because a guilty verdict required unanimity, prosecutors had to convince hostile jurors. Moreover, because African Americans were often eyewitnesses to or victims of the crimes and because community pressure prevented most whites from coming forward to testify against defendants, federal attorneys had to rely heavily on black testimony. Convincing hostile white jurors to change their minds on the basis of evidence offered by African Americans was not easy. As one distressed federal attorney explained, "The law is plain— the facts are plainer, but I can't make a white democratic juror believe colored witnesses nor force him to vote [for conviction]. I can't keep politics out of the human mind and I can't make the jury commissioners select more impartial men."[24]

Although it produced few convictions, the Justice Department's effort was not without effect. It served notice that northern Republicans had not abandoned civil rights and that efforts to deny African Americans the vote through literacy tests and poll taxes would meet resistance. To underscore this, Republicans in Congress conducted regular investigations of southern election fraud and violence. Combined with opposition from poor whites, who feared that poll taxes and literacy tests would disfranchise them, the government's campaign to protect the voting rights of blacks helped keep the disfranchisers in check during the 1870s and 1880s. Before 1890, only three states enacted legislation to disfranchise African Americans: Georgia and Virginia experimented with poll taxes and South Carolina created a complicated ballot that effectively disfranchised illiterate voters.

As long as they were not legally barred from voting, southern blacks remained politically active. Equating the franchise with freedom, personal dignity, and equal citizenship, they were well aware that political decisions had a significant bearing on their lives. Consequently, in most states of the former Confederacy, African Americans continued to vote at a high rate and occasionally mounted serious challenges to Democratic hegemony. In a number of heavily black counties, redemption did not bring an end to Republican control; candidates elected by former slaves continued to serve as state legislators, local officials, and sometimes even congressmen. In addition to retaining power in black belt enclaves, Republicans mounted periodic challenges that threatened Democratic control at the state level. In Tennessee, where Unionist whites in the mountainous eastern counties joined with blacks in the central and western counties to support Republican candidates, the party remained a threat to Democratic control. Indeed, the Republican gubernatorial candidate won election in 1880, when the Democrats divided, and the party won more than 40 percent of the vote in statewide elections during the remainder of the decade. In North Carolina, support from mountain Unionists in the west and African Americans in the east enabled Republicans to come within a whisker of regaining control of the state in 1880. During the next two decades, Republicans would remain a force to be reckoned with in North Carolina politics.

In other states, Republicans forged alliances with dissident Democrats. During the late 1870s and throughout the 1880s, independent political movements, backed mainly by poor white farmers alienated by the economic policies of conservative Democratic leaders, flourished. By joining forces with the dissidents, Republicans were able to mount serious challenges in Florida, Arkansas, and Texas. In Virginia, disaffected Democrats known as the "Readjusters" (who advocated reducing or "readjusting" the state debt, most of which was held by outside investors) formed an alliance with Republicans that shook the Old Dominion. Uniting white farmers and African Americans, they controlled the state between 1879 and 1883, when Democrats regained control in a campaign won through violence and fraud.

There were other indications that African Americans were not resigned to second-class citizenship. They continued to challenge discrimination through legal and political action. When Democrats resegregated the New Orleans public schools in 1877, the city's African Americans turned to the courts, arguing that segregation denied them the equal protection guaranteed by the Fourteenth Amendment. Although they were not successful, they refused to accept second-class citizenship and used the legal process to assert their rights. In other parts of the South, where segregated schools had emerged during Reconstruction, most African Americans accepted the redeemers' continuation of dual school systems; however, black conventions protested unequal funding for black schools and demanded that state governments devote equal resources to black and white schools. In Kentucky and North Carolina, where Democratic legislatures provided that taxes paid by members of each race be used to support their own schools, African Americans used legal and political action to have the laws reversed and to secure more equitable funding.

It was in the North, however, that blacks made the greatest gains against segregation during the 1880s. While the Supreme Court had ruled in 1883 that Congress lacked authority to ban discrimination in places of public accommodation, it left the way open for individual states to enact such measures. Making the most of this, blacks who met in Washington, DC, in 1883 to protest the Court's decision urged civil rights advocates to press for state legislation to replace the federal law struck down by the Court. In the North, where African Americans comprised only about 2 percent of the population, African Americans responded energetically. In Ohio, for example, African Americans formed a network of equal rights leagues to demand civil rights legislation. Between 1884 and 1887, Ohio and twelve other northern states passed laws prohibiting discrimination in hotels, restaurants, public transportation, and places of amusement. During the late 1880s and the 1890s, many of these states expanded the list of places covered by the acts, and four additional states passed antidiscrimination measures. Moreover, in enforcing these laws, state courts refused to permit businesses to make any distinction on account of color. In the three states where the issue arose, they ruled that restaurant and theater owners could not segregate African Americans within their establishments.

Northern blacks also continued their campaign for integrated schools. African Americans had won admission to white schools in most of New England prior to the Civil War, and during the late 1860s and 1870s they had used political and legal action to end school segregation in seven other states. Yet school boards in many northern states maintained separate schools for blacks, and state courts in Nevada, Ohio, California, and Indiana had ruled that separate schools did not violate guarantees of equality contained in the Fourteenth Amendment and state constitutions. During the 1880s and 1890s, African Americans and their white allies won legislation mandating integrated schools in seven additional northern states, including laws reversing the effects of prosegregation court decisions in California and Ohio. Throughout the North, black litigants enjoyed frequent success in cases they brought against school boards that operated separate schools for African Americans. In deciding these cases, state courts usually relied on state constitutional provisions and statutes to strike down segregation. As a result of litigation and political action, there were few segregated schools in the North by 1900.

Northern blacks' continued success in the battle against discrimination did not mean that racism was dead in the North. Interaction between whites and blacks was rare, aversion among whites to contact with blacks in public places remained widespread, and most whites did not consider blacks their equals. If anything, northern racism became stronger during the 1880s and 1890s, as respected biologists and social scientists placed the imprimatur of science on the myth of black inferiority by asserting that African Americans had not reached the same intellectual or moral level as whites. Given the persistence of racism, northern blacks continued to suffer discrimination and, despite the new public accommodations laws, were frequently denied admission to white theaters, hotels, restaurants, and amusements. The public accommodations laws gave African Americans remedies against such abuses, and they frequently sued those who discriminated against them; however, because confrontations with hostile proprietors were unpleasant and lawsuits were expensive, many African Americans chose to avoid places where they knew they were not welcome. White prejudice also consigned most African Americans to menial, low-paying jobs, depriving them of the opportunities offered by an expanding economy. And state law offered no redress against employment discrimination.

Nevertheless, northern blacks' political and legal victories were important. In practical terms, they gave black children access to white schools, which were better funded and offered greater educational opportunities than were available in the South's separate and unequal schools. Even though discrimination continued, greater fluidity in race relations existed in the North. Consequently, northern blacks, unlike their southern counterparts, were not subject to constant and blatant reminders that they were regarded as an inferior caste, unfit to associate with whites. Furthermore, the victories of the 1870s and 1880s established the principle of equal citizenship as part of the North's dominant public philosophy. As the Michigan Supreme Court noted in 1890, "there must be and is an absolute, unconditional equality of white and colored men before the law. . . . Whatever right a white man has in a public place, the black man has also."[25] This marked a significant change from the antebellum era, when most Republicans had assured their constituents that they did not support African American suffrage, much less African Americans' right to equal access to public accommodations. While the principle of equal citizenship often amounted to little more than empty rhetoric, it nevertheless upheld a standard that African Americans could press whites to honor in practice as well as in name. And given the political and legal techniques they had learned and the confidence they had gained in over half a century of agitation for reform, African Americans would not be bashful about holding whites to their promises.

The Triumph of Racism

While northern blacks' campaign for civil rights accelerated during the years after Reconstruction, southern blacks' gains were swept away by a rising tide of white supremacy. During the late 1870s and 1880s, southern blacks had refused to accept the Democratic counterrevolution, using political and legal means to defend their rights. Yet while they had won occasional victories, their position generally deteriorated. Beginning in the late 1880s and stretching into the first two decades of the twentieth century, southern Democrats launched a ferocious new offensive that reduced African Americans to second-class citizenship.

Despite Democrats' efforts to deter them, African Americans had continued to vote at a high rate in most states during the 1870s and 1880s. Indeed, they had frequently jointed with poor white farmers who had bolted the Democratic Party because of dissatisfaction with its economic policies, forming coalitions that forced the dominant Democrats to resort to even greater violence and fraud to maintain their power. This pattern continued in the 1890s, as many economically distressed white farmers left the Democratic Party to join the Populists. The new party pledged itself to use the power of government on behalf of working people, advocating nationalization of the railroads, a vigorous campaign against big business, wholesale reform of the financial system, and establishment of producer-operated cooperatives that would free farmers from dependence on merchants. Like the independent parties of the 1870s and 1880s, the Populists hoped to attract African American voters to their cause, uniting poor whites and blacks in a coalition that would drive the Democrats from power. In North Carolina, where Populists fused with the Republican Party, the strategy worked, at least temporarily; and in a number of other southern states, only widespread violence and unprecedented fraud by the Democrats defeated it.

Shaken by this challenge, southern Democrats moved to undercut the opposition by disfranchising African Americans. Aware that the Fifteenth Amendment prohibited them from openly denying blacks the right to vote, Democrats sought to accomplish their objective indirectly. By requiring voters to pay poll taxes (small annual head taxes usually amounting to less than three dollars per year), they could reduce the African American electorate substantially. The great majority of southern blacks were desperately poor agricultural laborers and sharecroppers. Trapped in a vicious credit system that kept many in debt from year to year, precious little cash passed through their hands. Consequently, a tax of only three dollars could put the ballot beyond their reach. The literacy test offered disfranchisers an even more effective tool. Given the legacy of slavery and the meager support for black schools in the aftermath of Reconstruction, illiteracy among African Americans remained high. In 1890, more than half of adult black males in the South could not read, and many others were barely literate. Fairly administered, literacy tests (which required prospective voters to prove that they could read a provision of the state or federal constitution) would deny the ballot to most black men; enforced by partisan white officials who were bitterly opposed to African American suffrage, they would cut even further into the black electorate.

For Democratic leaders, literacy tests and poll taxes had an added attraction. Although publicly they emphasized the effect these measures would have on African Americans, Democrats were well aware that they would also take their toll on poor whites. The region's depressed agricultural economy affected whites as well as African Americans, leaving many white farmers on the brink of ruin and forcing many others into the poverty of tenancy and sharecropping. Poverty also bred illiteracy; in 1900, 12 percent of southern whites could neither read nor write. The new voting requirements, therefore, excluded many whites from voting, and happily for Democratic leaders, these would be the men who had defected from the party during the 1880s and 1890s.

Although African Americans and dissident whites bitterly opposed dis-franchisement, conservative Democrats achieved their objective. Beginning with Florida and Tennessee in 1889 and Mississippi in 1890 and con-cluding with Georgia in 1908, measures designed to prune the electorate were adopted throughout the South. Each of the eleven states of the old Confederacy made payment of a poll tax a requirement for voting, and five heightened the effect of the tax by making it cumulative (i.e., requiring voters to pay all unpaid poll taxes before voting). Seven of these states coupled the poll tax with a literacy test, and seven adopted the secret ballot, which served as a de facto literacy test because illiterates were unable to read it. Except for Florida, each of these states supplemented the poll tax with a literacy test or the secret ballot or both. In five states, Democratic leaders established loopholes for whites—a concession necessary to obtain sufficient support for passage of the disfranchisement measures. Several exempted from the lit-eracy test those who owned a certain amount of property (usually $300) or enacted understanding clauses that enfranchised those who could explain a passage of the Constitution when it was read to them by the registrar. Several states supplemented these with grandfather clauses that waived literacy tests for those who were descendants of persons qualified to vote prior to 1867 (the year southern blacks gained the ballot) or who had fought for the Union or Confederacy.

The new requirements had a dramatic effect on the southern electorate. By 1910, black registration had decreased to 15 percent in Virginia and to less than 2 percent in Alabama and Mississippi. Although loopholes and dis-criminatory administration of the laws allowed many whites to dodge the effects of the literacy requirements, the new laws took their toll on whites as well. Many were too proud to admit that they could not read and declined to exploit the loopholes, while others were excluded from voting by their inability to pay a poll tax. Therefore, while white registration remained at approximately 80 percent in Virginia and Alabama, it decreased to about 50 percent in Louisiana and to 60 percent in Mississippi. As Morgan Kousser, the leading student of suffrage restriction, noted, the disfranchising meas-ures "insured that the Southern electorate for half a century would be almost all white; yet . . . [they] did not guarantee all whites the vote."[26]

Passage of legislation mandating segregation—the Jim Crow laws[27]—coincided with disfranchisement. Separation of the races in churches, schools, public transportation, hotels, and restaurants had become cus-tomary in the decades following the war. During the late 1870s and 1880s, however, some states began to codify custom, mandating segregation in prisons and public schools. Beginning in the late 1880s and continuing through the first two decades of the twentieth century, southern legislatures and city councils went to work with a new fervor, enacting a mountain of laws and ordinances to formalize and put the force of law behind customary arrangements.

Giving segregation the force of law was a predictable outcome of this turbulent era. As white Democrats launched disfranchisement campaigns, they stoked the fires of racial prejudice to convince those who were concerned about the impact on poor whites that disfranchisement was necessary at all costs. The disfranchisers repeatedly denounced African Americans as ignorant, lazy, criminally inclined, and venal, a race demonstrably unqualified to exercise political rights. In an atmosphere poisoned with racial hatred, laws designed to further degrade African Americans attracted broad support. Continued black assertiveness and activism in the decade after Reconstruction also contributed to the emergence of segregation. It reminded southern whites that they had not fully established white supremacy, the goal of the redeemers. In fact, many whites feared that a new generation of African Americans who had never known slavery was coming to maturity and that they might pose an even stiffer challenge to white supremacy than had their parents. Frustrated by their failure to restore black deference and concerned about the future, the establishment of legally sanctioned segregation offered white southerners a powerful means to assert dominance. Moreover, given the deep racism that existed throughout the South, adoption of segregation statutes by one or two states led legislators in neighboring states to follow suit, quickly spreading the poison across the region.

Jim Crow came to the South in three waves. Between 1887 and 1891, most states of the former Confederacy adopted laws requiring railroads to provide separate but equal accommodations for the two races. Then, beginning in 1901 with Virginia, most southern states passed laws requiring urban street railroads to separate black and white passengers. Finally, during the 1910s, states and localities created a complex web of regulations designed to extend the logic of separation to all spheres of southern life. A number of states forbade whites and blacks to be taught together, even in private schools; they also barred teachers and nurses from serving students or patients of another race. States and cities established separate parks and mandated residential segregation. Some states required manufacturers to designate different entrances for white and black employees, to maintain separate pay windows, toilets, and water buckets, and to separate workers by race on the job. Not content with segregating schoolchildren, North Carolina and Florida required that public school textbooks used by children of different races be stored separately. And, though not required by law, many courts kept separate Bibles for swearing black and white witnesses.

The results of the segregation campaign were devastating for southern blacks. Since the end of the Civil War they had lived in a public world increasingly separate from whites. Yet the triumph of Jim Crow infused this separateness with deeper meaning and force. By the early twentieth century, southern blacks' lives were circumscribed by signs designating "white" and "colored" facilities. Separate Bibles in courtrooms as well as separate waiting rooms in train stations served as constant reminders that whites considered them a degraded caste. The signs, together with the intricate set of laws establishing segregation, made African Americans adapt to ludicrous rules that varied from state to state and city to city, further underscoring whites' power.

In the face of the white onslaught, some black leaders renounced the battle for political and social equality. Most prominent was Booker T. Washington, principal of Alabama's Tuskegee Institute. While Washington worked behind the scenes on behalf of black voting rights, he believed that openly challenging segregation was futile and would destroy white support for the Institute. Washington argued that African Americans should be concerned not with integration, but with obtaining the education and skills that would enable them to advance economically and, gradually, to earn social acceptance by whites. In communities across the South, however, many African Americans rejected accommodationism as a dead end. As a powerless, proscribed group, they argued, African Americans would be even more vulnerable to white aggression and would find their efforts at advancement continually thwarted. Viewing segregation and disfranchisement as an effort "to humiliate, degrade, and stigmatize the negro," more militant leaders urged resistance "in order to maintain our self-respect."[28] In at least twenty-seven cities, blacks launched boycotts of segregated streetcars between 1900 and 1910, some lasting as long as two years. Black leaders also turned to the courts, charging that Jim Crow legislation violated the letter and the spirit of the Fourteenth and Fifteenth Amendments. Without the aid of a national organization to raise funds and develop legal strategy, a number of southern black communities raised money locally to support litigation aimed at derailing the movement for white supremacy.

African Americans' constitutional claims, however, were unequivocally rejected by the Supreme Court. During the 1870s and 1880s, the Court had been dominated by northern Republicans who, although quite conservative, nonetheless had come of age at the height of the struggle against slavery and who shared their party's commitment to emancipation and equal rights. Their rulings had narrowed the scope of the postwar amendments, restricting the government's authority to punish civil rights violations by private citizens. However, they had emphasized that the postwar amendments had been adopted to guarantee the former slaves equal rights, by clearly barring discriminatory state action, whether it was carried out through blatantly discriminatory laws or by more subtle means. The six new justices who came to the Supreme Court between 1888 and 1894 were of a different generation. Although most were northern Republicans, they had come of age at a time when northern interest in Reconstruction was dimming and scientists were giving respectability to racism. Consequently, the new justices were less inclined than their predecessors to protect the constitutional rights of blacks.

The first major test of the new justices' position on civil rights came in 1896, when the Court decided *Plessy v. Ferguson*. The case had been initiated by the American Citizens Equal Rights Association, a group organized by New Orleans blacks to challenge an 1890 Louisiana law requiring railroads to provide separate but equal accommodations for blacks. The association was represented by Albion Tourgee of New York, who had served on the front line of the Reconstruction-era battle for equality as a Republican leader in North Carolina and who had remained an eloquent advocate of the cause after returning to the North. Hewing to the arguments developed by abolitionist legal theorists and Reconstruction-era Republican congressmen, Tourgee denied that the law's guarantee of equivalent facilities satisfied the requirements of the Fourteenth Amendment's equal protection clause. The entire purpose of the postwar amendments, he emphasized, was to eradicate caste and establish a color-blind Constitution. By separating African Americans from whites, he concluded, the Louisiana statute stigmatized blacks, subjected them to invidious discrimination, perpetuated the spirit of caste, and therefore violated the US Constitution.

The Court's response suggested that the arguments of Reconstruction-era Republicans rang hollow to the new justices. Justice Henry Brown, a Michigan Republican who in 1890 had replaced Justice Samuel Miller, wrote the Court's opinion, sustaining the law's constitutionality. Reading the scientific racism of the 1890s back into the 1860s, Brown asserted that the amendment's framers must have understood that there was a deep natural aversion to racial intermingling. Consequently, he asserted, they had merely intended to guarantee "the absolute equality of the races before the law," not social equality. Brown concluded therefore that the amendment was satisfied by the Louisiana statute's requirement of equal but separate facilities. Blind to the campaign of racial hatred that was then raging in the South, he denied Tourgee's assertion that the statute "stamps the colored race with a badge of inferiority." "If this be so," the justice blithely explained, "it is not by reason of anything found in the act, but solely because the colored race chooses to put that construction upon it." Only John Marshall Harlan, a veteran of Reconstruction-era political battles who had served on the Court for nearly twenty years, dissented, predicting that "the judgment this day rendered will . . . prove to be quite as pernicious as . . . the *Dred Scott Case*."[29]

Three years later, when it decided *Cumming v. School Board of Richmond County, Ga.*, the Supreme Court demonstrated that it would not be overly scrupulous in guaranteeing that segregated facilities were actually equal. The case was brought by Augusta, Georgia, blacks to challenge the school board's decision to close the county's only African American high school. Since the board continued to support several white high schools, plaintiffs charged that it had deprived black children of opportunities afforded whites, thereby denying them equal protection. A unanimous Court turned aside their argument, however, signaling that under the guise of separate but equal African Americans might be consigned to grossly unequal schools, services, and accommodations.

The Court also sustained disfranchisement. While the new voting requirements disfranchised many poor whites, they were directed principally at African Americans. Not only did many states include understanding clauses, property tests, and grandfather clauses offering whites ways around the literacy tests, but the new laws had a much more drastic effect on blacks than on whites. Moreover, the rhetoric accompanying disfranchisement suggested that whites were determined to eliminate African Americans from politics. Despite the fact that the disfranchisement laws were racially neutral on their face, therefore, a good case could be made that they violated the Fifteenth Amendment.

African American activists and attorneys mobilized to challenge disfranchisement. They brought a dozen lawsuits to the US Supreme Court, asking the Court to set aside measures adopted by six southern states designed to exclude African Americans from voting. Like New Orleans blacks' challenge to segregation, none was successful. Attorneys' lack of experience in bringing novel constitutional challenges, the absence of a community of civil rights lawyers who could learn from one another, and, most important, the Court's unwillingness to stand against the rising tide of white supremacy doomed the effort. Two cases illustrate these challenges.

The first, *Williams v. Mississippi*, which the Court decided in 1898, grew out of the conviction of Henry Williams, an African American man who resided in Washington County, Mississippi, for murdering a lover who spurned him. Williams was represented by Cornelius J. Jones, a politically active African American attorney who had been born into slavery, educated in Freedmen's Bureau schools and at Alcorn State College, and apprenticed with white attorneys in Louisiana and Mississippi. Jones argued that his client had been denied equal protection of the laws because he had been indicted and convicted by all-white juries. The juries were lily white because only registered voters could serve, and the Mississippi Constitution of 1890 had effectively excluded African Americans from registering through a cumulative poll tax and a literacy test that was discriminatorily administered by local officials. In an opinion written by Justice Joseph McKenna, a Californian appointed by President William McKinley, the Court rejected Jones's argument, finding that it was not backed by adequate supporting evidence. McKenna quoted language from a recent Mississippi Supreme Court decision acknowledging that the state's suffrage scheme had been aimed surreptitiously at African Americans. "Restrained by the Federal Constitution from discriminating against the negro race," the state court had admitted, "the [constitutional] convention discriminated against its characteristics [poverty and low rates of literacy]." McKenna noted that, while aimed at African Americans, the constitution's language did not mention race. Therefore, it was incumbent on Jones to prove that the law had been administered in a way to prevent African Americans from registering to vote. McKenna concluded, however, that the record Jones presented did not demonstrate that the law had been applied in a discriminatory manner, even though evidence of racial animus in carrying it out was readily available and widely acknowledged.[30]

Alabama blacks mounted a well-orchestrated, skillfully developed challenge to the state's recently adopted voting requirements but fared no better. In 1902, Jackson Giles, an educated African American postal worker who was president of the Colored Men's Suffrage Association of Alabama, contested the suffrage provisions contained in Alabama's new constitution. That document created a convoluted system clearly designed to thin the African American electorate. It required prospective voters to pay a poll tax and pass a literacy test, but provided a lifetime exemption for former soldiers or their descendants and persons of good character. Anyone registering before 1903 who satisfied these requirements would be entitled to vote for the rest of their lives, while those who did not would have to demonstrate the ability to read and write or that they owned forty acres of land or $300 worth of real or personal property. Because relatively few black Alabamians or their descendants had served in the military or were able to persuade white officials of their good character, most African Americans would have to satisfy literacy or property requirements that many of them were unable to meet—especially when white officials judged applicants' literacy. In short, the constitution set up a maze that had a dead end for African Americans.

That is what Jackson Giles found. When he attempted to register prior to the 1902 election, Montgomery officials denied his request, ruling that, even though he was educated and a federal employee, he did not possess good character. This meant that Giles would have to pass the literacy or property test to vote, a requirement that most whites, who qualified under the military service and good character requirement, escaped. When Giles brought suit in federal court, he was represented by Wilford Smith, an accomplished African American lawyer. A graduate of Boston University Law School who practiced in New York City, Smith's legal fees were secretly paid by Booker T. Washington, who chafed at disfranchisement measures enforced in a manner that kept even educated African Americans from the polls. Producing voluminous evidence of the constitutional convention's intent to disfranchise African Americans as well as local officials' manipulation of the provisions to prevent even qualified blacks from registering, Smith argued that Alabama's scheme was a ruse to exclude African Americans from voting and therefore violated the Fourteenth and Fifteenth Amendments. Although his argument was sound and his evidence plentiful, the Court declined to order local officials to register Giles or to declare the constitution's suffrage provisions a violation of the US Constitution.

The Court's opinion, written by Justice Oliver Wendell Holmes Jr., underscored how far the justices were willing to bend to avoid questioning disfranchisement. If the Alabama constitution's suffrage provision were a scheme designed to circumvent the Fourteenth and Fifteenth Amendments, Holmes argued, the Court would "make . . . [itself] a party to the unlawful scheme by accepting it and adding another voter to its fraudulent lists." Better to forego a remedy guaranteeing Giles his constitutional right to vote than to tarnish the Court's reputation by doing so under the auspices of a tainted document—even if the Court allowed it to govern voting rights. Equally puzzling, Holmes insisted that whites' implacable determination to keep African Americans from voting made it impossible for the Court to act. "Unless we are prepared to supervise the voting in that state by officers of the court, it seems to us that all that the plaintiff could get from equity would be an empty form," Holmes concluded. "Apart from damages to the individual, relief from a great political wrong, if done, as alleged, by the people of a state and the state itself, must be given by them by the legislative and political department of the government of the United States."[31] Apparently, if the constitutional violation was sufficiently audacious and grew out of the political process, only the political branches—not the judiciary—could provide a remedy.

Smith brought two other lawsuits on behalf of Giles, but they fared no better. Indeed, the Court rejected all challenges brought against southern disfranchisement measures. By the end of the century, the postwar amendments' revolutionary promise lay unfulfilled. Given the ferocity of southern resistance, most white Americans' unwillingness to expand federal power significantly, the waning of concern for African American rights in the North, and the resurgence of racism nationwide, the nation reneged on promises made in the heat of the Civil War and Reconstruction. During the 1870s and 1880s, the Supreme Court had significantly restricted the scope of national power to protect individual rights, effectively curtailing (although not destroying) the revolutionary potential of postwar amendments and civil rights laws. With the addition of new members to the Supreme Court in the 1890s, the Court capitulated to the racist fury that swept the South. Placing form above substance, ignoring the purpose of the postwar amendments, and demonstrating a perverse ignorance of southern legislators' intent, the Court accepted segregation and disfranchisement.

Consequently, African Americans entered the new century stripped of the promise of the Reconstruction revolution. Northern blacks were in a better position than black southerners, but no thanks to federal Constitutional guarantees. Through political and legal action they had been able to win passage of legislation guaranteeing them equal civil rights, and state courts, relying on state constitutional provisions and statutes, had handed down decisions protecting these rights. Despite the law, however, racism remained powerful among northerners, as evidenced by the behavior of those who served on the Supreme Court, and frequently undercut the rights to which African Americans were entitled. It was in the South, however, where 90 percent of the nation's African Americans lived in 1900 that the capitulation to racism was most evident. There African Americans were subjected to a humiliating system of segregation that, despite the legal fiction of separate but equal, consigned them to separate and visibly unequal schools and other facilities. They were also systematically denied the ballot, the principal symbol of citizenship in the Republic. Marked by the law as members of an inferior caste and denied political power, they were left to the tender mercies of their white neighbors.

5

The Age of Segregation, 1900–1950

Born in 1895, the year Frederick Douglass died, Charles Hamilton Houston
would combine Douglass's passion for equality with sharply honed legal skills
to rekindle the struggle for equality—which was on life support at the time
of Douglass's death. Unlike Douglass, who was born a slave, Charles Houston
was the only son of a lawyer and a teacher. He attended Washington's M
Street School, perhaps the best African American high school in the nation,
and, after graduating first in his class, he went on to Amherst College, where
he was elected to Phi Beta Kappa and was valedictorian of the class of 1915.
After graduation, he taught in Washington and served in the army during
World War I, saving enough money to attend Harvard Law School. There he
became the first African American to serve on the *Harvard Law Review* and
caught the eye of future Supreme Court justice Felix Frankfurter, the human
dynamo who was an inspiring teacher, an exacting scholar, an avid civil libertarian, and an active public servant who urged his students to use their
talents to serve the community. After graduating fifth in his Harvard Law
class in 1922, Houston devoted one year to graduate work with Frankfurter
and then traveled to Spain and Italy for additional advanced study.

Houston was clearly an exceptional young man who led a seemingly
charmed life. Nevertheless, he was a black man in Jim Crow America, and
he could not insulate himself from the barbs of white racism. While Houston
attended Amherst, President Woodrow Wilson, a native Virginian, brought
segregation to the federal civil service, something that undoubtedly stung
Houston since many family friends worked in the federal bureaucracy.
During World War I, he fought in a Jim Crow army charged with making
the world safe for democracy, and he and other black soldiers returned from
France in 1919, not to a hero's welcome, but to a series of ugly race riots
that swept the nation. As he practiced law, he was repeatedly reminded of
the color line. Herbert Wechsler, a white lawyer who would go on to a distinguished career at Columbia Law School, the American Civil Liberties
Union, and the American Law Institute, recalled one incident. In 1931, while
clerking for Justice Harlan Fiske Stone, he encountered Houston, with whom

Promises to Keep. Donald G. Nieman, Oxford University Press (2020). © Oxford University Press.
DOI: 10.1093/oso/9780190071639.001.0001

he had become acquainted during his stay in Washington, DC, outside the Supreme Court's chambers. "I proposed that we have lunch in the Capitol," remembers Wechsler, "and he said no, we couldn't do that."[1] Washington, DC, was a Jim Crow town, and the Capitol restaurants were segregated.

Houston entered practice with his father and, despite the indignities of segregated Washington, could have made a good living. Perhaps because of personal experiences, perhaps because of Frankfurter's example, he had a burning desire to bring his legal skills and intellectual ability to the service of black America. In 1929, Howard University's president, Mordecai Johnson, offered him the opportunity to do just that, asking him to become dean of the Howard Law School and to revitalize a program that had floundered for years and had recently lost its accreditation. Houston accepted and during the next six years rebuilt the law school. Recruiting the best black legal talent in the nation, he created a rigorous program designed to produce top-notch lawyers. Thurgood Marshall, the future Supreme Court justice who was Houston's most prominent student, recalled:

> He was hard-crust. First off, you thought he was a mean so-and-so. He used to tell us that doctors could bury their mistakes but lawyers couldn't. And he'd drive home to us that we would be competing not only with white lawyers but really well-trained white lawyers. . . . I'll tell you—the going was rough. There must have been thirty of us in that class when we started, and no more than eight or ten of us finished up. He was so tough we used to call him "Iron Shoes" and "Cement Pants" and a few other names that don't bear repeating. But he was a sweet man once you saw what he was up to. He was absolutely fair, and the door to his office was always open.[2]

Houston was interested in more than educating first-rate lawyers. He instilled in his students a commitment to public service and created the nation's first public interest law program. "He kept hammering at us all those years that, as lawyers, we had to be social engineers or else we were parasites," explained Oliver Hill, who graduated in 1934, one year behind Marshall. Howard offered the first civil rights course in the country, and its law library became a treasure trove of books, memos, reports, lawyers' briefs, and other materials on segregated education, transportation, and housing; voting rights; and discriminatory law enforcement. Houston and his protégés demanded that the nation fulfill its long-delayed promise of equality, insisting that "the United States respect its own Constitution and laws." And they set out to create a generation of black lawyers who shared their commitment to equal rights and to using the law as a tool to effect social change. "Frankly, the purpose there was to learn how to bend the law to the needs of blacks," noted one Howard graduate. Moreover, like the abolitionists, Houston viewed lawsuits not only as a means to challenge legal rules that held blacks in thralldom but also as opportunities for rallying broad-based support in the African American community for the struggle for equality.[3]

During the following decades, Houston would continue to play a major role in that battle. In 1935 he became chief counsel for the National Association for the Advancement of Colored People (NAACP). In that post, which he held until 1938, he began a methodical campaign of litigation designed to undermine Jim Crow and nurture grass-roots civil rights

Figure 5.1. Left to right, Charles Hamilton Houston, Clarence Darrow, and Mordecai Johnson at Howard University https://americanhistory. si.edu/collections/search/object/siris_arc_179057. Photograph by Addison N. Scurlcok, ca. 1930s. Scurlock Studio Records, ca. 1905–1994, Archives Center, National Museum of American History. *Courtesy of the Smithsonian Institution.*

consciousness. After health problems forced him to return to private practice, he remained active in civil rights litigation throughout the 1940s. His greatest contribution, however, was at Howard University, where he created a first-rate law school that produced a generation of black lawyers who would reassert constitutional principles of equality and use them as a hammer to demolish the edifice of segregation.

Black America in the Age of Segregation

By the time Charles Houston left Amherst in 1915, the position of blacks in America approached its nadir. Disfranchisement and segregation shaped the contours of life for black southerners during the first half of the twentieth century, leaving them vulnerable to arbitrary white authority and sharply constricting their options. Segregated schools and whites' monopoly over political power had an especially devastating effect on black children. In 1910 the eleven states of the former Confederacy spent three times more per capita on white students than on their African American counterparts. Although absolute levels of spending increased during the following thirty years, per capita spending on black students remained one-third of that for whites on the eve of World War II. The results were predictable: black schools were run-down, overcrowded, and often without heat in the winter; buses were unavailable to transport black children to school (a major problem since the majority of black southerners lived in rural areas); and student-teacher ratios were far higher than in white schools. Opportunities to go beyond elementary school were limited. By the mid-1930s, only 19 percent of southern black children between the ages of fourteen and seventeen attended high school; the comparable figure for whites was 55 percent. African American teachers also suffered. In 1935, they taught classes that were 30 percent larger and took home paychecks that were 40 percent smaller than their white peers.

If blacks lost, whites gained from the system. Underfunding of black schools spared taxpayers the expense of maintaining separate and genuinely equal schools. In addition, tax dollars that should have gone to black schools were available to enhance educational opportunities for white children. The system also guaranteed that most African Americans remained poorly educated and therefore unable to compete with whites for good jobs. Finally, whites, confusing achievement with ability, cited blacks' low level of education as proof of their inferiority. This, they claimed, justified disfranchisement, segregation, and low levels of spending on African American education. The cycle was complete and self-perpetuating.

The caste system also narrowed employment opportunities for southern blacks, especially access to white-collar and professional jobs. African American poverty and white prejudice guaranteed that white-owned businesses dominated the southern economy. These establishments—from the local dry goods store to large firms like Coca-Cola—refused to hire blacks as clerks, secretaries, or salespersons, much less as managers. With government controlled by men committed to white supremacy, African Americans were excluded from managerial and clerical positions in state and local bureaucracies as well as from elective office. A few African Americans became physicians, dentists, and lawyers, but opportunities in these fields were limited. Whites shunned black professionals, and most blacks, being poor, sought medical and legal services infrequently. Those African Americans who could afford a lawyer often hired white attorneys, aware that they would have greater credibility with white judges and jurors. With medicine and law offering promising careers to only a few, white-collar and professional employment was, for all practical purposes, limited to teaching in black schools, preaching in black churches, and owning or working in black-owned businesses that served the black community. Consequently, African Americans' opportunities to achieve middle-class status were sharply restricted.

The situation was no better for blue-collar workers. African Americans were virtually excluded from jobs in textiles and oil and gas, the South's fastest-growing industries. They won employment in the construction, tobacco, railroad, iron and steel, turpentine, lumber, fertilizer, and mining industries, but these were unskilled, menial, dirty, hot, dangerous, and low-paying positions—jobs that whites shunned. Other African American workers took service positions in hotels, restaurants, laundries, and private homes, which paid meager wages for long hours and which most whites considered beneath their dignity. With good nonagricultural jobs closed to them, a majority of southern blacks continued to work the land, their fate tied to the cotton and tobacco economies. Given the low prices of these commodities and the fact that they worked as laborers and sharecroppers rather than owners and renters, rural blacks knew little but grinding poverty.

Regardless of their economic position, African Americans occupied a despised caste and stood outside the protection of the law. Virtually all law enforcement officials, justices of the peace, judges, and jurors were white men who shared their society's commitment to the principles of white supremacy. Most believed that the word of a white person, any white person, was superior to that of an African American, that blacks were lazy, shiftless, and given to lying and theft, and that whites must have adequate authority to keep African Americans in a position of subservience. The effect on the southern legal system was utterly corrosive. Law enforcement officers had little reason to fear complaints made against them by blacks, and consequently, police brutality and disregard for the rights of African Americans suspected of crime were pervasive. When African Americans were charged with crimes against whites, judges and jurors discounted the testimony of African American witnesses and readily convicted black defendants, even when the evidence against them was weak. Law enforcement officials generally refused to prosecute whites who assaulted or murdered blacks, especially if the perpetrators claimed that blacks had provoked the attacks by insolence or lack of deference. Finally, white officials showed little concern about crime within the African American community, failing to prosecute or imposing light punishments on blacks who assaulted, murdered, or robbed other blacks.

Lynching, the most horrific example of white supremacy, made a mockery of the rule of law. African Americans accused of serious offenses against whites or who flouted the conventions of white supremacy too conspicuously were frequently seized by angry mobs, subjected to gruesome torture, and executed, often before throngs of cheering whites. In 1911 a white mob in Livermore, Kentucky, dragged a black man accused of killing a white to a local theater and hanged him before an audience of white townspeople who paid admission. Those paying for orchestra seats were invited to empty their pistols into the victim's swinging body, while patrons in the balcony were each permitted one shot. State and local officials generally proved unable or unwilling to halt mobs or to prosecute participants, whose identities were widely known. Although the number of lynchings declined after the 1890s, an average of sixty-seven African Americans were lynched each year during the first two decades of the twentieth century. The horror of these grisly spectacles underscored black powerlessness and shaped African American consciousness. Indeed, it found expression in African American music, notably the ballad "Strange Fruit" popularized by Billie Holiday, as well as the poetry of Langston Hughes and the paintings of William H. Johnson and Jacob Lawrence.

Overwhelming support for segregation among white southerners did not prevent some from objecting to the flagrant denials of basic human rights they witnessed. Sometimes their vision of a more humane, more paternalistic form of white supremacy helped to curb the system's excesses. During the 1930s, for example, the Association of Southern Women for the Prevention of Lynching, led by Jessie Daniel Ames, publicized the horrors of lynching, warned southerners that it had tarnished the region's image, and pressed local officials to protect blacks from mobs. While their efforts contributed to a significant decline in lynching, the pangs of conscience felt by paternalistic southerners did little to stop the day-to-day injustices that were part of the fabric of African American life. To most whites, African Americans simply did not count, indeed were invisible. This made it easy for whites to ignore the problems blacks encountered and the barbarities of the caste system. And those whites who occupied positions to curb the excesses—especially lawyers, judges, and politicians—generally feared the social, political, and professional consequences of speaking out against injustice.

Injustice persisted not only because of the reluctance of most whites to risk taking a stand against it, but also because whites derived substantial benefits from the status quo. By degrading African Americans, the legal system assured that even poor whites were superior to African Americans. White taxpayers also benefited from the steady stream of African Americans convicted of petty crime and sentenced to serve on county chain gangs. Manacled, clothed in striped suits, and supervised by armed guards who had carte blanche to extract labor through flogging and other forms of violence, county convicts worked on roads and bridges, saving taxpayers millions of dollars annually. Planters and farmers also found the system useful. African Americans convicted of petty crimes provided a steady source of cheap labor. Eager to avoid the chain gang, they could not reject labor contracts offered by whites who agreed to pay their fines. When labor was scarce, local officials obligingly used the threat of prosecution for vagrancy to prod African Americans who supported themselves through odd jobs to come to terms with planters. The system also encouraged African American deference to white authority, creating outwardly pleasant relations between the races and placing a thin veneer over its oppression. Blacks realized that only a white patron or a reputation among whites as a "good Negro" could protect them should they get into trouble. Outwardly at least, most southern blacks, especially those in rural areas and small towns, accepted the conventions of white supremacy and were reluctant to challenge a system that brutally exploited them.

The oppression experienced by southern blacks, combined with the crisis of the cotton economy brought on by the boll weevil and falling cotton prices, drove successive waves of them to northern urban centers. More than 200,000 migrants trekked north between 1890 and 1910. The Great Migration of the 1910s saw a half-million African Americans leave the South for northern cities, and more than one million more followed in the next two decades. By 1940, more than 20 percent of the nation's African Americans lived in the North, with most concentrated in overcrowded ghettos in the region's great metropolises.

This migration produced new social tensions and increased racial prejudice among northern whites. As southern blacks moved into northern cities, they entered white working-class neighborhoods in search of low-cost housing. Proximity did not lead to greater understanding. Working-class whites—native-born as well as recent European immigrants—often greeted the new arrivals with suspicion, viewing them as competitors for jobs. Suspicion turned to hatred when white employers hired African Americans as strikebreakers, and hatred sparked violence. During the first two decades of the twentieth century, serious race riots erupted in New York (1900), Springfield, Illinois (1908), East St. Louis, Illinois (1917), and Washington, DC, Omaha, and Chicago (1919). In Chicago the fighting lasted thirteen days and left thirty-eight dead, more than five hundred injured, and a thousand black families homeless.

But racism was not the special preserve of working-class whites, and it was not only they who attacked African Americans in these melees. Prominent scientists purported to show that African Americans were inferior to whites; popular writers trumpeted the superiority of the Anglo-Saxon over darker-skinned peoples; historians depicted Reconstruction as a tragic era in which ignorant, venal black voters plunged the South into chaos; and the advertising and movie industries inundated Americans with images of childlike, irresponsible, lazy blacks. In this milieu, middle- and upper-class whites responded to African American migrants with hostility, viewing them as a potential threat to white neighborhoods, schools, and communities.

Although race relations remained considerably more fluid in the North than in the South, northern blacks encountered increasing discrimination during the 1910s and 1920s. Residential segregation was the norm in most northern cities. As African Americans settled in areas where low-cost housing was available, working-class whites began to move out. More recent black arrivals took their place as they joined relatives and settled in areas where black churches and community organizations had been established. Residential segregation may have emerged as a result of black settlement patterns, but whites worked to preserve it. White homeowners adopted restrictive covenants[4] barring sale of their property to non-whites. Adoption of these agreements was so widespread that by 1940, more than 25 percent of Chicago's South Side was closed to African Americans. Realtors' associations in many cities established guidelines prohibiting their members from showing homes in white neighborhoods to prospective black buyers. Lending institutions, afraid that integration would lead to white flight and lower property values, refused to make loans to African Americans who wished to purchase homes outside the ghetto. If these devices were not sufficient to deter them, African Americans who moved into white neighborhoods frequently encountered hostility and violence.

Most northern states did not require separate schools and many even had laws prohibiting school segregation. Consequently, many northern schools were racially mixed, and African American teachers occasionally taught white children. Nevertheless, residential segregation made neighborhood schools predominantly white or black. Race-conscious white school officials also contributed to segregation by drawing school district boundaries to maximize racial separation and by offering transfers to white children whose residences fell within heavily black districts. Officials in some northern cities went even further, creating separate classes for African Americans who attended integrated schools or even creating all-black schools in violation of state law. In states like Kansas and Indiana, which permitted segregation, some school boards established openly segregated schools.

African Americans in the North also encountered discrimination in employment and in public accommodations, although this discrimination was neither as pervasive nor as blatant as in the South. "Whites only" signs were rare in theaters, hotels, and restaurants, and some employers, notably the Ford Motor Company, offered black newcomers good jobs. Nevertheless, many white-owned businesses refused to serve blacks, and laws (enacted in the 1880s and 1890s) barring discrimination in public accommodations offered little relief from such indignities. In order to enforce their rights under these measures, victims of discrimination had to sue, a time-consuming and expensive proposition. As a result, the laws were seldom enforced, and most African Americans, unwilling to risk humiliation, avoided theaters, restaurants, and hotels that catered to whites. Employers generally refused to consider African Americans for white-collar and professional positions, fearful that their presence would anger white employees and alienate customers and clients. The blue-collar world was little different. Most of the unions affiliated with the American Federation of Labor (primarily craft unions that represented skilled workers) excluded African Americans, effectively denying them good jobs in union shops. When employers managed to keep unions out, blacks fared no better. Because of their own prejudice or because they feared unrest among white workers, most employers considered African Americans only for the most menial jobs, keeping them stuck at the bottom of the occupational ladder. The situation in Boston was typical of cities across the North: "As late as 1940, 6 out of 7 [blacks] worked in manual occupations," notes historian Stephan Thernstrom, "more than half were still confined to typical 'Negro jobs' as laborers, janitors, porters, servants, or waiters."[5]

The Attack on Discrimination Begins: 1910–1930

The North was not the promised land, but it offered African Americans significant advantages. Economic and educational opportunities, while constricted, were greater than in the South, and northern blacks could vote. Although fear of white reprisals had a chilling effect on black militance in the South, northern blacks encountered little opposition from whites when they organized to demand equal rights. As they had done in the antebellum era, therefore, northern blacks took the lead in the struggle for equality, organizing a host of protest organizations between 1890 and 1910. Groups such as the Afro-American League (led by T. Thomas Fortune, the militant New York editor), the Negro Fellowship League (organized by Ida Wells-Barnett, the fiery antilynching critic who had been driven out of Memphis by a white mob that demolished her newspaper), the New England Suffrage League (presided over by William Monroe Trotter, editor of the *Boston Guardian*), and the Niagara Movement (formed by the scholar and writer W. E. B. Du Bois) urged African Americans to demand that the nation honor the pledges of equality contained in the Declaration of Independence and the Reconstruction amendments.

Northern blacks were not alone in this endeavor. Although racism became more pronounced in the North in the early twentieth century, some whites remained committed to the abolitionist vision and worked closely with African American militants. The most long-lived and fruitful product of black-white collaboration was the National Association for the Advancement of Colored People (NAACP), founded in 1909 in New York City. Organizers included white heirs of the abolitionist tradition, including Oswald Garrison Villard (grandson of William Lloyd Garrison and editor of the *New York Post*) and Moorfield Storey (the distinguished Boston attorney who had served as Charles Sumner's clerk during Reconstruction); white social workers such as Mary White Ovington, Henry Moskowitz, and Jane Addams; white socialists William English Walling and Charles Edward Russell; and prominent black leaders such as Du Bois, Wells-Barnett, Trotter, Mary Church Terrell, and Francis Grimké. Although the dominant role that whites played in the NAACP's early leadership gradually declined during the 1920s and 1930s, the organization retained its commitment to integration and biracial collaboration.

From the beginning, black and white leaders agreed that the goal of the new organization would be to end disfranchisement and Jim Crow and to guarantee African Americans their rights as citizens. Like the abolitionists, NAACP leaders found inspiration in the Constitution. They insisted that it was a document intended to guarantee equality and called on Americans to reassert its equalitarian principles. "Besides a day of rejoicing, Lincoln's [centennial] birthday in 1909 should be a day of taking stock of the nation's progress since 1865," declared Oswald Garrison Villard in calling the meeting that created the NAACP. "How far has it gone in assuring to each and every citizen, irrespective of color, the equality of opportunity and equality before the law which underlie our American institutions and are guaranteed by the Constitution?"[6] In their effort to reclaim African Americans' constitutional rights, NAACP leaders came to the aid of individuals who were victims of racism and lawlessness. They also exposed the horrors of racism, believing (like the era's muckraking journalists) that they could bring about reform by pricking the nation's conscience. The ultimate goal of NAACP leaders, however, was to secure legislation and court decisions that would expand protection for the rights of African Americans.

During the 1910s and 1920s, as NAACP officials initiated their campaign of publicity, lobbying, and litigation, they found victories hard to achieve and progress slow. They were shocked by the resurgence of lynching that accompanied World War I and aware that mob violence struck a nerve with northern and southern blacks who understood that it was motivated by racial hatred and demonstrated that white power over blacks had changed little since the days of slavery. Consequently, NAACP leaders believed that a campaign against lynching would not only challenge gross injustice but draw African Americans to their fledgling organization. They made passage of federal antilynching legislation a top priority. As the 1910s progressed, the NAACP investigated lynchings and published articles, pamphlets, and studies exposing the horrors of lynching. Hoping to convince the public that federal antilynching legislation was necessary, the organization sponsored a well-publicized conference on lynching at New York's Carnegie Hall in 1919. The 2,500 persons who attended heard addresses by such prominent figures as Moorfield Storey, Charles Evans Hughes, and Anna Howard Shaw of the National American Woman Suffrage Association and passed resolutions demanding a federal anti-lynching law. Reviving Reconstruction-era ideas of national power, NAACP leaders also challenged the widespread belief that the state action doctrine precluded Congress from punishing civil rights violations perpetrated by private individuals.

James Weldon Johnson and Walter White of the NAACP staff worked closely with Congressman Leonidas Dyer, a St. Louis Republican, to capitalize on the change in public sentiment created by the antilynching campaign. In 1918 Dyer introduced in the House of Representatives legislation providing broad sanctions against lynchers as well as public officials and communities that tolerated lynching. Although the Republican Party had grown tepid in its support of black rights, its traditions and interest in keeping the growing number of northern blacks in the fold led it to give grudging support to Dyer's measure. In 1922, after four years of pressure, the House Republicans overcame solid Democratic opposition to pass the Dyer bill. Nevertheless, the threat of a southern filibuster[7] in the Senate, along with lukewarm support from the Republican leadership, killed the measure in the upper house.

Although antilynching advocates would not mount another sustained effort on behalf of federal legislation for another decade, the campaign of 1918–1922 had positive results. It exposed the ugliest side of American race relations, and challenged whites' complacency. The publicity generated by the campaign appalled and embarrassed some influential southern whites and prompted them to work against lynching. Debate over the Dyer bill also revived the tradition of broad construction of the Fourteenth Amendment, an essential step if the amendment were to be rescued from the narrow, formalistic reading given it by the Supreme Court in the 1880s and 1890s. Finally, the battle for the Dyer bill laid the groundwork for an alliance between blacks and Jews (themselves victims of prejudice, discrimination, and violence) to work for more vigorous national protection for civil rights. Louis Marshall of the American Jewish Committee, Felix Frankfurter of Harvard Law School, Herbert Lehman the New York banker who was prominent in state Democratic Party circles, and the Council of Jewish Women all supported the Dyer bill, beginning a fruitful and long-lived partnership.

NAACP leaders also carried the struggle to the courts. As they did so, the US Supreme Court signaled that it was ready to give substance to the guarantees of the Reconstruction amendments in a series of cases dealing with peonage, or forced labor to satisfy debts. During the first decade of the twentieth century, a number of prominent journalists exposed the evils of peonage in magazine exposés that reached middle-class homes. Offended by the brutality of the new slavery and concerned that it would retard the New South's economic progress, federal attorneys and judges in the South initiated a vigorous campaign against peonage, using a little-known 1867 federal statute that prohibited laws and practices that held persons in service for debt and established penalties for anyone "who shall hold, arrest, or return . . . any person . . . to a condition of peonage."[8]

In a series of decisions between 1905 and 1914, the Supreme Court sustained the campaign against peonage. In *Clyatt v. United States* (1905), a unanimous Court upheld the 1867 statute as a legitimate exercise of Congress's authority to enforce the Thirteenth Amendment's ban on involuntary servitude. Six years later, in *Bailey v. Alabama* (1911), the Court struck down an Alabama law that stipulated that an employee who received a cash advance from an employer and left before paying it back would be presumed to have taken the money with intent to defraud and would be subject to criminal penalties. Typical of statutes in other states, the law was used by planters and others to prevent indebted employees from leaving their service. The Court held that, because fraud was presumed, the law actually made breach of a labor contract a crime and thus compelled involuntary servitude. Finally, in *United States v. Reynolds* (1914) the Court banned southern criminal surety laws. These measures provided that persons convicted of petty crimes might sign contracts to labor for anyone who agreed to pay their fines, and they punished workers who fled before their contracts expired. Aware that many of the victims of these laws had often been convicted on trumped-up charges of vagrancy or disturbing the peace and that they had accepted contracts in order to avoid the horrors of the chain gang, the Court ruled that these agreements compelled involuntary servitude and were not enforceable.[9]

Despite the Court's vigorous stand against practices and laws that sustained peonage, its decisions did not root out the new slavery. Most victims of peonage were held in servitude through private terror and the extra-legal action of local officials rather than through enforcement of criminal fraud or criminal surety laws. While the *Clyatt* case gave federal prosecutors authority to punish persons engaged in such activity, US attorneys were often reluctant to undertake time-consuming prosecutions on behalf of poor blacks. And even if federal attorneys were willing to attack peonage, it proved impossible to uncover instances of forced labor in hundreds of out-of-the-way rural communities throughout the South. Not only did they lack the staff to investigate, but the victims, who were often ignorant of federal remedies or terrorized by their employers, rarely filed complaints. Despite the Court's rulings, then, many southern blacks continued to live in "the shadow of slavery."[10]

Nevertheless, the peonage cases encouraged NAACP activists to turn to the courts. Their initial venture into litigation came in 1915, when the US Supreme Court considered a challenge to the Oklahoma grandfather clause. Like similar provisions adopted by a number of southern states, it required prospective voters to pass a literacy test but waived the requirement for persons whose forebears had been entitled to vote on January 1, 1866, or who had resided in a foreign country on that date. Because only a few thousand African Americans who had resided in six northern states could vote in 1866, the obvious purpose of the law was to establish a literacy test that could be used to disfranchise blacks but not illiterate whites. Republicans needed black votes to carry the state, and the US attorney for Oklahoma, a Republican, moved promptly to prevent its enforcement. Charging that the grandfather clause violated the Fifteenth Amendment and was therefore void, he prosecuted state officials who enforced it and won convictions in federal court.

When the case, *Guinn v. United States,* reached the Supreme Court in 1913, the government was represented by John W. Davis, the solicitor general. At this point, the NAACP, viewing the case as an opportunity to challenge disfranchisement, authorized Moorfield Storey to file an amicus curiae brief.[11] Although the Court had upheld other disfranchising measures, in 1915 it heeded Davis and Storey and struck down the grandfather clause in a unanimous decision written by Chief Justice Edward D. White, a native of Louisiana. White ruled that the measure was a transparent attempt to establish an obstacle to voting that applied to African Americans but not to whites and therefore violated the Fifteenth Amendment. The victory was clear-cut but quite limited. Other states had adopted the grandfather clause as a temporary loophole; indeed, Georgia's, adopted in 1908, was the only one that had not expired when the Court heard *Guinn*. Moreover, White explained that the Court would not scrutinize the motive of state legislators who enacted voting requirements not on their face racially discriminatory and noted that literacy tests with grandfather clause loopholes removed were valid. Therefore, the case left literacy tests and poll taxes, which were the essential tools of disfranchisement, in place.[12]

The NAACP also mounted a vigorous campaign against residential segregation laws that spread across the South between 1910 and 1916. Although the ordinances varied, typically they barred whites who owned property on blocks that were more than 50 percent white from selling to African Americans and vice versa. Although two Baltimore ordinances were successfully challenged in the Maryland Supreme Court by that city's NAACP chapter, the most important attack on residential segregation came in *Buchanan v. Warley*, a case initiated by the Louisville NAACP chapter and carried to the US Supreme Court in 1917 by Storey.

The case presented a daunting challenge for the distinguished attorney. Not only had the Court consistently sanctioned segregation, but Chief Justice White and most of his colleagues shared the racial prejudice dominant in white America as the nation entered World War I. Storey made the best of a bad situation. He not only contended that the Louisville ordinance denied blacks equal protection by effectively restricting them to the least desirable areas of the city, but he exploited the justices' willingness to use the Fourteenth Amendment to protect property rights. Since the late 1890s, the Court had embraced the doctrine of liberty of contract, ruling that state laws that imposed unreasonable restrictions on contractual relations denied persons liberty without due process of law in violation of the Fourteenth Amendment. Storey grasped the opportunity that the doctrine offered, arguing that the Louisville ordinance denied property owners liberty without due process of law by placing unreasonable restrictions on their right to sell their property.

Storey's strategy was far more successful than he could have imagined. A unanimous Court struck down the Louisville ordinance in a surprisingly broad opinion written by Justice William R. Day, originally from Ohio.

Day held that the ordinance was a "direct violation of the fundamental law enacted in the Fourteenth Amendment . . . preventing state interference with property rights except by due process of law." Although ultimately he rested the decision on conservative due process grounds, Day gave civil rights advocates an unanticipated boost. At a time when the Court seemed to have forgotten that the Fourteenth Amendment had anything to do with protection of the rights of former slaves, Day quoted liberally from the *Slaughter-House Cases* and *Strauder v. West Virginia*, reminding his readers that the "chief inducement to the passage of the Amendment was the desire to extend federal protection to the recently emancipated race from unfriendly and discriminating legislation by the states." He also suggested that the Louisville ordinance violated the Civil Rights Act of 1866, which guaranteed "fundamental rights in property . . . upon the same terms to citizens of every race and color."[13]

Despite this improvement in the Court's memory, the victory was pyrrhic. *Buchanan* broke the back of efforts to legislate residential segregation, but it said nothing about the use of restrictive covenants, which were becoming an increasingly popular means of maintaining segregated housing, especially in northern cities. NAACP leaders were well aware of the problem and challenged the constitutionality of judicial enforcement of restrictive covenants in *Corrigan v. Buckley*, a case heard by the US Supreme Court in 1926. The Court dismissed the case, however, rejecting the argument that restrictive covenants denied individuals liberty to buy and sell property without due process of law. The covenants were private agreements, the Court noted, and did not come within the prohibitions of the Fifth and Fourteenth Amendments, which were merely restrictions on government action.[14] Thus even as the Court legitimized restrictive covenants, it encouraged white property owners and real-estate developers to use them to keep minorities out of their neighborhoods.[15]

NAACP lawyers won a significant victory in *Moore v. Dempsey*, a 1923 case growing out of white efforts to smash black protest in Phillips County, Arkansas. In the fall of 1919, violence erupted in the county when a deputy sheriff was killed as he and a posse tried to break up a meeting of a sharecroppers' union. The killing sparked a rampage by local whites in which dozens of African Americans were murdered. Although none of the whites was prosecuted, twelve blacks were convicted of murdering the white deputy after hasty trials that made a mockery of justice. All were sentenced to die in the electric chair. Some sixty-seven other blacks pled guilty to a variety of charges and received prison terms of as much as twenty years. Moore and the five other African Americans who appealed their case to the Supreme Court were among those sentenced to die. Moorfield Storey represented the defendants before the high court. He contended that they had not had the charges against them fully explained, had been denied adequate represen-tation, and had been convicted at trials permeated by a lynch mob atmos-phere. This made a fair trial impossible, Storey argued, and denied his clients due process of law in violation of the Fourteenth Amendment. The Court agreed, explaining that public passion and prejudice against the defendants had corrupted the trial and denied Moore and his co-defendants due process of law.[16]

The decision marked a new departure in civil rights law. Since the adop-tion of the Fourteenth Amendment, the Court had consistently refused to employ the due process clause as a restriction on state criminal procedure. It had denied that due process required states to honor the provisions of the Bill of Rights and had refused to reverse convictions when defendants had been denied the right to indictment by grand jury, the right to trial by jury, the right to confront witnesses against them, and the right to protection against self-incrimination. *Moore*, of course, did not hold that any of the guarantees of the Bill of Rights applied to the states. Nevertheless, it indicated that the Court would scrutinize state criminal proceedings to guarantee defendants justice, a matter of special concern to African Americans, the most frequent victims of kangaroo-court proceedings.

The Attack Broadens: The 1930s

The Great Depression of the 1930s brought economic privation to tens of millions of Americans as unemployment, bank failures, and foreclosures swept across the land. Black Americans bore a disproportionate share of the pain: they were more likely to be fired than whites, lost their hold on jobs that had previously been too menial to attract whites, and, especially in the South, encountered sharp discrimination in public-welfare programs. Nevertheless, the decade brought new hope to African Americans. The economic crisis of the 1930s shook the foundations of the American political order, increased blacks' political leverage, and made civil rights a salient issue.

During the 1930s, most black voters abandoned the party of Lincoln, which had offered them little but platitudes for thirty years. Courted by urban Democratic political machines in the North, impressed by the New Deal's commitment to working people, heartened by President Franklin D. Roosevelt's openness to them, and impressed by Eleanor Roosevelt's outspoken support for civil rights, most African Americans transferred their political loyalty to the Democratic Party. Although they had voted heavily for Herbert Hoover in the Democratic landslide of 1932, by 1936, according to the Gallup Poll, 76 percent of black voters cast their ballots for FDR.

As black voters entered the Democratic fold, their leaders forged alliances with important elements of the Democratic coalition, alliances that increased blacks' political influence during the 1930s and beyond. Perceiving the growing black vote as crucial to their success, northern urban Democratic politicians proved willing supporters. African American leaders also found powerful allies among the leadership of the influential Congress of Industrial Organizations (CIO). The CIO unions—the United Mine Workers, the United Auto Workers, and the United Steel Workers, among others—brought all workers, skilled and unskilled, in an industry into one union. Consequently, most CIO unions had significant black membership, and their leaders were forthright advocates of civil rights. African Americans also received firm support from liberal intellectuals, whose strength in party councils far outweighed their numbers. Influenced by new research in biology, psychology, and anthropology which debunked the myth of white supremacy, and sensitized to the consequences of racism by the spread of fascism in Europe, these men and women worked closely with African American leaders on behalf of civil rights. African Americans also strengthened their ties with Jews, whose experience with discrimination provided common ground for cooperation with blacks.

Growing militance further enhanced African Americans' political influence, making it more difficult for political leaders to duck their demands. Eager to win black support, the Communist party attacked the NAACP for its faith in gradual change and began an uncompromising, outspoken campaign against racism. Noncommunist radicals such as Howard University political scientist Ralph Bunche and W. E. B. Du Bois (who in 1934 broke with the organization he had helped to found) also criticized NAACP leaders for their reliance on litigation, their lack of concern for issues important to working-class blacks, and their faith in gradualism. Fearful that the radicals would steal its thunder, the NAACP responded by adopting new tactics. While refusing to abandon its program of lobbying and litigation, the organization devoted increasing attention to economic matters and

encouraged direct action against discrimination. The Communists' bold-
ness, combined with traditional civil rights leaders' growing militance, led
to an upsurge of black protest activity. African Americans in thirty-five cities
conducted "Don't Buy Where You Can't Work" campaigns, boycotting and
picketing white businesses that refused to hire blacks. Demonstrations by
Ohio blacks prodded the state employment service to encourage businesses
to hire minorities. In a dozen cities blacks marched to protest segregated
schools, and in many others they picketed theaters that showed racist films.
Although this grass-roots militance flourished primarily in northern cities,
it gave a new urgency to black demands and helped put civil rights on the
national agenda.

African Americans' growing political influence produced significant
changes in federal policy. FDR appointed more African Americans to significant governmental positions than had any president since Grant. He
named William Hastie of the NAACP to the bench, making him the first
black federal judge, and William Houston, the father of Charles Houston,
became the first black to serve as an assistant attorney general. In addition,
New Dealers named more than a hundred African Americans to administrative positions in federal agencies and opened professional positions in
the federal bureaucracy to several thousand others. Democratic lawmakers
wrote into law the principle of nondiscrimination, adding clauses
prohibiting "discrimination on account of race, creed, or color" to more
than twenty bills establishing federal programs. While it proved difficult
to translate principle into practice, African Americans witnessed some
gains. FDR created an interdepartmental committee popularly known as
the "Black Cabinet" to monitor discrimination in federal programs and to
assess how effectively those programs served blacks. By the late 1930s, important New Deal agencies that provided work for the unemployed, job
training, and loans for family farms had substantially eliminated discrimination from their programs. Attorney General Frank Murphy, a former
member of the NAACP Board of Directors, created a Civil Liberties Unit
in the Justice Department to afford "aggressive protection of fundamental
rights inherent in a free people."[17]

While the New Deal marked a break with the past, it neither eliminated
discrimination from federal programs, won enactment of federal civil rights
legislation, nor made civil rights issues a top priority. Southern Democrats
controlled key congressional committees and were a force to be reckoned
with on Capitol Hill. Consequently, many New Deal administrators were

reluctant to root out discrimination in relief and recovery programs in the South because they feared antagonizing powerful committee chairmen who controlled their agencies' appropriations. Southern legislative power—especially skillful use of the filibuster—also thwarted efforts by liberals to enact federal legislation outlawing lynching and the poll tax. FDR's relations with southern Democrats deteriorated during the mid-1930s. Nevertheless, during his first administration and later, between 1939 and 1941, as the nation moved toward war, he relied too heavily on southern support to lay down the gauntlet on civil rights. Even more important, civil rights failed to become a top priority for the president and for northern Democrats because it was overshadowed by problems of economic recovery and, after 1939, the outbreak of war in Europe.

Like the president, the Supreme Court took important, albeit halting, steps to expand national protection of civil rights during the 1930s. In a series of cases growing out of flagrant denials of justice to black defendants, the Court enlarged the due process rights of criminal defendants. In the process, it expanded the beachhead established by *Moore v. Dempsey* (1926) and provided greater checks on criminal justice officials who had long abused blacks. The Court decided these cases with a surprising degree of consensus considering how bitterly the justices disagreed on the questions of economic regulation and federal power that preoccupied them during the decade. However, members of the Court's conservative bloc were judicial activists who readily struck down state and federal policies they believed to be misguided. Indeed, they had long employed a broad, substantive definition of due process to strike down state and federal regulation of business that they considered arbitrary and unreasonable. Several of the conservatives followed the logic of this view to join their more liberal brethren in using the due process clause to expand the rights of the criminally accused.

The Court took the first step in expanding the meaning of due process in 1932, when it considered a case challenging the conviction of nine black youths in Scottsboro, Alabama, for raping two white women. With crowds of whites gathered outside the courthouse demanding vengeance, the nine went on trial for their lives, represented by an alcoholic attorney who met with them only twice before the trials began and was so poorly prepared that he offered no closing statement to the all-white jury. Even though the alleged victims gave contradictory testimony—within a year one of the women admitted that she had not been assaulted—and evidence offered by the physician who examined them strongly suggested that there had been no rape, jurors found the defendants guilty. Eight were sentenced to death, and the ninth, only thirteen years old, to life in prison.

The case attracted widespread attention in the national media and became a cause célèbre among northern liberals and radicals—a horrifying example of Jim Crow justice. The NAACP, ACLU, and International Labor Defense (ILD), a Communist party organization, took a keen interest in the case. The ACLU and ILD used statements made by individuals who claimed that the alleged victims had regularly engaged in prostitution with black and white clients to undermine their credibility—a common defense strategy. "Few people wondered whether privacy rights should protect the women from . . . having their sexual activities scrutinized in court," notes historian Leigh Ann Wheeler. "In cases that involved a black man charged with rape by a white woman, the deck seemed so stacked against the defendants that few progressives even considered the rights of the complainant."[18] The strategy was not only unfair, it proved counterproductive; prosecutors and most white southerners denounced it as an attack on white womanhood by outside agitators and doubled down on their belief that the defendants were guilty.

After a bitter struggle with the NAACP, the ILD won the confidence of the boys and their families and took the lead in representing them—in the court of public opinion as well as in court. For the ILD, the case was a golden opportunity to increase African American support for the Communist party—at the expense of the NAACP. It tirelessly publicized the "legal lynching" about to take place through newspaper and magazine articles, scores of rallies and marches, petitions, a demonstration outside the White House, mock trials, and even plays. Attorneys retained by the ILD filed appeals that ultimately found their way to the US Supreme Court and persuaded it to overturn the convictions. In *Powell v. Alabama*, a 7–2 majority ruled that the trial court denied the defendants due process of law by failing to provide them with meaningful representation. The right to counsel was a critical element of due process, the majority held, and in capital cases states had the obligation to provide indigent defendants with effective representation.[19]

In the years following *Powell*, the Court announced decisions in a series of cases brought by black defendants that further curbed the arbitrary authority of state and local officials. In *Brown v. Mississippi* (1936), the justices considered an appeal by three African Americans convicted of murdering an elderly white man. Confessions made after authorities had beaten them served as the only evidence of their guilt. Indeed, when the three men had appeared at their trial the bruises and lacerations inflicted by the county sheriff and his deputies were clearly visible. Although the Court had ruled in 1908 that "exemption from compulsory self-incrimination in the courts of the States is not secured by any part of the Federal Constitution,"[20] it now unanimously reversed the convictions. "It would be difficult to conceive of methods more revolting to the sense of justice than those taken to procure the confessions of these petitioners," wrote Chief Justice Charles Evans Hughes, "and the use of the confessions thus obtained [as evidence] . . . was a clear violation of due process."[21] Four years later, in *Chambers v. Florida* (1940), the Court considered the appeal of a black man who had been convicted of murdering a white man on the basis of a confession obtained after an interrogation that lasted five days and culminated in an all-night grilling. Again, the Court deemed use of evidence obtained through coercion, whether physical or psychological, a denial of due process of law.

The Court's rulings in *Powell, Brown,* and *Chambers* dealt with general issues of criminal procedure and applied to white as well as black defendants. Nevertheless, they had a special relevance for African Americans. They began the process of transforming the due process clause into an effective means of guaranteeing procedural fairness in state criminal trials. By doing so, they expanded federal courts' ability to supervise the actions of state and local criminal justice officials and established a check on the repressive methods typically employed against blacks. Justice Hugo Black captured the racial dimensions of these rulings in his *Chambers* opinion. Due process, he explained, was designed to bar "secret and dictatorial proceedings" of the sort employed by "tyrannical governments . . . to make scapegoats of the weak, or of helpless political, racial, or religious minorities."[22]

The Court also challenged exclusion of blacks from juries, a widespread practice that lay at the root of the South's racially oppressive criminal justice system. The Scottsboro affair again produced the pivotal case *Norris v. Alabama* (1935). After the Supreme Court had reversed the initial convictions, the Scottsboro boys had been retried and convicted by all-white juries. The trial judge, who was convinced of their innocence, set aside the verdicts and ordered a new trial. A third round of trials produced the same result as lily-white juries once again found the nine guilty. The youths' repeated convictions made it clear that procedural rights, effective representation, and mountains of evidence meant little as long as judgment was passed by white jurors. In *Norris,* defense lawyers appealed the latest round of convictions, charging systematic exclusion of blacks from the juries that had indicted and tried their clients. This, they argued, had denied them the equal protection of the laws in violation of the Fourteenth Amendment. The Court agreed in a unanimous decision written by Chief Justice Hughes. His opinion rejected the state's claim that proof of discrimination required evidence that local officials had consciously and intentionally excluded potential black jurors on account of their race. Instead, he ruled that the evidence produced at the trial—which showed that for decades no blacks had served on juries in the counties in which the defendants had been indicted and tried—was sufficient proof of discrimination.[23]

Four years later, in *Smith v. Texas* (1940), the Court extended its ruling in *Norris*. Although the Harris County, Texas, grand jury that had indicted Smith was all-white, token numbers of blacks had served as grand jurors in the county during the 1930s. Defense lawyers pointed out that while more than 20 percent of the county's residents were blacks, only six blacks had served on the thirty-two grand juries that sat in Harris County between 1931 and 1938. This token representation, they contended, served as proof of systematic discrimination that denied their client equal protection. The justices unanimously accepted this argument and reversed Smith's conviction. By doing so, they suggested that mere token representation of blacks on juries did not get local officials off the hook and might, in fact, be used to prove discrimination.[24]

While important, these decisions did not guarantee that black defendants received justice. White law enforcement officials still arrested and charged them, white judges presided over their trials, and, with rare exceptions, white juries still determined their fate. Consider the outcome of the Scottsboro cases. After the Supreme Court twice reversed convictions that carried the death sentence, the state initiated a new round of prosecutions in 1936. Consistent with the Court's ruling in *Norris*, it included African Americans in the jury pool, but none was selected; several, clearly uncomfortable with the prospect of serving, asked to be excused, and the prosecutor used peremptory challenges to eliminate the rest. Predictably, four defendants were again convicted, with one receiving the death penalty and the others life in prison. Only a compromise negotiated between desperate defense attorneys and prosecutors embarrassed by six years of bad publicity brought the episode to an end. The state dropped charges against four defendants who had not been retried, and the governor agreed to commute Clarence Norris's death sentence to life imprisonment. Five of the defendants, however, remained in prison. Three were paroled and one escaped from prison and fled the state in the 1940s, while Norris remained behind bars until

1978. Procedural guarantees were important, but they did not prevent the Scottsboro defendants from serving years and even decades in prison.

The most important legal development of the decade resulted from the NAACP's campaign against segregated education. In the early 1930s, the organization's legal staff had envisioned an ambitious program of litigation challenging segregation in elementary and secondary education. When Charles Houston became chief counsel in 1935, however, he realized that the organization lacked adequate resources to implement the original plan. Consequently, Houston and his protégé, Thurgood Marshall, who joined the staff in 1936, attacked segregation at the periphery. Emphasizing the equality requirement implicit in the separate but equal rule established by *Plessy*, they initiated suits challenging unequal pay for black teachers and discrimination in graduate and professional education.

This approach was attractive for several reasons. First, discrimination in these areas was blatant; most states maintained graduate and professional programs for whites but not for blacks, and school districts' salary schedules clearly showed that black teachers received substantially lower pay than whites with comparable training and experience. Consequently, limited research would be required to prove discrimination, making the cases less expensive to litigate. Second, the salary cases would revitalize moribund NAACP chapters by drawing African American teachers into the organization and would thus help raise civil rights consciousness at the grassroots. Third, by winning precedents requiring absolute equality under segregation, Houston and Marshall would, at the very least, improve the quality of African American schools and might even make segregation too expensive for the South to maintain. Especially at the graduate level, states might find it more practical to admit African Americans to white schools than to establish expensive programs for the small number of blacks who sought advanced education. And this would be the first crack in the South's wall of segregation.

Houston and Marshall scored their first victories in two law school cases. In 1935 they represented Donald Murray, a graduate of Amherst College who had been denied admission to the University of Maryland's all-white law school. Like most other southern states, Maryland had no graduate or professional programs in its black colleges. Instead, it had established tuition grants to black residents who attended programs in other states. The legislature, however, had not funded the program, so no money was actually available. Houston and Marshall charged that the state clearly had denied Murray equal opportunity for legal study. Even if the tuition-grant program were funded, they contended, it would not give Murray the same rights as whites. While white students would be able to attend school in Maryland, their client would have to incur the inconvenience and expense of leaving the state to obtain a legal education. Both the trial court and the Maryland Supreme Court, which heard the case on appeal in 1936, agreed, ordering Murray's admission to the state's white law school.[25]

A Missouri case offered the opportunity to bring these issues before the US Supreme Court. After graduating in 1935 from Lincoln University, the state's Jim Crow college, Lloyd Gaines applied for admission to the University of Missouri Law School. Because the school did not admit African Americans, university officials rejected Gaines's application. They advised him that the state met the needs of African Americans by providing grants for them to attend law school in another state and by offering to establish a law school on demand at Lincoln University. With the aid and encouragement of the

Figure 5.2. Left to right, Thurgood Marshall, Donald Murray, and Charles Hamilton Houston preparing for Murray's lawsuit to win admission to the University of Maryland School of Law in 1934 or 1935 https://www.flickr.com/photos/washington_area_spark/32285321446/in/photostream/. *Flickr.*

St. Louis chapter of the NAACP, Gaines sued, demanding admission to the all-white law school. The black St. Louis lawyers who filed the case promptly called on Houston's expertise, and he argued the case when it went to trial in Missouri and later, in the US Supreme Court. In 1938, when the high court announced its decision in *Missouri ex rel Gaines v. Canada*, it handed Houston a major victory. "The admissibility of laws separating the races in the enjoyment of privileges afforded by the State rests wholly upon the equality of the privileges which the laws give to the separated groups within the State," noted Chief Justice Hughes. But Missouri fell short of this standard. The promise to establish a legal program at Lincoln remained a "mere declaration of purpose," while the subsidy program denied blacks a right enjoyed by whites, the right to obtain a legal education without leaving the state.[26]

Gaines did not end segregation in graduate education, and many southern states attempted to hold the line against integration by establishing graduate and professional programs at their all-black colleges. The decision's implications were, nevertheless, far-reaching. By rejecting Missouri's subsidy program—which offered blacks legal education at out-of-state schools that were fully equal to the University of Missouri—the Court suggested that segregation must be accompanied by absolute equality. Even if it were financially feasible for southern states to establish graduate and professional programs that would pass the Court's muster, *Gaines* spelled trouble for the South. The standard of absolute equality presumably applied to all levels of education, and southern states would be financially hard-pressed to bring black elementary and secondary schools up to the level of white schools.

Litigation demanding an end to separate and unequal salaries suggested that the courts would carry *Gaines*'s demand for genuine equality beyond graduate education. Between 1936 and 1940, Thurgood Marshall worked with local groups of black teachers in Maryland who initiated lawsuits to demand equal pay for black and white teachers with similar qualifications. In most counties, school officials agreed to salary equalization before the cases went to trial. And in Anne Arundel County, where the school board refused to settle, the US district court ruled in 1939 that the substantial discrepancies between the salaries of black and white teachers was based on race and therefore violated the equal protection clause.[27] As the Maryland cases moved toward a successful conclusion, Marshall was already working with teachers in Virginia. In 1940, close on the heels of his victories in Maryland, he convinced the Fourth Circuit Court of Appeals to strike down Norfolk's discriminatory salary structure in *Alston v. School Board of Norfolk*. The victory was particularly noteworthy because the US Supreme Court declined to hear the case when the school board appealed, thereby affirming the lower court's decision. By 1940 the federal courts had clearly indicated that segregation was acceptable only in the presence of absolute equality.[28]

Jim Crow at the Crossroads: The 1940s

As the nation moved toward war in 1940–1941, African Americans' demand for equality became more insistent. Their expectations raised by promising developments in the 1930s, black leaders were outraged that the so-called arsenal of democracy marched to war to a beat laid down by Jim Crow. As defense orders revived industry and brought millions of the unemployed back to work, African Americans encountered systematic discrimination by employers and government-training programs designed to remedy the shortage of skilled workers needed in defense plants. Discrimination also permeated the armed forces. The army practiced segregation and maintained a quota that sharply restricted African American enlistment, the navy accepted blacks only as messmen, and the marines and the air corps excluded them altogether. African American leaders and journalists unleashed a barrage of criticism, demanding a swift end to discrimination. "Our war is not against Hitler in Europe, but against Hitler in America," thundered the African American columnist George Schuyler. "Our war is not to defend democracy, but to get a democracy we never had." Fearing a defection by black voters in the 1940 election, FDR moved quickly to mollify blacks. He directed federal agencies that supervised the defense industry to develop plans guaranteeing nondiscrimination in employment and training; ordered the War Department to issue a statement that "colored men will have equal opportunity with white men in all departments of the Army"; created a new air corps training unit for blacks; and promoted Colonel Benjamin Davis, a black career officer, to brigadier general.[29]

Disappointed that Roosevelt had not established concrete policies to end discrimination in the defense industry, African Americans increased the pressure. The NAACP announced that it would represent any black person who wished to challenge discrimination by the armed forces, and black community groups protested employment discrimination in cities across the country. But it was the March on Washington Movement (MOWM), spearheaded by the black union leader and socialist A. Philip Randolph, that galvanized black protest and forced FDR to take meaningful action. In early 1941 Randolph announced that on June 24 African Americans would stage a mass march on Washington. During the ensuing months, MOWM chapters emerged in communities across the country, and march leaders confidently predicted that 100,000 would join the protest. Fearing that a confrontation between marchers and whites might spark violence and further divide the nation as it prepared for war, the president reached an agreement with Randolph and other African American leaders. He promised to issue an executive order barring discrimination in employment and training programs in the defense industry. He also pledged to establish an administrative agency, the Committee on Fair Employment Practices (FEPC), to investigate complaints, provide redress for victims of discrimination, and recommend policies to achieve equal employment opportunity. In return, Randolph agreed to call off the march.

These concessions were significant. FEPC secured greater economic opportunity for black workers, and the demonstration of black political power emboldened African Americans. In the aftermath of Pearl Harbor, African American leaders threw their support behind the war effort, but they insisted that the nation defend freedom and democracy at home as well as abroad. "Prove to us," Walter White of the NAACP demanded, "that you are not hypocrites when you say this war is for freedom." Philip Randolph, who transformed MOWM into a permanent organization, was more specific, demanding an end to "Jim Crow in education, in housing, in transportation, and in every other social, economic, and political privilege; full enforcement of the Fourteenth and Fifteenth amendments; abolition of all suffrage restrictions and limitations; prohibitions on private and government discrimination in employment; and expansion of the role of Negro advisors in all administrative agencies."[30] Moreover, as support for the march on Washington suggested, assertiveness at the grass roots was growing. The NAACP grew from 355 branches with 50,000 members in 1940 to 1,073 branches with a membership of almost half a million in 1946. Southern as well as northern blacks participated in this growing militance. In South Carolina, for example, NAACP membership grew from 800 to more than 14,000 during the war years, and by the end of the war the Progressive Democrats, an African American group formed to end disfranchisement, claimed almost 50,000 members.

Propelled by these wartime achievements, African Americans won important victories in the postwar years. In many northern states the New

Figure 5.3. Meeting of the Montgomery, Alabama, NAACP chapter, 1947
http://www.loc.gov/pictures/item/2015648524/. Visual materials from the Rosa
Parks Collection. *Library of Congress.*

Deal coalition of blacks, big city politicians, labor leaders, Jews, and liberals
secured important new civil rights laws. The new measures marked a mile-
stone in the history of civil rights by attacking discrimination in housing and
employment. During the late 1940s, eleven states and twenty cities passed
laws against discrimination by employers, and nine states barred discrimination in public housing. Moreover, most of the measures established effective means of enforcement. Rather than relying on lawsuits initiated by
individuals—which were too expensive for most citizens to undertake—the
new laws created administrative agencies to enforce the rights they established. Victims of discrimination could file complaints with these agencies,
which, in turn, had authority to investigate and issue cease-and-desist orders
which were enforceable by the courts.

African Americans also achieved important victories at the national
level. Joined by white allies, they pressed Harry S. Truman to use the power
and prestige of the presidency on behalf of equal rights. Democrats were

concerned that black voters in northern cities might drift back to the GOP, whose likely presidential nominee in 1948—Governor Thomas Dewey of New York—had a strong civil rights record. Truman responded decisively, becoming the first president in the twentieth century to urge passage of a comprehensive civil rights program. In February 1948, he urged Congress to pass antilynching legislation, tough federal action against employment discrimination and segregation in interstate transportation, and measures to guarantee African Americans the right to vote. In addition, he promised to end Jim Crow in the armed forces by executive order.

Truman's commitment to civil rights achieved tangible results. The Justice Department filed an amicus curiae brief in an NAACP suit to challenge the constitutionality of restrictive covenants, thereby ending the government's neutrality in civil rights litigation. In July 1948 the president issued an executive order calling for "equality of treatment and opportunity" in the armed forces and establishing a committee to supervise desegregation. Although the army bureaucracy doggedly resisted implementation and only accepted full integration after the outbreak of the Korean War in June 1950, Truman's action marked the first time that the federal government had challenged segregation since it enacted the Civil Rights Act of 1875.

Equally important was the fair employment practices bill that the administration sponsored in Congress, a measure that harnessed recently expanded federal commerce power on behalf of civil rights. During the mid-1930s, the Supreme Court's slender conservative majority had used a narrow definition of Congress's power to regulate interstate commerce to strike down New Deal legislation regulating industry, agriculture, and labor relations. In 1937, under the threat of FDR's court-packing proposal, the Court changed course. It accepted the government's contention that the commerce clause gave Congress full authority to regulate any activity that affected interstate commerce. In the following years, as conservatives left the bench and New Dealers replaced them, the Court used the new understanding of federal commerce power to justify a wide range of federal regulatory activity. This shift in doctrine had important implications for civil rights. While the state action theory might limit congressional authority under the Fourteenth Amendment to ban discrimination by private employers and labor unions, the newly invigorated commerce power offered the means to regulate the activities of private individuals and organizations involved in interstate commerce. The Truman administration's fair employment bill drew on this reservoir of power, banning discrimination by employers and labor unions involved in interstate commerce and establishing a federal commission with authority to issue cease-and-desist orders against violators.

The accomplishments of the Truman administration, however, fell far short of its promises. The administration's civil rights package, including the fair employment bill, died in Congress. Republican control on Capitol Hill limited Truman's influence, and southern senators used the filibuster to stall civil rights legislation. Truman, however, bears some responsibility for his program's failure. Although the president forthrightly supported his civil rights proposals, he neither made them a top priority nor launched an all-out effort to win their passage. Concerned about other legislative programs and unwilling to risk a complete break with southern Democrats, he chose not to throw all of his resources into the civil rights battle. African Americans had gotten the attention of national political leaders, but had not persuaded them to expend political capital to secure legislative success.

African Americans fared better in the courts than in Congress. Roosevelt appointees dominated the Supreme Court in the 1940s. Many—Hugo Black, Felix Frankfurter, Wiley Rutledge, William Douglas, and Frank Murphy—staunchly opposed segregation, while the others—Stanley Reed and the mercurial Robert Jackson—sympathized with the cause of civil rights. Truman's four appointees—Fred Vinson, Sherman Minton, Tom Clark, and Harold Burton—were undistinguished jurists not known for passionate devotion to human rights. Nevertheless, like Reed and Jackson, they made concessions to civil rights advocates.

Changes in public opinion encouraged the justices to take a bolder stand on civil rights, assuring them that more liberal rulings would not generate such widespread opposition that they would be unenforceable. Passage of state antidiscrimination laws and President Truman's bold civil rights initiatives suggested growing public support for civil rights. The fight against Nazism had made obvious to many whites the contradictions between segregation and democracy. Moreover, as the Cold War began, many Americans found segregation an embarrassment that threatened the nation's status as the leader of the free world and that gave Soviet propagandists ammunition "to prove our democracy an empty fraud, and our nation a consistent oppressor of underprivileged people."[31] Although few whites became outspoken critics of segregation and most found it convenient to ignore racial discrimination, outside the South, at least, support for Jim Crow weakened.

More liberal civil rights decisions were not simply the result of changes in the Court's membership or shifting white public opinion. The Court acts only when individuals initiate lawsuits and bring cases before it. African American plaintiffs and lawyers kept civil rights issues before the justices, pushing them to expand earlier rulings and forcing them to choose between adherence to legal precedent and the nation's equalitarian promises.

Civil rights advocates won two notable victories that expanded the definition of state action and thus increased the reach of the Fourteenth and Fifteenth Amendments and federal civil rights legislation. The first came when the Court ended the twenty-year battle over the Texas white primary. In the one-party South, Democratic primaries were hotly contested, but those who won nomination were assured victory in the general election. Concerned that African Americans who had not been disfranchised by poll taxes, literacy tests, or intimidation might hold the balance of power in close primaries, the Democratic Party in most southern states had limited participation to whites. Although black Texans and the NAACP had waged a determined fight against the white primary during the 1920s and 1930s, the Court had ultimately turned aside their objections in *Grovey v. Townsend* (1935). According to the Court, the Texas Democratic Party was a private organization and therefore not subject to the Fourteenth and Fifteenth Amendments. Consequently, it could deny blacks membership, thereby prohibiting them from participating in the elections that really mattered.[32]

Black Texans refused to give up. By the early 1940s, changes in the Court's membership and a recent decision that recognized primaries as integral to the state's election process suggested that *Grovey* was ripe to be overturned. In *Smith v. Allwright,* which the NAACP Legal Defense and Education Fund (LDF)[33] carried to the Supreme Court in 1944, black plaintiffs renewed the challenge and won an important victory. The Court not only reversed *Grovey,* but indicated that it was willing to take a broad view of state action. Justice Stanley Reed explained that primaries "are conducted by the party under state authority," thereby making the party "an agency of the State in so far as it determines the participants in a primary election." In concluding, Reed emphasized that legal fictions would not be permitted to stand in the way of constitutional rights, noting that the "right to participate in the choice of elected officials without restriction by any State because of race . . . is not to be nullified by a State through casting its electoral process in a form which permits a private organization to practice racial discrimination."[34]

African American lawyers also pushed the Court to accept a broader view of state action by challenging judicial enforcement of restrictive covenants. Although in 1927 the Court had suggested that these private agreements did not come within the purview of the Fourteenth Amendment, NAACP lawyers were eager to bring the issue before the Court again. They got their chance in 1948, when the Court heard *Shelley v. Kraemer,* a St. Louis case, and two other restrictive covenant cases appealed from Detroit and Washington, DC. Accepting the organization's analysis, all six members who heard the cases concurred that the agreements were unenforceable. "These are not cases . . . in which the States have merely abstained from action, leaving private individuals free to impose such discriminations as they see fit," wrote Chief Justice Vinson. "Rather, these are cases in which the States have made available to such individuals the full coercive power of government to deny to petitioners, on the grounds of race or color, the enjoyment of property rights."[35]

The Court also clearly indicated its dislike for segregation in public accommodations. Facing a steady stream of complaints from blacks about the indignities of Jim Crow buses and trains, NAACP strategists mounted an imaginative challenge to segregated transportation. In *Morgan v. Virginia,* which reached the Court in 1946, they argued that segregation in interstate transportation was unconstitutional, not because it violated the equal protection clause, but because it impeded interstate commerce. They drew on a long line of precedents voiding state laws and regulations that unduly burdened commerce or dealt with matters that required uniform national regulations. Thurgood Marshall contended that state segregation laws disrupted interstate commerce by forcing passengers to change seats as they went from one state to another and by imposing a multiplicity of complex regulations on interstate carriers. With only one member in dissent, the Court agreed, holding that state segregation statutes unduly burdened interstate commerce and could not be enforced against interstate carriers.[36]

The decision did not apply to travelers within a single state. Nor did it effectively end segregation for interstate travelers. Because *Morgan* struck down state laws, but not carrier-imposed regulations, most southern railroads and bus companies continued to enforce rules requiring segregation. The decision, nevertheless, presaged the future. Had the justices not been predisposed to whittle away at segregation, they would not have found the NAACP's rather strained argument convincing. Indeed, had the Court followed its recent trend of allowing states greater freedom to regulate businesses involved in interstate commerce, it would have rejected the NAACP's argument. Thus the decision indicated the justices' hostility to segregation and that, while they were not yet ready to take the dramatic step of overruling *Plessy,* its days were numbered.

The NAACP's campaign against segregation in graduate and professional education, which continued after World War II, brought the Court
even closer to the precipice. Thurgood Marshall, who succeeded Houston as
chief counsel in 1938, moved cautiously toward a direct attack on the separate but equal doctrine. The LDF staff mushroomed in the postwar years,
and many of these young African American lawyers were impatient with
the strategy of working within the confines of the separate but equal doctrine to erode segregation. Marshall himself understood the limitations of
this approach. During the 1940s, as the campaign to equalize the salaries
of African American teachers had spread beyond Maryland and Virginia,
progress slowed considerably. School officials in most states developed systems of rating teachers that allowed white administrators to make subjective
judgments about merit and performance, thus perpetuating discrimination
through less obvious means. Challenging this more subtle form of discrimination required extensive research and a multiplicity of complicated lawsuits
that achieved fewer concrete results. Consequently, Marshall realized that
the old strategy of using the separate but equal doctrine to force equalization
of black and white schools in hopes of making segregation too expensive was
more likely to wear down the NAACP than its opponents. Yet Marshall was
not simply driven to undertake a direct attack by the young turks on his staff
or by the failure of the indirect approach. His own reading of the postwar
political climate suggested to him that the time was ripe to challenge *Plessy*.

A Texas case, *Sweatt v. Painter*, offered the best opportunity to present a
direct challenge to the separate but equal doctrine. When Heman Sweatt,
a black mail carrier, sued to win admission to the University of Texas Law
School, the state promptly created a makeshift black law school in Austin,
renting three rooms in a building across the street from the state capitol,
assigning faculty from the white law school to teach in the new school, and
offering black law students access to the state law library, a substantial collection located in the capitol. The black law school, while not fully equal to
the university's law school, was not a complete travesty. Indeed, the quality
of its faculty and library compared favorably to those of the University of
Texas Law School. This made the case more difficult, yet also offered the
opportunity to press the Court to reconsider the legitimacy of separate but
equal. When the case came before the Supreme Court, Marshall argued
that the law school did not meet the requirements of separate but equal;
the state law library was open to the public and not designed primarily for
the use of students, and the black school had no law review or moot court

program. He also broadened the argument, contending that even if the two schools were physically equal, the black school could never accord African Americans an equal education. Intangible factors—the superior reputation of the established white law school, the greater opportunity it offered for developing professional contacts, its wide network of influential alumni—doomed the black school's ability to offer its students opportunities open to their white counterparts. Thus separate but equal in professional education was an oxymoron.

The ball was in the justices' court. Justice Tom Clark, himself a graduate of the University of Texas Law School, urged the justices to confront the issue squarely and to declare that separate but equal had no place in graduate education. "If some say this undermines *Plessy* then let it fall, as have many Nineteenth Century oracles," he urged in a memo to his colleagues. With Chief Justice Vinson and several other justices unwilling to issue an opinion openly questioning *Plessy*, the Court rejected Clark's counsel. Nevertheless, the unanimous decision in *Sweatt*, written by the chief justice, was a severe blow to *Plessy*. Although Vinson found the physical facilities of the black law school inferior, he suggested that the black school would be wanting even if it were physically equal to the white law school:

> What is more important [than the disparity in physical facilities], the University of Texas Law School possesses to a far greater degree those qualities which are incapable of objective measurement but which make for greatness in a law school. Such qualities, to name but a few, include reputation of the faculty, experience of the administration, position and influence of the alumni, standing in the community, traditions and prestige.[37]

This emphasis on intangibles had important implications for the future. "Given the discussions within the Court, invoking the intangibles committed the justices as much as any doctrine could to the position that equality could not be achieved in separate graduate and professional schools," notes Mark Tushnet.[38] Once separate but equal fell in the realm of higher education, it was only a matter of time before it fell in secondary and elementary education. Indeed. *Sweatt* (as well as the Court's decision in another 1950 case, *Henderson v. United States*, which effectively invalidated carrier-imposed segregation in interstate commerce[39]) heartened NAACP attorneys and encouraged them to launch an all-out offensive against the separate but equal doctrine. By mid-century, then, the stage was set to bring down the legal framework that perpetuated the caste system. African American leaders had developed the arguments, secured the precedents, built the political alliances, and, perhaps most important of all, fostered grass-roots support for civil rights in black communities across the nation. The dream of equality not only remained alive but within reach.

6

The Civil Rights Movement and American Law, 1950–1969

Rosa Parks, a forty-two-year-old Montgomery, Alabama, tailor, boarded the Cleveland Avenue bus for the long trip home when she left work on Thursday, December 1, 1955. Like the other African American riders, Mrs. Parks moved toward the back of the bus, taking a seat in the first row of the "colored" section. As more riders boarded at succeeding stops, black passengers stood in the aisles, even though a few seats in the white section remained vacant. By the third stop the last "white" seat was taken, leaving one white man standing at the front of the bus. In keeping with company policy (which was to expand the white section row by row as it became filled), the driver brusquely ordered Parks and the other three African Americans in her row to surrender their seats. The others complied, but Parks refused to move—even when the driver stopped the bus and threatened to have her arrested for violating the city's bus segregation ordinance. A civil rights activist and secretary of the Montgomery NAACP chapter, she deeply resented the bus company's humiliating policies and had resolved that she would never surrender her seat to a white. Several minutes later, police officers responded to the driver's call for help, arrested Mrs. Parks, and took her to the police station, where she was booked and placed in the city jail. Although the US Supreme Court had declared segregation in education unconstitutional one and a half years earlier, Montgomery officials, like most other southern whites, remained determined to preserve Jim Crow.

Parks's arrest set off feverish activity in the Montgomery black community. E. D. Nixon, the president of the local NAACP chapter, learned of her arrest, quickly posted bond to secure her release, and drove her home. Later that evening, Nixon conferred with Jo Ann Robinson, a black English professor at Alabama State College and the president of the city's Women's Political Caucus (WPC). The two had long wished to organize a bus boycott and agreed that Parks's arrest offered the perfect opportunity to mobilize Montgomery blacks. Robinson and her colleagues in the WPC immediately went to work. They

Promises to Keep. Donald G. Nieman, Oxford University Press (2020). © Oxford University Press.
DOI: 10.1093/oso/9780190071639.001.0001

spent the night at the college mimeograph machine cranking out thousands of copies of a flier urging blacks to protest Parks's arrest by staying off the buses on Monday. As bleary-eyed WPC members began to distribute the handbills the next morning, Nixon was on the phone, summoning Montgomery's African American leaders to assemble that evening to discuss the boycott. Those who attended agreed to endorse a boycott and to convene a mass meeting at the Holt Street Baptist Church on Monday evening to determine whether there was sufficient community support to continue the protest.

On Monday, December 5, the movement developed greater momentum. The boycott was almost completely effective on its first day, even though most blacks depended on buses for transportation. That afternoon, African American leaders met again, endorsing a series of resolutions drafted by Nixon. Acknowledging white intransigence, they demanded not integration, but a more humane form of segregation. They proposed that blacks could seat themselves from the rear to the front, whites from the front to the rear, and no black, once seated, would be ordered to surrender his or her seat. They also formed a new organization, the Montgomery Improvement Association (MIA), to coordinate the protest and to negotiate with city officials. The group then chose as its president a twenty-six-year-old minister who had recently come to the pulpit of the prestigious Dexter Avenue Baptist Church after completing his Ph.D. in theology at Boston University. His name was Martin Luther King Jr.

That evening, a huge crowd packed the Holt Street Church, spilling out into the surrounding churchyard. King electrified the throng with a largely improvised speech. In rolling cadences, he assured his listeners that they were not wrong to resist "being trampled over by the iron feet of oppression." "If we are wrong—the Supreme Court of this nation is wrong," he insisted. "If we are wrong—Jesus of Nazareth was merely a Utopian dreamer who never came down to earth! If we are wrong—justice is a lie." He urged the audience to employ nonviolent protest to call attention to the evils of segregation and to compel whites to do justice. "First and foremost we are American citizens," he explained. "We are not here advocating violence. . . . The only weapon that we have in our hands this evening is the weapon of protest," and "the great glory of American democracy is the right to protest for right." Moved by King's call for action, the audience roared its approval and agreed to continue the boycott until city officials capitulated.[1]

In the days following Monday's meeting, MIA leaders organized a vast carpool that transported thousands of boycotters, while thousands of other

African Americans braved the elements and walked to jobs, schools, and stores. Even though the boycott drove the bus company into the red, city officials remained resolute, refusing to accept the MIA's moderate demands. In the face of white intransigence, African Americans continued to walk, and African American attorney Fred Gray filed a lawsuit in federal district court that transformed the MIA's cause. No longer seeking merely to modify segregation, they asked that Jim Crow bus service be declared unconstitutional. As the boycott dragged on, whites bombed the homes of King and other MIA leaders, arrested carpool drivers on trumped-up speeding charges, and charged more than a hundred boycott leaders with violating an obscure state law outlawing boycotts "without just cause or legal excuse."[2] White aggression only steeled blacks' resolve, and throughout the spring, summer, and fall of 1956, working-class African Americans continued the boycott, despite the great personal inconvenience. Although white officials were equally resolute, black persistence ultimately paid off. In June the US district court declared Montgomery's bus segregation statute unconstitutional. City attorneys appealed to the Supreme Court, but the justices unanimously sustained the lower court when it decided the case, *Gayle v. Browder*.[3] Just before dawn on December 21, 1956, one year and twenty days after Rosa Parks refused to give up her seat, King and other boycott leaders ceremoniously boarded a city bus and took seats near the front as photographers snapped photos and reporters scribbled notes.

The triumph the journalists reported was a portent of the following turbulent decade. Court decisions and statutes attacking the South's caste system would meet massive, determined, ingenious, and often violent resistance from whites determined to preserve their power and privilege. In the face of such resistance, court decisions and laws could not, by themselves, guarantee equality. African Americans would have to mobilize and challenge the caste system if they were to breathe life into pronouncements from Washington and force cautious judges and politicians to make civil rights a priority. Yet the success of the Montgomery movement also suggested that community mobilization, while vital, had its limits. After all, not until the Supreme Court spoke did city officials capitulate. Neither law nor mass protest could, by itself, end the caste system; only a combination of the two would accomplish that monumental task and bring the long-deferred promise of equality closer to realization. Martin Luther King Jr. understood that as he donned the mantle of leadership that December evening in 1955. "Not only are we using the tools of persuasion, but we've got to use tools of coercion," he prophetically told the audience at the Holt Street Baptist Church. "Not only is this thing a process of education, but it is also a process of legislation."[4]

Challenge and Response, 1950–1960

The massive protest in Montgomery was triggered, in part, by the successful culmination of the NAACP's long legal battle against segregation. Since the 1930s, Thurgood Marshall and his colleagues on the NAACP legal staff had crisscrossed the South, arguing scores of cases designed to chip away at segregation. Their campaign had produced a long string of important victories and had brought the Supreme Court to the verge of abandoning the separate but equal doctrine. Encouraged by the trend of the Court's decisions and by growing support for black equality, Marshall and his staff sought to push the Court further. In 1951, attorneys from the NAACP Legal Defense Fund, representing black parents in Delaware, Virginia, South Carolina, Kansas, and the District of Columbia who sought to have their children admitted to white schools, challenged the constitutionality of segregated education. *Sweatt v. Painter*'s emphasis on the intangible aspects of education, they argued, meant that segregated schools were necessarily unequal. They cited social science research conducted by the African American psychologist Kenneth Clark demonstrating that segregation had a devastating effect on black children, destroying their self-esteem and their incentive to learn. Therefore, even if physical facilities were equal, the black lawyers contended, segregated schools denied African Americans equality.

In 1952 the Supreme Court agreed to hear appeals in these cases, consolidating the four state cases under the title of the Kansas case, *Brown v. Board of Education of Topeka*, while addressing the somewhat different constitutional issues posed by the District of Columbia appeal separately in *Boiling v. Sharpe*.[5] In doing so, the justices set the stage for a full-scale debate over the constitutionality of segregated education, a debate that forced often anguished consideration of the nature of judicial power. All of the justices except Kentuckian Stanley Reed found segregation and the *Plessy* precedent distasteful. Nevertheless, most had reservations about the wisdom of declaring segregation unconstitutional. They realized that most white southerners passionately supported segregation and would bitterly resist its demise. Southern opposition, they feared, might lead to an endless stream of cases that would drag the Court into day-to-day management of local school

Figure 6.1. The NAACP attorneys who argued *Brown v. Board of Education*
http://digitalcollections.nypl.org/items/8e0ab460-3604-4be6-e040-
e00a18063fa6, left to right, Louis Redding, Robert Carter, Oliver Hill,
Thurgood Marshall, Spottswood Robinson III, Jack Greenberg, James Nabrit
Jr., and George E. C. Hayes. *Schomburg Center for Research in Black Culture,
Photographs and Prints Division, The New York Public Library.*

districts. And if the Court's mandate were not backed by the president and
the Congress, it might prove unenforceable, severely damaging the Court's
authority.

Several justices, notably Felix Frankfurter and Robert Jackson, also
worried that the Court might exceed the proper limits of its authority if it
reversed *Plessy*. They had long criticized conservative judges for using the
general language of the due process clause to declare state laws regulating
business unconstitutional and to write their personal preference for laissez-
faire economic policy into the law. In a democracy, they believed, elected
officials should make public policy, and judges should invoke the power of
judicial review only when legislation clearly violated the Constitution. This

philosophy of judicial self-restraint made the *Brown* case a difficult one for Frankfurter and Jackson. Both found racial segregation repugnant; however, the Fourteenth Amendment's equal protection clause did not expressly prohibit it, and evidence that the amendment's framers intended to do so was inconclusive at best. In addition, Congress (which had express authority to enforce the equal protection clause) had supported segregated schools in the District of Columbia since the 1860s—a strong indication that it did not view segregation as unconstitutional. Furthermore, for fifty-six years the Supreme Court had maintained that segregation and equal protection were not incompatible. Consequently, Frankfurter and Jackson worried that in striking down segregation they would be writing their personal preferences into law and usurping authority best left to legislators—the very things for which they had taken conservatives to task. Although both men would later overcome these doubts, in early 1953 neither was ready to reverse *Plessy*.

The Court was thus in disarray as the justices considered *Brown* during the spring of 1953. Justice Reed determined to uphold segregation, Chief Justice Vinson leaned in that direction, and several other justices remained undecided. Because even the staunchest foes of segregation believed that a divided Court would fuel southern resistance, the justices agreed to postpone their decision. In June 1953 they ordered the case held over for reargument, creating a one-year delay that would profoundly affect the outcome. In early September, barely one month before the Court reconvened, Chief Justice Vinson died, and President Dwight Eisenhower appointed Governor Earl Warren of California as his successor. Vinson had been noncommittal, but Warren firmly believed that segregation denigrated blacks and clearly denied them equal protection. He used his formidable political skills and powers of persuasion to win over doubters and forged unanimous support for a decision declaring segregated schools unconstitutional.

Warren did not doubt the proper outcome, but he hoped to avoid "precipitous action that would inflame [the white South] more than necessary."[6] This concern, rather than abstract legal principles, shaped his opinion in *Brown*, which was announced on May 17, 1954. To avoid antagonizing whites, Warren refrained from attacking segregation as part of a caste system designed to preserve white supremacy and deny African Americans equal protection. Rather than suggesting that *Plessy* had been wrongly decided and that southerners had supported a blatantly unconstitutional institution for more than a half century, he contended that recent developments had made segregation incompatible with the guarantees of equal protection. Public education had become far more important than it had been when the Fourteenth Amendment was adopted and *Plessy* was decided. In fact, it now was "a principal instrument in awakening the child to cultural values, in preparing him for later professional training, and in helping him to adjust normally to his environment." Relying on recent social science research conducted by Kenneth Clark and featured in the NAACP brief, Warren argued that segregation denied African American children the full benefit of education and thus put them at a considerable disadvantage. "To separate them from others of similar age and qualifications," he explained, "solely because of their race generates a feeling of inferiority . . . that may affect their hearts and minds in a way unlikely ever to be undone." Therefore, the chief justice concluded, "separate educational facilities are inherently unequal."[7]

An important question remained: how would legal principle translate into practice? If segregation was unconstitutional, black children presumably had the right to attend nonsegregated schools immediately. Warren and his colleagues refused to issue such an order, however, fearing that if they moved too quickly they would antagonize white southerners. Believing that democracy ultimately relied on consent rather than force, they were determined to win at least grudging acceptance from southern whites. Massive resistance would, they feared, produce chaos, block compliance with the decision, humiliate the court, and threaten the rule of law. Consequently, Warren's opinion postponed a decision on implementation until the Court's next term, reassuring whites that the Court would not act rashly or demand immediate integration.

In May 1955, the Court issued another decision (commonly known as "*Brown II*"), addressing the thorny problem of enforcement. Eager to conciliate whites, Warren's *Brown II* opinion emphasized that implementation would proceed gradually and would take into account local conditions. He ordered the cases returned to the courts in which they had been tried, giving judges who were familiar with each local situation responsibility for implementation. While the Supreme Court instructed the lower courts to require that school officials "make a prompt and reasonable start" toward compliance, it also urged judges to consider the complex problems involved and give local officials adequate time to deal with them. Judges were to implement *Brown* "with all deliberate speed," Warren concluded, using an oxymoron that would plague civil rights advocates for the next decade. In their desire to defuse white resistance, the justices placed responsibility for implementing

Brown on lower federal courts but gave them vague and even contradictory instructions regarding how to proceed.[8]

Any hope that the white South would accept *Brown* quickly faded. Although some school districts in the border states grudgingly acquiesced, whites in the Deep South bitterly denounced the decision as an unconstitutional act of judicial tyranny and vowed to resist. In 1955, Mississippi whites organized the Citizens' Council to hold the line against integration. It quickly spread across the Deep South, claiming 250,000 members by 1956 and orchestrating a campaign of economic reprisals against African Americans and whites who dared to challenge segregation. Some whites demanded sterner measures. The months following *Brown* witnessed a resurgence of the Ku Klux Klan and a wave of bombings, murders, beatings, and cross burnings aimed at intimidating black activists. In Mississippi, three prominent African American leaders were murdered during the summer and fall of 1955—one, Lamar Smith, shot to death in broad daylight on the grounds of the Pike County Courthouse. In 1956, mobs prevented African American students from enrolling at the University of Alabama and in the public schools of Mansfield, Texas, and Clinton, Tennessee. Nor did the violence subside. In 1957, as Birmingham blacks began efforts to desegregate the public schools, a black man was savagely beaten and castrated by a group of whites who told him, "This is what will happen if Negroes try to integrate the schools."[9]

With the South aflame, Southern politicians and politics shifted sharply rightward. "Candidates tried to show that they were the 'most blatantly and uncompromisingly prepared to cling to segregation at all costs,'" legal historian Michael Klarman explained. "Moderation became 'a term of derision' as the political center collapsed."[10] Governors like Orval Faubus in Arkansas, once considered a moderate on race, embraced massive resistance to *Brown*, and aspiring politicians like George Wallace learned that anything less than full-throated defense of segregation would doom their careers. With extremism ascendant, state legislatures quickly crafted measures to defy the Court. Several states passed laws prohibiting school officials from obeying court orders to integrate. Others ordered integrated schools closed and offered to pay private school tuition to white children in communities that closed their public schools. Less bombastic, but more effective, were the pupil placement laws enacted by most southern states. These measures purported to meet *Brown*'s requirement for gradual desegregation by establishing ostensibly nonracial criteria for assignment of new students to schools and by allowing students already enrolled to apply for transfers to any school in their

Figure 6.2. Left to right, Arthur Shores, Robert Carter, Fred Gray, and Orzell Billingsley in Alabama circuit court in Montgomery in 1956 or 1957 as they challenged the state's attempt to stop the NAACP from conducting business in the state and to compel it to turn over membership lists. *Alabama Department of Archives and History.*

district. When assigning new students to schools or considering applications for transfers, school officials were directed to consider such things as the academic preparation, moral character, and home environment of the pupil, "the effect of admission of the pupil upon the academic progress of other students, . . . [and] the possibility of . . . disorder among pupils or others."[11] These criteria were flexible enough to permit white officials to assign black children to all-black schools and to deny the applications of black children who had the temerity to request transfers to white schools. Moreover, the laws established a procedural maze that students must follow to challenge school officials' decisions. The latter requirement was particularly important. Because federal law required individuals to exhaust all administrative remedies before suing in federal courts, time-consuming and complicated local procedures were guaranteed to keep all but the most determined black litigants out of court.

In the face of determined white resistance, proponents of desegregation received little support or encouragement from the president or Congress, something the justices had feared. President Eisenhower worked behind the scenes to promote desegregation in the District of Columbia, but he had (as an aide noted) a "basic insensitivity" about racism, feared that vigorous support for desegregation would reverse the progress that the Republican Party had made in attracting white southerners, and considered the *Brown* decision ill-advised.[12] Consequently, Ike refused to endorse *Brown* publicly, thus declining to use his enormous popularity to reconcile white southerners to the decision. On more than one occasion when he was asked about desegregation, Ike responded that moral beliefs could be changed only by education, not by law. Congress did no more to assist desegregation. Although liberals pressed for legislation authorizing the Justice Department to bring desegregation suits, an alliance of southerners and northern conservatives blocked passage.

With the political branches inert, enforcement of *Brown* depended on lawsuits initiated by blacks in hundreds of communities across the South, guaranteeing that widespread desegregation would be a long time coming. African Americans—especially those who lived in rural areas and small towns—invited economic and physical retaliation if they challenged segregation; not surprisingly, most hesitated to press their rights under *Brown*. In 1955, for example, blacks in five Mississippi towns petitioned for school desegregation, but intense pressure from the Citizens' Council deterred them from going to court. Besides, lawsuits were too expensive for most African Americans to undertake. Even when local attorneys volunteered their services or the Legal Defense Fund sent counsel to manage a case, plaintiffs still paid approximately $15,000 (the equivalent of $138,000 in 2019 dollars). By 1961, few lawsuits targeted school districts in the Deep South.

Despite the intimidation and expense, southern blacks did bring several dozen school cases before the federal courts during the late 1950s. US district courts, presided over by a single judge, initially heard most of these. If a plaintiff requested an injunction barring enforcement of an allegedly unconstitutional state law (as was sometimes done in desegregation suits), a special three-judge district court would hear the case instead. Although parties could appeal the decisions of three-judge district panels directly to the Supreme Court, appeals from the decisions of single-judge courts went first to the courts of appeals for consideration. The nation was divided into ten circuits, each supervised by an appeals court consisting of between three and nine judges depending on the circuit's caseload. Five of these tribunals had jurisdiction over at least one southern state (the third circuit included Delaware; the fourth Virginia, the Carolinas, Maryland, and West Virginia; the fifth, Florida, Georgia, Alabama, Mississippi, Louisiana, and Texas; the sixth, Kentucky and Tennessee; and the eighth, Arkansas) and therefore played an important role in supervising desegregation.

The judges who presided over these courts and who enjoyed enormous discretion in overseeing school desegregation under *Brown II* were white southern men. Most had grown up in a society that viewed segregation as necessary and moved in professional and social circles that staunchly defended it. A few—John Minor Wisdom, John R. Brown, Elbert Tuttle, and Richard Rives of the US Court of Appeals for the Fifth Circuit, and District Judges Frank Johnson of Alabama and J. Skelly Wright of Louisiana—defied friends and associates to become forceful advocates of integration. Most southern federal judges, however, opposed integration and believed that the Supreme Court had decided *Brown* incorrectly. Although only a minority let personal prejudices prevail over constitutional duty, most were more inclined to emphasize deliberation than speed in implementing *Brown*. Indeed, given the absence of support from the president and Congress and the vague instructions dispensed by the Supreme Court, their caution was understandable.

Where federal judges' devotion to segregation was stronger than their commitment to carry out their oaths of office, they blocked desegregation. Consider the tortuous pace of litigation in Dallas. Although black plaintiffs initiated a desegregation suit in September 1955, District Judge William Atwell, an outspoken segregationist, refused to act for two years. After the Fifth Circuit Court of Appeals had twice overruled Atwell's dilatory tactics, it issued a third opinion, in September 1957, ordering the school board to develop a desegregation plan. When no plan was forthcoming two years later, the plaintiffs went back to the district court to compel action. Atwell had retired, but another segregationist, T. Whitfield Davidson, had taken charge of the case. After admonishing blacks to recognize "that the white man has a right to maintain his racial integrity and it can't be done so easily in integrated schools," he directed school officials to "study this question and perhaps take further action, maybe an election." The court of appeals again intervened, directing the school board to come up with a desegregation plan soon. When the board complied and presented Davidson with a proposal to admit a few black first graders to white schools in the fall of 1961 and to integrate another grade each year until the process was completed in 1973, Davidson rejected it as too radical. " 'The Dallas Plan,' would lead . . . to an amalgamation of the races," he exclaimed hypocritically.[13] (In fact, the "amalgamation" Davidson feared was quite common and largely the product sexual exploitation of black women by white men.) Once again the court of appeals reversed Davidson's decision. It suggested that the school board's twelve-year plan was too slow and would have to be accelerated, but it ordered the board to begin on schedule. In 1961, after six long and costly years of litigation, token desegregation began in Dallas.

Even when district judges did not engage in obstruction, progress was slow, as judges' response to the pupil placement laws suggest. Appeals courts struck down Virginia and Louisiana placement statutes that were part of legislative packages prohibiting integration; however, they took a more charitable view of those laws that did not openly announce their opposition to integration. Until the early 1960s, the US Court of Appeals for the Fourth Circuit held that these measures were adequate steps toward desegregation and ruled that blacks could not sue until they had exhausted the administrative appeals established by the acts. The fifth circuit court was somewhat more skeptical of the pupil placement laws. In 1959, a federal district judge in Florida refused to order Dade County (Miami) school officials to present a desegregation plan, ruling that the Florida pupil placement law constituted such a plan. The fifth circuit judges quickly reversed his decision, explaining that such statutes were insufficient if districts remained segregated. Although the court did not order desegregation, Miami school officials soon began token integration in order to forestall action by the federal courts.

As the Miami case suggests, even when federal judges acted in good faith, the result was generally only token integration. After four years of litigation, District Judge J. Skelly Wright finally imposed a grade-a-year desegregation plan on New Orleans in 1960. Although Wright stood firm in the face of defiance by state officials, the plan brought only five black first graders into white schools when it was implemented in November 1960. The story was the same in Atlanta. In late 1959, under pressure from Judge Frank Hooper, the school board adopted a plan admitting a few black seniors to previously all-white schools and moving down one grade each year thereafter. Although interference from the state legislature blocked implementation in the fall of 1960, the plan took effect the following year, and by September 1962, forty-four black high school students were enrolled in ten previously all-white schools.

As federal judges inched toward implementation of *Brown*, the Supreme Court remained aloof. It routinely affirmed without comment or refused to review lower court rulings that accepted the validity of pupil placement statutes, grade-a-year plans, and token desegregation. There were several reasons for its timidity. Justice Frankfurter remained a force to be reckoned with until his death in 1962. While he had played an important role in unifying the justices in *Brown* and remained an opponent of segregation, Frankfurter believed that the Court's power should operate in a narrow compass and was reluctant to become deeply involved in the management of southern schools. Moreover, he and most of his colleagues believed that white resistance and the absence of support for desegregation from the president and Congress dictated caution. Although the lower federal courts moved slowly, they were nonetheless translating *Brown*'s call for desegregation into reality, demonstrating to southerners that the world would not end if African Americans went to school with whites, and establishing a beachhead in the fight for integration.

The Court's only major statement on school desegregation came in response to the Little Rock crisis of 1957–1958. Under a desegregation plan approved by a federal court, nine African Americans were scheduled to enter Little Rock's Central High School in September 1957. Seeking to bolster his chances for reelection the following year, Governor Orval Faubus blocked the Court's order. On September 3, the first day of classes, he deployed units of the Arkansas National Guard to prevent admission of the black students. District Judge Ronald Davies, who continued to supervise the city's school desegregation plan, promptly directed school officials to proceed with desegregation. On September 4, as several hundred hostile onlookers taunted and spat on the black students, National Guardsmen turned the nine youths away from the school. Intent on preventing Faubus from nullifying federal law, Davies issued an injunction on September 20, ordering the governor and members of the National Guard to stop further interference with the court-approved desegregation plan. On Monday, September 23, when the nine African American students arrived at Central High, the National Guard had left, but a mob had taken its place. School officials succeeded in getting the black children past the angry whites and into the school, but integration proved short-lived. Fearing a violent assault on the school, school leaders evacuated the African American students later that day.

Confronted with open violation of federal law and a clear threat to federal supremacy, President Eisenhower finally acted. Invoking his authority to use the military to remove obstructions to national authority, he sent units of the 101st Airborne Division to Little Rock, called the National Guard into federal service, and deployed these forces at Central High to quell resistance to the federal court's desegregation order. Although Ike still declined to endorse *Brown*, he refused to accept open defiance of federal authority. Failure to intervene, he informed Senator Richard Russell of Georgia, "would be tantamount to acquiescence in anarchy and the dissolution of the union."[14] On September 24, protected by a thousand troops, the nine black students entered the high school. In the face of continued white harassment and an epic war of wills, eight of them would remain for the entire school year, escorted at all times by the federal troops assigned to guarantee their safety. Faubus's antics may have earned him derision in the national media, but they played well with his base. He won a landslide victory in 1958 and went on to three subsequent victories in gubernatorial races before stepping down in 1967.

In February 1958, with troops still present at Central High and tensions running high, the school board asked that the black children be withdrawn and desegregation postponed until September 1960. Although the district judge accepted this proposal, a unanimous Supreme Court reversed him, ruling in *Cooper v. Aaron* (1958) that the black children must remain. In an unprecedented step, all nine justices signed the Court's opinion, emphasizing their commitment to *Brown* and their determination to stay the course on school desegregation. "The principles announced in that decision and the obedience of the States to them, according to the command of the Constitution, are indispensable for the protection of the freedoms guaranteed by our fundamental charter for all of us," they explained. "Our constitutional ideal of equal justice under law is thus made living truth." The Court also declared its unwillingness to tolerate evasion: "The constitutional rights of children . . . declared . . . in the *Brown* case can neither be nullified openly and directly by state legislators or state executive or judicial officers, nor nullified indirectly by them through evasive schemes for segregation whether attempted 'ingeniously or ingenuously.'"[15] Despite the Court's strong language, Faubus and his supporters had the last word. With the backing of the legislature, Faubus prevented integration by closing the public schools during the 1958–1959 school year.

The Court's strong stand in *Cooper v. Aaron* was, nevertheless, significant. Reinforced as it was by Eisenhower's action, it warned white southerners that the federal government would not capitulate. The Court reinforced this message in a series of cases dealing with other civil rights issues. Between 1955 and 1958, prodded by Thurgood Marshall and other Legal Defense Fund attorneys, the Court extended its ban against segregation from education to other public facilities, including parks, buses, golf courses, and beaches.[16] Although in the absence of congressional legislation it did not extend the ban to privately owned businesses, the Court did expand the definition of what constituted a public facility. Thus in 1961, it ruled that a privately owned restaurant that operated in a city parking garage was so closely tied to the city that discrimination by it was tantamount to state action and therefore impermissible under the Fourteenth Amendment.[17] Moreover, it shielded the NAACP from harassment by southern officials, barring them from compelling the organization to reveal the names of its members. Such disclosure, the Court ruled, would subject NAACP members to retaliation and thus inhibit their First Amendment right to freedom of expression and association.[18]

Even Congress acted to promote civil rights. With northern voters closely divided between the two major parties in the crucial industrial states, northern Democrats were intent on holding the black vote while Republicans were determined to woo African Americans back to the party of Lincoln. Consequently, civil rights legislation attracted strong bipartisan support as 1956, an election year, dawned. Eager to place the resources of the Justice Department behind plaintiffs in school desegregation cases, liberals urged that the attorney general be given authority to seek injunctions against all civil rights violations. Their efforts were defeated by a coalition of conservative Republicans and southern and western Democrats. The bill that eventually emerged from Congress, the Civil Rights Act of 1957, was a weak measure concerned principally with voting rights. It elevated the civil rights section of the Justice Department to a division directed by an assistant attorney general for civil rights, provided for appointment of a Commission on Civil Rights to investigate voting discrimination, made it a federal offense to interfere with the right to vote, and authorized the attorney general to prosecute voting rights cases.

Dissatisfied with this half-hearted measure, liberals pressed for bolder action. They demanded a comprehensive civil rights bill that would authorize the Department of Health, Education, and Welfare (HEW) to draft school desegregation plans for communities that refused to do so, empower the attorney general to seek injunctions in all cases involving civil rights violations, and prohibit employment discrimination. Liberals also wanted to put teeth in federal voting rights law. They urged that the Commission on Civil Rights be empowered to investigate complaints of voting discrimination and to dispatch federal officials to register voters in any county in which it discovered evidence of discrimination.

Once again liberals went down to defeat as Congress enacted another mild bill. Like the 1957 law, the Civil Rights Act of 1960 dealt mainly with voting. It required state officials to preserve records of federal elections for at least two years, thus preventing destruction of incriminating documents before complaints of fraud could be investigated. It also strengthened the hand of federal judges in voting cases. If they determined that local voter registration officers were guilty of discrimination, judges could dispatch federal referees to supervise registration. Although this involved the time-consuming process of litigation, it offered a potentially effective tool to combat southern officials' often ingenious manipulation of registration requirements to prevent African Americans from voting. Finally, the act established criminal penalties for anyone who obstructed federal court orders (a provision aimed at nullificationists like Faubus) or who crossed state lines to engage in bombings or arson.

The Pace of Change Quickens, 1960–1965

If the slow pace of change symbolized by the tepid civil rights bills of 1957 and 1960 frustrated most black leaders, it nevertheless spurred African American college students to challenge the status quo. They had grown up on a steady diet of Cold War rhetoric that extolled the openness of American society and proclaimed the United States the leader of the free world. *Brown*, handed down when they were in their early teens, led them to believe that the nation was finally prepared to make good its professions of democracy and equality. The slow pace of change in the late 1950s, however, undermined these expectations, giving birth to a new militance that shook the foundations of the old order.

Four neatly dressed African American freshmen at North Carolina Agricultural and Technical College in Greensboro walked into the local Woolworth store on February 1, 1960, sat down at its whites-only lunch counter, and politely asked to be served. When the waitress refused, the young men remained at the counter, studying quietly, until the store closed. During the weeks that followed, more than a thousand students joined these four pioneers, as the sit-ins spread to other Greensboro lunch counters, and local African Americans closed ranks with the students, picketing and boycotting Woolworth and other variety stores that discriminated against blacks. The Greensboro sit-ins sparked a direct action campaign that spread across the South like wildfire. In dozens of towns and cities, in every southern state, black youths defied segregation at lunch counters, restaurants, motels, swimming pools, beaches, libraries, and theaters and staged massive demonstrations. Using the tactics of nonviolent resistance, the demonstrators politely asserted their moral right to equal treatment and turned the other cheek when whites verbally and physically abused them. Thousands of demonstrators were arrested and chose jail over bail to highlight the repressiveness of the caste system. In Orangeburg, South Carolina, home to South Carolina State College, police filled the city and county jails and incarcerated three hundred more African American student protesters in a hastily improvised stockade.

The sit-ins marked a turning point in the civil rights struggle. In response to this new militance, more than two hundred cities began desegregate public accommodations. Although most towns and small cities in the Deep South refused to budge, students boasted that in six months they had moved the South closer to integration than the federal courts had done in the six years since *Brown*. Even more important, the students demonstrated a new sense of urgency, indicating that they were tired of gradualism and were no longer willing to wait until judges and politicians decided the time was ripe for them to enjoy their rights. "We cannot tolerate, in a nation professing democracy and among people professing Christianity, the discriminatory conditions under which the Negro is living today," Atlanta sit-in leaders proclaimed. "We do not intend to wait placidly for those rights which are already legally and morally ours to be meted out to us one at a time."[19]

This impatience and militance was not a flash in the pan. Ella Baker, executive director of the Southern Christian Leadership Conference (SCLC)—founded by Martin Luther King Jr. in the wake of the Montgomery bus boycott—brought student leaders together in Atlanta in April 1960.

Recognizing the students' potential for militant action and suspicious of more cautious civil rights leaders, she encouraged the students to create an independent organization. The result was the Student Non-Violent Coordinating Committee (SNCC, pronounced "snick"), which trained members in nonviolent civil disobedience. Just as the young radicals were influenced by older civil rights leaders like Baker, their actions affected established civil rights groups. The Congress of Racial Equality (CORE), a small northern interracial group that had brought nonviolent resistance to the civil rights effort in the 1940s, sent representatives to the conference that gave birth to SNCC and advised the young activists on the tactics of direct action. CORE was itself invigorated by the success of the students and, in the year following the sit-ins, expanded its activities into the South. King's philosophy and tactics of nonviolent resistance, developed during the Montgomery bus boycott, had inspired the students, and King himself had participated in the Atlanta sit-ins. At the same time, the students reaffirmed the potential of direct action for King and his colleagues in the SCLC, prompting them to try more militant tactics.

When John F. Kennedy entered the White House in January 1961, African American leaders were becoming increasingly impatient. Despite his youthful vigor and personal dislike for segregation, the new president spoke the language of gradualism and moved cautiously on civil rights, aware that his legislative agenda and reelection prospects depended on support from Southern Democrats. African Americans had played a crucial role in his razor-thin victory in 1960 and would be rewarded with federal appointments (Thurgood Marshall, for example, was named to the US Court of Appeals for the Second Circuit in 1961), vigorous enforcement of the voting rights laws, and an economic policy that promised higher wages to working-class Americans. Kennedy refused to ask Congress for comprehensive civil rights legislation. It had no chance of passing, he believed, and would cost him too much.

The administration also resisted providing federal intervention to protect civil rights activists in the South. Attorney General Robert Kennedy resolutely maintained that the federal system gave the states responsibility for general law enforcement; the federal government had neither the constitutional authority nor the personnel to take responsibility for maintaining law and order. He pointed out that the Supreme Court's venerable state action interpretation of the Fourteenth Amendment denied the federal government authority to prosecute private individuals who used violence and intimidation to deny blacks equal rights and due process. The attorney general also pleaded that the federal government did not possess a police force capable of preserving the peace. Both the US Marshals Service and the Federal Bureau of Investigation had far too few officers to take responsibility for general law enforcement in the South. Moreover, he maintained that the creation of a national police force was a threat to liberty because it could afford a ruthless president the means to suppress dissent.

Although these objections had some merit, they also "accord[ed] nicely with the political needs of the Kennedy brothers," according to historian Michal Belknap.[20] The state action restriction made successful prosecution of anti–civil rights violence problematic, but the Supreme Court might be convinced to reverse itself, as it had in *Brown*. There may have been too few federal officers to police the entire South, but there were enough to handle selected cases. And a small number of prosecutions might deter future violence. Federal intervention was neither impossible nor a potential threat to liberty. It was, however, calculated to anger white southerners and therefore politically risky.

The administration's response to the freedom rides of 1961 illustrates its position. In December 1960, the Supreme Court ruled that the Interstate Commerce Act forbade discrimination in bus terminals serving interstate carriers.[21] The following May, CORE and SNCC activists left Washington, DC, for a bus trip into the Deep South to test compliance with the Court's decision. On May 14, in Anniston and Birmingham, and on May 20, in Montgomery, mobs of Alabama whites wielding chains, pipes, and baseball bats attacked and beat three separate groups of freedom riders. Although local police refused to protect the protesters, Robert Kennedy resisted calls for federal intervention, choosing to work behind the scenes to defuse the crisis. He pressed the Interstate Commerce Commission to issue regulations compelling obedience to the Court's decision. (In November, the commission barred interstate carriers from using segregated terminals, forcing most southern terminals to capitulate.) He also prodded state officials to preserve order, repeatedly urging Governor John Patterson of Alabama to protect the riders and sending aides to Montgomery to confer with Patterson and to monitor the situation.

The Justice Department intervened only when state officials demonstrated that they would not act. On the evening of May 21—after a week of pleading and cajoling—the attorney general finally gave up on state officials when Montgomery police refused to respond as a mob threatened a church where Martin Luther King Jr. spoke in honor of the freedom riders. Fearing bloodshed, department officials deployed one hundred US marshals to hold the angry crowd at bay. Yet this was the exception. As the freedom riders moved into Mississippi, the attorney general, fearing a repetition of events in Alabama, negotiated a deal with state officials. The state agreed to guarantee the safety of the riders on the condition that the Justice Department would not interfere with local prosecution of the young activists. While protected from Mississippi mobs, more than three hundred freedom riders languished in Mississippi jails by summer's end.

Although unsympathetic to direct action, the Kennedys supported the aspirations of African Americans. They believed that equality could be achieved gradually and with a minimum of confrontation if barriers to black voting were destroyed. Like Reconstruction-era Republicans, they contended that once blacks possessed the ballot, state officials would respond to their demands for justice. Thus the rights of blacks could be protected without dramatically altering the federal system or confrontations with state officials. In the bargain, most new black voters would join the Democratic Party and help reverse the steady erosion of Democratic strength in the post–World War II South.

During late 1961 and 1962, administration officials urged civil rights activists to shift their efforts from direct action to voter registration. Justice Department officials participated in a series of meetings that led to the creation of the Voter Education Project, a two-and-one-half-year campaign to register southern blacks that was financed by $870,000 from northern foundations. SCLC, CORE, and NAACP all readily agreed to participate. SNCC leaders were suspicious of cooptation by the administration, but they believed voter registration efforts would raise rights consciousness among rural southern blacks and encourage them to challenge white supremacy.

As the campaign began, the Justice Department itself devoted greater attention to voting rights. Especially in the rural black belt, whites had developed a variety of techniques to keep African Americans politically inactive. Although the literacy rate among blacks had increased dramatically, local officials manipulated literacy tests to deny literate black citizens the right to vote. Often going beyond the letter of state law, they asked African Americans difficult questions about the Constitution and state and local government—questions they never asked whites. In addition, officials developed complex voter registration forms and refused to register blacks (but not whites) who made even minor errors in completing them. Registration boards also foiled blacks' efforts to register by meeting infrequently and irregularly and by not publicizing the hours they were open for business. Officials were only part of the problem. In small towns and rural areas, blacks who attempted to register might be fired, turned off the land they farmed, denied credit by local merchants, or worse. In this climate, few African Americans attempted to register. In 1962, only one-fourth of voting-age southern blacks were registered; in Mississippi the figure stood at 5 percent and in Alabama, 13 percent.

Intent on rooting out these practices, Robert Kennedy dramatically increased the size of the Civil Rights Division staff and directed it to begin wholesale prosecution of voting rights cases. The primary weapons in the campaign were the provisions of the Civil Rights Act of 1957 permitting the Justice Department to seek injunctions against those who prevented citizens from registering or voting. Government lawyers won injunctions barring officials from refusing to register African Americans who made minor mistakes on their applications and from imposing more stringent literacy tests on blacks than on whites. They also challenged private intimidation of blacks by securing injunctions against those who retaliated against African Americans for challenging discriminatory registration practices.

The campaign's results were mixed. In tandem with the Voter Education Project, Justice Department litigation helped increase the proportion of southern black adults who were registered from 26 to 40 percent between 1962 and 1964. Nevertheless, department officials had to proceed county by county, conducting in-depth investigations to establish proof of discrimination or economic coercion. The process was time-consuming and limited the number of localities in which cases could be initiated. Furthermore, the injunctions department attorneys won only ordered individuals to stop a particular practice. Local whites were generally resourceful enough to devise other means to hinder black registration, forcing department lawyers to conduct further investigations and return to court. By the end of 1964, only 7 percent of the black adults residing in the forty-six counties in which the government had initiated suits were registered, and black registration was below 10 percent in one hundred southern counties.

The administration's hope that voter registration would ease tensions produced by the sit-ins and the freedom rides was soon disappointed. SNCC took its voter registration campaign into black belt counties in Georgia and Mississippi, where whites viewed black political empowerment as a dire threat. Predictably, whites launched a campaign of terror designed to drive out SNCC workers and to intimidate local blacks. Although state officials failed to punish the perpetrators of this violence, the Justice Department refused to make arrests or initiate prosecutions, clinging to its position that responsibility for law enforcement lay primarily with state officials. Only in October 1962, when Mississippi officials and an armed mob prevented enforcement of a court order admitting James Meredith to the University of Mississippi, did the administration act forcefully to curb racist violence. As Eisenhower had done in the Little Rock crisis, Kennedy dispatched US marshals and troops to the campus to break resistance to federal authority and to enable Meredith to enroll.

Events in Birmingham during the spring of 1963 finally forced President Kennedy to abandon his cautious approach to civil rights. During the winter of 1962–1963, Martin Luther King Jr. and his closest advisors devised a bold plan for massive demonstrations in Birmingham, the toughest, most segregated city in the South. Invited to the city by the Reverend Fred Shuttlesworth, a fiery activist and co-founder of the SCLC, King knew that he would meet bitter resistance from the police commissioner, Eugene "Bull" Connor, a hard-line segregationist with a short fuse. Connor, who had earned his spurs during the 1930s in a brutal campaign to keep the unions out of Birmingham's steel mills, ruled the city with an iron fist and could be counted on to respond with violence. Consequently, the city offered King an opportunity to focus the nation's attention on the brutality of segregation, to precipitate a crisis that would force the administration off dead-center, and to win a stunning victory that would reinvigorate a sagging civil rights movement. Wyatt Tee Walker, the SCLC staff member who drafted the Birmingham plan, called it "Project C"—for confrontation.

The Birmingham campaign began in early April with a boycott of downtown merchants, sit-ins at segregated lunch counters, and marches on city hall. Connor responded by arresting protesters and obtaining an injunction against further demonstrations, but the protest continued and grew larger after King himself was arrested on April 12. During the remainder of the month, white leaders refused to negotiate, demonstrations and arrests continued, and police brutality increased. King and his lieutenants had won the attention of the national media, but they found it difficult to recruit new demonstrators. Adults with jobs, mortgages, and children to support found the consequences of arrest too great. During the first week in May, the SCLC took the audacious step of recruiting African American children to demonstrate, filling the city's jail and pushing Connor over the edge as more children appeared every day to demonstrate and go to jail. The police commissioner responded to the "children's crusade" by unleashing club-swinging patrolmen, snarling police dogs, and high-pressure water hoses on peaceful demonstrators and bystanders, bruising their bodies, tearing their flesh, breaking their bones, and cracking their heads.

King's strategy worked. As pictures of police brutality appeared on the front pages of newspapers and on TV screens across the nation, civil rights again took center stage, and northern support for national action mounted. The president sent Justice Department mediators to Birmingham to arrange a set-tlement and pressured the city's business elite to compromise. Negotiations began promptly and were successfully concluded on May 10, when King announced that whites had agreed to desegregate lunch counters, drinking fountains, rest rooms, and department store fitting rooms and had pledged to implement a nondiscriminatory hiring program in the city's industries. The victory over Bull Connor emboldened African Americans across the South, touching off more than eight hundred boycotts and demonstrations in two hundred southern towns and cities during the summer of 1963. Birmingham kindled a new assertiveness among blacks, leading them to reject tokenism and to demand fundamental and immediate change.

Figure 6.3. Walter B. Gadsden, a Birmingham, Alabama, high school student, attacked by a police dog, May 3, 1963, during demonstrations against segregation. *Alabama Media Group Collection, Alabama Department of Archives and History.*

Birmingham also forced John Kennedy to make civil rights a top priority—
something that no president since Ulysses Grant had done. He realized
that blacks were no longer willing to wait patiently and feared that unless
sweeping changes were initiated, racial confrontation would tear the nation
apart. Indeed, while King continued to espouse nonviolence, many African
Americans had grown tired of turning the other cheek. On May 11, in response to a wave of racist bombings orchestrated by the Klan and local police,
Birmingham blacks took to the streets, pelting police with rocks and bottles
and burning several white-owned businesses located in the ghetto. Elsewhere,
black writer James Baldwin wrote of *The Fire Next Time*, and Malcom X, the
militant black nationalist who appeared on television more than any other
African American leader in 1963, insisted that "the day of nonviolent resistance is over."[22] Faced with a growing racial crisis and sensing greater support
for action, Kennedy appeared on national television on June 11 to announce
that he was sending sweeping civil rights legislation to Congress. He appealed
to principle, arguing that the nation confronted a moral issue "as old as the
scriptures and . . . as clear as the American Constitution." But he also warned
that the issue could no longer be avoided. "The events in Birmingham and
elsewhere," he suggested, meant that legislation was essential "if we are to
move this problem from the streets to the courts."[23]

The president moved quickly. He submitted legislation strengthening
voting rights laws, authorizing the attorney general to file school desegregation suits, empowering the president to end federal financial assistance to
discriminatory state and local programs, and banning discrimination in employment and places of public accommodation such as motels, restaurants,
theaters, retail stores, and gas stations. Kennedy could count on the votes
of northern Democrats and support from many labor leaders, the major
national Jewish organizations, and liberal groups such as Americans for
Democratic Action. But he needed support from Republican leaders to offset
opposition by southern Democrats and to overcome the inevitable Senate filibuster. The president worked hard to line up Republican support, and when
liberal Democrats jeopardized his efforts by attempting to broaden the bill,
he intervened, convincing liberals to keep amendments to a minimum and
preserving bipartisan support. When an assassin's bullet felled Kennedy in
November 1963, his successor, Lyndon Johnson, made the civil rights bill his
top legislative priority. Strengthening the bipartisan alliance Kennedy had
forged and drawing on his unparalleled knowledge of Senate rules and culture, Johnson secured congressional approval for the bill in June 1964.

The Civil Rights Act of 1964 translated most of the objectives of the early civil rights movement into law, harnessing the principle of equal rights to the engine of federal power. At the heart of the bill lay the goal of banishing segregation from American life, thereby realizing the principle announced ten years earlier in *Brown*. Titles III and IV authorized the attorney general to institute lawsuits challenging discrimination in public schools and other facilities "owned, operated, or managed by or on behalf of any State or subdivision thereof," thus removing from private individuals the entire burden of desegregation. Title VI used the power of the purse to attack discrimination. It directed federal agencies to adopt regulations banning discrimination in all programs receiving federal funds and to cut the flow of federal dollars if they failed to comply. With many state and local governments becoming increasingly dependent on federal largesse, especially to finance public education, this provision offered a potent weapon against discrimination.

The law also set its sights on discrimination in privately owned and operated businesses that served the public. Relying on a broad interpretation of the commerce power bequeathed by the New Deal, Title II prohibited discrimination on account of race, color, religion, or national origin by restaurants, hotels, motels, gas stations, theaters, stadiums, concert halls, or other places of entertainment that "affected" interstate commerce. Although victims of discrimination might institute lawsuits and recover monetary damages, the act's sponsors realized that private citizens might be reluctant to sue. Consequently, they authorized the attorney general to initiate suits against business that violated the act.

The law also attacked employment discrimination, a target of black leaders and congressional liberals since the 1930s. Title VII prohibited discrimination on account of race, color, religion, national origin, or sex by employers and labor unions with more than twenty-five employees or members and by employment agencies. Introduced by a Virginia segregationist to undermine support for the bill, the ban on sex discrimination remained in the bill as finally passed through the efforts of a handful of women in the House. It marked the beginning of an alliance between civil rights advocates and feminists that would blossom in the 1970s and beyond. To assure Title VII's effectiveness, liberals pressed for establishment of an administrative agency to investigate complaints of employment discrimination and issue cease-and-desist orders against violators. Modeled on FDR's wartime FEPC, this approach afforded a far more effective remedy than litigation. To maintain Republican support, however, sponsors accepted weak enforcement provisions. They established a five-member Equal Employment Opportunity Commission (EEOC) and authorized it to investigate complaints of employment discrimination. When it found evidence of discrimination, EEOC's only recourse was to negotiate with the employer or union to end its discriminatory practices. If that failed, the victim of discrimination could go to court or the commission could ask the attorney general to initiate a lawsuit.

With the Civil Rights Act on the books, President Johnson turned to the problem of disfranchisement. As the administration consulted civil rights leaders and prepared new legislation, events in Selma, Alabama, lent greater urgency to the issue. Despite several years of voter registration efforts and Justice Department lawsuits, only 2 percent of the black adults in Dallas County had registered to vote. In January and February 1965, SNCC and SCLC staged massive demonstrations at the county courthouse in Selma to focus attention on the problem. Local officials responded by arresting more than three thousand protesters. On March 7, as five hundred protesters defied a state court injunction and began a march from Selma to the state capitol in Montgomery, some sixty miles away, state police and a mounted posse led by the sheriff moved against them. As the panic-stricken demonstrators fled, they were trampled by horsemen, shocked with electric cattle prods, and beaten with clubs and chains. That evening the television networks interrupted programs—ABC was airing *Judgment at Nuremberg*—to show the attack. The next morning Selma occupied headlines in newspapers across the country. Lyndon Johnson seized the moment, promptly submitting a sweeping voting rights bill to Congress and making a nationally televised speech to demand speedy passage. "It is not just Negroes, but really it is all of us who must overcome the crippling legacy of bigotry and injustice," the president told legislators. After a brief pause, he concluded with the movement's own language: "And we shall overcome."[24] Lawmakers quickly fell into line, completing action on the bill in less than five months.

Cutting through state registration requirements and procedures that purported to be racially neutral, the authors of the Voting Rights Act of 1965 established formulas to identify and effective means to end discrimination. The act set its sights on the literacy test, historically the most notorious disfranchising device. In any state or county where fewer than 50 percent of the adults were registered to vote, the act automatically suspended the operation of any "test or device" that served as a prerequisite for voting. Congress also provided a remedy for other types of discrimination. In counties in which twenty or more residents filed complaints of or the attorney general initiated a voting discrimination case, federal examiners would be appointed to register voters. Moreover, lawmakers attempted to prevent southern officials from developing new techniques of discrimination. States and localities covered by the act were required to obtain preclearance from the attorney general or a three-judge district court in Washington, DC, before implementing any new voting requirements or procedures.

After years of temporizing, the president and Congress had finally acted boldly, drawing on the deep reservoirs of federal power to promote equality. The Supreme Court quickly gave its blessing. In two 1964 cases, *Heart of Atlanta Motel v. United States* and *Katzenbach v. McClung*, the Court considered the Civil Rights Act's ban on discrimination by motels and restaurants. Drawing on a long line of cases that gave Congress broad authority to regulate businesses affecting interstate commerce, the Court unanimously upheld the statute. The *McClung* case emphasized the breadth of Congress's authority. The business involved, Ollie's Barbeque, was a small Birmingham restaurant that served a local clientele. The Court noted that Ollie's came within the scope of the law because it was open to interstate customers and because some part of the food it sold had moved in interstate commerce. Moreover, it ruled that Congress had "a rational basis" for believing that such businesses affected interstate commerce and for subjecting them to regulation. They not only purchased food and other goods from interstate suppliers, but their discriminatory policies made interstate travel by African Americans difficult.[25]

Two years later, in *South Carolina v. Katzenbach* (1966), the Court gave its blessing to the Voting Rights Act. Chief Justice Warren emphasized that in enforcing the Fifteenth Amendment, Congress was free to choose the means best suited to eliminate racial discrimination in voting. Surveying the provisions adopted by Congress—suspension of literacy tests, appointment of federal examiners, and judicial supervision of changes in voting procedures—he concluded that they were clearly designed to meet problems that Congress had encountered in its long struggle to overcome state and local officials' ingenious and persistent efforts to deny African Americans the right to vote. Consequently, while the act represented an unprecedented exercise of federal power, it did not exceed Congress's authority to enforce the Fifteenth Amendment.[26]

The Court not only sustained the Voting Rights Act but went where Congress had feared to tread and struck down the poll tax. This device was a far less serious obstacle to African American voting than discriminatory administration of literacy tests; by 1960, all but four states—Virginia, Alabama, Mississippi, and Texas—had repealed it. Nevertheless, in those states it deterred the very poor from voting and had a disproportionate effect on African Americans. Anti–poll tax legislation had long received strong support on Capitol Hill, and in 1962 Congress had passed the Twenty-fourth Amendment (which was ratified two years later) banning the poll tax as a requirement for voting in *federal* elections. Although liberals made a strong effort to extend the prohibition to state elections in the Voting Rights Act, doubts about its constitutionality torpedoed their effort. Opponents argued that, unlike literacy tests, which were administered in a discriminatory fashion, the poll tax was applied to whites and blacks alike and therefore did not violate the Fifteenth Amendment. One year later, however, the Supreme Court gave opponents of the poll tax the outright victory that had eluded them for decades. In *Harper v. Virginia Board of Elections* (1966), the Court ruled the tax unconstitutional, resting its decision on the Fourteenth rather than the Fifteenth Amendment. Writing for the majority, Justice Douglas asserted that the poll tax discriminated against the poor and thus violated the equal protection clause.[27]

The Court also expanded the government's authority to punish anti–civil rights violence. By early 1965, growing northern outrage over violence against civil rights workers convinced the Justice Department to initiate prosecutions in several highly publicized cases of racist violence. Because the federal system gave states primary responsibility for criminal justice, crimes such as assault and murder were state, not federal, offenses. There were, however, Reconstruction-era federal statutes that punished persons who deprived others of their civil rights, and it was these that federal prosecutors employed. Justice Department officials relied on Title 18, section 241 of the *United States Code*, which had been adopted as part of the Enforcement Act of 1870 and punished persons who conspired to use force or intimidation to prevent anyone from exercising rights secured by the Constitution or laws of the United States.

Although the law appeared adequate to the task, many questioned whether it could be used to prosecute perpetrators of racist violence. First, many lawyers and scholars doubted whether the rights protected by section 241 included Fourteenth Amendment rights of equal protection and due process. In 1951, the Court had divided 4–4 on the question: four justices held that section 241 covered denials of equal protection and due process, four (led by Justice Frankfurter) insisted that it did not, and one wrote a concurring opinion that ignored the issue altogether. Writing for the four-member plurality, Frankfurter maintained that rights mentioned in section 241 were limited to those created by the Constitution (such as the right to vote in *federal* elections), not rights that government was prohibited from violating (such as the Fourteenth Amendment rights of equal protection and due process and the rights mentioned in the Bill of Rights). Otherwise, Frankfurter believed, the federal government would have carte blanche to usurp law enforcement activities that properly belonged to the states. Although Frankfurter's opinion did not represent a majority and was not binding, it cast a shadow over the government's authority to prosecute perpetrators of racist violence on grounds that they denied their victims equal protection or due process.[28] In addition, many observers believed that the state action rule precluded prosecution of private citizens under section 241. Given the long line of Supreme Court rulings that held that the Fourteenth Amendment authorized Congress to provide remedies against state, but not private, denials of equal protection and due process, many doubted that section 241 could be employed against private citizens, even if it were interpreted to protect Fourteenth Amendment rights. Although the Court had whittled away at the state action limitation on the Fourteenth Amendment, it had not abandoned it, as *Heart of Atlanta Motel* and *McClung* had suggested.

Two 1966 rulings swept these doubts aside. In *United States v. Price*, which involved the prosecution of eighteen whites implicated in the cold-blooded murder of three civil rights workers in Neshoba County, Mississippi, the Court ruled that section 241 protected Fourteenth Amendment rights. Justice Abe Fortas pointed out that section 241 had its origins in Reconstruction legislation (the 1870 Enforcement Act) designed to enforce the guarantees of the Fourteenth and Fifteenth Amendments. "In this context," he concluded, "it is hardly conceivable that Congress intended [it] . . . to apply only to a narrow and relatively unimportant category of rights." Unquestionably, its "purpose and effect" was "to reach assaults upon rights under the entire Constitution . . . not merely under part of it."[29]

In a companion case, *United States v. Guest*, the Supreme Court considered whether Congress could punish private as well as state interference with Fourteenth Amendment rights. Although Justice Potter Stewart's opinion for the Court ducked the issue, concurring opinions by Justices William Brennan and Tom Clark (which were joined by six justices) were much bolder. Challenging the limitations imposed on Congress in the *Civil Rights Cases* (1883), Justice Brennan insisted that Congress enjoyed broad power to enforce the amendment's guarantees. "Section 5 [of the Fourteenth Amendment] authorizes Congress to make laws that it concludes are reasonably necessary to protect a right created by . . . that Amendment," he wrote, "and Congress is thus fully empowered to determine that punishment of private conspiracies interfering with the exercise of such a right is necessary to its full protection." In short, Brennan concluded, Congress is authorized "to exercise its discretion in fashioning remedies to achieve civil and political equality for all citizens."[30]

The *Price* and *Guest* cases did not bury the state action rule. They suggested that Congress's authority to enforce the amendment (expressly conferred in section 5) gave it broad discretion to strike at state and private action. Yet the justices did not claim such authority for themselves. When the Court enforced the equal protection clause (rather than congressional legislation), it would still require the presence of state action to prohibit discrimination. Nevertheless, *Guest* and *Price* gave the government the authority necessary to prosecute anti–civil rights violence. In 1966 and 1967, government lawyers used the newly reinvigorated section 241 to win convictions in several of the most brutal cases of violence against African Americans and civil rights workers. More important, the decisions unshackled Congress from the state action theory, offering it greater authority to protect individual rights. Lawmakers promptly took advantage of the Court's largesse. In Title I of the Civil Rights Act of 1968 they established a much clearer definition of federally protected civil rights than did the maddeningly vague section 241. Additionally, they gave the attorney general broad authority to prosecute anyone who used force or intimidation to interfere with these rights.

Consolidation, Expansion, and Opposition, 1965–1969

After a decade of frustration, civil rights advocates had scored major victories, dramatically expanding federal civil rights authority and establishing effective remedies against discrimination. With Lyndon Johnson in the White House, the government moved swiftly and surely, using the new legislation to destroy Jim Crow. Faced with the threat of lawsuit, most public facilities and private businesses covered by the public accommodations provisions of the Civil Rights Act of 1964 opened their doors to African Americans. Those that refused faced Justice Department lawyers who were determined to compel obedience. When it received complaints of discrimination, the department warned offenders that their practices were illegal and, if the warnings failed, took them to court. By 1968 the attorney general reported "widespread voluntary compliance" with the public accommodations section of the 1964 act and that most of the complaints that the department received involved "small eating establishments in the more rural areas." By the end of the decade, most white southerners grudgingly accepted what a few years earlier they had viewed as intolerable—blacks and whites eating in the same restaurants, attending the same theaters and ball parks, and staying in the same motels.[31]

The problem of school segregation proved tougher to resolve, but by the end of the decade the executive and judicial branches, working together, had transformed the face of southern education. In 1964, a decade after *Brown*, only 2 percent of the black children living in the states of the former Confederacy attended school with whites. Officials in the Department of Health, Education and Welfare (HEW) promptly invoked their authority under the Civil Rights Act to compel desegregation. In December 1964 they informed southern school officials that they must submit desegregation plans to remain eligible for federal funds, and four months later, issued guidelines for schools to follow in drafting plans. Almost 95 percent of southern school districts responded, with most adopting so-called freedom of choice plans. Ostensibly these plans were color-blind, offering students the opportunity to attend the school of their choice. In reality, however, they were designed to minimize integration. Whites almost never chose to send their children to black schools, and many African Americans, fearing reprisals by employers and merchants, kept their children in all-black schools. White officials did their best to deter African Americans from entering white schools as well. Frequently they required black parents and children to appear in person to apply for transfers to white schools, informed black parents that buses serving the white school did not run through the black section of town, warned black children that they would not be permitted to join the band, school clubs, or athletic teams, and turned away black applicants on the grounds that the white schools were too crowded.

Although these plans offered little actual freedom of choice, they did produce some integration in most southern districts. Moreover, HEW soon indicated that freedom of choice plans, by themselves, were not enough. Faced with southern whites' use of race-neutral policies to preserve segregation, it issued new guidelines stipulating that districts would be judged on their actual progress toward desegregation and requiring them to establish goals and timetables to speed up the process.

The federal courts reinforced HEW policy, signaling to school officials that even if they chose to forgo federal money (which amounted to almost 10 percent of their funding by 1966), efforts to perpetuate segregation would not fly. In December 1966, Judge John Minor Wisdom of the US Court of Appeals for the Fifth Circuit shocked southern school officials with his landmark opinion in *United States v. Jefferson County Board of Education.* Wisdom not only endorsed the HEW guidelines and directed all judges in the fifth circuit to follow them, but he also announced that compliance with the guidelines was the first step on the road to full integration. The Louisiana native acknowledged that the Constitution prohibited discrimination but did not mandate integration. He held, however, that where segregation had been imposed by law, officials had a responsibility to take positive action to undo the results of their unconstitutional behavior. And that meant integration. "*The only adequate redress for a previously overt system-wide policy of segregation directed at Negroes as a collective entity,*" he asserted, "*is a system-wide policy of integration.*" Although Wisdom did not disallow freedom of choice plans, he emphasized that district judges should accept them only if they led to integration:

> What the decree contemplates, then, is continuing judicial evaluation of compliance by measuring the performance—not merely the promised performance—of school boards in carrying out their constitutional obligation "to disestablish dual, racially segregated school systems and *to achieve substantial integration in such systems*" [emphasis added]. . . . If school officials in any district should find that their district still has segregated faculties or schools *or only token integration* [emphasis added], their affirmative duty to take corrective action requires them to try an alternative to a freedom of choice plan, such as a geographic attendance plan . . . or some other acceptable substitute.[32]

Wisdom's opinion—which was endorsed by the twelve judges of the US Court of Appeals for the Fifth Circuit sitting en banc—was significant. Written as a directive to judges throughout the circuit, it would guide the process of school desegregation in most of the Deep South. Consequently, the decision signaled that school districts must comply with HEW's demands and could not hide behind policies that appeared color-blind on their face but preserved segregation. They would be pushed relentlessly to integrate. Wisdom's *Jefferson County* opinion also indicated a major shift in the federal courts' approach to civil rights law. Rejecting the notion that the Fourteenth Amendment merely required states to cease discriminating, it announced a result-oriented interpretation of the equal protection clause. In those places in which segregation had been imposed by law and public policy, race-neutral policies would perpetuate the effects of segregation. In these states and communities, officials had a legal obligation to take affirmative action to dismantle the effects of their unconstitutional actions and wipe the slate clean by achieving integration. *Jefferson County* also signaled a shift to color-consciousness. Although Wisdom acknowledged that the equal protection clause aimed to create color-blind public policy, he suggested that the courts must take color into account (e.g., measuring the degree of racial balance in schools) to root out the effects of past discrimination and achieve genuine equality.

Less than two years later, in *Green v. County School Board* (1968) the US Supreme Court endorsed Wisdom's approach. The case involved a challenge to a freedom of choice plan in a largely rural Virginia county whose population divided equally between whites and blacks. The county had operated two schools, a white school on the east side and a black school on the west side. Despite little residential segregation in the county and the freedom of choice plan—which permitted children to choose either school—no whites had elected to attend the black school and only 15 percent of African Americans had entered the formerly all-white school. The Court declared the county's desegregation efforts inadequate. *Brown II*, Justice Brennan pointed out, required school officials in states and localities where segregation had been established by law "to effectuate a transition to a racially nondiscriminatory school system." This meant that they were "clearly charged with the affirmative duty to take whatever steps might be necessary to convert to a unitary system in which racial discrimination would be eliminated root and branch." With 85 percent of its black children still in all-black schools, Brennan concluded, the county had failed to meet that requirement. "The burden on a school board today," he asserted, "is to come forward with a plan that promises realistically to work, and promises realistically to work *now*." The message was clear. Formerly segregated school districts had the obligation to integrate promptly, and the Court would look carefully at the racial balance in the schools to determine whether they had met their obligation.[33]

Confronting HEW guidelines that annually grew more stringent, an increasing number of Justice Department lawsuits, and courts that demanded results, southern school districts capitulated. In 1968,

18 percent of southern black pupils were attending white majority schools; two years later the figure stood at 39 percent, and in 1972, it had risen to 46 percent, making southern schools the most integrated in the nation. (In 1972 only 28 percent of black pupils in the North and West were enrolled in white-majority schools.) Desegregation gave southern black children access to better schools and improved their educational performance. That was not the only benefit, however. "As long as schools were segregated by law, southern blacks lived in a society whose public authority defined them as inferior and where, for them, democratic principles were a mockery," notes historian Allen Matusow.[34]

The Johnson administration also moved forcefully against voting discrimination. Under the Voting Rights Act, literacy tests were suspended in six states—Virginia, South Carolina, Georgia, Alabama, Mississippi, and Louisiana—and in parts of North Carolina. While this eliminated the most potent disfranchising device, many officials continued to employ dilatory tactics to prevent blacks from registering. To overcome this resistance, the Justice Department dispatched federal registrars to fifty-eight counties between 1965 and 1968. Civil rights activists pressed for appointment of more registrars, pointing out that they had been sent to only a third of the counties in which fewer than half of the adult African Americans were registered. Nevertheless, the presence of federal registrars not only ended disfranchisement in the counties in which they operated, but convinced officials in neighboring counties to register blacks to avoid federal intervention.

The results of the campaign were impressive. Between 1964 and 1969, voter registration increased from 36 to 65 percent of African American adults in the region. In Mississippi, where only 7 percent of adult blacks had been registered in 1964, the figure rose to 67 percent by 1969. Moreover, black voting quickly produced significant results. By 1968, in the five states in which federal registrars had been deployed (South Carolina, Georgia, Alabama, Mississippi, and Louisiana), more than 120 blacks had won elective office. Granted, most of these served in county and municipal government, but their success marked a dramatic departure in a region in which blacks had not been permitted to vote, much less hold office, for more than seventy years. Nevertheless, blacks were minorities in every southern state, and most whites continued to follow the color line in politics. Consequently, African American candidates could reasonably expect success only if they ran in black-majority or near-black-majority districts. And this meant that they had little chance of victory in statewide contests or in most local elections.

African American voting, however, was not in vain. Even in districts with black minorities, African American voters frequently held the balance of power and could defeat openly racist office seekers. Consequently, white politicians soon learned that appeals to racism were likely to backfire and largely abandoned the scurrilous race-baiting that had been a staple of southern politics. This opened the way for a new generation of moderate white politicians such as Jimmy Carter, Reubin Askew, Ernest Hollings, and Dale Bumpers who emerged in the 1970s, and ultimately convinced even the formerly staunch segregationist George Wallace to court black voters. Furthermore, most white elected officials, aware of the growing power of black voters, became more responsive to them. Dr. John Cashin, the head of Alabama's all-black National Democratic Party, noted that black voting had an especially salutary effect on law enforcement. "It's no longer standard operating procedure for whites to kill blacks at will," he explained in 1973. "And it's all because of politics."[35] Although southern blacks had a long way to go if they were to exercise effective political power, the Voting Rights Act radically altered southern politics and government.

The late 1960s witnessed the demise of disfranchisement and Jim Crow, bringing a campaign by three generations of black activists to a successful conclusion. As important as this victory was, however, it highlighted how much remained to be done. Because of discrimination by employers and labor unions and low levels of educational achievement, far too many blacks were stuck in menial, poorly paying jobs or were chronically unemployed. Trapped in poverty, with little hope of improving their lot, they attached little importance to the right to vote or to be served in restaurants they could not afford. Poverty, combined with the practices of banks, realtors, and city and suburban governments, guaranteed that urban blacks remained in the nation's decaying inner cities. There they lived in substandard housing owned by landlords who often extracted exorbitant rents from a captive market. Furthermore, residential segregation meant that black children attended segregated schools. In 1962, for example, two-thirds of the black students in Gary, Indiana were enrolled in schools that were at least 99 percent black. Predictably, these schools were more crowded, less modern, and less conducive to learning than predominantly white schools.

These problems were by no means exclusively southern. Indeed, they were perhaps most acute in northern cities. Consequently, as the 1960s progressed, national civil rights leaders focused increased attention on the North. In the process, they shattered the complacency of many whites who considered racism a southern problem. During the 1950s and early 1960s, CORE and black community organizations in cities large and small boycotted segregated schools, picketed segregated housing projects and businesses guilty of employment discrimination, and staged rent strikes to force landlords to bring their buildings up to standards mandated by city codes. In 1966, with black activism growing in northern cities, Martin Luther King Jr. focused national attention on the racial problems of the North by going to Chicago, where he led a massive campaign against housing discrimination. There, King's marchers met mobs of virulently racist whites—some waving Confederate flags and wearing Nazi helmets—determined to keep blacks in the ghetto. These white mobs were backed by Mayor Richard Daley, head of the most powerful political machine in the nation. King left Chicago after nine months with little to show for his efforts, merely confirming what those who had been in the trenches already knew: the problems that existed in the North would be even more difficult to solve than those the movement had encountered in Birmingham and Selma.

Deadly uprisings erupted like clockwork during the long, hot summers of the mid- and late 1960s, shifting public attention to the urban North. Beginning in Harlem in 1964 and Watts the following summer, uprisings swept 43 cities in 1966 and 164 urban areas in 1967. Frustrated by the contradiction between the promise of the civil rights movement, the resistance of local officials to their demands, and the hopelessness of their situation, urban blacks unleashed the rage produced by three centuries of oppression. They struck at the most visible symbols of white domination: policemen who treated African Americans disrespectfully and too often employed unnecessary force and white-owned ghetto businesses that preyed on poor customers who had few options. And they struck hard. In the Watts neighborhood of Los Angeles, the uprising lasted for four days and left 34 dead, more than 1,000 injured, and almost 1,000 buildings damaged or destroyed. Three years later, in Detroit, the toll was even worse: 43 persons died, well over 1,000 were injured, and 1,300 buildings were burned.

Although the causes of northern blacks' dissatisfaction—poverty, employment discrimination, police brutality, and segregated schools and housing—were obvious, solutions proved elusive. The Civil Rights Act of 1964 created the EEOC to supervise implementation of a nationwide ban on discrimination by employers and labor unions with at least twenty-five employees or members. Although the 41,000 complaints brought between 1965 and 1969 suggest broad awareness of the law's provisions, the commission's small

Figure 6.4. Fires from burning buildings on Detroit's West Side light up the early morning sky on July 24, 1967. *Walter P. Reuther Library, Archives of Labor and Urban Affairs, Wayne State University.*

staff proved inadequate to the task at hand. By 1969, it had determined that 24,000 of the complaints had merit, but had completed investigations in only 18,000 of these, leaving a backlog of 6,000 cases. After the staff completed its investigation, cases went to the five-member commission, which determined whether the evidence showed that a violation had occurred and then drafted its decision. A critical bottleneck developed at this point. By 1969, the commission had written decisions in only 4,800 cases (finding for the complainants in 2,500) and was taking an average of eighteen to twenty months to resolve each case. This not only delayed relief for complainants, but meant that many cases had become moot by the time decisions were announced.

Another problem was lack of enforcement authority. If it found reasonable cause that discrimination had occurred, the commission could attempt to resolve the case through negotiation. If that failed, it had two options: advise the complainant that he or she could sue or, if the case revealed a widespread pattern of discrimination, request the Justice Department to initiate litigation. With the threat of sanctions remote, EEOC staff enjoyed little success in arranging voluntary settlements with employers. By 1969, it had attempted to settle 3,360 cases, but succeeded in only 683 cases affecting 14,000 persons.

The other major federal employment discrimination program accomplished even less. In September 1965, President Johnson issued Executive Order 11246, prohibiting job discrimination by firms that supplied goods or services to the federal government or held federal construction contracts. The order authorized the secretary of labor to establish regulations outlining fair employment practices and to terminate contracts with employers who failed to comply. Because companies holding government contracts employed an estimated one-third of the workforce, vigorous enforcement promised substantial results. After issuing the order, however, the administration—increasingly preoccupied with the Vietnam War and reluctant to ruffle the feathers of politicians, businessmen, and labor leaders—quickly forgot it. The Office of Federal Contract Compliance (OFCC), created by the Labor Department to oversee enforcement, was poorly staffed and lethargic. It failed to draft clear guidelines for government agencies to follow in dealing with contractors and imposed no sanctions until May 1968.

Although the federal attack on job discrimination was weak, it achieved some modest gains. EEOC won redress for several thousand victims of discrimination and began to attack systemic forms of discrimination. Tests that measured educational achievement created barriers for many African Americans (who for decades had endured Jim Crow schools), so the commission began a campaign against the use of employment tests that measured knowledge or skills not directly relevant to the job. The commission's effort would bear fruit in the 1970s. While the Justice Department initiated few job discrimination suits, it won several major victories in the lower federal courts, invalidating seniority systems that perpetuated the effects of earlier discriminatory practices common among unions in the construction industry. Moreover, evidence of employment discrimination publicized by the civil rights movement and the EEOC helped raise consciousness about the issue and alter public opinion. A 1968 poll, conducted in fifteen cities, for example, indicated that only 23 percent of those interviewed opposed enforcement of equal employment laws.

Although labor shortages and rapid economic growth played an important role, changes in public opinion and the presence of legal sanctions against discrimination helped African American workers score steady gains during the 1960s and early 1970s. The percentage of African Americans employed as managers, professionals, and skilled workers almost doubled between 1958 and 1973, while the proportion engaged in service work and farm and nonfarm labor declined by one-third. Black women experienced especially dramatic changes during these years; the proportion working as domestic servants decreased from 33 to 15 percent, while the proportion employed in clerical, sales, and professional jobs increased from 19 to 40 percent. Black workers also saw gains in income. In 1959, black men, on average, earned only 53 percent as much as white men; by 1971, they earned 66 percent as much as whites. During the same period, the income of African American women also increased, moving from 66 percent to 90 percent of the earnings of white women—whose earnings were only 65 percent of white men's. Racism and sexism had forged a job market segmented by race and gender, consigning African Americans and women to low-paying employment. While the civil rights movement challenged racial segmentation, opening new opportunities for African American men, the barriers women faced were deeply entrenched and would be eroded only by the successes of the feminist movement in the 1970s.

Impressive as they appear, these gains should not be exaggerated. African Americans who became managers, professionals, and skilled workers generally made it to the lowest rungs of those categories. In the professions, African Americans were concentrated in teaching and social work rather than in the more highly remunerative fields of law and medicine. For those trapped in the ghettos who lacked the education, skills, and hope necessary to take advantage of a more favorable job market, little changed. They still worked at menial jobs, suffered high rates of unemployment, and often left the job market altogether. The result was broken families, substance abuse, and crime, problems barely touched by laws guaranteeing equality of opportunity.

Aware that poverty and civil rights were intertwined, President Johnson declared war on poverty in his 1964 State of the Union address. Convinced that the most prosperous nation in history must open opportunity to all its citizens, he methodically pushed landmark legislation through Congress with the deft touch he used to win passage of major civil rights legislation. His Great Society program funded federal programs to provide food, medical, and housing assistance to the poor; offer job training to the unemployed; improve educational achievement among children from poor families; and support formation of community organizations that encouraged the poor to advocate for themselves and shape the policies of government agencies that served them.

African American women did not need Johnson's Great Society to encourage them to organize, although its community action program facilitated the process. The everyday humiliation experienced by single mothers supported by Aid to Families with Dependent Children (AFDC), the nation's principal welfare program, proved sufficient. Created as part of the Social Security Act of 1935, AFDC provided monthly payments to support children whose fathers had died or abandoned their families. The federal government provided matching payments to states that established levels of support and set rules for eligibility. Given high rates of unemployment among African Americans in the urban North and the rural South, black women and children were overrepresented among AFDC recipients in the decades following World War II. As the proportion of African American beneficiaries grew, monthly payments declined—even as payments to the blind, disabled, and elderly increased—and eligibility requirements became more stringent. These reflected an assumption, widespread among whites, that beneficiaries were lazy, immoral, undeserving, and needed watching: case workers who inspected homes and dispensed advice could cut off support if they found evidence of a man in the house or determined that recipients did not keep a "suitable home."

Stingy monthly payments that made it hard to put food on the table, arbitrary and degrading rules, and racist case workers sparked grass-roots organizing by black women in cities across the United States in the late 1950s and early 1960s. With the support of ministers and middle-class antipoverty activists, these groups protested cuts in welfare budgets, capricious policies, and humiliating treatment by case workers and welfare department functionaries. They also assisted individuals whose payments had been terminated and challenged case workers' decisions about eligibility. In the process, they "came to believe that they should not have to be humiliated to receive a welfare check . . . and that they had rights that ought to be protected," notes historian Premilla Nadasen.[36]

Leaders of local organizations such as Johnnie Tillmon, founder of Aid to Needy Children in Los Angeles, and Jeanette Washington, a leader of New York's Westside Welfare Recipients League, also sought a national voice. Along with representatives of more than twenty local welfare rights organizations, they gathered in Chicago in 1966 to form the National Welfare Rights Organization (NWRO). While it did not supplant the work of local organizations, NWRO became a powerful force and shaped the conversation about poverty policy in the late 1960s and beyond. It helped win important victories that increased monthly benefits, established welfare as a right that could not be terminated without due process, curbed case workers' authority to investigate recipients' private lives, ended the "man-in-the-house" policy, and forced discussion of a guaranteed annual income.

Poverty and the problems faced by the poor attracted even more attention in the wake of urban uprisings that shook the nation's cities in the mid-1960s. After violence again erupted across the nation in the summer of 1967, Johnson appointed a commission headed by Illinois governor Otto Kerner to investigate the causes and make recommendations about how to prevent them. "The criminals who committed these acts of violence against the people deserve to be punished," Johnson asserted as he announced the commission. But he also stressed that "the only genuine, long range solution for what happened lies in an attack on . . . discrimination, slums, poverty, disease, not enough jobs."[37] After an exhaustive investigation, the Kerner Commission delivered its report in February 1968. Noting that "our nation is moving toward two societies, one black, one white—separate and unequal," the body made a bold set of recommendations to address the underlying causes of the uprisings. [38] These included creating one million public sector jobs within three years; constructing six million units of low- and moderate-income housing within five years; desegregating urban schools; increasing support for early childhood education; assuring that welfare benefits were at least equal to the poverty level; passing legislation to end housing discrimination; and a taking steps to improve relations between law enforcement and minority communities. The report met with great fanfare; it was covered widely in the press, and the Government Printing Office sold 740,000 copies within two weeks of its release. Nevertheless, it exercised little influence on public policy. Confronting budget deficits, rising inflation, defeat in Vietnam, and growing criticism from the right and left, Johnson offered only tepid support. And Congress showed little appetite for the bold initiatives the commission proposed.

If politicians shied away from tackling the problem, civil rights leaders demanded action to address the intertwined issues of race and class. Few attracted more attention to the issue than Martin Luther King Jr. Deeply disturbed by a war in Vietnam that he considered immoral and concerned that it siphoned resources from the War on Poverty, in 1967 King called for US withdrawal from Southeast Asia and a domestic Marshall Plan that would guarantee economic justice to African Americans. Anticipating much of what would appear in the Kerner Commission report, he advocated a guaranteed annual income, preferential hiring practices to compensate for centuries of discrimination against African Americans, and construction of a half million units of low-income housing annually. To assure that the president and Congress understood the urgency of the situation, King began planning a Poor People's March. The women who led the NWRO helped King, a middle-class black preacher, better understand the problems faced by African American women and children who struggled with poverty and the oppressive welfare system. Their support enabled King and his lieutenants to mobilize tens of thousands of poor people for a march on Washington that would show the nation and its leaders the face of poverty and promote militant civil disobedience to compel action.

While planning the march, King went to Memphis, Tennessee, in April 1968 to show solidarity with African American sanitation workers whose strike for decent wages and working conditions embodied the campaign for economic justice that he was about to take to the Capitol. Gunned down by a sniper on April 4, King did not live to lead the march. His murder ignited renewed rage in African American communities across the nation. Uprisings erupted in 130 cities, resulting in property destruction estimated at $100 million, 20,000 arrests, and deployment of 130,000 troops. With the nation shaken by yet another series of uprisings, the march went forward in May as a tribute to the slain civil rights leader. However, it was met with indifference or outright hostility by Johnson and many members of Congress, beset by internal conflict, and unsuccessful in winning a hearing for an Economic Bill of Rights.

Like poverty, northern school segregation proved an elusive target. In northern cities, residential segregation bred highly segregated neighborhood schools. Observers labeled the outcome de facto segregation to distinguish it from the South's legally imposed, or de jure segregation. The label was misleading. Northern school officials themselves often played a role in creating segregated schools by developing student transfer policies, drawing school attendance zones, locating new schools, and assigning faculty with an eye toward keeping black and white children separate. The federal courts generally refused to challenge de facto segregation, ruling that the Fourteenth Amendment did not require integration but merely prohibited public officials from segregating students on the basis of race. Even when the federal courts began to require southern schools to integrate, little changed in the

North. Federal judges pointed out that southern schools were obligated to integrate to correct wrongs that resulted from de jure segregation, but that this obligation did not extend to northern schools, where segregation seemed to be the result of residential patterns rather than state law. Although some courts did order desegregation when plaintiffs proved that school officials had adopted policies intended to encourage segregation, this requirement created a heavy burden and made northern school suits difficult to win. Moreover, until 1973 the Supreme Court remained silent, offering no encouragement to opponents of de facto segregation.

Because residential segregation contributed to school segregation and trapped blacks in economically depressed inner-city neighborhoods, federal fair housing legislation became a high priority for civil rights leaders. In 1966, as Martin Luther King's Chicago campaign focused attention on the consequences of housing discrimination, President Johnson recommended a fair housing bill. Liberals eagerly supported the bill, but it encountered rough sailing as many northern legislators joined southerners in opposition. As long as discrimination had been as open, obvious, brutal—and remote—as that practiced in the South, many northerners had supported legislation to eradicate it. Housing discrimination in the North, however, was another matter. As King's reception in Chicago suggested, many northern whites, who had fled their old neighborhoods when blacks had entered or who feared that integration would lower the value of their property, bitterly opposed open housing legislation. Consequently, Congress stalled for two years before passing a weak bill in 1968—the only action it took to adopt recommendations from the Kerner Commission.

The new legislation applied to more than 80 percent of the nation's housing stock. When it became fully operational in December 1969, the law banned discrimination on account of race, religion, or national origin in the sale or rental of most apartments and homes. The only dwellings excepted were single-family homes sold or rented without the assistance of a realtor and small apartment buildings with resident owners. The law also prohibited discriminatory lending practices by banks. Unfortunately, its enforcement provisions were as weak as its coverage was broad. Instead of creating an enforcement agency with authority to issue cease-and-desist orders, the act empowered the Department of Housing and Urban Development to investigate complaints and to negotiate voluntary agreements with those found guilty of discrimination. If this conciliatory approach failed, the attorney general was authorized to bring lawsuits in cases that revealed broad patterns of discrimination. Otherwise, individual victims of discrimination would have to initiate their own lawsuits—an expensive and time-consuming process that could drag on for years. Not surprisingly, the fair housing law did little to alleviate the problem of housing discrimination. Because it failed to afford timely redress, victims of discrimination considered it unhelpful and filed fewer than 1,500 complaints during its first two years of operation.

At the same time that Congress passed the Fair Housing Act, the Supreme Court addressed the issue in its landmark decision in *Jones v. Alfred H. Mayer Co.* (1968). The case involved a suit brought by an African American couple against a St. Louis real estate developer under Title 42, section 1982 of the United States Code. Originally enacted as part of the Civil Rights Act of 1866, section 1982 provided all citizens the same right "as is enjoyed by white citizens . . . to inherit, purchase, lease, sell, hold, or convey real and personal property." The Court rejected Mayer's contention that the statute had been aimed solely at state-enacted black codes and did not apply to private action. Justice Potter Stewart held that Congress, under the Thirteenth Amendment (which contained no state action limitation), had intended to erase all badges of servitude, whether imposed by state law or by private action. Moreover, he concluded that Congress had been fully justified in prohibiting discrimination in the sale of real estate. "At the very least, the freedom that Congress is empowered to secure under the Thirteenth Amendment includes the freedom to buy whatever a white man can buy, the right to live wherever a white man can live," Stewart wrote. "If Congress cannot say that being a free man means at least this much, then the Thirteenth Amendment made a promise the Nation cannot keep."[39]

Although the ruling required victims of housing discrimination to go to court to win redress, it was significant nonetheless. It applied to all housing, even units not covered by the housing act. In addition, *Jones* suggested that the Court would take a broader view of the Reconstruction amendments and federal civil rights laws, offering civil rights lawyers a wider array of weapons against private discrimination. For example, section 1981, also originally enacted as part of the Civil Rights Act of 1866, provided that all persons "shall have the same right . . . to make and enforce contracts . . . as is enjoyed by white persons." Under the *Jones* precedent, persons who were denied employment or admission to private schools because of their race could seek damages under section 1981, claiming that they had been denied the same rights as white persons to make contracts.[40] Although the Civil Rights Act of 1964 offered remedies against employment discrimination, suits under section 1981 could still prove useful. They could be initiated without first going through the EEOC complaint process, and they offered victims of discrimination monetary damages not available under the 1964 act.

Even as the Court became bolder, enthusiasm for civil rights among northern whites waned. Indeed, by the late 1960s, many commentators spoke of a "white backlash." As the movement tackled discrimination in education, employment, and housing rampant in the North, many whites decided that change had gone far enough. They reacted strongly against black militants who rejected nonviolence, advocated Black Power, charged that America was racist to the core, and claimed that achieving meaningful change by working through the system was impossible. And they responded with disbelief and anger when the nation's inner cities burned. Oblivious to the ways in which racism continued to permeate their own assumptions as well as political, legal, educational, and economic institutions and practices, many whites believed that the victories of the 1960s guaranteed African Americans the same rights whites possessed. Blacks should be grateful, they asserted, and take advantage of the opportunities now open to them rather than dwell on the past.

As many northern whites soured on civil rights and reacted viscerally against white students who burned draft cards and American flags to protest the Vietnam War, many who had voted for John Kennedy and Lyndon Johnson threw their support to flag-waving conservatives who promised to restore law and order and asserted that individual initiative was the best anti-poverty program. In the 1966 congressional campaign, Republicans picked up forty-seven House seats, while Ronald Reagan, the new darling of the Republican right, won the California gubernatorial election in a landslide. Two years later, the liberals' old nemesis, Richard M. Nixon, captured the White House, by wooing southern whites, promising to restore law and order, and pledging to secure peace with honor in Vietnam.

By 1969, as liberals lost control of the presidency, civil rights advocates had cause for alarm. Granted, the 1960s had witnessed unprecedented advances: the destruction of the South's deeply entrenched system of Jim Crow and disfranchisement; a dramatic expansion of federal power to protect civil rights; a growing assertiveness and political sophistication among African Americans that ensured continued pressure for advances in civil rights; and an altered national consciousness that made it difficult for political leaders to ignore civil rights. Nevertheless, difficult, perhaps intractable, problems remained. Yet for many whites these problems were less visible and seemed less pressing than the blatant discrimination and brutality that the civil rights movement had challenged in the South. Moreover, the conservative resurgence suggested that civil rights advocates would encounter growing resistance to new initiatives designed to achieve the long list of objectives that remained unfulfilled.

7

The Elusive Quest for Equality, 1969–1989

Controversy gripped Boston as the public schools prepared to open in September 1974. After protracted litigation initiated by African American activists, Federal District Judge W. Arthur Garrity had ruled that the city's schools were unconstitutionally segregated. As a remedy for the violation of African American children's constitutional rights, Garrity had established a desegregation plan that relied heavily on busing. Black children would be transported from predominantly black neighborhoods to schools in white neighborhoods, while whites would be bused to schools in African American communities. On the average, students would spend thirty minutes per day in transit. Although few whites cheered the ruling, opposition was most intense in the tightly knit Irish working-class neighborhoods of Charlestown and South Boston. There, residents harbored a century-old antipathy to blacks and deep devotion to their community schools that fueled adamant opposition to sending their children to schools in heavily black neighborhoods. Whipsawed by the economic stagnation and inflation of the early 1970s, they bitterly resented what they perceived as the government's special concern for minorities—they called it "reverse racism." Moreover, they denounced the inequity of busing, charging that the wealthy could avoid integration by moving to the suburbs or by sending their children to private schools, options unavailable to the working-class residents of Charlestown and South Boston. "Someone's got to explain it to me," demanded one white parent. "I'll listen to anybody, but someone's got to tell me how this Garrity guy, this big deal judge gets all this power to move people around, right the hell out of their neighborhood, while everybody else in the world comes out of it free and equal."[1]

White resentment exploded on September 9, 1974, three days before classes were to begin, as eight thousand white parents staged an antibusing rally outside the John F. Kennedy Federal Building in Boston. Hoping to stem the antibusing tide and to prevent disruptive behavior when classes began, Senator Edward M. Kennedy made a surprise appearance at the rally. His presence only inflamed the crowd. A strong advocate of civil rights, the senator

Promises to Keep. Donald G. Nieman, Oxford University Press (2020). © Oxford University Press.
DOI: 10.1093/oso/9780190071639.001.0001

had helped defeat antibusing legislation in Congress, so demonstrators felt betrayed by him. As he approached the microphone, the crowd responded with boos and catcalls: "Impeach him. Get rid of the bum! . . . Why don't you put your one-legged son on a bus! Yeah, let your daughter get bused, so she can get raped!"[2] Drowned out by the crowd, Kennedy left the microphone and started across the plaza to the Federal Building. His antagonists began lobbing tomatoes and eggs at him, and several ran after him, shouting insults. An angry woman with a small American flag in her hair struck Kennedy on the shoulder, while another heckler landed an elbow in his ribs. Finally, the senator reached the Federal Building and hurried inside, his assailants held at bay by security guards. Seething with anger, the crowd pounded at the windows, sending a huge pane of glass shattering across the lobby.

The attack on Kennedy set off a turbulent autumn. When classes began on September 12, buses transporting black students from the Roxbury ghetto to South Boston High School passed graffiti reading, "Niggers Go Home" and "This Is Klan Country." And when the buses arrived at school, they were met by mobs of rock- and bottle-throwing whites. Although police moved in before anyone was injured seriously, tensions remained high. On October 2, a melee between black and white students left eleven persons injured, prompting city officials to assign three hundred police officers to patrol the school's corridors. The police restored order, but resentment continued to smolder. On December 11, a white mob, incensed after a black student stabbed a white boy, laid siege to South Boston High, menacing 135 black students for four hours until police could spirit the black youths out of the building. Officials promptly closed the school, reopening it one month later under the watchful eyes of an expanded force of five hundred city and state police.

Although most Boston schools desegregated peacefully and violence gradually subsided in the antibusing hotbeds of South Boston and Charlestown, the city's battle over busing foreshadowed the future of civil rights. Lobbying, litigation, and fund-raising techniques perfected during the long struggle for equality, as well as landmark legislation and court decisions won during the 1960s, gave African American leaders weapons to attack the structural racism that survived the death of Jim Crow. Combined with the growing political strength of African Americans, they enabled civil rights leaders to win surprising victories in the less hospitable climate of the 1970s and 1980s. Thus, as in Boston, civil rights lawyers prodded federal courts to attack school segregation in northern cities, something that they had studiously avoided during the previous decade. The consensus on civil rights that had emerged in the mid-1960s, however, did not survive the decade, as events in Boston made painfully clear. New remedies designed to attack the deeply rooted effects of discrimination encountered growing resistance, and victories won during the Indian Summer of the civil rights movement in the 1970s proved difficult to protect as the nation approached the Constitution's bicentennial.

School Segregation: Advance and Retreat

The 1960s, which began with the youthful optimism of the sit-ins, ended with the civil rights movement in disarray and on the defensive. Although the NAACP and the NAACP Legal Defense Fund methodically continued their lobbying and litigation, other civil rights groups fared less well. By 1968, CORE and SNCC, which had served as the movement's shock troops, were reeling from internecine conflict and dwindling membership. The assassination of Martin Luther King Jr. in April 1968 deprived the movement of its most charismatic leader and most eloquent and effective spokesperson. Moreover, Richard Nixon's victory in the 1968 presidential election was cause for alarm. During the campaign, Nixon had successfully wooed white southern voters, promising them relief from federal demands for school desegregation. Although liberals remained a force to be reckoned with on Capitol Hill, the new president controlled the federal agencies responsible for enforcing the civil rights laws. With good reason, civil rights leaders feared that Nixon would abandon the vigorous enforcement effort begun during the Johnson administration.

Such fears proved well founded. During the summer of 1969, with several hundred southern school districts still holding out against integration, the administration signaled its intention to slow down the desegregation process. In July, officials at HEW recognized the difficulties desegregation posed and declined to hold school districts to deadlines established by the department's previous guidelines. Six weeks later, the Fifth Circuit Court of Appeals heard *Alexander v. Holmes County Board of Education*, a suit against thirty-three Mississippi counties that continued to operate segregated schools fifteen years after *Brown*. In a dramatic reversal, Justice Department lawyers appeared on behalf of the state of Mississippi, urging the court to delay desegregation. President Nixon also lashed out against busing. In March 1970, he denounced recent court decisions that "raised widespread fears that the nation might face a massive disruption of public education: that wholesale compulsory busing may be ordered and the neighborhood school virtually doomed."[3] Shortly after Nixon's statement, the Justice Department intervened in the Charlotte, North Carolina, case, challenging a court-ordered desegregation plan that used a variety of techniques, including busing, to desegregate the city's schools.

Even more alarming to African American leaders, Nixon worked to reshape the Supreme Court. During the 1968 campaign, Nixon had criticized the Court, charging that liberal judges had interpreted the Constitution too broadly and placed undue restrictions on elected officials. Although his remarks aimed primarily at the landmark decisions of the 1960s that expanded the rights of the accused, his pledge to appoint conservative judges who adhered to a philosophy of strict construction and self-restraint alarmed civil rights advocates. During the 1960s, an activist Court had read the guarantees of the Thirteenth, Fourteenth, and Fifteenth Amendments broadly, sweeping away precedents that had long prevented effective national protection of civil rights and imposing restrictions on state and local government, schools, and private businesses to guarantee substantive equality. Civil rights proponents feared that Nixon's appointees would take a narrow view of the Reconstruction amendments and civil rights statutes to deny African Americans effective remedies against such systemic problems as urban school segregation and employment discrimination.

Concern grew as four justices retired during Nixon's first term, giving him a historic opportunity to reshape the high court. In 1969, Chief Justice Earl Warren, the guiding force behind the Court's civil rights revolution, left the bench. To replace him, Nixon chose Warren Burger, known as a proponent of strict construction during his ten years on the prestigious Court of Appeals for the District of Columbia. Even before Nixon had selected Burger, another seat on the Court became vacant when Justice Abe Fortas, a staunch supporter of civil rights, resigned under threat of impeachment for alleged financial improprieties. Prodded by the Black Congressional Caucus, the NAACP, and other civil rights organizations, a Democratic majority in the Senate killed the nominations of two conservative southerners, Clement Haynsworth and G. Harrold Carswell, whose records on civil rights and labor issues were suspect. The president then nominated Harry Blackmun, a conservative federal appeals court judge from Minnesota, and the Senate, exhausted by the bruising battle over Fortas's successor, quickly gave its assent. When Justices Hugo Black and John Harlan retired in 1971, Nixon moved the Court further to the right. He replaced the legendary Black with Lewis Powell, a distinguished Virginia attorney of decidedly conservative views. To fill Harlan's seat, he appointed William Rehnquist, a trenchant and outspoken critic of the Warren Court's activism.

The Burger Court quickly disappointed the president. In October 1969, the Court considered the administration's effort to slow the pace of southern school desegregation. In August, the Fifth Circuit Court of Appeals had decided the *Alexander* case, accepting a Justice Department request to delay desegregation in thirty-three Mississippi counties. When the NAACP Legal Defense Fund, which represented the plaintiffs, appealed, a unanimous Supreme Court promptly issued a terse one-paragraph opinion, reversing the lower court and prohibiting further delay. "Under explicit holdings of this Court the obligation of every school district is to terminate dual school systems at once," the court emphasized, "and to operate now and hereafter only unitary schools."[4]

Several weeks later, the Court made it clear that "now" meant immediately. In implementing *Alexander*, the fifth circuit judges ordered desegregation to take place in two steps. Faculty, transportation, and student activities were to be desegregated by February 1, 1970. Owing to the difficulty of assigning students to new schools during the middle of the year, however, the court ruled that they could remain in their old, segregated schools until the following September. When the fifth circuit court applied this formula to another group of school cases, plaintiffs in one of these, *Carter v. West Feliciana Parish School Board*, appealed. The high court promptly reversed the appeals court, ordering full desegregation of facilities and students no later than February 1, 1970. *Alexander* and *Carter* ended the South's hopes of avoiding desegregation and undermined the administration's last-ditch effort to reward its southern supporters. During 1970 and 1971, the federal courts compelled holdout districts to desegregate, and when classes resumed in the fall of 1972, southern schools were the most integrated in the nation, with 46 percent of African American students attending white-majority schools.

Although *Alexander* and *Carter* struck a blow against segregation in the public schools of the rural South, a majority of African Americans lived in cities, where schools remained highly segregated. Urban desegregation posed special problems. In rural areas, with little residential segregation, assigning students to schools nearest their homes produced integration. In towns and small cities, school attendance zones could easily be drawn to achieve integration. But large cities often sprawled over several hundred square miles and had highly segregated residential patterns. Indeed, the movement of whites to the suburbs in the decades after World War II had intensified racial isolation in the nation's metropolitan areas. Consequently, no matter how school attendance zones were drawn, most neighborhood schools would remain highly segregated. Meaningful desegregation was possible only if children were bused to schools outside their neighborhoods. Without busing, segregated schools would continue to perpetuate racial polarization and deny African American children the educational advantages of integrated schools.

Yet busing was a potentially explosive policy, as events in Boston demonstrated. The school bus had long been an accepted part of American life, used by rural school districts to carry children to far-off consolidated schools and by urban districts to relieve pressure on overcrowded schools and to transport children to schools with special programs. By 1970, 40 percent of the nation's students were bused to school, and North Carolina proudly called itself "the schoolbusingest state in the Union." Busing to achieve desegregation was another matter, however, and most white parents bristled at transporting children to schools in black neighborhoods. Many parents who had purchased homes in affluent (and highly taxed) neighborhoods known for high quality—and predominantly white—schools were outraged that their children would not be permitted to attend those schools. Others resisted busing because they believed that neighborhood schools gave children and parents a closer identification with them, made it easier for parents to be involved, and allowed children greater access to after-school activities. Moreover, many white parents feared for their children's safety in inner-city schools they perceived to be dangerous.

The Supreme Court first confronted the busing dilemma in 1971, when it decided *Swann v. Charlotte-Mecklenburg Board of Education*. The case had begun in 1964, when blacks in Charlotte, North Carolina, went to court to compel school desegregation. As the case dragged on, school officials stepped up the token desegregation they had begun in the late 1950s. Nevertheless, when District Judge James B. McMillan took charge of the case in 1968, 60 percent of the city's African American students attended schools that were at least 99 percent black. Encouraged by the Supreme Court's ruling in *Green v. County School Board* (1968), Julius LeVonne Chambers, the young African American attorney who represented Charlotte blacks, pressed Judge McMillan to end tokenism and order meaningful desegregation. In 1969, the judge responded with a sweeping new desegregation decree. He ruled that the persistence of segregation meant that the school board had not met the constitutional obligation established by the *Green* case to "take whatever steps might be necessary" to eliminate the effects of past discrimination.[5] Because blacks were concentrated in the northwest quarter of the city, McMillan concluded that even the most careful redrawing of school attendance zones would leave the schools segregated. Therefore, he adopted a plan that required 13,000 of the district's 84,000 students to be bused to produce schools ranging from 9 to 38 percent African American.

As local whites launched a massive antibusing campaign, the Charlotte school board, assisted by an amicus curiae brief filed by the Justice Department, appealed Judge McMillan's ruling, ultimately bringing the highly charged busing issue before the Supreme Court. With two Nixon appointees (Burger and Blackmun) now on the bench, most observers predicted that the *Swann* case would splinter the Court, ending its unanimity on school desegregation. Although the justices were divided in their early discussions of *Swann*, the force of precedent and tradition led them to uphold the district court's decision. A ruling against busing meant that the wrongs of the past would remain unremedied and segregation would persist in urban America. The *Green* precedent, with its demand for affirmative action to root out the effects of past discrimination, and the weight of the Court's role as the champion of civil rights made such an outcome

Figure 7.1. Julius LeVonne Chambers in 1971. *Charlotte Observer Collection, Robinson-Spangler Carolina Room, Charlotte Mecklenberg Library.*

unacceptable to most of the justices. With a solid majority supporting the lower court, the Nixon appointees probably did not wish to enter a dissent that would make them appear to be puppets of the president. In a decision that confounded pundits, a unanimous Court endorsed busing in an opinion written by Chief Justice Burger.

Following the logic of the Court's holding in *Green*, the chief justice ruled that where school officials had been guilty of discrimination, as in Charlotte, they had an obligation to dismantle segregation. If they failed to do so, the federal courts had broad authority to devise remedies that would work, even if they required transportation of students. "Desegregation plans cannot be limited to the walk-in school," the chief justice emphasized. He acknowledged that busing "may be administratively awkward, inconvenient . . . and may impose burdens on some." But he asserted that this "cannot be avoided in the interim period when remedial adjustments are being made to eliminate the dual school systems." Although Burger rejected the use of rigid racial quotas to guarantee that all schools in a system have the same racial mix as the system as a whole, he held that the district court had not erred in taking racial balance into account in devising a desegregation plan. "As we said in *Green*, . . . a district court's remedial decree is to be judged by its effectiveness," Burger wrote. "Awareness of the racial composition of the whole school system is likely to be a useful starting point in shaping a remedy to correct past constitutional violations."[6] Color-conscious remedies were appropriate, the Court insisted, to remedy the persistent effects of segregation.

Civil rights advocates were pleased that the Court had upheld busing, but one aspect of the opinion troubled them. Burger had emphasized repeatedly that the federal courts could impose desegregation plans only to remedy past discrimination by school officials. While this gave the green light to desegregation in southern cities, where segregation had been established by law, it created an obstacle to desegregation in the North. In the decades before *Brown*, few northern states had enacted school segregation laws, and many had explicitly banned segregation. Therefore, plaintiffs in northern school desegregation cases had to prove that, in the absence of laws, school officials had acted covertly to create segregated schools. This required time-consuming investigations and protracted trials to show that officials had chosen school sites, drawn school attendance zones, and adopted transfer policies designed to maximize segregation.

Although the Court did not remove this burden, it lightened it in deciding *Keyes v. School District No. 1, Denver, Colo.* in 1973. When the case was tried in federal district court, lawyers from the Legal Defense Fund had shown that in the Park Hill section, where one-third of Denver's blacks lived, school officials adopted policies that had created segregated schools. In response, the court ordered a desegregation plan for the schools in Park Hill; however, even though blacks living in other parts of the city attended segregated schools, the judge refused to order a city-wide desegregation plan without proof that schools in other neighborhoods had been intentionally segregated. The implications were clear: plaintiffs would have to demonstrate, school-by-school, that segregation was the result of policies intentionally adopted to achieve that end. This would increase the already considerable time and expense required to litigate northern desegregation cases.

In *Keyes*, the Supreme Court considerably reduced the burden on plaintiffs. Writing for the Court, Justice William Brennan ruled that adoption of a city-wide plan did not require school-by-school proof of intentional segregation. "Where plaintiffs prove that the school authorities have carried out a systematic program of segregation affecting a substantial portion of the students, schools, teachers and facilities," Brennan explained, "it is only common sense to conclude that there exists a predicate for a finding of the existence of a dual school system."[7] Only if school officials could prove that their policies had neither created nor contributed to segregation in other schools, he concluded, would they be able to avoid imposition of a city-wide desegregation plan. The Court sent the case back to the district court, which subsequently adopted a system-wide busing plan.

In the wake of *Swann* and *Keyes*, NAACP attorneys initiated desegregation suits on behalf of grass-roots groups in cities across the North, and federal courts responded with desegregation orders that relied heavily on busing. Predictably, as busing spread northward, white opposition mounted. Critics charged that the Constitution prohibited segregation but did not mandate integration. Indeed, by assigning students to schools by race to achieve racial balance, they argued, busing plans violated a central principle of the Constitution—that law and public policy must be color-blind. Ironically, many of these critics were recent supporters of segregation who found that color-blind principles allowed them to defend segregation without employing overtly racist arguments. James J. Kilpatrick, the pundit who had led Virginia's massive resistance campaign, called *Swann* "a scheme of racist lunacy" that flew in the face of *Brown*. "The Brown decision said . . . pupils could not be assigned to schools by reason of their race," he thundered, "[while Swann] lay[s] down precisely the opposite rule: Pupils must be assigned to schools by reason of their race."[8]

In 1972, bills that would restrict federal courts' authority to order busing gained broad support in Congress, and only a filibuster by Senate liberals prevented them from passing. Two years later, similar bills were defeated by one vote in the upper house. In the face of these narrow defeats, antibusing sentiment became more powerful, and congressional opponents of busing redoubled their efforts. Although ultimately they could not end the federal courts' authority to order busing, in early 1976 the antibusing forces enacted legislation stripping HEW of authority to cut off federal aid to school districts that refused to adopt busing plans to achieve integration.

As antibusing pressure grew in Congress, the Supreme Court itself imposed a significant restriction on the tools available to remedy segregation. In 1971, a federal district court ruled that the Detroit school board had engaged in a wide range of activities consciously designed to promote school segregation. Because African Americans constituted 65 percent of the city's school-age population, however, any desegregation plan that was limited to the city itself would leave many schools between 75 and 90 percent black. Moreover, it would accelerate "white flight" to the suburbs, undermining even the minimal desegregation achieved. To devise an effective remedy, the court joined the Detroit school district with fifty-three surrounding suburban districts and ordered that black children be bused to the suburbs and white suburban children be transported to schools in the city.

When the Detroit case, *Milliken v. Bradley*, reached the Supreme Court in 1973, the future of urban school desegregation hung in the balance. Like Detroit, most large American cities had growing black majorities in their schools, guaranteeing that a desegregation plan limited to the city itself would leave African American children in segregated schools and hasten white flight to the suburbs. In these circumstances, metropolitan plans were essential because they permitted meaningful integration while reducing the incentive for white flight.

In June 1974, with Justice Potter Stewart joining the four Nixon appointees to form a 5–4 majority, the Court reversed the district court, dealing a crippling blow to metropolitan desegregation. The federal courts could not arbitrarily interfere with local school district lines, Chief Justice Burger wrote for the majority, asserting that "[n]o single tradition in public education is more deeply rooted than local control over the operation of schools."[9] Only if the state had drawn school district boundaries with intent to establish segregated schools or if the suburban districts themselves had adopted policies that contributed to segregation would cross-district busing be justified. Burger concluded, however, that while abundant evidence demonstrated that Detroit school officials pursued practices that contributed to segregation within the city, boundaries between the Detroit school district and the suburban districts had not been drawn with segregative intent and the policies of the suburban districts had not contributed to segregation within the city. Consequently, the district court lacked authority to order cross-district busing.

The four dissenters blasted the chief justice's analysis. Pointing out that school districts were merely administrative subdivisions of the state, Justice Byron White charged that the majority had unjustifiably transformed school district lines into artificial barriers that blocked effective desegregation. "I cannot understand," White wrote, "why a federal court may not order an appropriate inter-district remedy, if this is necessary or more effective to accomplish this constitutionally mandated task [i.e., desegregation]."[10] Justice Thurgood Marshall, who during his long career with the NAACP had relentlessly pressed the Court to strike down segregation, warned that the majority had taken "a giant step backwards." Marshall argued that the Court had consistently held that where officials of the state or any of its political subdivisions were guilty of discrimination, the state had a duty to eliminate the consequences of their action. Since that could only be done in Detroit through cross-district busing, the district court's desegregation plan was fully justified. Not only was the majority's legal analysis misguided, Marshall concluded, but the consequences of its ruling would be disastrous. "In the short run," he predicted, "it may seem to be the easier course to allow our great metropolitan areas to be divided up each into two cities—one white, the other black—but it is a course, I predict, our people will ultimately regret."[11]

The ensuing years demonstrated the truth of Marshall's claim. In cities with metropolitan-wide school districts (such as Charlotte), *Milliken* did not pose a barrier to desegregation. In cities such as Louisville, Kentucky, or Wilmington, Delaware, where civil rights attorneys could show that school district boundaries had been drawn with segregative intent or that the policies of suburban districts contributed to segregation in the city, federal courts remained free to impose metropolitan desegregation plans. Nevertheless, *Milliken* meant that in most of the nation's large cities—New York, Chicago, Atlanta, Philadelphia, Kansas City, among others—the courts' hands were tied. When they ordered city-wide plans—as they did in Detroit—they ended up spreading a few white students among predominantly black schools. They could—as they did in Kansas City and Chicago—devise plans that compensated for past discrimination by enhancing the quality of inner-city schools. This, however, seemed more like a reversion to the separate but equal doctrine than a fulfillment of *Green*'s promise of rooting out segregation. By devising plans that called for establishing schools with special curricula (so-called magnet schools), judges could attract white as well as black students to selected inner-city schools, thereby creating pockets of integration in a sea of predominantly black schools. In the absence of cross-district busing, however, the federal courts lacked the tools to desegregate most cities. Consequently, the rapid progress toward school integration that had occurred during the late 1960s and early 1970s came to a halt.

Under pressure from the Congressional Black Caucus (CBC), Congress passed legislation in the 1970s and 1980s designed to address housing discrimination, one of the principal factors that produced segregated schools. The Home Mortgage Disclosure Act of 1975 attacked redlining, a practice lenders used to deny mortgages on properties in neighborhoods that were becoming racially mixed—and therefore the very areas likely to become integrated. Two years later, Congress passed the Community Reinvestment Act, which encouraged banks and savings and loans to provide mortgages to customers in low- and middle-income neighborhoods, another step to combat redlining. Ten years later, in the wake of the savings and loan crisis, the CBC succeeded in winning passage of legislation that provided funding to nonprofit groups that challenged housing discrimination and also strengthened penalties against lenders that discriminated. Taken together, these measures put teeth in the Fair Housing Act of 1968, and, combined with a growing African American middle class, facilitated modest gains in residential integration. Nevertheless, poverty and persistent racism kept far too many African Americans in segregated neighborhoods in cities and their inner suburbs, perpetuating school segregation. By the late 1980s, schools in most of America's metropolitan areas were more segregated than they had been in 1968.

Employment Discrimination and the Affirmative Action Controversy

Like school desegregation, elimination of employment discrimination had eluded civil rights advocates in the 1960s and remained at the forefront of the civil rights agenda in the 1970s. Deeply rooted discrimination in the North as well as the South relegated most blacks to unskilled, menial, and low-paying jobs and had produced a high rate of poverty among African Americans. Discrimination, poverty, and inferior schools undermined many young blacks' incentive and ability to finish high school, thereby locking them into low-paying, dead-end jobs or out of employment altogether. Title VII of the Civil Rights Act of 1964 had attempted to deal with the economic problems of blacks by prohibiting discrimination by private employers and creating the Equal Employment Opportunity Commission (EEOC) to monitor compliance. The civil rights act and changing attitudes generated by the civil rights movement eliminated much of the most blatant ("no colored need apply") discrimination and contributed to significant gains in employment and earnings for African Americans. Yet discrimination did not disappear; it became more subtle, harder to detect, and more difficult to prove. Even more troubling, those who had been denied education, job training, and employment experience by past discrimination continued to find economic opportunity elusive.

Employment discrimination was not only a problem for black men; it was also sorely felt by women of both races. The 1960s and 1970s saw increasing numbers of women enter the workforce as families adapted to changing social patterns and increased expectations of material comfort. Higher divorce rates left many women and the family members they supported dependent on their paycheck. Increasing numbers of college-educated women aspired to careers that would make them life-long, full-time members of the workforce. Moreover, the consumer culture that blossomed in the postwar decades added to the economic pressures on both married and single women. As material expectations rose, women in the workforce increasingly regarded themselves as primary breadwinners. As more women came to regard jobs and careers as integral parts of their lives and livelihoods, they chafed under employment practices established by men that excluded them from competition for good jobs and occupational advancement. Under the influence of a burgeoning Second Wave Feminist movement, white women realized striking parallels between their position and that of African American men and women: they were ghettoized in poorly paid, dead-end jobs and excluded from positions that offered security, advancement, fringe benefits, and fair compensation. Like African Americans of both sexes, women of both races demanded vigorous action against employment discrimination.

The 1970s proved a less propitious time than the 1960s to tackle these difficult problems. Not only had the conservative political tide deprived civil rights leaders and feminists of allies in the White House, but the economic climate militated against further efforts to redress the effects of past discrimination. The dynamic economic growth of the 1960s slowed during the 1970s, and sharply rising inflation alarmed most Americans, making it seem harder to make ends meet and to maintain their standard of living. (In fact, real income and purchasing power grew during the decade.) Afraid that the pie was no longer growing, many whites felt threatened by programs that promised a bigger piece to blacks, and many men were equally resentful of gains made by women. Consequently, like busing, the issue of employment discrimination became highly charged and hotly debated.

Nevertheless, the combined efforts of civil rights and women's groups produced important gains in a conservative decade. In 1972, a wide array of civil rights and women's groups prodded Congress to pass the Equal Employment Opportunity Act, broadening the coverage of Title VII and increasing the EEOC's power. The law extended Title VII's coverage to state and local government and to employers and unions with fifteen or more employees or members (originally the number was twenty-five). It also conferred greater enforcement power on the EEOC. Whereas Title VII originally had denied the agency authority to issue cease-and-desist orders or to sue parties found guilty of discrimination, the 1972 law gave it authority to sue employers or unions that refused to abandon discriminatory practices.

Congress also substantially enlarged the budget and staff of the EEOC. During the late 1960s, the agency had been woefully underfunded and had insufficient personnel to investigate the avalanche of complaints it had received or to follow up on settlements that it had negotiated with employers. Between 1970 and 1981, its budget increased by a factor of ten, growing from $13 million to more than $140 million and enabling it to expand both the size of its staff and the range of its activities. Indeed, by 1977, EEOC's Office of General Counsel employed more than three hundred attorneys to litigate discrimination cases.

Despite these changes, problems continued to plague the agency during the early 1970s. Although resources grew, so did the number of complaints, increasing from around 15,000 in 1970 to 75,000 in 1981. Although such a dramatic increase would have posed a difficult challenge under the best of circumstances, ineffective leadership compounded the problem. Because President Nixon and his successor, Gerald Ford, did not assign a high priority to the federal effort against discrimination, the commissioners and commission staff turned over rapidly. As a result, the agency drifted. The backlog of cases mushroomed, the time required to resolve complaints grew to two years, and the commission did not monitor settlements to assure compliance. This began to change in 1977, when President Jimmy Carter appointed Eleanor Holmes Norton, a Yale Law School graduate and former head of the New York City Commission on Human Rights, to chair EEOC. Under Norton's vigorous leadership, the commission slashed its backlog, investigated new cases more expeditiously, increased the number of employment discrimination suits it filed, and became a force to be reckoned with.

Figure 7.2. Elizabeth Holmes Norton in 1977 https://www.loc.gov/item/ 2017651398/. *Library of Congress.*

Until Norton's appointment, private attorneys shouldered most of the responsibility for enforcing Title VII's guarantees. Beginning in 1965, the Legal Defense Fund devoted a substantial portion of its resources to employment discrimination cases. With a staff of only twenty full-time lawyers assisted by two hundred cooperating attorneys (privately employed lawyers who volunteered their services), the Legal Defense Fund lacked the vast resources of the EEOC. Nevertheless, as it had done thirty years earlier in its campaign against school segregation, the organization focused its resources on cases that promised to establish important legal precedents. In addition to the Legal Defense Fund, other civil rights groups—the ACLU, the Lawyers' Constitutional Defense Committee, the Employment Rights Project of the Columbia Law School, and the Lawyers' Committee for Civil Rights Under Law—and many private attorneys also took employment discrimination cases. Indeed, after 1976, when Congress authorized the federal courts to award attorneys' fees to victorious parties in civil rights suits, private enforcement activity grew even faster, subjecting employers charged with discrimination to expensive litigation, bad publicity, and potentially costly awards.

The private enforcement effort chalked up significant victories in the federal courts, which dramatically expanded the scope of Title VII. The most important of these came in 1971, when the Supreme Court issued its landmark decision in *Griggs v. Duke Power.* Prior to 1965, when attorneys from the Legal Defense Fund initiated the suit, black employees at the company's Dan River, North Carolina, plant had been assigned exclusively to the Labor Department, where the highest wage was lower than the lowest wage paid to employees in other departments. In 1965, when the company opened jobs in other departments to African Americans, it required all applicants to have a high school diploma or pass an aptitude test. Although the new policy established ostensibly race-neutral criteria, it adversely affected African Americans. Only 12 percent of North Carolina's black males, compared with 34 percent of the state's white men, had graduated from high school. And given their heritage of separate and unequal education, black applicants scored lower on the aptitude test. The requirements appeared unrelated to the unskilled jobs the black employees sought; at the time the case was filed, whites who had won promotions out of the Labor Department before the new requirements took effect "continued to perform satisfactorily and achieve promotions."[12]

A group of African American employees denied transfers from the Labor Department challenged the company's policies. Energized by the civil rights movement, they turned to Charlotte attorney and activist Julius LeVonne Chambers. The young African American attorney, who would later head the Legal Defense Fund, argued that company policies violated Title VII because they were not job related and made it more -difficult for African Americans than whites to advance.

Writing for a unanimous Court, Chief Justice Burger again surprised court watchers with a bold opinion declaring the company's policies illegal. Burger held that Congress's objective in passing Title VII had been "to achieve equality of employment opportunities and remove barriers that have oper-ated in the past to favor an identifiable group of white employees over other employees." Consequently, employment policies that had a discriminatory effect were suspect under Title VII, even if adopted without intent to dis-criminate. The chief justice added that employment criteria that had an ad-verse impact on blacks could be justified only if employers could prove that they were job related. "The touchstone is business necessity," he wrote. "If an employment practice which operates to exclude Negroes cannot be shown to be related to job performance, the practice is prohibited."[13] Since neither a high school diploma nor a passing score on the aptitude test was related to actual performance of the unskilled jobs the Duke employees had sought, Burger concluded, the company's policies violated Title VII, even though they were nondiscriminatory in appearance. *Griggs* was an important vic-tory because it lightened the burden on plaintiffs in employment discrimi-nation cases. Once complainants demonstrated that employment practices had an adverse impact on blacks and women, the burden of proof shifted to employers, who had to prove that there was a genuine relationship between the hiring criteria they had established and applicants' ability to perform the job they sought.

By the early 1970s, affirmative action programs also offered a potentially effective if controversial and misunderstood remedy for discrimination in the workplace. In 1965, President Johnson had issued Executive Order 11246, prohibiting discrimination by firms doing business with the federal govern-ment and requiring them to take "affirmative action" to remedy the effects of past discrimination. The Labor Department, which was given responsibility for enforcement, established the Office of Federal Contract Compliance (OFCC) to monitor federal contractors and to terminate contracts with violators. Between May 1968 and December 1971, OFCC issued a series of orders that clarified employers' obligations. Employers were to determine the percentage of minorities and women in their workforce and compare this with the percentage of these groups in the labor pool. If the firm was "deficient in the utilization of minority groups and women," it was to establish "goals and timetables" for redressing this imbalance.[14]

OFCC guidelines had a limited impact on government contractors. Affirmative action plans might make employers aware of standards to which they should aspire and might even encourage them to work to increase the number of women and blacks on their payrolls; however, they faced little pressure to achieve the goals or to stick to the timetables. OFCC's only means of enforcing compliance was to terminate contracts with businesses that failed to make a good-faith effort to carry out their plans. Doing so was politically risky because it threatened to hurt companies and bring down the wrath of members of Congress. Consequently, OFCC rarely used its authority. Employers could go through the motions of creating goals while making little effort to achieve them, knowing that their chances of losing federal contracts were nil.

Although OFCC proved to be a paper tiger, its affirmative action guidelines were not without effect. EEOC soon took the position that all employers, not just federal contractors, should adopt affirmative action programs. In 1974, for example, the commission warned employers that "equal employment opportunity usually requires positive *affirmative action* beyond establishment of neutral 'nondiscriminatory' and 'merit-hiring' practices."[15] A number of factors gave weight to the EEOC's call for affirmative action: the commission's newly won authority to sue employers it deemed guilty of discrimination; the dramatic growth of employment discrimination suits (from 340 in 1970 to 5,480 nine years later); the federal courts' deference to EEOC guidelines; and plaintiffs' success in employment cases. Consequently, firms became increasingly sensitive to the threat of litigation, and many adopted and even implemented affirmative action programs as a hedge against lawsuits.

Affirmative action also won endorsement from the federal courts. When employment cases revealed intentional, invidious, illegal discrimination, federal judges imposed mandatory, court-supervised programs to remedy the effects of the discrimination. In 1969, for example, the Court of Appeals for the Fifth Circuit found the Asbestos Workers' Union—which controlled access to employment by referring workers to particular jobs—guilty of systematic discrimination against African Americans. As a remedy, it ordered union officials to alternate between blacks and whites in assigning workers to jobs. Similarly, when a federal court found the Minneapolis Fire Department guilty of discriminatory hiring practices, it ordered department officials to hire at least one black for every three whites until there were twenty minority firefighters.

Like busing, affirmative action generated passionate arguments that reverberated throughout the 1970s and beyond. Taking on the mantle of nondiscrimination, critics charged that it amounted to "reverse discrimination" by giving special preferences to blacks and women. They also argued that by assigning rights on the basis of race, affirmative action violated the principle of color-blind citizenship. Critics cited the words of the conservative constitutional scholar Alexander Bickel to support their position: "The lesson of the great decisions of the Supreme Court and the lesson of contemporary history have been the same for at least a generation: discrimination on the basis of race is illegal, immoral, unconstitutional, inherently wrong, and destructive of a democratic society."[16] This was true, the critics argued, whether the discrimination was against blacks or in their favor. The moral force of the argument was rendered suspect by the fact at least some of those making it— like Republican presidential hopeful Ronald Reagan—had opposed passage of civil rights legislation in the 1960s.

Proponents of affirmative action responded that rules that appeared equal often served to perpetuate discrimination and inequality. Although it generally took more subtle forms, they asserted, discrimination against African Americans and women continued to be a reality. White men generally controlled hiring decisions in business, government, and education. Even when not consciously prejudiced, they frequently felt most comfortable with applicants who were like themselves, believed that they would "fit in" better than blacks and women, and thus subtly slanted hiring decisions in their favor. According to its defenders, affirmative action would serve as a check against these subtle forms of discrimination.

Advocates of affirmative action agreed that a color-blind society was a laudable goal but argued that color must be taken into account to remedy the continuing effects of racism. Otherwise, institutional racism would continue and the nation's promise of equality would remain hollow, much like *Plessy*'s promise of separate but equal. Generations of white men, they pointed out, had benefited from a de facto affirmative action program that had reserved the choicest jobs for them. Moreover, they argued that the legacy of segregation, unequal education, and poverty made it difficult for blacks to overcome the historic advantages enjoyed by whites and threatened to leave them stuck at the bottom of the economic ladder. "To break this cycle requires, as a matter of common sense, special treatment for the victims of past discrimination," explained J. Skelly Wright of the US Court of Appeals for the District of Columbia. "Such special treatment may appear unnatural—even unfair in the short run—but the only alternative is to allow the effects of our history of discrimination to plague our civic life in perpetuity."[17] The temporary protection afforded by affirmative action, Judge Wright and others concluded, was designed to achieve equality and therefore was fully in keeping with the spirit of the Fourteenth Amendment and the civil rights movement.

Opponents countered that affirmative action penalized persons who themselves were not guilty of discrimination to rectify wrongs committed by previous generations. By giving special consideration to African Americans, they argued, affirmative action meant that equally or even better qualified white males were passed over for jobs and promotions. Consequently, they would be made to suffer, not because of wrongful behavior on their part, but because of their race. Concomitantly, individual black applicants would benefit, not because they themselves had been the victims of discriminatory acts, but because members of their race had been subject to discrimination. Furthermore, critics pointed out that for many lower-class whites who came from disadvantaged backgrounds, affirmative action would be one more obstacle to overcome. Indeed, middle-class blacks would reap the benefits of affirmative action programs, even though they were not disadvantaged, while whites would be penalized, regardless of their background.

To claim that special treatment for blacks inflicted wrongs on innocent whites, proponents of affirmative action responded, denied the reality of white privilege. Even if blatant, systematic discrimination against African Americans was less common, they argued, its effects continued to burden young African Americans who had never known the harshness of Jim Crow. High rates of poverty, unemployment, illiteracy, and broken homes in the black community were the legacy of centuries of discrimination. As a result, young blacks all too frequently lacked the supportive home environment crucial to success in school, grew up without role models to encourage success, found schools frustrating places that were irrelevant to them and dropped out, and lived in urban ghettos where high unemployment made it difficult to obtain essential work experience. Ignoring the legacy of racism would only condemn them to compete in a game whose rules were stacked against them and perpetuate injustice in the name of policies that were formally neutral but actually gave decided advantages to whites. While defenders of affirmative action admitted that there were disadvantaged whites, they pointed out that, as a group, blacks labored under a heritage of discrimination that was far more severe than that whites had ever known. Indeed, irrespective of their class or level of education, African Americans routinely endured suspicion and indignities few white men ever encountered.

Questions of justice aside, opponents charged that affirmative action subverted the principle of reward according to merit and thus threatened to elevate mediocrity. Although they admitted that most affirmative action programs did not establish quotas, critics contended that they put almost irresistible pressure on employers to hire African Americans and women regardless of their qualifications. They argued that this made race rather than merit the crucial factor in hiring decisions. At a time when American firms were coming under increasingly sharp competition from abroad, they insisted, the nation could ill afford to promote mediocrity.

Defenders of affirmative action strenuously denied these charges. Pointing to the *Griggs* case, they argued that employers frequently established arbitrary qualifications that were irrelevant to job performance but effectively screened out African Americans and women. Proponents charged that the critics had created a largely imagined golden age, before the onset of affirmative action, when employment decisions were made solely on the basis of merit. They pointed out that employment decisions frequently had been based on race and gender, excluding blacks and women from consideration regardless of their qualifications, or on family influence and personal connections rather than ability and experience. Plenty of mediocre and incompetent white men had found their way into jobs without raising the hue and cry that greeted affirmative action. By encouraging the hiring and promotion of African Americans and women, proponents argued, affirmative action would bring diverse perspectives to the workplace by breaking down the "old boy" networks that had long favored white males.

As the debate became sharper, both sides looked to the Supreme Court for a resolution. In 1977 the justices signaled their willingness to tackle the issue when they agreed to hear *Regents of the University of California v. Bakke*. It dealt not with employment but with medical school admissions. While African Americans made up 11 percent of the nation's population in 1970, they claimed only 2 percent of its doctors. As a result, many black communities suffered from a shortage of physicians, and African American children were deprived of professional role models. Although the medical school at the University of California at Davis had been established in 1968 and had no history of discrimination, it instituted a voluntary affirmative action plan designed to increase the enrollment of minorities. The school set aside

sixteen of the hundred seats in its entering class for minorities and admitted
some minority students who had lower college grades and test scores than
many whites who were denied admission. Allan Bakke, an aerospace engi-
neer and Marine Corps veteran in his early thirties, was one such white applicant. After twice being rejected while minority applicants with lower grades
and test scores won admission, Bakke brought suit in the California courts,
charging that the medical school's policy constituted racial discrimination
that was prohibited by the Fourteenth Amendment and the Civil Rights Act
of 1964. When the California Supreme Court agreed with Bakke, the university appealed, bringing the case and the troubling questions raised by affirmative action before the US Supreme Court.

Like the rest of the country, the Court was badly divided over the use
of quotas as a tool of affirmative action. Four justices—Warren Burger,
William Rehnquist, Potter Stewart, and John Paul Stevens—concluded that
the University had denied Bakke admission on account of his race in violation of the Civil Rights Act of 1964. Four of their colleagues—William
Brennan, Thurgood Marshall, Harry Blackmun, and Byron White—
disagreed, arguing that the civil rights act and the equal protection clause
had been adopted to root out America's racial caste system. To read them
to prohibit programs designed to overcome the effects of past discrimination, they charged, was to transform them into barriers to genuine equality.
"In order to get beyond racism, we must first take account of race," Justice
Blackmun explained. "And in order to treat some persons equally, we must
treat them differently. We cannot—we dare not—let the Equal Protection
Clause perpetuate racial supremacy."[18]

Justice Lewis Powell, the conservative Virginian, cast the decisive vote
and wrote the opinion of the Court. Powell went beyond his conservative colleagues to argue that the Davis admissions program violated the
Constitution's equal protection clause as well as the civil rights act. By setting
aside sixteen seats for minorities, it created a special privilege for minorities,
thereby denying whites equal rights on the basis of race. "The guarantee of
equal protection cannot mean one thing when it is applied to one individual
and something else when applied to a person of another color," he wrote.
"If both are not accorded the same protection, then it is not equal."[19] Powell
admitted that courts might impose quotas in cases in which an employer or
school had been found guilty of discrimination, but noted that this was not
relevant to the *Bakke* case, where the medical school had been found guilty
of discrimination.

Although Powell took a hard line against the use of quotas to compensate for past discrimination, he broke ranks with the other conservative justices by holding that less rigid affirmative action programs were acceptable. Schools had a legitimate educational interest in obtaining diversity, Powell noted, and were free to take race into account in the selection process in order to achieve it. Indeed, he praised Harvard College, which openly admitted that in the interests of diversity, race, as well as geographic origin and socioeconomic background, played a role in its admissions decisions.

Powell's effort to take a middle course produced a curious decision. That part of his decision striking down quotas in the absence of proof of discrimination had the backing of the four opponents of affirmative action, who believed that the medical school was forbidden to take race into account in considering applications; however, his assertion that schools could use race as one criterion prevailed because of the support of the four proponents of affirmative action. If by the slimmest of margins and the most circuitous of routes, the Court gave its blessing to flexible affirmative action programs.

Subsequently, the Court underscored its cautious, qualified acceptance of affirmative action. In *United Steel Workers v. Weber* (1979), it considered a voluntary affirmative action program adopted by Kaiser Aluminum and the steelworkers union to redress the almost complete absence of African Americans in skilled jobs at the company's plants. Kaiser established a program to train unskilled employees for higher-paying craft positions and specified that half of the openings in the program would be reserved for blacks until the percentage of black craft workers approximated the percentage of blacks in the local labor force. In a 5–2 decision (Justices Powell and Stevens did not participate), the Court upheld the program against charges that it violated Title VII's ban on racial discrimination. Writing for the Court, Justice Brennan emphasized that the Kaiser program did not involve state action (and thus did not violate the Fourteenth Amendment) and that it was temporary. He also denied that the program violated Title VII, which, he claimed, had been adopted to remedy deeply rooted economic discrimination against blacks. "It would be ironic indeed if a law triggered by a Nation's concern over centuries of racial injustice," Brennan explained, "constituted the first legislative prohibition of all voluntary, private, race conscious efforts to abolish traditional patterns of racial segregation and hierarchy."[20]

One year later, in *Fullilove v. Klutznik* (1980), the Court gave its blessing to a controversial congressionally mandated affirmative action program established in 1977 to redress discrimination that had stifled the growth of minority businesses. Congress stipulated that 10 percent of all money expended on state and local public works projects undertaken with federal funds must go to firms owned by minorities. In a 6–3 decision, with the opinion written by Chief Justice Burger, the Court sustained the legislation. While the federal courts could provide remedies only for specific acts of discrimination, Congress's power was far broader, Burger argued. Congress enjoyed express authority to enforce the equal protection clause, he explained, and if it believed that equality necessitated a program to remedy past discrimination, it could act. "It is not a constitutional defect in this program that it may disappoint the expectations of nonminority firms," Burger explained. "When effectuating a limited and properly tailored remedy to cure the effects of prior discrimination, such 'a sharing of the burden' by innocent parties is not impermissible."[21]

Voting Rights and Black Political Power

As they attempted to expand the meaning of equal employment opportunity, black leaders also worked to extend their newly won political rights. Although the Voting Rights Act of 1965 had opened the polls to southern blacks, African American voters continued to confront barriers to effective use of the ballot. Given the prevalence of racial bloc voting, African American candidates could usually hope to win elections only in districts with a majority or near-majority of black voters. White politicians sought to minimize the number of African American elected officials—and thereby reduce the effect of black voting—by establishing multi-seat electoral districts and at-large elections. For purposes of illustration, consider a hypothetical city with a five-member city council and a black population of 40 percent. If the city were divided into five wards, each electing one councilmember, blacks would be likely to have majorities in two wards and elect two black councilmembers. Yet if members were elected at-large, with voters throughout the city casting ballots for all five seats, the white majority could preserve a all-white council.

Sharp debates emerged over whether the Voting Rights Act prohibited such electoral changes. In states and counties with a history of discrimination, the act required preclearance of any change in "voting qualification or prerequisite to voting, or standard, practice, or procedure with respect to voting" by the Justice Department or a district court in Washington, DC. The change would be permitted only if the attorney general or the court agreed that it had neither a discriminatory purpose nor effect. Civil rights advocates attacked laws establishing at-large elections and other electoral changes that diluted the black vote as illegal because of their discriminatory effect. Conservatives disagreed, arguing that the Voting Rights Act only prohibited laws and regulations designed to prevent individuals from registering and voting. They charged civil rights advocates with attempting to transform a measure that had been adopted to protect the right to vote into a guarantee of proportional representation for blacks. Like affirmative action, they contended, this gave African Americans a privilege that no other group possessed, amounted to "reverse racism," and was at odds with color-blind principles established by the Constitution.

The Supreme Court quickly swept aside southern states' arguments for a narrow interpretation of the law. In *Allen v. State Board of Elections* (1969), a suit brought by the Legal Defense Fund, the Court held that a law replacing single-member districts with multi-seat districts and at-large elections needed to obtain preclearance and could not take effect if it diluted black votes. According to the Court, the Voting Rights Act gave "a broad interpretation to the right to vote, recognizing that voting includes 'all action necessary to make a vote effective.'" Procedures diluting the votes of African Americans would "nullify their ability to elect the candidate of their choice just as would prohibiting some of them from voting" and therefore came within the act's purview.[22] Four years later, in *Georgia v. United States* (1973), the Court ruled that Georgia's plan for reapportioning seats in the state legislature was covered by the preclearance requirement and suggested that it could be rejected if it hindered the ability of African Americans to elect candidates of their choice.

The Voting Rights Act's preclearance requirement was to remain in effect for only five years. Fearful that expiration would encourage adoption of new laws designed to minimize black political power, in 1969 members of the Black Congressional Caucus, Clarence Mitchell (the NAACP's veteran lobbyist), and representatives of the Leadership Conference on Civil Rights (which represented a number of civil rights organizations) began to press for renewal. The Nixon administration, adhering firmly to its southern strategy, opposed extension, arguing that it imposed on the South a humiliating requirement that did not apply to the rest of the nation. Nevertheless, in 1970, Democratic leaders in Congress, with crucial support from northern Republicans, extended the preclearance requirement for five years. (It was extended for seven years in 1975, twenty-five years in 1982, and an additional twenty-five years in 2006.) Moreover, black leaders rallied congressional liberals to press a reluctant Justice Department to adopt tougher procedures for screening electoral changes. In May 1971, the department announced guidelines that placed the burden of proof on state and local officials; if they could not prove that proposed changes were nondiscriminatory, the department would block implementation. Vigorously enforced by career lawyers in the Civil Rights Division, the guidelines proved an effective tool against vote dilution.

The rigorous preclearance process, however, applied only to new laws, not to measures in force before 1965. During the 1970s, blacks began to challenge pre-1965 laws establishing at-large elections and multi-seat districts, many of which had been enacted around the turn of the century as part of a disfranchisement campaign. Initially, the Supreme Court proved receptive to claims that these laws were discriminatory and therefore violated the Voting Rights Act and the Fourteenth and Fifteenth Amendments. In *White*

Figure 7.3. Clarence Mitchell in 1971 https://www.loc.gov/item/2017651388/. *Library of Congress.*

v. Regester (1973), the Court established a flexible standard for establishing unconstitutional discrimination. According to Justice White, who wrote the opinion for a 5–4 majority, whether an electoral scheme was discriminatory depended on "an intensely local appraisal" by the district court of its *"design and impact* [emphasis added] . . . in light of past and present reality, political and otherwise."[23] Therefore while the discriminatory effect of an established electoral practice did not by itself establish proof of illegal discrimination, it went a long way toward doing so. With the burden on plaintiffs lightened, civil rights lawyers enjoyed considerable success in challenging established electoral practices.

In 1980, however, the Court dealt civil rights advocates a severe blow in *City of Mobile v. Bolden,* increasing the burden of proof on challenges to voting laws adopted before 1965. To establish discrimination, the Court held, plaintiffs must prove that the electoral practice they challenged had been adopted and maintained with actual intent to discriminate against blacks. "Racially discriminatory motivation," wrote Justice Stewart, "is a necessary ingredient of a Fifteenth Amendment violation."[24] The new standard was not impossible to overcome; indeed, when the *Mobile* case was retried in the district court under the new intent standard, the plaintiffs succeeded in proving that the city's at-large elections had been adopted with the intent to dilute black votes and violated the Fifteenth Amendment. Nevertheless, establishing proof of discriminatory intent was time-consuming and expensive, making cases more difficult to win. After the Supreme Court remanded the *Mobile* case to the district court, for example, the plaintiffs required nearly two years to establish proof of discriminatory intent.

The Reagan Administration and Civil Rights in the 1980s

For civil rights advocates, the Court's decision in the *Mobile* case provided less cause for alarm than Ronald Reagan's landslide victory in the 1980 presidential election. A leader of the Republican right since the mid-1960s, Reagan had long been at odds with African American leaders. As a prominent supporter of Barry Goldwater's unsuccessful bid for the presidency in 1964, he had vigorously defended the candidate's opposition to the Civil Rights Act. And in his own successful campaign for the California governorship two years later, Reagan skillfully exploited the white backlash generated by the Watts riot. During the 1970s he became reconciled to the Civil

Rights Act but continued his running battle with black leaders, fervently denouncing busing and affirmative action.

Nor were civil rights leaders concerned only with Reagan's pedigree. Pursuing the Southern Strategy pioneered by Richard Nixon, Reagan kicked off his general election campaign in Philadelphia, Mississippi, where three civil rights workers had been murdered in 1964. Using code words that echoed his opposition to the Civil Rights Act, he proclaimed, "I believe in states' rights."[25] Conservative southern whites, members of the religious right, and northern Democrats who had left their party because of its support for civil rights, were important elements of the Reagan coalition and would exert pressure on his administration to roll back the civil rights gains of the 1970s. Appointments to crucial civil rights enforcement positions suggested that the new president was prepared to accede to their demands. Reagan named William Bradford Reynolds, a sharp critic of color-conscious remedies for past discrimination, assistant attorney general for civil rights. For chair of the Civil Rights Commission, he appointed Clarence Pendleton, a black conservative who decried affirmative action as "a bankrupt public policy."[26]

Administration officials denounced color-conscious remedies as "reverse racism" even though civil rights advocates viewed them as essential to root out the vestiges of slavery and Jim Crow. In an address at the 1982 meeting of the American Bar Association, Reynolds asserted that color-conscious remedies like affirmative action, advocated by contemporary civil rights leaders, threatened Martin Luther King Jr.'s vision of a society in which individuals "would not be judged by the color of their skin but by the content of their character." Insisting that the nation could not "get beyond racism by borrowing the tools of the racist," he insisted that "we must not again allow consideration of race to intrude upon the decisional processes of government." The quest for equality, he concluded, "should not be jeopardized by bureaucratic regulations and decisions which rely on quotas, ratios and numerical requirements to exclude some individuals in favor of others."[27] Oblivious to the legacy of discrimination that confronted African Americans, Reynolds's remarks were a dog whistle to whites who believed that women and minorities had made gains at their expense—and who were part of Reagan's base.

The administration lost no time in showing its hand on civil rights, coming to the defense of policies that were anything but color-blind. Bob Jones University, a nonprofit fundamentalist institution that prohibited interracial dating between students, challenged its loss of tax-exempt status under an Internal Revenue Service (IRS) policy that denied exemptions to institutions that practiced discrimination. In January 1982, shortly after the Supreme Court agreed to hear its case, the administration bent to pressure from Senator Trent Lott, the Mississippi Republican, and announced that it would file a brief on behalf of the university. Ultimately, that decision backfired. A torrent of protest led administration officials to scramble for cover. Denying their support for discrimination, they claimed to have challenged the IRS policy only because it had been adopted without authorization by Congress. Then in a rapid about-face, they announced support for legislation giving express statutory authority to the very IRS policy they were challenging in court. When the Court announced its decision in 1983, an 8–1 majority curtly upheld the IRS decision. Although the *Bob Jones* fiasco did no damage to the civil rights cause, it did reveal the administration's agenda.

While the *Bob Jones* controversy played out, the administration was locked in battle with civil rights leaders over voting rights. In 1981, African American leaders pressed Congress to extend the preclearance provisions of the Voting Rights Act, which were to expire the following year. They also urged adoption of an amendment to the act that would void existing electoral laws and regulations that had a discriminatory effect, thereby reversing *Mobile v. Bolden*. A bill incorporating their demands sailed through the House of Representatives, winning approval by a 389–24 margin in early October. Although Reagan understood that opposing reauthorization was not politically feasible, administration officials nevertheless launched a campaign to preserve the intent test as the bill moved to the Senate, charging that the effect standard amounted to political affirmative action. In mid-December, Reagan claimed that abandoning the intent standard would mean that "all of society had to have an actual quota system."[28]

Administration officials kept up the attack during the first three months of 1982. In February, William Bradford Reynolds denounced "race conscious remedies which require preferential treatment for minorities" in a speech to the Delaware Bar Association. And in late March, Attorney General William French Smith lambasted "the abhorrent notion that blacks can only be represented by blacks and whites can only be represented by whites" in an attack on the House bill that appeared on the Op-Ed page of the *New York Times*.[29] Nevertheless, the administration offensive failed miserably, and Senate Republican leaders agreed to a compromise bill that satisfied Democrats and civil rights advocates. The compromise extended the preclearance provision for twenty-five years and swept aside the Court's ruling in the *Mobile* case. It banned existing electoral laws and practices that, given "the totality of the circumstances" (including minorities' success in winning office), afforded minorities "less opportunity than other members of the electorate . . . to elect representatives of their choice."[30] In June the compromise passed the Senate by a 86–8 margin and won quick acceptance from the House. As he signed the bill at a White House ceremony attended by more than three hundred guests, President Reagan made the best of a bad situation. Forgetting his opposition, he cited the law as evidence of "our unbending commitment to voting rights."[31]

Despite the president's disingenuous words, the Justice Department continued to demonstrate opposition to the effect standard. For one and a half years after the new law was adopted, department lawyers ignored it, failing to challenge electoral practices that had discriminatory effects. Although the department finally initiated some vote dilution cases, it remained quite sluggish in enforcing the effect standard. Despite its substantial resources, private groups brought ten times more lawsuits challenging discriminatory electoral practices than did the Justice Department during the Reagan years. Moreover, in 1985 when the Supreme Court agreed to hear *Thornburg v. Gingles*, a case that involved interpretation of the 1982 law, the department filed an amicus curiae brief calling for a narrow reading of the effect standard. Although the Court rejected the department's argument, the case demonstrated the administration's continued opposition to effective remedies for vote dilution.[32]

Nor were Justice Department officials especially vigilant in executing their preclearance responsibilities. In 1981, for example, in the course of redrawing the state's congressional districts, Louisiana legislators deftly divided the New Orleans black community between two congressional districts, thereby splitting a large concentration of African American voters between two districts with white majorities and avoiding creation of a district with a black majority. A Republican who had served in the Nixon Justice Department characterized the plan as "a blatant intentional racial gerrymander,"[33] and career attorneys in the Civil Rights Division urged their boss to reject it. Nevertheless, Assistant Attorney General Reynolds overrode these objections and approved the plan; only a lawsuit brought by African American voters prevented the scheme from taking effect. Nor was this a momentary lapse. During the Reagan administration, a significantly higher proportion of electoral changes submitted for preclearance were approved than during the previous fifteen years.

The Reagan Justice Department also clashed with civil rights advocates over appropriate remedies for employment discrimination. Department officials denounced affirmative action plans and even opposed court orders establishing hiring and promotion goals for employers who had been found guilty of discrimination. The Fourteenth Amendment and Title VII of the Civil Rights Act of 1964, they argued, banned all forms of race and sex discrimination, including discrimination against white men. In addition, they maintained that when employers were found guilty of discrimination, judges could only order them to end their discriminatory practices and to hire or promote individuals who had proven that they had been wrongfully denied jobs or promotions. Critics pointed out that by limiting remedies to individuals who proved discrimination—an extremely expensive and time-consuming process—the administration's approach would freeze into place the effects of past discrimination. Nevertheless, officials in the Justice Department remained adamant that "public policy must be racially neutral" and that "counting by race is a form of racism."[34]

Committed to reversing precedents favorable to affirmative action established in the 1970s, the Reagan Justice Department took the offensive, regularly going to court on behalf of white males who challenged affirmative action. In 1983 it intervened in *Firefighters v. Stotts*, seeking to overturn a federal district court decision that set aside the seniority rights of white firefighters. The district court had concluded that because African Americans had been excluded from the force by discrimination until recently, layoffs based on seniority would perpetuate the effects of past discrimination. Consequently, it had ordered the department to adopt a layoff plan that would not reduce the proportion of blacks on the force, even if that meant laying off whites who had more seniority than blacks more recently hired. In 1984 the Supreme Court reversed the lower court. A slender majority of five justices, speaking through Justice White, ruled that under Title VII federal courts could set aside seniority systems only if they had been adopted and maintained with discriminatory intent.[35]

Although the *Stotts* ruling was quite limited, Justice Department officials were buoyed by language in Justice White's opinion suggesting that Title VII denied the courts' authority to establish goals and quotas. They pounced on White's cryptic remark, using it to challenge consent decrees that established hiring and promotion goals in more than fifty fire and police departments. (A consent decree is a voluntary agreement between the parties to a lawsuit that is accepted by the judge and promulgated in a court order settling the case.) Moreover, during the next two years the department filed amicus curiae briefs in several important affirmative action cases, hoping for a clear-cut ruling against affirmative action.

During 1986 and 1987, however, the Court dealt the Reagan administration a series of sharp reversals. In *Wygant v. Jackson Board of Education* (1986), the Court struck down a layoff plan—voluntarily adopted by a teachers union and a school board—that compromised the seniority rights of white teachers. Nevertheless, Justice Powell's decision for the majority rejected the administration's contention that race-conscious remedies were never acceptable. "We have recognized," Powell explained, "that in order to remedy the effects of prior discrimination, it may be necessary to take race into account. As part of this nation's dedication to eradicating racial discrimination, innocent persons may be called upon to bear some of the burden of the remedy." He carefully distinguished between preferential treatment for minorities in carrying out layoffs and other forms of affirmative action, noting that hiring goals "simply do not impose the kind of burden that layoffs impose."[36]

As Powell's comments suggested, a majority was willing to accept race-conscious remedies as long as they were narrowly drawn. In *Local 28 of the Sheet Metal Workers' International Association v. Equal Employment Opportunity Commission* (1986) and *United States v. Paradise* (1987), the Court approved lower court decisions that established hiring and promotion quotas to remedy the effects of intentional discrimination by an employer and a union. Both opinions were written by Justice Brennan and were heavily qualified, limiting the use of court-imposed quotas to cases of egregious discrimination and emphasizing that they were temporary remedies and did not require employers to hire unqualified candidates. Nevertheless, the cases dealt a blow to the Justice Department's agenda. "The plain language of Title VII," noted Justice Powell, in his concurring opinion in *Local 28*, "does not clearly support a view that all remedies must be limited to benefitting victims."[37]

The Court also accepted voluntary affirmative action plans, refusing to retreat from its 1979 ruling in the *Weber* case. In *Local Number 93, International Association of Firefighters v. City of Cleveland* (1986), the Court turned back the Justice Department's challenge to consent decrees that set hiring and promotion goals as voluntary agreements rather than orders imposed by a court. "There is no reason to think that voluntary race conscious affirmative action such as was held permissible in *Weber* is rendered impermissible by

Title VII simply because it is incorporated into a consent decree," Brennan concluded.[38] One year later, in *Johnson v. Transportation Agency* (1987), the Court rejected a challenge to a local government's voluntary affirmative action program. The case had been initiated by a white man who had been passed over for promotion in favor of a woman who had received a passing but slightly lower score (73 as opposed to 75) on her interview. Justice Brennan, who again wrote for the majority, pointed out that the plan did not reserve any positions for women and minorities but merely used race and gender as two factors among many in hiring and promotion decisions. "Such a plan is fully consistent with Title VII," Brennan concluded, "for it embodies the contribution that voluntary employer action can make in eliminating the vestiges of discrimination in the workplace."[39]

These decisions were sharp setbacks for the Reagan administration, demonstrating that it had not convinced the Court to jettison race-conscious remedies. During his first seven years in office, Reagan had filled two vacancies on the Court. In 1981, he had named Sandra Day O'Connor to fill the seat vacated by Potter Stewart, and when Chief Justice Warren Burger had resigned in 1986, he had elevated the Court's most conservative member, William Rehnquist, to the chief justiceship and appointed another pronounced conservative, Antonin Scalia, to the position vacated by Rehnquist. However, the Reagan appointments did not shift the balance of power on civil rights. Four justices—Brennan, Marshall, Blackmun, and Stevens—accepted the constitutionality of color-conscious remedies, and a fifth—Justice Powell—consistently supported affirmative action programs that were narrowly drawn and did not place severe burdens on white men. That left only four justices—Rehnquist, O'Connor, Scalia, and White (who had become increasingly conservative on civil rights)—who were hostile to affirmative action. Moreover, Justice O'Connor, though highly skeptical of affirmative action, did not reject color-conscious remedies out of hand and occasionally defected from the conservative bloc.

Affirmative action did not just survive the conservative assault. Embraced by many businesses and most educational institutions, it helped minorities and women enter occupations and professions that had previously been closed to them and, in the process, improve their income and career opportunities. Although the earnings gap remained, women closed it from 60 to 73 cents on the dollar between 1960 and 2000, and they moved from 10 percent to more than 25 percent of practitioners in such high-profile fields as law and medicine. The gains made by African Americans were also impressive. By

2000, 18 percent of African Americans over twenty-five had earned a college degree—up from just 5 percent in 1960;[40] 27 percent held management or professional positions[41]—compared with 11 percent[42] in 1970; and 55 percent had achieved middle-class status—a jump from 38 percent in 1967.[43] Concomitantly, the percentage of blacks living in poverty declined from over 40 percent in 1967 to 21 percent in 2000.[44] Popular culture celebrated the black middle class in television sitcoms like *The Jeffersons* (1975–1985), whose theme, "Movin' On Up," conveyed the sense of optimism many felt, and *The Cosby Show* (1984–1992), which showed the possibility of a happy, successful upper-middle-class black family. Indeed, Cliff Huxtable, the family's patriarch, topped *TV Guide*'s "50 Greatest TV Dads of All Time" in 2014, eclipsing Ben Cartwright, the wise, firm, empathic father on the 1960s hit Western *Bonanza*.

Of course, the lives of the Huxtables were far removed from the experience of millions of African Americans living near or below the poverty line, whether they resided in the rural South or the nation's cities. As agricultural production became mechanized and farms larger, rural America and its small towns lost population, leaving more residents, black and white, isolated, poor, and without access to good jobs. In cities—which continued to lose population to the suburbs and manufacturing jobs to rural and suburban communities as well as to China, Mexico, and other low-wage economies—many African Americans found themselves trapped in blighted neighborhoods. Good jobs—sometimes any jobs at all—were hard to come by, and unemployment rates high. From the 1970s through the mid-1990s, black unemployment typically ranged from 10–15 percent—always at least double white unemployment—and reached a high of 20 percent during the recession of the early 1980s. Among black youths, the unemployment rate exceeded 30 percent for most of the 1980s and 1990s, but rose to over 50 percent in the recession of the early 1980s. While African American high school dropout rates declined from over 20 percent in 1972 to 10 percent in 2000, far too many young African Americans lacked even the minimal education necessary to get a job.

The growth of the black middle class—coupled with passage of the Fair Housing Act of 1968, the Equal Credit Opportunity Act of 1974, and the Community Reinvestment Act of 1977—produced a modest decline in urban residential segregation between 1970 and the end of the century. Nevertheless, many African Americans lived in highly segregated neighborhoods in the urban core or older, inner suburbs like Ferguson,

Missouri. Major metropolitan areas such as New York, Chicago, Detroit, and Philadelphia remained hypersegregated, a term the sociologists Douglas Massey and Nancy Denton developed to describe cities in which African Americans clustered in neighborhoods joined together in a geographically contiguous area.[45] Segregation persisted because cities and suburbs blocked construction of low-income housing in white neighborhoods, whites fled when blacks entered their neighborhoods, many realtors and lenders continued to discriminate against black homebuyers and renters, and far too many African Americans lacked the financial resources to leave the ghetto. As a result, many African Americans remained trapped in neighborhoods where jobs were scarce, schools poor, crime common, and banks and supermarkets unknown. These communities offered limited opportunities for their residents, increased the likelihood of intergenerational poverty, and eroded hope, encouraging many young people to turn to crime.

In the mid-1980s, as crack cocaine entered the nation's ghettoes, life became even more fraught for residents. Although whites—and the media that served them—had long associated drugs with African Americans, a major study of drug use in the United States by the Department of Health and Human Services in 2000 concluded that the rate of drug use was the same among whites, blacks, and Hispanics. In the 1970s and 1980s, cocaine became popular among affluent whites, a trend highlighted by the drug-related death of *Saturday Night Live* icon John Belushi in 1982, as well as popular movies such as *Looking for Mr. Goodbar* and Eric Clapton's 1977 hit song, "Cocaine." Cocaine use by whites raised concern, but when crack cocaine entered the nation's black neighborhoods in the mid-1980s, it became an "epidemic," generating sensational news coverage and triggering a bipartisan war on drugs that proved as devastating for African American communities as the drug itself.

While powder cocaine remained popular in affluent communities, crack gained traction in poor black communities. Made by cooking powder cocaine with water and baking soda, crack takes on a crystalline form that can be smoked, entering the bloodstream quicker and creating a stronger but shorter high. Because a tenth of a gram of powder cocaine yielded a dose of crack, it was far cheaper than powder cocaine, selling for as little as $5–$10 per dose. Inner-city residents found that 100 grams of powder cocaine could be used to produce a thousand rocks of cheap crack that found a market among even young and poor residents in their neighborhoods. As a result, the number of producers and dealers grew dramatically in cities across the

United States, and crack was sold openly on the streets and from homes. As dealers battled each other for turf, guns proliferated. They included 9 mm semiautomatic handguns with magazines of two dozen or more rounds that could be fired in a matter of seconds. Crack and semiautomatic weapons were a lethal combination. Dealers and their henchmen gunned down rivals and settled scores with customers unable to pay. After hitting a fifteen-year low of 7.9 murders per 100,000 population in 1984, the nation's murder rate climbed steadily, peaking at 9.5 in 1993 (after which it declined by more than 50 percent, to 4.4 in 2014—its lowest in more than half a century). Urban areas were the center of this carnage. Washington, DC, became known as the nation's murder capital; homicides tripled there between 1985 and 1991, hitting a peak of almost 500 per year. The victims were predominantly young African American men, aged fifteen to twenty-four; the homicide rate for this group climbed from about 60 per 100,000 in 1980 to 160 in 1993— approximately 2.5 times the rate of young Hispanic males and 8 times the rate of young white men.

Even before the crack epidemic struck fear in the public, the Reagan administration launched a war on drugs. In 1982, a sharp recession drove unemployment to 10 percent on the eve of congressional elections, which escalated criticism of Reagan and his wife, Nancy, for their lavish lifestyle. Reeling from the charges that she was out of touch, Nancy Reagan adopted as her cause as First Lady a campaign against drugs in schools, and the president announced a war on drugs. "We're making no excuses for drugs. Drugs are bad and we're going after them," Reagan said sternly in his October 2 radio address. "And we're going to win the war on drugs."[46] The administration's first "victory" was passage of the Comprehensive Crime Control Act of 1984. Drafted by the Justice Department, the bill ultimately received bipartisan support, as most Democrats did not wish to be on the wrong side of an issue that responded to widespread public fear. The law created a mandatory minimum sentence for anyone who used a firearm in the commission of a violent federal crime and a mandatory sentence of fifteen years to life for anyone convicted of a third federal felony. It abolished parole for federal prisoners and sharply limited the federal judiciary's discretion by creating a sentencing commission that established guidelines federal judges must follow in imposing sentences. The law also provided an incentive for law enforcement to target drug offenders by allowing police departments to retain the majority of the cash and property they seized in drug raids. The law had a dramatic effect; within two years, it resulted in a 32 percent increase in the federal prison population.[47]

In 1986, as the Crime Control Act began to take its toll, the media's obsession with illegal drugs, and especially crack, peaked. *Newsweek* published cover stories on cocaine and crack on March 17 and June 20, 1986—"Kids and Cocaine" and "Crack and Crime"—and on Sunday, May 18, all three major New York daily newspapers—including the *Times*—ran lengthy articles on crack and its consequences. On June 30, *Sports Illustrated*'s cover story—"Death of a Dream"—reported on the shocking death of Len Bias, a University of Maryland basketball star and second pick in the 1986 NBA draft, who died of a cocaine overdose. In September, NBC and CBS aired TV specials on crack. Across the nation, many African American leaders joined the mainstream media in sounding the alarm and demanding quick action against what many described as a plague that was destroying black communities and black youth. At Bias's funeral, the civil rights activist Jesse Jackson told mourners, "ropes never killed as many of our young people as the pushers of drugs,"[48] likening drug dealers to white lynch mobs.

Politicians responded quickly, with Democratic leaders in Congress—including most members of the Congressional Black Caucus—jumping on the issue. Smarting after twenty years of being portrayed by Republicans as "soft on crime" and deeply concerned about the consequences of crack in minority communities, they demanded that Congress pass comprehensive legislation before the 1986 midterm elections. Republicans, worried that their opponents would steal the issue, quickly jumped on board. The result was speedy passage of the Anti-Drug Abuse Act of 1986, which President Reagan signed on October 17, 1986. The hastily drafted bill proved a poor fit for the problem at hand. It did nothing to address the underlying causes of the crack epidemic—poverty, unemployment, and failing schools—and provided minimal funding for drug education and treatment, which many believed critical to break the cycle of drug dependence. Most of the funds were earmarked for building new prison cells, for hiring additional federal drug enforcement officials, and for funding to enable state and local law enforcement agencies to increase firepower and further militarize their operations. These would be sorely needed because the law created mandatory minimum sentences for trafficking and a sharp differential between punishment for dealers of cocaine and crack. Those selling 5 grams of crack would receive a mandatory minimum sentence of five years, the same penalty assigned to dealers caught with 500 grams of cocaine. Two years later, Congress extended these mandatory minimums—and the differences between the amount of crack and cocaine that triggered them—to cover possession as well as trafficking.

The new federal mandatory minimum drug laws—along with a spate of laws passed by states—flew in the face of the color-blind rhetoric that justified Republican civil rights policy. Penalties for crack—which was more heavily sold and used by poor blacks—were one hundred times greater than those for cocaine—a drug primarily sold and used by whites. The popular media and many politicians justified the difference by asserting that crack was more highly addictive than cocaine and therefore merited harsher punishment. However, Congress conducted little research before adopting the new drug laws, and no scientific evidence justified the disparity. Indeed, most experts agreed that while crack provided quicker stimulation, chemically it was almost identical to cocaine and no more addictive.

The law devastated minority communities. Although many of the nation's largest cities had African American police chiefs and significant numbers of black and Hispanic officers by the late 1980s, suspicion and mistrust between the police and minority communities persisted. Federal funding provided by the 1970s war on crime and augmented by the new drug law militarized police departments with military-grade firepower, including semiautomatic weapons, assault rifles, tanks, airplanes, and helicopters. Facing a surge of violent crime and criminals armed with semiautomatic weapons, police deployed their new weaponry and resorted to aggressive tactics in encounters with young African Americans. When confronted by what they deemed suspicious behavior—often simply being young, black, male, and hanging out on the street—officers questioned and searched young African Americans on the slightest pretense. Police also routinely stopped cars driven by African Americans, usually on the pretext of having defective tail lights or making a turn without signaling, and used the stop as an excuse to search the car and its occupants. Officers found evidence that justified arrests in a small percentage of searches, but the encounters intensified hostility to and suspicion of the police that had long existed in African American communities. All too often, police resorted to violence. For example, in 1991, Rodney King, a black Los Angelino on parole for robbery, was brutally beaten by four police officers who arrested him after he led them on a high-speed chase. Captured on video, the beating showed the entire country what African Americans experienced all too frequently. When the four officers were acquitted, South Central Los Angeles exploded in an uprising even more devastating than the violence that swept the same neighborhood twenty-five years earlier during the Watts riot.

Equally serious were the new laws' harsh sentencing provisions. Emboldened by the mandate conferred by the war on drugs and armed with aggressive tactics, police arrestedtens of thousands of African Americans and charged them with dealing or using drugs, violent crimes that the drug culture bred, robbery or burglary committed to support a drug habit, or use of guns to commit a crime. Once arrested, they entered a criminal justice system—whether state or federal—that held them in overcrowded jails and methodically processed, convicted, and imprisoned them. Driven by a commitment to put away "bad guys" who destroyed communities, prosecutors resolved the vast majority of cases through plea bargains rather than trials. Armed with mandatory minimum sentencing laws that prescribed draconian penalties, they drove hard bargains to convince the accused to plead guilty to lesser—but still serious—charges and to provide evidence against others. As the US Sentencing Commission noted in 1991, "the value of a mandatory minimum sentence lies . . . in its value as a bargaining chip to be given away in return for the resource-saving plea to . . . a more leniently sanctioned charge."[49] Because most defendants were poor, they depended on overworked public defenders who lacked the time and resources to gather exculpatory evidence. Unable to mount strong defenses, they typically advised their clients to accept plea bargains that sent them to prison but reduced the time they would serve.

The upshot was a dramatic and sustained growth in the number of African Americans incarcerated in federal and state penitentiaries. The US prison population jumped from about 300,000 in 1980 to over one million in 1995 and peaked at 1.5 million in 2010. The number of Americans enmeshed in the criminal justice system—in prison or jail, on probation or parole—was even larger, growing from about 1.8 million in 1980 to over 7 million by 2010, more than 2 percent of the population. Given urban police departments' focus on inner-city neighborhoods, African American men were far more likely to be incarcerated than whites. Between 1980 and 2000, the incarceration rate for black men rose from under 1,000 per 100,000 (1 percent) to 3,500 per 100,000 (3.5 percent) while the rate for white men rose more modestly, from around 200 per 100,000 (0.2 percent) to about 500 (0.5 percent).

The result of the war on crack was perhaps the most significant and sustained assault on the rights and well-being of African Americans in a century—what Michelle Alexander called "the new Jim Crow."[50] Millions of African Americans, most of them young men, lost years of their lives to prison. When they were released their opportunities were even more limited than when they entered. Branded as felons, many lost the right to vote. A 2013 study conducted by the NAACP, the NAACP Legal Defense Fund, Inc., the ACLU, and several other civil rights organizations found that almost six million Americans were barred from voting because they had been convicted of felonies and a disproportionate number—2.2 million—were African Americans. Indeed, almost 8 percent of adult African Americans lost the right to vote because of a felony conviction—compared with fewer than 2 percent of non–African Americans.[51] In many states, those convicted of drug offenses were ineligible for public assistance and food stamps, thanks to legislation passed by Congress in 1996 barring them from these benefits unless states waived the ban. Most employers also shied away from hiring felons. For young black men who lacked a high school degree and had limited work experience, a felony conviction made prospects for employment even more remote. And without a job, ex-convicts were likely to return to crime and, before long, to prison, where they faced even harsher sentences as repeat offenders.

The war on drugs was anything but color-blind. Penalties were much harsher for crack than cocaine, police focused enforcement on black communities, and the disparity between the number of blacks and whites sent to prison was staggering. Nevertheless, a 1987 Supreme Court ruling in a death penalty case, *McCleskey v. Kemp*, foreclosed the possibility of a constitutional challenge to the discrimination woven into the fabric of the war on drugs. McCleskey, a black man, was found guilty of first-degree murder for killing a white police officer in the course of a robbery in Atlanta. The jury impaneled in the sentencing phase of McCleskey's trial found that there were aggravating circumstances that warranted imposition of the death penalty. The defense appealed the conviction, relying principally on research by David Baldus, a University of Iowa law professor, that demonstrated a statistically significant relationship between race and the imposition of the death penalty in Georgia. Baldus found that juries were far more likely to impose the death penalty when the victim was white than when he or she was black and that black defendants were more likely to receive the death penalty than whites. In short, McCleskey was more likely to be sentenced to death because he had killed a white man and was himself black. Therefore, his counsel contended, he had been denied equal protection of the laws in violation of the Fourteenth Amendment.

The Court rejected McCleskey's argument by a 5–4 margin, with Justice Powell casting the deciding vote and writing the opinion of the Court. Powell concluded that to make a successful equal protection claim, the defendant had to prove that he had suffered "purposeful" discrimination in the course of his trial, conviction, and sentencing, not merely that the system was discriminatory. Statistical analysis showed probabilities and patterns but could not prove that discrimination had occurred in a specific case. To rule otherwise, Powell explained, would eliminate the "discretionary judgments . . . essential to the criminal justice process" and, even more disturbingly, open Pandora's box by inviting challenges to disparities in sentencing for other crimes—including drug offenses. Writing for the four dissenters, Justice Brennan found that the state had violated the Eighth Amendment's ban on cruel and unusual punishment as well as the Fourteenth Amendment's guarantee of equal protection. The statistical evidence presented, he explained, demonstrated that Georgia's system of sentencing in capital cases was arbitrary and capricious, thereby violating the basic standard established in *Gregg v. Georgia* (1976). It was also "influenced by racial considerations," in violation of the equal protection clause. Georgia's "legacy of a race conscious criminal justice system" buttressed the statistical evidence, he concluded, strengthening McCleskey's claim that he had suffered discrimination because of his race. Indeed, Brennan emphasized, "it would be unrealistic to ignore the influence of history in assessing the plausible implications of McCleskey's evidence."[52]

Despite Brennan's sharp disagreement with Powell's position in *McCleskey*, the conservative Virginian had often supported race-conscious remedies for institutional racism. His landmark opinion in *Bakke* permitted universities to take race into account in admissions, and he supported narrowly tailored affirmative action hiring plans and federal minority construction set-aside programs. Therefore, when Powell announced his decision to retire in 1987, court watchers saw it as an opportunity for Reagan to achieve what had eluded him for six years: a conservative majority on the high court. The president leaped at the opportunity, nominating Robert Bork, an outspoken conservative and judge on the US Court of Appeals for the District of Columbia Circuit, to succeed him. Civil rights and women's organizations launched a well-coordinated offensive against the nominee and convinced the Senate to block Bork's nomination. Southern Democrats, fearful of alienating black constituents who adamantly opposed the nomination, played a crucial role in the outcome, attesting to the impact of the Voting Rights Act on southern politics. Reagan's second nominee, Douglas Ginsburg, withdrew his name from consideration when reports surfaced that he had smoked marijuana while a member of the Harvard Law School faculty—an embarrassing revelation for an administration that had launched a war on drugs. The third try proved to be the charm, however. In early 1988, the Senate, weary from the bruising battle over Bork, confirmed Anthony Kennedy, a cautious conservative who had served on the US Court of Appeals for the Ninth Circuit.

Although little was known of Kennedy's views on civil rights when he joined the court, his voting during his first term (1988–1989) suggested that Reagan had forged a new conservative majority. In three major civil rights cases, the freshman justice joined Rehnquist, Scalia, White, and O'Connor in decisions that represented major setbacks for civil rights advocates. In *Martin v. Wilks*, the new majority struck a severe blow at voluntary affirmative action agreements embodied in consent decrees. Even though white workers affected by the decree in question had declined to enter the case at the outset and had their objections considered by the judge, the majority ruled that they might institute a new lawsuit challenging the terms of the decree. The ruling meant that consent decrees would not protect employers from further litigation, one of their chief benefits. The result, many predicted, would be protracted litigation that would increase the time and expense required to challenge employment discrimination. Indeed, the case under consideration by the Court—which originated in a lawsuit by black firefighters and the Birmingham, Alabama, chapter of the NAACP against the city's fire department—had been in the courts for fifteen years. And the Supreme Court's ruling guaranteed that it would remain there several more years.[53]

The same 5–4 majority also badly weakened one of the principal weapons against job discrimination. Since 1976 the Court had held that Title 42, section 1981 of the United States Code (all persons "shall have the same right . . . to make and enforce contracts . . . as is enjoyed by white persons") applied to private contracts. As a result, black plaintiffs increasingly had relied on section 1981 in employment discrimination suits. In its 1989 decision in the highly publicized case of *Patterson v. McLean Credit Union*, the conservative majority agreed that section 1981 was applicable to private contracts; however, it read the provision narrowly, holding that although it prevented discrimination in hiring, it did not offer a remedy against racially motivated harassment on the job. In an opinion reminiscent of the narrow formalism that had enabled the Court to accept the separate but equal doctrine in 1896,

Justice Kennedy explained that section 1981 "extends only to the formation of a contract, but not to problems that may arise later from the conditions of continuing employment."[54] Granted, a victim of on-the-job discrimination had a remedy under Title VII, as the majority pointed out; however, section 1981 offered monetary damages that Title VII did not.

The new conservative majority dealt its severest blow to civil rights advocates in *Ward's Cove Packing Company v. Atonio.* Since 1971, when it had decided the *Griggs* case, the Court had maintained that plaintiffs in job discrimination suits need not prove intentional discrimination, only a discriminatory effect. Thus the challenged employer assumed the burden of proving that its policies were justified by business necessity. In *Ward's Cove,* however, the Court pulled back from the *Griggs* rule, holding that the burden of proof remained on the plaintiffs—not the employer—to prove that employment practices were not necessary.[55] Although the dispute concerned a technical point, the Court's ruling would make it substantially more difficult for minorities and women to prove job discrimination.

A fourth case decided during the 1988–1989 term called into question the constitutionality of voluntary affirmative action programs. In *Richmond v. Croson,* Justice Stevens joined the conservative bloc in a 6–3 decision striking down a Richmond, Virginia, ordinance that required businesses in possession of municipal construction contracts to subcontract at least 30 percent of the dollar value of their jobs to minority-owned firms. Writing for the majority, Justice O'Connor noted that government programs that gave preference on the basis of race were inherently suspect. They were not permissible to redress general societal discrimination that historically had denied minorities opportunity for economic advancement and had contributed to the paucity of minority entrepreneurs. Rather, such programs were justified only as remedies for actual discrimination against the parties that would benefit from them. The present case, O'Connor explained, contained no evidence of systematic discrimination against minority-owned construction firms and therefore no justification for the city's policy. She was careful to distinguish Richmond's policy from a strikingly similar congressional program that the Court had sustained in *Fullilove v. Klutznik* (1980). Unlike states and cities, she explained, Congress had express authority to enforce the guarantees of the Fourteenth Amendment's equal protection clause. It might use this broad discretionary authority to adopt measures designed to redress the effects of societal discrimination if necessary to achieve equality.[56] Although this concession offered some consolation to civil rights advocates, the decision suggested that voluntary affirmative action programs established by state and local government (and perhaps by private businesses) were in trouble. Indeed, in the year following *Croson*, lower courts struck down programs establishing set-asides for minority-owned businesses in six cities and one state.

The 1989 decisions suggested to many that the Reagan position on civil rights had finally triumphed. "The decisions left no doubt," according to *New York Times* legal reporter Linda Greenhouse, "that Ronald Reagan, out of office five months, finally succeeded in a goal that had appeared to elude him for much of his eight years in the White House: to shift the Supreme Court's direction on civil rights."[57] Conservatives had effectively mobilized the language of the civil rights movement to challenge race-conscious remedies necessary to remedy the continuing effects of the nation's centuries-old racial caste system. Arguing that the Constitution was color-blind and that race-conscious remedies like affirmative action constituted "reverse racism," they mounted a powerful challenge to the hard-earned victories civil rights advocates won in the 1970s and 1980s. By the late 1980s, their arguments proved increasingly influential among a growing conservative bloc on the high court. From the bench, Justice Harry Blackmun, the Nixon appointee who had become a staunch civil rights advocate, lamented the direction of the Court. "One wonders whether the majority still believes that race discrimination—or more accurately, race discrimination against nonwhites—is a problem in our society," he mused, "or even remembers that it ever was."[58]

Painfully aware that the United States had not become color-blind and that African Americans' lives were shaped by the nation's racist history, African American leaders shared Blackmun's gloomy assessment. Recalling that a century earlier the nation had reneged on its promise of equality, they became increasingly pessimistic. During the previous two decades they had moved against the tide, skillfully building on the historic victories of the 1960s to expand guarantees for civil rights. They had prodded the courts and Congress to adopt measures designed to breathe life into formal guarantees of equality. Nevertheless, as the 1980s came to an end, race remained the most divisive, the most explosive, and the most intractable problem confronting the nation. America's cities and schools remained highly segregated, hundreds of thousands of African Americans were in prison, and, despite a concerted campaign for equal employment opportunity, legal victories offered little to poor blacks trapped in poverty. Yet in the conservative atmosphere of post-Reagan Washington, quotas and "reverse racism" were, for many disgruntled whites, the biggest challenges. The bold new initiatives necessary to deal with the legacy of Jim Crow seemed unlikely to receive serious consideration. Indeed, the Supreme Court's 1988–1989 term suggested that civil rights leaders would be hard-pressed merely to protect the hard-won gains of the 1970s and 1980s.

8

The Color-Blind Challenge to Civil Rights, 1990–Present

Justice Thurgood Marshall stunned Washington, DC, as the Supreme Court's term ended on June 27, 1991, by announcing his retirement. Marshall had shaped civil rights law for sixty years. As an NAACP attorney and head of the NAACP Legal Defense Fund, he developed and executed the legal strategy that toppled Jim Crow, winning twenty-nine of thirty-two cases he argued before the Supreme Court as well as dozens of cases in state and lower federal courts. Appointed to the high court in 1967 by President Lyndon Johnson, Marshall and his ally William Brennan became the Court's conscience, supporting expansive interpretations of the Constitution and 1960s civil rights legislation designed to root out the vestiges of white supremacy. By the 1980s, however, the two were on the defensive, as a succession of justices nominated by Republican presidents moved the Court slowly but surely rightward. Arguing that the Constitution was color-blind, members of the emerging majority questioned and limited the use of race-based remedies to root out the persistent effects of racial privilege. After Brennan stepped down in 1990, Marshall, who was eighty-two, in poor health, and increasingly isolated on the Court, decided it was time to retire.

Conservatives were ecstatic. They believed that Marshall's retirement at long last paved the way for them to cement control of the Court and reverse decades of liberal jurisprudence in areas ranging from affirmative action and voting rights to abortion and defendants' rights. When Brennan had retired the previous year, President George H. W. Bush disappointed the right by naming David Souter, a moderate Republican whose judicial record on the New Hampshire Supreme Court gave no evidence of fealty to conservative principles. Seeking to assuage conservatives and at the same time name a candidate who could muster a majority in the Democratic-controlled Senate, Bush nominated as Marshall's replacement Clarence Thomas, a member of the prestigious Court of Appeals for the District of Columbia and former chair of the Equal Employment Opportunity Commission (EEOC).

Promises to Keep. Donald G. Nieman, Oxford University Press (2020). © Oxford University Press.
DOI: 10.1093/oso/9780190071639.001.0001

It was a master stroke. Conservatives, including members of the religious right, saw Thomas as one of their own. The product of a Catholic education and member of a fundamentalist congregation in suburban Washington, he was that rare breed—an African American critic of affirmative action who argued that the policy stigmatized its ostensible beneficiaries and undermined the constitutional command of equal protection without respect to race. Thomas had a powerful advocate in the Senate, the body that would determine his fate. John Danforth, his mentor, was a highly respected Republican moderate and a key supporter of the civil rights bill that Congress was then reconsidering after Bush vetoed it the previous summer. Thomas was also a difficult target for Democrats. He was an All-American success story: an African American who grew up dirt poor in Pin Point, Georgia, was raised by his grandfather, graduated from Holy Cross and Yale Law School, and reached the highest levels of public service. Even though his views were controversial and leading civil rights and women's organizations opposed his nomination, many Democratic senators—all of them white men—found taking down a black nominee with such a compelling personal story distasteful and politically risky. For six Southern Democrats who would rely heavily on black votes to win reelection in 1992, opposition could prove lethal, given strong support for Thomas among southern blacks.

The Senate Judiciary Committee began its hearings on September 10. In testimony spanning parts of five days, Thomas hewed closely to a strategy developed in concert with the White House. He and his supporters on the committee lost no opportunity to remind listeners that he had pulled himself up by his bootstraps. Thomas's background had a powerful appeal to Democrats and Republicans alike. As Senator Wyche Fowler, a Georgia Democrat, put it, "the fact he grew up poor . . . would bring a perspective to a court that was mostly white and privileged."[1] Thomas also deflected efforts by Democrats to probe his views on constitutional interpretation and controversial issues that might come before the Court. When pressed about speeches he had given endorsing the writings of conservative legal theorists whose views lay well outside the mainstream, the candidate admitted to finding them intellectually interesting but not a guide for constitutional interpretation. When pressed about his views on abortion, he indicated support for a constitutional right to privacy but said repeatedly he had never discussed with anyone the merits of the Court's 1973 decision in *Roe v. Wade* upholding a woman's right to an abortion. Even when a committee member reminded him that he had been in law school when the controversial decision came down and suggested that he must have discussed it with peers, Thomas demurred, saying that he was too busy working to support himself and his family—another reminder of the barriers he overcame. Although many found his performance wooden and unconvincing, Thomas did not appear to be a conservative ideologue and certainly not an elitist, the qualities that had sunk Robert Bork's candidacy just four years earlier.

Just as it seemed that Republicans had deflected Democratic opposition, Thomas's nomination ran into a buzz saw. In July and August, rumors circulated in Washington social and political circles that Thomas had sexually harassed a female staff attorney who worked for him at the US Department of Education's Office of Civil Rights and subsequently at the EEOC. As the hearings began, staff in the offices of several Judiciary Committee members contacted the woman, Anita Hill, a law professor at the University of Oklahoma. She told them that during the two years she worked for Thomas, he had pressured her to date him, made comments about her body and dress, boasted about the size of his penis and his enjoyment of oral sex, and described in great detail the pornographic movies he liked, including those featuring a character known as Long Dong Silver. On one occasion when they were in Thomas's office, Hill recalled, he glanced at his can of Coke and asked, "Who has put pubic hair on my Coke?"[2] Several days after the hearings concluded, Hill submitted a signed statement and was interviewed by the FBI. Shortly thereafter, FBI agents questioned Thomas, who categorically denied the charges.

Although Hill's charges circulated among committee members, the chair, Joseph Biden of Delaware, decided against reopening the hearings to explore Hill's allegations, despite their relevance to Thomas's fitness to serve on the Court. Perhaps Biden declined to act because sexual harassment was an issue that most Americans—including the white men who sat on the Judiciary Committee—neither understood nor appreciated. Biden and his colleagues also disliked the optics of conducting hearings to investigate Hill's allegations: a panel of privileged white men grilling an African American nominee about charges that conjured up stereotypes of black men as sexual predators. While the committee chose not to consider Hill's allegations publicly, they influenced its vote. The committee deadlocked 7–7, as several members who would have reluctantly supported confirmation voted against Thomas. The nomination thus went to the full Senate without a recommendation, but with a final vote scheduled for the evening of Tuesday, October 8.

Biden's effort to keep Hill's charges under wraps proved futile. On Sunday, October 6, Nina Totenberg of National Public Radio broke the story, detailing Hill's charges. Although Senate leaders initially rejected calls to postpone the vote, public outrage and pressure from a group of female legislators led by Senator Barbara Mikulski and Representatives Eleanor Homes Norton (former EEOC chair) and Patricia Schroeder compelled them to reevaluate. Senate leaders reluctantly agreed to conduct three days of hearings to explore Hill's allegations, from Friday, October 11, to Sunday, October 13, with a final vote by the Senate scheduled for Tuesday, October 15.

Americans were mesmerized by the televised hearings, which lasted for more than thirty hours, ending in the wee hours of Monday, October 14. On Friday evening, approximately 30 percent of households with a television tuned in, reducing the audience for the competing Toronto-Minnesota baseball playoff game to the smallest in playoff history.[3] Thomas categorically denied Hill's allegations and deftly placed off limits questions about his personal life that could have exposed any penchant for pornography. He put Democrats on the defensive by invoking racism—something that

Figure 8.1. Eleanor Holmes Norton, Patricia Schroeder, and other members of the House of Representatives walking to the Senate in October 1991 to demand hearings on Anita Hill's allegations of sexual harassment against Clarence Thomas https://www.loc.gov/resource/ppmsca.38877/. *Library of Congress.*

he was reluctant to recognize in the cases he adjudicated. Thomas charged that his accusers appealed to racist stereotypes to take down a successful, independent-minded black man. The fabricated charges against him "play into the worst stereotypes about black men in this society," he insisted, before calling the committee's proceedings a "high-tech lynching for uppity blacks."[4]

During more than seven hours of testimony, Hill appeared composed, sincere, and believable in the face of withering cross-examination by Republicans. After Hill ended her testimony, however, Republicans lost no opportunity to attack her credibility as they questioned Thomas—who appeared a second time following Hill's testimony—and witnesses called by each side. Republican senators found her failure to press charges against Thomas in a timely manner suspicious, insinuated that she was motivated by politics or even anger at Thomas for spurning her, and charged that she had fabricated many of the most lurid details contained in her allegations. Senator Orrin Hatch implied that words Hill attributed to Thomas—about pubic hair on his Coke can and Long Dong Silver—came from *The Exorcist* and a pornography case decided by a federal appeals court—but produced no evidence that Hill had read the book or the decision. Alan Simpson went further, telling the panel that he had "letters hanging out of my pockets" from "former law professors, from people that knew her, statements from Tulsa, Oklahoma, saying, watch out for this woman." The names of the writers and contents of their communications remained a mystery, but Simpson's claim raised questions about Hill's character. Arlen Specter, a Pennsylvania Republican, struck the lowest blow. After Hill completed her testimony and left the hearing room, Specter charged her with perjury because a statement she had made was contradicted by a quote by a friend that appeared in a press account. Because Hill had already corrected her statement, it was not perjury. Nevertheless, Specter's charge damaged Hill's credibility.

Republican attacks on Hill took their toll, as did Biden's decision not to call key witnesses. Several witnesses corroborated her story, testifying that Hill had told them about Thomas's behavior when she worked for him. Nevertheless, many critics found it strange that no other witnesses came forward to testify that Thomas had harassed them. If the person described by Hill was the real Clarence Thomas, surely others had experienced or heard about his unwanted advances. In fact, two women who worked for Thomas at the EEOC reported experiences strikingly similar to Hill's. Neither knew Hill nor one another. Both came to Washington to tell their stories to the committee, but neither was called because Republicans dragged out questioning of witnesses called by Thomas, and Biden blinked. Aware that Republicans would seek to discredit both women, exhausted by the marathon hearings, and wounded by charges that he had let the hearings turn into a circus, Biden did not call them to testify. His decision was crucial. Whatever questions Republicans might have raised about the women, the similarities between their experiences and Hill's would have strengthened Hill's credibility. The hearings ended with polls showing that twice as many Americans believed Thomas over Hill, and the Senate quickly confirmed Thomas by a 52–48 vote, with eleven Democrats—seven of them from the South—voting in favor and two Republicans voting against.

The hearings were pivotal in several respects. The battle against Thomas's confirmation reinforced the long-standing alliance between women's groups and civil rights organizations, fortifying a civil rights community increasingly on the defensive. The confirmation fight also helped Americans understand that the demeaning, threatening experiences women routinely endured in the workplace were not just offensive but constituted legal offenses. A year after the hearings, public opinion shifted dramatically, with more Americans reporting that they believed Hill than Thomas. By 1998, the EEOC received almost three times as many sexual harassment complaints as it had in 1991. Appalled that members of the all-male Judiciary Committee did not understand the demeaning treatment many women experienced, the number of women seeking election to Congress mushroomed; in 1992, twenty-four additional women won House seats and the number of women in the Senate jumped from two to six. But perhaps the most important outcome of the hearings was that Clarence Thomas replaced Thurgood Marshall on the US Supreme Court, cementing conservatives' grip on the Court and paving the way for the triumph of a color-blind constitutionalism that limited effective remedies for the institutional racism that survived the collapse of Jim Crow.

The Affirmative Action Debate

Thomas joined a Court that President Ronald Reagan had pushed sharply to the right by elevating its most conservative member, William Rehnquist, to the chief justiceship and appointing activist conservative Antonin Scalia and moderate conservatives Sandra Day O'Connor and Anthony Kennedy as associate justices. The results became apparent almost immediately. At its 1988 term, the Court handed down a series of decisions that significantly eroded major civil rights victories of the previous two decades. The biggest blow was *Ward's Cove v. Atonio Packing Co.*, which undermined *Griggs v. Duke Power*, the landmark 1971 employment discrimination ruling. When hiring practices, such as education or height qualifications, had a disparate impact on women or minorities, *Griggs* held, employers must demonstrate that the practice was justified by "business necessity." It encouraged employers to eliminate arbitrary job qualifications and exposed them to lawsuits if their workforce lacked diversity, a powerful tool for opening the workplace to those who had been historically excluded—and continued to be screened out by requirements unrelated to job performance. Other cases decided during the 1988 term weakened protections for historically disadvantaged groups: *Patterson v. McLean Credit Union* denied employees the right to seek monetary damages for discrimination by their employers under Title 42, section 1981 of the US Code; *Martin v. Wilks* allowed third-party challenges to voluntary affirmative action plans established by consent decrees in employment discrimination cases; and *City of Richmond v. Croson* declared unconstitutional a municipal ordinance requiring that minority-owned firms receive a share of construction contracts awarded by the city.

A coalition of civil rights and women's groups, led by Ralph Neas, the executive director of the Leadership Conference on Civil Rights, that included the NAACP, the NAACP Legal Defense Fund, the National Organization for Women, and the Women's Legal Defense Fund, immediately turned to Congress. There the coalition could count on support from Democrats who held solid majorities in both houses as well as a large group of Republican senators receptive to their concerns. In early 1990, Senator Edward Kennedy and Representative Augustus Hawkins introduced a bill to reverse several of the Court's most damaging 1989 rulings. Their bill required employers to demonstrate that job requirements that had a discriminatory effect on the hiring and promotion of women and minorities had "a substantial and demonstrable relationship to effective job performance" (reversing *Ward's Cove*), stipulated that section 1981 prohibited racial discrimination on the job as well as in hiring (reversing *Patterson*), and overturned *Martin* by barring challenges to consent decrees by third parties who had the opportunity to object before they were issued.

The Kennedy-Hawkins bill aimed to end a historic anomaly in civil rights law by leveling the playing field between individuals who suffered employment discrimination on the basis of race and those who experienced discrimination because of their sex, national origin, or religion. Section 1981, which originated in Reconstruction-era civil rights legislation, provided monetary damages to employees who proved that employers discriminated against them because of their race. Title VII prohibited employment discrimination on the basis of sex, religion, and national origin as well as race, but it offered successful plaintiffs only the job they had been wrongfully denied as well as back pay. The bill eliminated this anomaly by authorizing monetary damages to those who suffered intentional employment discrimination on account of sex, religion, or national origin as well as race.

While the bill commanded majorities in both houses of Congress, sponsors feared that they might not have the votes to override a veto. Therefore, they began negotiations with the White House to find a mutually agreeable compromise. Discussions focused on provisions reversing *Ward's Cove* and restoring the *Griggs* standard. President George H. W. Bush and his advisors maintained that by returning the burden of proof to employers when plaintiffs demonstrated that hiring practices adversely affected women and minorities, the legislation would compel employers to create hiring quotas to escape litigation. The Leadership Conference's Neas, along with Vernon Jordan, a Democratic political insider and former executive director of the Urban League, and William Coleman, president of the NAACP Legal Defense Fund and an influential Republican, insisted that restoration of the *Griggs* standard was essential to prevent discrimination.

When the bill's supporters refused to accept watered-down language demanded by the administration, Bush vetoed the bill in October 1990. In his veto message, he appealed to color-blind principles conservatives used to challenge affirmative action and other remedies against institutional racism. "When our efforts, however well intentioned, result in quotas, equal opportunity is not advanced but thwarted," he asserted. "The very commitment to justice and equality that is offered as the reason why this bill should be signed requires me to veto it."[5] The bill's supporters mustered the necessary two-thirds majority in the House to override, but fell one vote short in the Senate, even though eleven Republicans supported the bill. Republican support reflected a continuing, if shrinking, consensus on civil rights that had been key to civil rights victories for a quarter century. It also signaled many northern Republicans' concerns about alienating women and exacerbating the gender gap that emerged during the Reagan years as well as their desire to distance themselves from the rising tide of white supremacy. Senator Rudy Boschwitz, a Minnesota Republican who initially opposed the bill, voted to support the override when he saw David Duke, the former Ku Klux Klan leader and current Republican candidate to represent Louisiana in the US Senate, sitting in the gallery, ready to proclaim victory when Congress sustained the veto.

Given broad congressional support, the bill's sponsors revived it during the next session, naming it the Civil Rights Restoration Act of 1991. It sailed through the House, but with the prospect of another Bush veto, its sponsors renewed negotiations with the White House that dragged into October, as the Thomas hearings reached their conclusion. Ironically, Senator John Danforth, Thomas's most dogged supporter, emerged as the key figure in forging a compromise that secured most of what Democrats wanted while bringing along enough Republicans to make it clear that a veto would fail. A moderate Republican who was deeply concerned about growing racial divisions, Danforth saw his mission as "reconstituting a political consensus in our country that had been threatened."[6] The bill Danforth brokered reversed *Ward's Cove*, the issue that had torpedoed efforts at compromise a year earlier. It provided that when hiring practices resulted in women and minorities being hired at lower rates than their percentage of the workforce, employers bore the burden of proving that the practices were "job-related for the position in question and consistent with business necessity." Danforth's formulation was strengthened by a study completed by the prestigious New York law firm Fried, Frank, Harris, Shriver, and Jacobson for the NAACP Legal Defense Fund showing that in the eighteen years the courts had applied this standard, employers had prevailed in 28 percent of lawsuits in disparate impact cases—a blow to Bush's charge that the new legislation was a "quota bill."

The Danforth compromise also stipulated that section 1981 allow victims of racial discrimination in hiring *and* on the job to obtain monetary damages and barred individuals from reopening consent agreements in employment discrimination cases if they had the opportunity to object before the settlement was adopted. Finally, the bill amended Title VII by allowing monetary damages to individuals who suffered employment discrimination on the basis of sex, national origin, or religion as well as race, although it limited the amount of damages plaintiffs could collect. Bush disliked the bill but signed it when he realized that Danforth had assembled sufficient Republican support to make it veto-proof. In the end, the coalition of civil rights and women's groups that had helped shape civil rights law and policy since the 1960s mobilized Democratic and Republican allies in Congress to carry the day. Yet even they realized that they were fighting a rearguard action against conservative adversaries who appealed to color-blind principles to dismantle remedies for the discrimination that remained woven into the fabric of American culture.

Although they were unable to block passage of the civil rights bill, conservatives continued to attack color-conscious remedies necessary to the legacy of slavery and Jim Crow. President George H. W. Bush's attacks on quotas in the battle over the Civil Rights Restoration Act resonated with many white men and reverberated in heated debates over affirmative action that flared in the mid-1990s. Developed to address persistent racial and gender discrimination and its enduring effects in employment, government contracting, and university admissions, affirmative action programs created in the 1960s and 1970s took a variety of forms. Some were aspirational, setting goals and timetables for achieving greater diversity, while others established hiring and admissions quotas or required that a certain percentage of construction contracts be allocated to minority-owned companies. The US Supreme Court ruled that quotas violated the equal protection clause unless mandated by courts to remedy proven acts or patterns of discrimination or agreed to voluntarily by employers and unions. While the Court declared quotas impermissible, it held that universities and employers had a legitimate interest in assembling a diverse student body or workforce. Consequently, they could use race and sex as one among many considerations in admissions and hiring, as the Court held in *Regents of the University of California v. Bakke* (1978). In the case of government contracts, the Court drew a distinction between federal and state minority set-aside programs. Congress's spending power and authority to enforce the Fourteenth Amendment allowed it to establish minority set-asides. The equal protection clause, however, barred states from establishing quotas based on race, including when they awarded construction contracts.

The Court's rulings on affirmative action represented a complex and sometimes contradictory compromise on a highly charged issue, leaving many dissatisfied. Conservatives—including some who once had been staunch segregationists—argued that the Constitution was color-blind and prohibited any consideration of race, whether by federal, state, or local government. Many suspected that universities and employers surreptitiously used affirmative action to create de facto quotas that privileged race over merit—and disadvantaged white men. In the context of the late 1980s and early 1990s, when many workers suffered as a result of deindustrialization, these concerns resonated with many white voters who had traditionally voted Democratic. Republican politicians exploited these fears. In vetoing the Civil Rights Act of

1990, George Bush won kudos from the right for labeling it "a quota bill." No one, however, used the issue more effectively than Jesse Helms, the conservative ideologue who faced a formidable challenge in the 1990 North Carolina Senate race from Harvey Gantt, an African American architect and former mayor of Charlotte. Helms ran a television ad featuring the hands of a white man crumpling a letter as a voice-over proclaimed, "You needed that job, and you were the best qualified. But they had to give it to a minority because of a racial quota. Is that really fair?"[7] It worked, helping Helms win reelection by a 53–47 percent margin.

Debate over affirmative action ebbed in the early 1990s, as the recession of 1990–1991 and the continuing economic pain that accompanied the nation's shift from an industrial to a service economy became the focus of the 1992 presidential campaign, a three-way contest between George Bush, Democrat Bill Clinton, and independent Texas billionaire Ross Perot. Clinton, a moderate Democrat, steered away from divisive social and cultural issues. "It's the economy, stupid!" became his mantra as he focused on matters vital to struggling working- and middle-class voters, many of whom Ronald Reagan had peeled away from the Democratic Party. This strategy—and the votes Perot siphoned from Bush—helped Clinton become the first Democrat in more than a decade to win the presidency. Clinton's undisciplined personal style, the failure of major policy initiatives on health care and gays and lesbians in the military, and the historic tendency for an incumbent president's party to lose seats in midterm elections resulted in a Democratic rout in the 1994 congressional elections. Republicans reclaimed the Senate and won control of the House for the first time in forty years.

Ascendant in Congress and seeing an opportunity to win control of the presidency in 1996, Republicans once again used affirmative action as a wedge issue to attract working- and middle-class white voters. As a Republican advisor explained, "the issue of . . . racial preferences is very close to the top" of the party's priorities because it "is a no-lose proposition." In February 1995, Senate majority leader Bob Dole, eyeing a presidential bid, asked the Congressional Research Service to assemble a list of federal laws that involved preferences based on race or gender. Other Republican presidential hopefuls—Senator Phil Gramm of Texas, Governor Pete Wilson of California, and former secretary of education Lamar Alexander—attacked affirmative action, promised to end it if elected, and supported a ballot initiative gaining steam in California.

Proposition 209, initiated by two white professors in the California State University system, barred the use of "race, sex, color, ethnicity, or national origin as a criterion for either discriminating against, or granting preferential treatment to, any individual or group in the operation of the State's system of public employment, public education, or public contracting." Wilson had become a supporter of the measure, even before he announced his bid for the presidency. When the effort faltered because of poor management and finances, he enlisted his friend and longtime ally Ward Connerly to help. An African American businessman and member of the University of California Board of Regents, Connerly already had his sights trained on affirmative action in admissions in the UC system. At Wilson's behest, Connerly assumed leadership of the campaign for Proposition 209. He succeeded on both fronts. In July 1995, the California Regents voted to end affirmative action in admissions throughout the system; seven months later, in February 1996, with the presidential primaries in full swing, Proposition 209 won a place on the November ballot.

In July 1995, with Republicans on the attack and the election little more than a year away, President Clinton chose to address the issue in a highly publicized speech. While he admitted that affirmative action should not continue forever and that some abused it, he embraced it as an essential tool in the nation's long struggle for equal rights. It reflected the nation's commitment to equal opportunity, had been initiated with bipartisan support, and strengthened businesses, the military, government, and universities by increasing diversity in their ranks. Affirmative action did not mean quotas or hiring or admitting individuals who were unqualified, Clinton claimed, but it was necessary to battle historically rooted and continuing discrimination against women and minorities. Emphasizing that "the job of ending discrimination in this country is not over," he pledged to continue affirmative action programs while fixing their shortcomings. "We should have a simple slogan," the president asserted. "Mend it, but don't end it."[8]

Clinton proved more persuasive than his Republican critics. Polls showed that while a majority of Americans opposed special treatment for minorities and women, an equally large majority favored affirmative action designed to help blacks and women get better jobs and education.[9] If affirmative action meant quotas, few supported it; if it meant creating opportunity, few opposed it. California's Proposition 209, which was framed as prohibiting preferential treatment, sailed to victory by a 54–46 percent margin. However, even before the 1996 campaign ended, opposition to affirmative action lost its allure for the GOP. Republican leaders in Congress abandoned their bill to eliminate federal affirmative action programs, and most candidates dropped the issue. "Heading into the final eight weeks of the election . . . the affirmative action issue has virtually fallen from view," the *Washington Post* exclaimed.[10] Americans' ambivalence, concern about alienating women, and Clinton's skillful reframing of the issue increased the risk and decreased the benefit of attacking affirmative action. Far from serving as a wedge issue to help Republicans take back the White House, it fizzled as Clinton cruised to a comfortable victory over Republican nominee Bob Dole.

As politicians debated affirmative action, the US Supreme Court handed down a major—if inconclusive—ruling on federal set-aside programs in construction, *Adarand Constructors v. Peña* (1995). Adarand, a Colorado firm that installed highway guardrails, was the low bidder on a highway construction project won by Mountain Gravel & Construction. However, Mountain Gravel passed over Adarand and awarded the guardrail contract to Gonzales Construction Company because the US Department of Transportation gave contractors a financial incentive for subcontracting with "disadvantaged business enterprises (DBEs)." Under federal law, DBEs were presumed to be small businesses owned by minorities and women, although other individuals had the opportunity to prove that their small firms were socially disadvantaged. Adarand claimed that the department's presumption that minority-owned firms like Gonzales qualified for the incentive gave them an advantage, were discriminatory, and therefore violated the Constitution's guarantee of equal protection. The Court agreed, ruling 5–4 that because the department's policy constituted a racial classification it was subject to strict scrutiny. "Our action today," wrote Justice O'Connor for the majority, "makes explicit [that] federal racial classifications, like those of a State, must serve a compelling governmental interest and must be narrowly tailored to further that interest."

The conservative majority's decision overturned long-established precedent that gave Congress broad authority to establish minority set-aside programs under its power to enforce the Fourteenth Amendment's equal protection clause. Not surprisingly, it invited a sharp rebuke from the minority. Emphasizing that women and minorities still did not enjoy a level playing field in the construction industry, Justice Stevens challenged the majority's reliance on color-blind principles as overly simplistic, uninformed by history, and insensitive to current realities. He chided the majority for its inability to distinguish between invidious discrimination against minorities and programs designed to compensate for the continuing effects of that discrimination. "There is no moral or constitutional equivalence," Stevens wrote, "between a policy that is designed to perpetuate a caste system and one that seeks to eradicate racial subordination."[11]

Federally funded projects constituted a significant portion of construction in the United States, so many feared that *Adarand* would end programs that had helped women and minorities enter a field long dominated by white men. However, Justice O'Connor's opinion offered hope that set-aside programs could be adapted to withstand the Court's new requirement. Rejecting "the notion that strict scrutiny is 'strict in theory, but fatal in fact,'" she acknowledged "the unhappy persistence of both the practice and the lingering effects of discrimination against minority groups in this country" and asserted that "race based action" to combat it would meet constitutional muster if narrowly tailored.

The Clinton administration took the hint and issued regulations that encouraged awarding 10 percent of federal construction funds to DBEs as a target, not a quota, made it easier for small business owners who were neither women nor minorities to gain certification as disadvantaged, and gave preference to minority contractors only in those industries and parts of the country where the data demonstrated that their success in winning contracts was less than would be expected given the number of minority firms in the market. The new regulations were favorably received in the federal courts, allowing the program to continue. Even many Republicans came on board. In 1998, with fifteen Republican senators voting in favor, Congress extended the stipulation that 10 percent of the funds expended on projects supported by the Department of Transportation should go to small businesses controlled by socially and economically disadvantaged individuals. Republicans worried that voting to kill the program would damage the party's ability to close the gender gap and attract Hispanic voters. As Senator John McCain explained, "the danger exists that our ... intentions will be misperceived, dividing our country and harming our party."[12]

While many conservative politicians shied away from discussion of affirmative action, conservative activists continued to fight it in the courts. At the forefront was the Center for Individual Rights (CIR), a nonprofit public interest law firm founded in 1989 to advance a libertarian agenda. Adopting the model established by such liberal organizations as the ACLU, the Women's Legal Defense Fund, Public Citizen, and the NAACP Legal Defense Fund, the Center recruited conservative lawyers who practiced in private firms to represent individuals whose cases offered opportunities to establish precedents that would advance the conservative agenda in areas like affirmative action. The time was right to launch a libertarian public interest venture; many attorneys who cut their teeth in the Reagan and Bush administrations had left government service for private law firms and were eager to work with the Center and its clients. Conservative donors and foundations also opened their checkbooks to provide financial support.

The Center's affirmative action litigation centered on higher education, with the goal of overturning *Bakke*. In 1992, it found the perfect case. Steven Wayne Smith, a conservative Austin attorney who subsequently won election to the Texas Supreme Court, contacted white students with strong academic records who had been denied admission to the University of Texas (UT) School of Law. Four of them—including Cheryl Hopwood, a twenty-eight-year-old mother who had worked her way through college, earning a 3.8 GPA and a competitive LSAT score—became plaintiffs in a case challenging the school's admissions policies. UT was an easy target because its law school created an admissions index number—a combination of GPA and LSAT score—and had one classification scale for African American and Hispanic applicants and another for all other applicants. Not surprisingly, the US Court of Appeals for the Fifth Circuit ruled the school's admissions policy unconstitutional. But it went further, asserting that Justice Powell's opinion in *Bakke* "is not binding precedent on this issue" because it did not command a majority of the justices when it was decided. After dismissing *Bakke* as precedent, the court asserted that "any consideration of race or ethnicity by the law school for the purpose of achieving a diverse student body is not a compelling interest under the Fourteenth Amendment."[13] The Supreme Court declined to consider the case on appeal, so the circuit court's opinion was neither overruled nor endorsed as the law of the land. However, it did become binding in the Fifth Circuit, effectively outlawing affirmative action by universities in Texas, Louisiana, and Mississippi.

The civil rights community gave no ground to the CIR. Venerable public interest litigation groups such as the NAACP Legal Defense Fund monitored, helped with strategy, and litigated affirmative action cases. As the Fifth Circuit struck a blow to affirmative action in *Hopwood*, a case involving teacher layoffs threatened a conservative victory in the Supreme Court. In the process of reducing staff to meet budget cuts, the Piscataway, New Jersey, public school administration decided to eliminate one position from its business education department. The two instructors with the least seniority—and therefore first in line to be fired—were Sharon Taxman and Debra Williams, both of whom had been hired on the same day. However, Taxman was white and Williams African American. Because Williams was the only African American teacher in the department, the district decided to terminate Taxman, thereby preserving diversity that it considered critical to its educational mission. Taxman sued, claiming that by basing its decision on race, the district violated the equal protection clause and federal civil rights laws. She prevailed in the district court and the Court of Appeals for the Third Circuit, in part because the school district's attorneys had not presented evidence that demonstrated the importance of diversity to the district's mission. When the US Supreme Court decided to hear the case in 1997, the Legal Defense Fund saw a disaster in the making. Elaine Jones, the executive director, concluded that the record developed by the school board's attorneys failed to demonstrate that diversity was a compelling interest of the district, making the chances of success before the Court low and the risk of a decision crippling affirmative action high. She rallied other civil rights organizations to pay 70 percent of the $450,000 necessary to settle the case before it reached the high court.

While affirmative action defenders dodged a bullet in New Jersey, another challenge loomed in Michigan. In 1996, Carl Cohen, a University of Michigan philosophy professor, used the state's freedom of information law to obtain the university's admissions policy, which clearly gave preference to minority students. A lifelong Democrat, former president of the state ACLU, and author of a book critiquing affirmative action, Cohen took his findings to the state legislature. There he found an ally in Representative Deborah Whyman, a conservative Republican. Whyman contacted the CIR, and together they developed a plan to find clients. Whyman made frequent media appearances to call attention to the University's policy, hoping that unsuccessful applicants would come forward as plaintiffs. After vetting the two hundred names Whyman generated, the CIR selected Jennifer Gratz, who had earned a 3.8 GPA and membership in the National Honor Society at a suburban Detroit high school, as the lead plaintiff. Not surprisingly, the publicity surrounding Michigan's use of affirmative action in undergraduate admissions sparked suspicion among unsuccessful white applicants to the University's prestigious law school. One of these, Barbara Grutter, a forty-three-year-old mother of two who boasted a 3.8 undergraduate GPA and scored in the eighty-sixth percentile on the LSAT, came to the attention of the CIR. After interviewing her, its attorneys selected her as the lead plaintiff in a second case, challenging the law school's use of affirmative action in admissions. Two cases naming University of Michigan president Lee Bollinger as the defendant—*Gratz v. Bollinger* and *Grutter v. Bollinger*—were filed in US district court in October 1997.

Gratz and *Grutter* challenged different approaches to affirmative action, making them ideal vehicles to foreclose different paths to diversity and drive a stake in *Bakke's* heart. The undergraduate admissions policy at issue in *Gratz* used an index derived from a variety of factors, including high school GPA, ACT or SAT scores, geographic residence, unusual circumstances in the individual's life, diversity attributes, and relationships with alumni, to rank students. Of the 100 points necessary to guarantee admission, 20 were awarded to underrepresented minorities—African Americans, Hispanics, and Native Americans. As a result, minority students with lower GPAs and ACT scores were admitted while Gratz was denied the opportunity to attend the state's flagship school. The law school policy challenged by Grutter was more nuanced. It employed a holistic review of candidates, including undergraduate GPA, the quality of the applicant's undergraduate institution and the difficulty of undergraduate courses taken, LSAT scores, letters of recommendation, the applicant's essay, and the applicant's contributions to diversity. The policy defined diversity more broadly than race, but emphasized a commitment to "one particular type of diversity," namely "racial and ethnic diversity with special attention to the inclusion of students from groups which have been historically discriminated against, like African Americans, Hispanics, and Native Americans, who without this commitment might not be represented in our student body in meaningful numbers." The result was that minority applicants with lower GPAs and LSAT scores than Grutter were admitted to the law school.

As the cases wended their way through the lower federal courts, the University of Michigan mounted a herculean defense of its policies. Unlike the Piscataway school board, the university mustered its considerable academic prowess and connections to produce a mountain of evidence demonstrating its compelling interest in a diverse student body. While the Bush administration and more than a dozen individuals and organizations such as the Cato Institute and Ward Connerly filed amicus curiae briefs on behalf of the plaintiffs, over sixty universities, professional associations, businesses, advocacy organizations, and retired military officers filed briefs on behalf of the university. Especially notable was the so-called military brief joined by three former chairs of the Joint Chiefs of Staff, three former superintendents of the service academies, and a former secretary of defense. It emphasized the importance of diversity to military leadership and the nation's security. "A highly qualified racially diverse officer corps educated to command our nation's racially diverse enlisted ranks is essential to the military's ability to fulfill its principal mission to provide national security," the brass argued, adding that "limited race-conscious recruiting and admissions policies" to the academies and ROTC was essential to achieve this imperative. A brief from General Motors, the university's neighbor, argued that companies needed a diverse workforce that had "learned to work productively . . . with individuals from a multitude of races and ethnic, religious and cultural backgrounds" if they were to "maintain America's competitiveness in the increasingly diverse and interconnected world economy." "A ruling proscribing the consideration of race and ethnicity in admissions decisions," GM asserted, "would dramatically reduce diversity at our nation's top institutions and thereby deprive students who will become the core of our nation's business elite of the interracial and multicultural interactions in an academic setting that are so integral to their cross-cultural skills."[14] The outpouring of support for affirmative action from leaders in academia, business, defense, and the professions was a testament to how America's elite had embraced diversity and underscored the durability of the compromise forged by Justice Powell in his *Bakke* opinion twenty-five years earlier.

When the US Supreme Court handed down its much anticipated rulings in *Gratz* and *Grutter* in June 2003, diversity triumphed and *Bakke* survived, even though the university prevailed in *Grutter* but not *Gratz*. The Court declared the undergraduate admissions policy unconstitutional in a 6–3 vote in *Gratz*. By awarding minority applicants one-fifth of the points necessary to secure admission, the majority concluded, the university's policy was "not narrowly tailored to achieve the interest in educational diversity that respondents claim justifies the program." However, a 5–4 majority in *Grutter* not only upheld the law school's holistic admissions policy but also offered a ringing endorsement of Justice Powell's *Bakke* opinion. "We endorse Justice Powell's view that student body diversity is a compelling state interest that can justify the use of race in university admissions," Justice O'Connor wrote. A diverse student body, she explained, "promotes 'cross-racial understanding,'" makes classroom discussions more robust, and "better prepares students for an increasingly diverse workforce and society, and better prepares them as professionals." More broadly, O'Connor explained, diversity was critical to social stability. Because many graduates of elite law schools served in

Congress and as governors, and federal and state judges, it was "necessary that the path to leadership be visibly open to talented . . . individuals of every race" if the nation was to "cultivate a set of leaders with legitimacy in the eyes of the citizenry." The law school's affirmative action policy not only served a compelling interest, but it was narrowly tailored to achieve that goal. It did not establish a quota or give a fixed number of points to minority candidates. Rather, it was "flexible enough to ensure that each applicant is evaluated as an individual and not in a way that makes an applicant's race or ethnicity the defining feature of his or her application." In short, it was a model of how a university could take race into account without running afoul of the equal protection clause.[15] Affirmative action remained alive, if constricted.

The New Face of Disfranchisement

Civil rights advocates also found themselves on the defensive in voting rights cases. In the wake of the 1990 census, states began the complicated, high-stakes, intensely political process of redistricting. Revisions to the Voting Rights Act adopted in 1982 banned electoral practices—including redrawing electoral districts—that made it more difficult for minorities to elect candidates of their choice. Electing candidates of their choice, of course, included the opportunity to elect minorities. In the South that was only likely in districts with heavy concentrations of minorities because most whites were unwilling to vote for African American candidates. As a result, civil rights advocates argued that the Voting Rights Act required politicians, where possible, to create districts with a majority or at least a high percentage of minorities. Their arguments carried weight. When states had the opportunity to draw districts with a high percentage of minorities and chose not to, they could be sued for violating the Voting Rights Act. In the South, where the act required all redistricting to be approved by the Justice Department, states faced even more immediate pressure to create majority minority districts (i.e., districts in which minorities constituted a majority of the residents). The Bush Justice Department refused to approve redistricting plans that did not include the maximum number of heavily minority districts feasible. By doing so, it hoped to concentrate African Americans—the most reliably Democratic voters—into a few districts, thereby making Republicans more competitive in other districts. The upshot was a spike in congressional districts with substantial minority populations and a concomitant surge in

African American and Hispanic membership in Congress from thirty-two in 1990 to fifty-one in 1992.

Predictably, challenges to the new electoral maps quickly emerged. They relied on a growing body of conservative scholarship that portrayed efforts to increase minority representation as antithetical to the civil rights movement's goal of creating a color-blind society and a violation of the equal protection clause. The most influential conservative voice was Abigail Thernstrom, whose 1987 book *Whose Vote Matters* resonated with conservative politicians, lawyers, and judges. Thernstrom argued that the intent of the Voting Rights Act was to eliminate laws and practices that kept minorities from voting, not to guarantee that they won elections. Through court decisions and amendments to the Voting Rights Act, she insisted, the civil rights lobby had transformed the act into a mechanism for assuring proportional representation for minorities. By creating racial quotas for elected positions, Thernstrom concluded, these changes injected the evils of affirmative action into politics. They rested on the pernicious assumption that only African Americans could represent African Americans, threatened to racially balkanize American politics, and denied Martin Luther King's dream that all Americans would be judged "by the content of their character rather than the color of their skin."[16] Her analysis ignored continued efforts by whites to exclude minorities from positions of power as well as the fact that whites' voting behavior had already created racial balkanization in American politics. Nevertheless, her book became a weapon for conservative judges, lawyers, and intellectuals.

North Carolina provided the test for Thernstrom's critique. In redistricting after the 1990 census, the state created one majority minority district in the eastern part of the state, opening the way for the first African American to represent North Carolina in Congress since 1901. The Bush Justice Department refused to approve the state's redistricting plan, however, insisting that the state create a second majority minority district. The state complied, redrawing the boundaries of 12th congressional district so that it contained an African American majority. The district stretched 150 miles along the I-85 corridor from Charlotte to Durham and was sometimes so narrow that people on different sides of the interstate voted in different districts. As one prominent Democrat quipped, "I love the district because I can drive down I-85 with both doors open and hit every person in the district."[17] Although creation of two majority minority districts reversed ninety years of law and policy that had kept North Carolina blacks from having one of their own seated in Congress, the odd shape of the district and the role race played in creating it made the 12th a target for opponents of race-conscious redistricting.

In early 1992, Robinson Everett, a Democrat, retired chief judge of the US Court of Military Appeals, and faculty member at Duke University Law School, recruited Ruth Shaw and three other white Democrats to join him in a lawsuit asking the US district court to enjoin implementation of the redistricting plan. Asserting that "the Constitution is color-blind," Everett charged that the redistricting plan imposed on the legislature by the Justice Department amounted to "racial gerrymandering" and "a racial quota system."[18] A three-judge district court dismissed the case, concluding that the plaintiffs had not established "the requisite discriminatory purpose and effect on them as individuals or a cognizable group" required by the law. Undeterred, Everett appealed to the Supreme Court, hoping its newly reinforced conservative majority would prove more responsive.

In 1993, when the Court issued its decision in *Shaw v. Reno*, Everett felt vindicated. Writing for a 5–4 majority, Justice O'Connor stopped short of declaring the 12th district unconstitutional, but remanded the case to the district court for a full trial. Nevertheless, her opinion cast a long shadow over the constitutionality of majority minority districts. While admitting that the Court "never has held that race-conscious decision making is impermissible [under the equal protection clause] in all circumstances," O'Connor ruled that if race was the predominant motive in creating a district, it would be a racial classification subject to strict scrutiny and justified only if the state could demonstrate a compelling justification. And she strongly suggested that race motivated those who created the 12th district because its odd shape disregarded "traditional districting principles such as compactness, continuity, and respect for political subdivisions." Seemingly oblivious to North Carolina's long history of excluding African Americans from voting and office holding and the well-documented aversion of white North Carolinians to vote for black candidates, O'Connor ignored any consideration of why majority minority districts might be necessary to give African Americans a full voice in the political process. Instead, she catalogued the evils of "racial gerrymandering." Relying on race to draw districts, she argued, segregated voters, "balkanize[s] us into competing racial factions," and "reinforces the perception that members of the same racial group . . . think alike, share the same political interests, and will prefer the same candidates." Indeed, racial classifications "of any sort pose the risk of lasting harm to our society," she asserted, by reinforcing the belief that "individuals should be judged by the color of their skin."[19] According to O'Connor, race-conscious remedies for entrenched racism were a greater threat to a color-blind society than the actual behavior of North Carolina whites who refused to consider voting for a black candidate.

Two years later, in *Miller v. Johnson*, the Court underscored its hostility to majority minority districts created by states to comply with the Voting Rights Act. When Georgia sought approval from the Justice Department for the new congressional districts it created following the 1990 census, the department rejected the plan because only two of the state's eleven districts had black majorities even though the state's population was 27 percent African American. The legislature created a third black majority district, the 11th, which was not irregular in shape but stretched 260 miles from Atlanta to Savannah. White plaintiffs challenged it as the kind of racial gerrymander that *Shaw* subjected to strict scrutiny. A three-judge US district court ruled that race had been the motivating factor in creating the district, that the state had not demonstrated a compelling justification for doing so, and therefore had violated the equal protection clause.

Writing for a 5–4 majority, Justice Anthony Kennedy upheld the district court's ruling. Even though the 11th district was not "so bizarre that it is inexplicable other than on the basis of race," Kennedy explained, the record demonstrated that "race was the predominant factor motivating the drawing of the 11th district," so the state must show a compelling reason for its action. Complying with the Justice Department's guidance was not a compelling justification, he argued, because any interpretation of the Voting Rights Act that required race-based districting "raises a serious constitutional question." Like O'Connor in *Shaw*, Kennedy seemed oblivious to the difference between invidious segregation practiced in the Jim Crow era and race-conscious remedies designed to overcome Jim Crow's legacy. "Just as a State may not, absent extraordinary justification, segregate citizens on the basis of race in in its parks, buses, golf courses, beaches and schools," Kennedy asserted, "it may not separate its citizens into different voting districts on the basis of race."[20] The fundamental difference between Jim Crow's stigmatizing restrictions and policies designed to combat its persistent effects eluded Kennedy. Like O'Connor, he seemed to believe that invoking color-blind principles was like waving a magic wand that would usher the nation into a post-racial age.

The Court's decisions not only threatened the vitality of the Voting Rights Act, they made little sense to those familiar with the complexities of the redistricting process. With access to block-level census data, powerful computers, and robust mapping software, politicians could slice and dice the population to create districts that maximized outcomes for themselves and their party. A variety of demographic factors helped predict the political orientation of a particular neighborhood or community—party registration, wealth, education levels, age—but none was more reliable than race, especially in the South where blacks voted Democratic at a rate of 90 percent or higher. The Court's decisions recognized political advantage, including incumbent protection, as a legitimate consideration in districting but made race suspect even though it was the most reliable predictor of how individuals would vote. But how could race be separated from party considerations given its predictive value? Weren't the two inseparable? And if politicians chose to divide black populations among districts rather than concentrate them, weren't they deliberately creating districts that made it more difficult for African Americans to elect representatives of their choice, thereby violating the Voting Rights Act? "Every time districts are drawn in states containing 'significant' numbers of minority voters, those voters have to be 'placed' somewhere," historian J. Morgan Kousser observed. "If [the statements in Justice Kennedy's *Miller* opinion] . . . take on an independent life, as Supreme Court opinions often do . . . then any districting plan whatsoever in such states might end up in court."[21]

Perhaps the implications of *Miller* led the Court—or at least Justice O'Connor—to temper application of color-blind principles—as she had in *Adarand* and would in *Grutter*. Ironically, it was continued litigation over North Carolina's 12th congressional district that provided the vehicle for a recalibration. In *Shaw v. Reno* (1993), the Court had remanded a challenge to the constitutionality of the 12th congressional district to the district court. After a full trial, that court ruled that, while the legislature had used race in drawing the district, it had a compelling interest in doing so, namely complying with the Voting Rights Act. Robinson Everett—still guiding the case— appealed to the Supreme Court, which ruled in *Shaw v. Hunt* (1996) that race had been the predominant factor in creating the 12th district, that the state had not demonstrated a compelling interest in doing so, and the district must be redrawn. In 1997, the legislature responded to the Court's directive, drawing a new 12th that was less irregularly shaped than the original, divided fewer counties and precincts, and was only 47 percent African American. Not surprisingly, it did not satisfy Everett, who persuaded the district court to issue a summary judgment, ruling that the legislature had again been primarily motivated by race and that the district had therefore been created in violation of the equal protection clause. In *Hunt v. Cromartie* (1999), the high court sent the case back to the district court for a full trial. After a trial in which politicians involved in creating the district testified, emails exchanged among those who drew the district lines were entered as evidence, and expert testimony was considered, the district court again found that racial consid- erations had predominated in creating the district. It found unpersuasive the state's argument that political motives—creating a safe Democratic district and protecting the incumbent congressman—motivated the legislature.

When the Supreme Court decided the case, *Easley v. Cromartie*, in 2001, it surprised many observers with a 5–4 decision overruling the district court. The opinion was written by Stephen Breyer, a Clinton appointee, and joined by Justice O'Connor, the author of *Shaw*. Breyer's opinion did not revisit the constitutional principles established in *Shaw* and *Miller*; instead, it simply concluded that the evidence did not support the district court's conclusion that race was the legislature's predominant motive in creating the district. Rather, Breyer found that the legislature was motivated by traditional consid- erations, namely partisan advantage—creating a safe Democratic district— and incumbent protection. Legislators took race into consideration, Breyer concluded, because it was the most reliable predictor of voting: blacks voted overwhelmingly Democratic while whites who registered as Democrats often voted Republican. While they could have created a more compact dis- trict that had a majority of registered Democrats and a smaller percentage of African Americans, such a district would most likely have voted Republican. "Because race in this case correlates closely with political behavior," Breyer wrote, the plaintiffs had to demonstrate that "the legislature could have achieved its legitimate political objectives in alternate ways . . . comparably consistent with traditional districting principles."[22] However, they did not.

Cromartie did not signal a major doctrinal shift in the Court's redistricting jurisprudence. When race was found to be the dominant factor in redistricting decisions, those decisions were subject to strict scrutiny and states would have to prove that their approaches were narrowly tailored and justified by a compelling interest. However, the complexities of the redistricting process, the Court's willingness to bless partisan motives as le- gitimate considerations, and the high correlation of race and political beha- vior meant that challenges to districts that were heavily African American or Hispanic would be difficult. As a result, the Court's color-blind turn had a limited effect on redistricting. Indeed, the 115th Congress, which took office in January 2017—the same month that Donald Trump entered the White House—was the most diverse in history.[23]

As the battle over redistricting cooled, attention once again focused on efforts to limit the right to vote. Most Republicans opposed measures championed by Democrats that made it easier to register and vote, fearing that they would increase turnout by minorities and the poor. "I don't want everybody to vote," said Paul Weyrich, conservative activist and founding director of the Heritage Foundation. "As a matter of fact, our leverage in elections . . . goes up as the voting populace goes down."[24] In the early 1990s, when Democrats pushed the National Voter Registration Act, popularly known as "motor voter," Republicans opposed it. The bill required states to make voter registration forms available to everyone applying for or renewing a driver's license as well as at offices that provided public assistance and serv-ices for persons with disabilities. When Congress approved the measure in 1992 over Republican opposition, President Bush vetoed it, invoking con-cern about voter fraud. He argued that the bill opened the "election process to an unacceptable risk of fraud and corruption without any reason to believe that it would increase electoral participation to any significant degree."[25] Although Bill Clinton signed motor voter into law a year later, Republicans continued to express fear of fraudulent voting.

Voter fraud emerged as a major issue—and some argued a pretext for vote suppression—in the wake of the 2000 presidential election, the closest and most controversial since 1876. Al Gore, the Democrat, won the popular vote, but George W. Bush secured a six-vote electoral vote majority by winning Florida's twenty-five electoral votes after carrying the state by only a few hun-dred ballots. Amid charges of massive irregularities—individuals unable to vote because of long lines at the polls or because the state had wrongfully purged their names from voting lists, voting machines that malfunctioned, and a confusing ballot used in one heavily Democratic county—the Florida Supreme Court ordered a manual recount. However, the US Supreme Court, with the five justices appointed by Reagan and George H. W. Bush forming a one-vote majority, reversed the Florida court, sealing Bush's victory. Amid widespread concern about the electoral process, Congress passed legisla-tion in 2002 that promised funding to states to replace antiquated voting machines and train election workers. It also required states to issue provi-sional ballots to those whose names did not appear on voter registration lists and to pass legislation defining what constituted a valid vote. Republicans' concern with fraudulent voting also resurfaced, resulting in a provision that required that anyone registering to vote provide a driver's license number or the last four digits of their Social Security number and that individuals who registered by mail must provide identification—a driver's license, bank statement, or utility bill—when they voted.

Bush's attorney general, John Ashcroft, who believed that fraud had denied him reelection to his US Senate seat in 2000, made combating illicit voting a priority. The department's orientation complemented Republican efforts to stop fraudulent voting through state legislation requiring voters to produce official identification—often a driver's license—before they entered a voting booth. Studies showed that in-person fraudulent voting—as opposed to stuffing the ballot box with votes by deceased or nonexistent voters—was very rare. Nevertheless, Republican governors, legislators, and members of the Bush Justice Department claimed that it was a major threat to the nation's democracy. Critics pointed to the obvious advantage voter ID laws gave Republicans: poor and minority voters were less likely than others to have a driver's license or other official photo IDs. In 2005, Georgia passed legislation requiring voters to produce an official photo ID—a driver's license, a Georgia ID card, a US passport, a government ID card, a military ID, or tribal ID—before voting. Under the Voting Rights Act, the law could only take effect if the Justice Department concluded that it did not have an adverse effect on minority voting. Although data showed that African Americans would be adversely affected by the act, testimony by the bill's sponsor suggested racial animus, and four of the five Civil Rights Division professional staff members who reviewed the case recommended that the law be rejected, Ashcroft allowed it to take effect. After a Georgia judge declared the law a violation of the state constitution, the legislature modified it to provide free state-issued IDs to voters. The Georgia Supreme Court then allowed it to take effect.

In 2008, the US Supreme Court gave proponents of voter ID laws the green light when it considered the constitutionality of an Indiana ID law that was the most restrictive in the nation. Passed in 2005 without a single Democratic vote, it required voters to produce a state or federal ID, which meant, in practice, a passport, a driver's license, or state-issued photo ID that was free but required individuals to present a birth certificate or passport to obtain. Plaintiffs in the case, *Crawford v. Marion County Election Board*, argued that there was no evidence of in-person voter fraud and that the law had a disparate impact on the poor, the elderly, and the disabled. In a 6–3 ruling in which Justice Stevens—who usually voted with the Court's liberal bloc—joined the five-member conservative majority, the Court turned back the challenge.

Stevens, whose opinion commanded the greatest support, albeit not a majority, wrote that the state had a legitimate interest in preventing election fraud and that the plaintiffs had not produced sufficient evidence that the law interfered unduly with the right to vote. While his opinion did not foreclose future challenges, critics found no consolation in this prospect. Justice David Souter's dissent pointed out the virtual nonexistence of in-person voter fraud and reminded his colleagues that "interest in combatting voter fraud has too often served as a cover for unnecessarily restrictive electoral rules."[26]

The 2008 presidential election and its aftermath only intensified the battle over voter ID laws. Defying all odds, Barack Obama, a first-term African American US Senator from Illinois, won the presidency by appealing to voters' desire for change, offering them an optimistic message of hope for a better future, and deploying savvy political strategists, sophisticated data analysts, and droves of idealistic volunteers to get his supporters to the polls. Obama's election was historic, not only because he was the first African American to win the nation's highest office, but because Americans voted at a higher rate than any time since 1968, and for the first time African Americans turned out at a higher rate than whites. Indeed, voter turnout and especially African American mobilization played a key role in the outcome.

Those who believed that Obama's victory was the dawning of a post-racial age were quickly disappointed. Critics accused him of playing the race card when he criticized police for arresting Harvard professor Henry Louis Gates in his own home and for responding to the killing of Trayvon Martin, an unarmed seventeen-year-old black youth, by a white neighborhood watch captain by saying, "if I had a son, he'd look like Trayvon."[27] "Birthers" dogged him throughout his presidency as several prominent television and radio personalities, members of Congress, and his unlikely successor, Donald Trump, denied that he had been born in the United States and maintained that he was, therefore, ineligible to serve as president. Hatred for Obama on the right, fueled by his success in pushing health care reform through Congress and serving as president while black, coupled with the historic tendency of an incumbent president's party to lose seats in midterm elections, resulted in crippling losses for the Democrats in 2010. Republicans picked up sixty-three seats in the House of Representatives to regain the majority they lost in 2006, increased the number of states in which they controlled both houses of the legislature from nineteen to twenty-six, and augmented the number of governorships they occupied from twenty-three to twenty-nine. Gains at the state level gave Republicans greater control over the redistricting that followed the 2010 census and put additional weight behind their legislative agenda.

High on the list of the GOP's priorities was voter ID laws. The stated goal was stamping out in-person voting fraud—an imagined evil that masked the party's efforts to reduce Democratic voting strength. This goal became more important in the wake of Obama's success in mobilizing minorities and young, first-time voters. "In the decades after 1965, the fight over voting rights had centered on the value of the vote, not on the right to vote itself," wrote journalist Ari Berman. "But after Obama's election, the climax of decades of struggle to win greater representation, vote denial efforts returned with a vengeance."[28] Between 2011 and 2015, eight states adopted voter ID laws that required prospective voters to produce photo IDs before casting ballots. In 2011 and 2012, courts blocked many of the new laws from taking effect, and Eric Holder, Obama's attorney general, took a strong stand against them, likening Texas's voter ID law to poll taxes of yesteryear. Because Texas was covered by section 5 of the Voting Rights Act, it had to win approval of the new law by the Justice Department or a three-judge panel of the US District Court for the District of Columbia. Seeking to avoid Holder and his lieutenants, the Lone Star State took its case to the district court, which ruled that the law had a disproportionate impact on minorities and the poor. Even though the Texas law allowed prospective voters who did not have a driver's license to obtain a free state-issued voter ID, it could only be obtained at offices of the Department of Motor Vehicles, and almost a third of the state's counties had no DMV offices. As a result, Hispanic voters were far less likely than whites to have the requisite ID.

Even as the Obama Justice Department and civil rights groups succeeded in fighting back new efforts to suppress the vote, Republicans mounted a major constitutional challenge to sections 4 and 5 of the Voting Rights Act, which had played such a critical role in preventing southern states from devising new procedures to prevent minorities from voting or to make it more difficult to elect their preferred candidates. During his two terms, George W. Bush made two appointments to the US Supreme Court, replacing Sandra Day O'Connor with Samuel Alito, a hard-line conservative, and naming John Roberts as chief justice to replace William Rehnquist. Roberts, who had clerked for Rehnquist in 1980 and 1981, shared his opposition to an expansive reading of the Voting Rights Act. As Congress considered renewal of the act in 1982, Roberts had found himself in the Reagan Justice Department, serving as special assistant to the attorney general and leading the charge against legislation that renewed the act and strengthened remedies against minority vote dilution. Roberts opposed changes to section 2 that banned electoral procedures that made it more difficult for minorities to elect candidates of their choice. He deployed the color-blind arguments that had become the mantra of conservatism to attack the changes. "In their zest for the colorblind society they professed to see," remembers a career attorney in the department, Roberts and his colleagues "didn't recognize that the long couple hundred years of segregation and discrimination continued to have present-day effects."[29] In a memo to his colleagues, Roberts warned of the dangers of a muscular section 2, arguing that it "would establish essentially a quota system for electoral politics," make violations "too easy to prove," and encourage "the most intrusive interference imaginable by federal courts into state and local processes."[30] Roberts lost the battle. In 1982, with overwhelming support from Republicans as well as Democrats, Congress renewed the act for twenty-five years and strengthened section 2.

But Roberts lived to fight another day. In 2013, he sat as chief justice of a conservative Court that considered a challenge to the constitutionality of a key provision of the Voting Rights Act. The law, which Roberts had fought so hard against extending in 1982, had been renewed for another twenty-five years in 2006 with a unanimous vote in the Senate and only thirty-three dissenting votes in the House. A challenge to it originated with intervention by the Department of Justice in redistricting in Calera, a small town in Alabama, one of nine southern states singled out in section 4 of the Voting Rights Act for its history and ongoing record of discrimination against minority voters. As a result, Alabama and subdivisions like Calera were required by section 5 to receive approval—or preclearance—from the Justice Department or a three-judge panel of the US District Court for the District of Columbia before altering laws or practices related to voting. In 2008, Calera made changes to the borders of its city council districts that made it harder for blacks to elect a candidate of their choice, and the Justice Department used its power under section 5 to block the town's action. That's when Ed Blum got involved. Something of a legend in conservative circles for identifying cases that were ripe for challenging the Justice Department's application of the Voting Rights Act, Blum noticed the department's objection to Calera's redistricting while visiting the department's web site. He contacted the county attorney, and a constitutional challenge to sections 4 and 5 of the Voting Rights Act—*Shelby County v. Holder*—was born.

Although federal district and appeals courts rejected the county's challenge, the US Supreme Court brought an end to the preclearance process in a 5–4 decision with the opinion written by Chief Justice Roberts. By subjecting some states to the onerous requirements of preclearance, Roberts ruled, section 4 violated state equality, a bedrock constitutional principle. When section 4 became law in 1965, Roberts noted, placing special burdens on the states identified in the section made sense because their laws and practices disfranchised African Americans. However, the formula for determining the states singled out by section 4 had not changed in almost fifty years, despite the fact that the law had rooted out discrimination in voting and blacks and whites participated in the political process at the same rate. As a result, Roberts found no rational basis for Congress to treat states covered by section 4 differently from other states. He pointed out that the decision did not strike down section 5's preclearance process and that Congress could continue to employ it to screen changes in voting practices if it developed new criteria for determining which jurisdictions were subject to preclearance. But that was a big if because a highly partisan Congress was unlikely to agree on criteria for coverage or states to be covered.

Writing for the minority, Justice Ruth Bader Ginsburg took Roberts's flaccid reasoning apart. She emphasized that Congress had acted deliberately when it renewed the act in 2006. It had held twenty-one separate hearings, received testimony from scores of witnesses, completed numerous investigative reports, and documented an ongoing need for the preclearance process in the areas covered by section 4. Indeed, those areas experienced a disproportionate number of successful challenges to electoral discrimination under section 2 of the act. Ginsburg acknowledged that the act had opened the ballot box to African Americans and that in the states covered by section 4, blacks and whites voted at roughly the same rate. However, she noted that "the covered jurisdictions have a unique history of problems with racial discrimination in voting and that Congress had determined that discrimination in these areas 'had evolved into subtler second-generation barriers,' and that eliminating preclearance would risk the loss of gains that had been made." "Throwing out preclearance when it has worked and continues to work to stop discriminatory changes," Ginsburg observed, "is like throwing away your umbrella in a rainstorm because you are not getting wet."[31]

Roberts and Ginsburg understood race discrimination differently. Both agreed that, as Roberts put it, "history cannot be ignored." Yet for Roberts, the relevant history was almost fifty years of progress in which "voting tests were abolished, disparities in voter registration and turnout due to race were erased, and African Americans attained office in record numbers." For Ginsburg, history reached back further and included centuries of slavery, segregation, and exclusion of African Americans from voting and office holding. In her view, that history continued to affect the present notwithstanding the enormous progress the country had made since the 1960s. She understood William Faulkner's profound insight about the South: "The past isn't dead. It isn't even past." Roberts believed that color mattered less than it ever had and that extraordinary measures like requiring states that had disfranchised African Americans fifty years earlier to seek preclearance for routine policy changes required justification. Ginsburg acknowledged the progress, but understood that the legacy of white supremacy persisted, manifesting itself in more subtle forms of discrimination that required continued vigilance. The triumph of Roberts's view—rooted in his commitment to color-blind jurisprudence—had serious consequences. With section 5 dormant and unlikely to be revived, measures that had a discriminatory effect could not be blocked through the preclearance process. Instead, civil rights advocates would have to rely on section 2 to challenge them in costly, protracted litigation that played out while the changes remained in effect.

The ground had truly shifted, and many states governed by Republicans took advantage. On the day *Shelby County* was announced, Texas implemented the same strict photo ID law that the Justice Department had blocked. Several days later, Republicans in the North Carolina legislature revised a pending photo ID bill to make it even more restrictive. The measure quickly cleared both houses without a single Democratic vote and was signed into law by Governor Pat McCrory. Although civil rights attorneys challenged both laws under section 2 of the Voting Rights Act, the litigation dragged on for years while the ID laws remained in effect. In the case of Texas, the Court of Appeals for the Fifth Circuit, one of the most conservative appeals courts, ruled that the state's photo ID law discriminated against minorities, forcing the state to adopt new legislation that allowed voters who signed an affidavit explaining why they could not obtain one of the seven approved photo IDs to show an alternative form of identification such as a utility bill or a bank statement. That measure was upheld by the Fifth Circuit in 2017. Civil rights advocates' challenges to North Carolina were more successful. In 2016, the Court of Appeals for the Fourth Circuit ruled that its photo ID law violated the Voting Rights Act because legislators adopted it after receiving evidence of its adverse effect on blacks. A year later, the US Supreme Court refused to hear the state's appeal. These cases suggested that civil rights attorneys were not without options, but that those options were far more difficult to pursue than preclearance had been.

The Battle against Mass Incarceration

As battles over voting rights, affirmative action, and employment discrimination continued, civil rights advocates focused greater attention on criminal justice and mass incarceration. The Reagan-era war on drugs continued unabated in the 1990s, with devastating consequences for African Americans. While bipartisan support remained widespread, some began to question the harsh tactics that put so many African Americans behind bars. Changing attitudes were reflected in the Violent Crime Control and Law Enforcement Act, which President Bill Clinton pushed through Congress in 1994. Seeking to avoid criticism—frequently aimed at Democrats by Republicans—that he was soft on drugs and crime, Clinton included provisions that extended some of the most draconian measures adopted in the 1980s, while walking back others and embracing approaches to drugs advocated by members of the Congressional Black Caucus and white liberals. The bill included concessions to those who demanded continuation of the draconian approaches of the 1980s by providing more foot soldiers for the war on drugs, authorizing $10 billion for state and local governments to hire additional police officers, and appropriating an additional $10 billion to construct more prison cells. It also toughened sentencing laws, expanding the number of federal capital crimes to sixty and imposing mandatory life sentences for persons convicted of a third violent felony. Concessions to liberals included a federal ban on the manufacture and sale of nineteen types of semi-automatic assault weapons, significant funding for drug education and rehabilitation, initiatives to divert first-time offenders from prison, and programs to combat delinquency and violence against women. Liberals also won modest sentencing reform, securing a provision that authorized judges to drop mandatory minimum sentences for first-time, non-violent drug offenders.

Despite concessions to liberal demands, the new law continued the harshly punitive approach that characterized the war on drugs and underwrote expansion of the carceral state. Not surprisingly, then, efforts to repeal or even modify draconian penalties continued to meet resistance. In 1995, the US Sentencing Commission—created by the 1984 drug law to establish

guidelines federal judges had to follow in sentencing, reduce judicial discretion, and bring about more uniform punishment—recommended that
the penalty for sale and possession of crack and cocaine be equalized. The
100-1 ratio, which required the same punishment for the sale of 5 grams
of crack and 500 grams of cocaine, was unjustified, it concluded. Sensing
the political difficulty of persuading Congress to accept the recommendation and concerned about reelection, President Bill Clinton supported
reducing the ratio to 10-1. Even that was too much for Congress, which
rejected the commission's proposal and kept the 100-1 ratio in place. When
Clinton signed legislation maintaining the status quo, African American
leaders took him—and the sentencing laws—to task. The Congressional
Black Caucus argued that the disparity "makes a mockery of justice," and
civil rights veteran and former presidential hopeful Reverend Jesse Jackson
charged that Clinton "is willing to sacrifice black youth for white fear."[32]
Some in the mainstream media joined African American leaders, with the
New York Times criticizing Clinton for being "afraid to appear remotely soft
on drugs" and charging that "[i]t is shameful to maintain a disparity with
no rational basis."[33]

Over the next decade, members of the Congressional Black Caucus continued to challenge the ratio, although it never became a top priority. And
even if it had been, Republican majorities on Capitol Hill (1995–2007) and
a centrist Democratic president (1993–2001) limited their leverage. In 1993,
Charles Rangel, once a staunch supporter of the war on drugs, introduced
legislation to equalize punishment for crack and cocaine possession and sale
and to end mandatory minimum sentences for crack convictions. Although
the bill did not make it to the floor for debate and a vote, Rangel introduced
it in every session of Congress for the following sixteen years. Initially, the
bill attracted no co-sponsors, but beginning in 1995, it picked up twelve co-
sponsors, principally members of the CBC. By 1999, thirty-five co-sponsors,
most of whom were members of the caucus, had signed on. Others followed
Rangel's lead. In 1999, Maxine Waters, a House member representing South
Central Los Angeles and a former chair of the caucus, introduced her own
legislation abolishing the crack-cocaine disparity and all mandatory minimum sentences in drug cases. Rangel and Waters brought drugs, crime, and
mass incarceration into the political conversation, but they failed to move
Congress or the White House. Young black men sentenced to long terms in
prison did not rouse sufficient public sympathy to generate changes in criminal law and the criminal justice system.

Nevertheless, criticism begun by the CBC grew as mainline civil rights organizations, more members of Congress, and several prominent public figures found their voice on the issue. In 1996, the NAACP Legal Defense Fund took up the case of Kemba Smith, a nineteen-year-old African American college student who was sentenced to prison when prosecutors established that she had an incidental relationship with a drug ring in which her boyfriend was involved. Even though Smith had no criminal history and was trapped in an abusive relationship from which she struggled to free herself, under federal mandatory minimum sentencing laws, she was sentenced to twenty-four years in prison. Despite the draconian sentence imposed on a young woman who was little more than a bystander, challenging it was risky for an organization that relied on the financial support of middle-class blacks. Elaine Jones, the LDF's executive director, recalled that gaining their support was challenging. She hired a limousine and took the presidents of two prominent African American sororities to the penitentiary to meet Smith and help them see that what had happened to her might have befallen a daughter or a niece. The trip proved successful, helping to build support for a commutation that President Clinton issued less than a month before leaving the White House in 2001. The commutation, however, did nothing for tens of thousands of African Americans serving lengthy sentences.

Public criticism of the war on drugs also slowly emerged. In 1998, NAACP executive director Kweisi Mfume joined Walter Cronkite, the retired CBS News anchor, George Shultz, the former secretary of state, and numerous academics in signing an open letter to UN secretary-general Kofi Annan urging the General Assembly's Special Session on Drugs to reconsider the global war on drugs. While acknowledging "the threat drugs pose to our children, our fellow citizens, and our society," the signatories asserted that "the global war on drugs is now causing more harm than drug abuse itself," adding that "human rights are violated . . . and prisons inundated with hundreds of thousands of drug law violators."[34] Two years later, Wade Henderson, executive director of the Leadership Conference on Civil Rights, testified before Congress, highlighting his organization's extensive study of discrimination in the law enforcement and criminal justice systems, *Justice on Trial*. He called for an end to the crack/cocaine disparity and mandatory minimum sentences. "Disparities in law enforcement threaten to render irrelevant fifty years of hard-fought civil rights progress," Henderson argued.[35]

Support for the war on drugs and the harsh sentencing laws it generated dwindled in the early 2000s in response to a steadily declining crime rate and the rising costs of mass incarceration. In 2001, Senator Jeff Sessions, a staunchly conservative Alabama Republican, introduced legislation to reduce the crack-cocaine ratio to 20-1. Although the bill kept the ratio bewilderingly high, it still failed to pass. Nevertheless, it indicated growing bipartisan support for revisiting the nation's harsh drug sentencing laws.

Some federal judges also called lopsided punishments for crack into question, imposing lower sentences than those mandated by the 100-1 sentencing guidelines. In 2007, the US Supreme Court recognized judges' discretion to stray from the guidelines in a 7–2 decision in *Kimbrough v. United States.* Derrick Kimbrough was convicted after being arrested for possession of 58 grams of crack, 98 grams of powder cocaine, and a firearm, all of which were found when his car was searched by police. Based on the combination of the charges—possession of crack and cocaine with intent to sell as well as possession of a firearm in furtherance of a drug-related crime—the sentencing guidelines dictated a sentence between 19 and 22.5 years—even though Kimbrough had no previous felony convictions. Taking into account "the nature and circumstances of the case" and the defendant's "history and characteristics," the federal district judge who presided over the trial sentenced Kimbrough to 15 years in prison. He did so by weighting the crack and the cocaine offenses equally, noting that the extremely harsh penalty indicated by the guidelines was the result of the "disproportionate and unjust effect that crack cocaine guidelines have in sentencing." The Court of Appeals for the Fourth Circuit reversed the sentence because the judge failed to follow the sentencing guidelines, in effect taking it on himself to equalize the punishment for crack and powder cocaine. Writing for the majority, Justice Ginsburg reversed the Fourth Circuit and reinstated the district judge's sentence. She ruled that the guidelines were advisory and that the judge exercised appropriate discretion, considering the circumstances of the case and imposing a sentence that was "sufficient but not greater than necessary" to accomplish the goals of the guidelines.[36]

As the Court gave judges greater flexibility, support grew in Congress for revisiting inequities in drug sentencing. In 2007, two bills emerged in the Senate—a Republican measure that reduced the crack-cocaine ratio to 20-1, and a Democratic alternative that equalized penalties. Both bills also repealed mandatory minimum sentences for first-time offenders. Neither succeeded, but as the presidential campaign got underway, Barack Obama pledged to eliminate the disparity between penalties for crack and powder cocaine and to review mandatory minimum sentences. Although once elected, his top legislative priorities became economic recovery and health care, bipartisan support allowed Obama to achieve the first significant change in federal drug policy since the war on drugs began in the 1980s. The Fair Sentencing Act, which he signed in 2010 reduced the disparity in punishment between crack and powder cocaine from 100-1 to 18-1 and, equally important, ended the federal five-year mandatory minimum sentence for possession of crack.

Further legislative action floundered after Republicans won control of Congress in the 2010 elections and made their top priority, as Senate Republican leader Mitch McConnell put it, "to deny President Obama a second term in office."[37] Obama and his attorney general, Eric Holder, pivoted from legislative initiatives to executive action. Holder directed US attorneys to "decline to pursue charges triggering a mandatory minimum sentence" in drug cases when the crime did not involve violence and the defendant did not have ties to a large-scale drug trafficking organization or a significant criminal history.[38] Holder also worked closely with the US Sentencing Commission to modify the sentencing guidelines to reduce the number of sentencing points judges assigned to approximately 70 percent of drug trafficking offenses. That action had the effect of reducing average drug sentences by almost one year. When Congress let the changes stand, the commission applied them retroactively—to those already convicted and sentenced—triggering the release of over 6,000 federal prisoners.

As Obama's second term neared its end, he continued to press for change. "Mass incarceration makes our country worse off, and we need to do something about it," he told the NAACP annual convention in 2015, just days before becoming the first president to visit a federal penitentiary.[39] His focus on mass incarceration helped muster support for the Sentencing Reform and Corrections Act, which reduced mandatory sentences for repeat offenders, gave federal judges greater discretion in tailoring sentences to defendants' circumstances, and provided greater support for inmates reentering society. Although the bill attracted significant bipartisan support, it remained stuck in committee as the 2016 presidential election approached. Obama's presidency marked significant progress; he was the first president since Jimmy Carter to leave office with a smaller federal prison population than when he entered. Nevertheless, there were six times as many federal prison inmates as when Reagan became president in 1981.

As important as reform at the federal level was, the vast majority—about 90 percent—of prisoners were held in state prisons. Advocates for easing mandatory minimums and reducing the crack-cocaine disparity as well as penalties for marijuana possession pressed their case at the state level, where they found politicians responsive. In some states, like New York, concern about racial justice drove reform. The state's first African American governor, David Paterson, who had long championed repeal of the punitive 1970s Rockefeller drug laws, brokered a deal with the legislature in 2009 to ease mandatory minimum sentences. In most states, the motivation was fiscal. Across the country, spending on prisons had ballooned since the 1980s, becoming a significant—and ever-growing—claim on state revenues. Between 1990 and 2012, for example, Georgia's spending on corrections had doubled and was second only to spending on education. To contain spiraling costs, many states moved to ease mandatory minimum sentences and restore to judges the flexibility to tailor punishment to fit the perpetrator, the severity of the crime, and the threat the perpetrator posed to the community. As a result, state prison populations declined by about 10 percent between 2009 and 2015, falling from 443 inmates per 100,000 residents to 402. The changes were important, but left the United States with far higher incarceration rates than other democracies and even authoritarian states like China and Russia. Moreover, further progress would require that reform efforts extend beyond drug sentencing. While a majority of federal prisoners had been convicted of drug-related offenses, fewer than a quarter of state prisoners had been sentenced for drug crimes; a majority were incarcerated for violent crimes.

With sentencing and criminal justice reform progressing at a snail's pace, young African American activists brought a renewed sense of outrage, commitment to direct action, and facility with social media to the fight against mass incarceration and institutional racism. The new insurgency was sparked by a series of highly publicized police killings of unarmed African American men and women. These killings—some of which were captured on cell phone videos—underscored for many young African Americans that despite the election of a black president, racial disparities and racism remained woven into the fabric of American life. In 2013, following the acquittal of a neighborhood watch captain who shot and killed Trayvon Martin, a seventeen-year-old unarmed African American who was visiting his father's fiancée in a gated community in Sanford, Florida, protests erupted across the country. The killing, acquittal, and protests dominated the news, prompting President Obama to make a rare, unannounced visit to the White House briefing room to comment. "Trayvon Martin could have been me 35 years ago," he said, adding, "it's important to understand that the African American community is looking at this issue through a set of experiences and a history that doesn't go away."[40] For most African Americans and many whites, the killing and acquittal were painful reminders that even though the country had elected a black president, many whites viewed African Americans with fear, suspicion, and contempt. As a result, African Americans' everyday activities received scrutiny that whites escaped; police routinely stopped, questioned, arrested, and sometimes killed African Americans in far greater numbers than whites. An unarmed seventeen-year-old black boy had been accosted and shot to death because he was walking down the street of a gated community wearing a hoodie, and his killer went unpunished. The color-blind vision that animated conservative rhetoric, constitutional theory, and policy did not reflect the realities of African American life.

Millions of Americans responded to the acquittal of Martin's killer with disbelief, shock, rage, shame, and pain. One of them, Alicia Garza, an activist living in Oakland, posted a message on Facebook that she called "a love note to black people." "Black people, I love you," she wrote. "I love us. Our lives matter."[41] Garza's friend and fellow activist, Patrisse Cullors, shared the post with her friends, using the hashtag #blacklivesmatter. Subsequently, Garza, Cullors, and their social media–savvy friend Opal Tometi used the hashtag to build Facebook and Twitter platforms. Although the #blacklivesmatter hashtag generated little traffic during its first year, it exploded a year later, in August 2014, in the wake of the killing of an unarmed eighteen-year-old African American, Michael Brown, by a white policeman in Ferguson, Missouri. As crowds gathered in Ferguson, a poor, predominantly black suburb of St. Louis, to protest Brown's killing, Garza, Cullors, and Tometi followed the events closely and posted information about the killing and the protests. Through the power of social media and the phrase itself, #blacklivesmatter lit up, generating an avalanche of tweets and helping to spread awareness of and outrage over the killing. The tweets were also picked up by news organizations across the country, amplifying the message, attracting new eyes to the story, and lending credibility to the hashtag. But Garza, Cullors, and Tometi did more. They used Twitter and Facebook to launch Black Lives Matter "Freedom Rides" that recruited over five hundred activists from eighteen cities across the country to drive to Ferguson to join the protest. And as the protests grew, chants of "Black Lives Matter" filled the air in Ferguson and captured public imagination.

Ferguson transformed Black Lives Matter into a nationwide movement. The name was misunderstood by many whites, who wondered—and sometimes asked—"Don't ALL lives matter?" But it resonated with African Americans and many white supporters who understood that, in a society in which African Americans too often endured disrespect and even violence because of their race, asserting that *black* lives mattered was essential. No one questioned whether white lives mattered, but the realities of American life suggested that black lives did not. Asserting that they did, therefore, was imperative, especially when high-profile acts of police violence against African Americans continued. In November 2014, Tamir Rice, a twelve-year-old black boy, was killed by Cleveland police who responded to reports that a black male was wielding a gun at a local recreation center. The gun turned out to be a toy. In April 2015, Walter Scott, a forty-eight-year-old black man, was shot in the back by a police officer in North Charleston, South Carolina, when he fled from his car after being stopped for a malfunctioning brake light. Three months later, Sandra Bland, a twenty-eight-year-old black woman, was found dead in her jail cell in Waller County, Texas, after she was arrested for a traffic violation, and Samuel DuBose, a forty-two-year-old unarmed African American, was shot to death when he pulled away from a University of Cincinnati police officer who had stopped him for a missing front license plate. The police shootings would continue and so would the movement against them. Local Black Lives Matter organizations emerged in the eighteen cities that had sent freedom riders to Ferguson and other cities as well. By 2016, approximately thirty US cities had chapters. The founders created an umbrella group, the Movement for Black Lives, that provided support and coordination for local organizations as well as several dozen other black-led organizations focused on combating the racism embedded in political, social, economic, and legal institutions.

This loosely organized coalition relied heavily on direct action, leading some to compare it to the Student Non-Violent Coordinating Committee, the organization that had mobilized young people to challenge segregation and disfranchisement in the 1960s. Intent on communicating the urgency of their cause, activists often disrupted public events, demonstrating that there would be no peace until their demands were heeded. During the 2014 and 2015 Christmas shopping seasons, local Black Lives Matter organizations orchestrated protests—including "die-ins" in which hundreds of protesters lay on floors in public places—at malls and shopping districts in Minneapolis, Chicago, Boston, Memphis, Seattle, and Washington, causing some to close. Protesters shut down Oakland's Bay Area Rapid Transit and disrupted travel at the Minneapolis airport. At suburban Minneapolis's Mall of America, where three thousand protesters shut down a portion of the nation's largest shopping mall, protesters chanted, "While you are on your shopping spree, black people cannot breathe,"[42] a reference to Staten Island's Eric Garner who died the previous July after New York City police used a chokehold while arresting him for selling single cigarettes from packs without tax stamps. Local organizations also protested at political events, disrupting Mayor Eric Garcetti's town hall meeting in South Los Angeles in 2015, preventing progressive presidential hopeful Bernie Sanders from holding a rally in Seattle in August 2015, and confronting Democratic presidential candidate Hillary Clinton at a fundraiser in February 2016 to demand an apology for her support of President Bill Clinton's 1994 crime bill.

While Black Lives Matter's use of civil disobedience hearkened back to SNCC, its leadership, structure, strategies, and goals were different. Black Lives was a highly decentralized group that relied on local chapters and several dozen allied organizations. It also rejected SNCC's model of charismatic black male leadership. Started by black women, it did not rely on a chairman and strong executive committee that spoke for the organization, developed strategy, and executed tactical decisions. Female, lesbian, and transgender people were prominent and filled key roles. When admonished that they would never succeed without strong leadership, organizers responded that the movement was "leaderful," not leaderless.

Figure 8.2. Black Lives Matter protestors, November 10, 2015 https://www.flickr.com/photos/johnnysilvercloud/28476745294. Photo by Johnny Silvercloud. *Flickr.*

The Black Lives agenda was as broad as its leadership, envisioning a fundamental restructuring of American society. While many members and chapters focused on law enforcement and criminal justice, the movement also critiqued American capitalism as a system that concentrated power and wealth in the hands of the few and the white. They actively supported gender equality, LGBTQ and workers' rights, single-payer health care, and efforts to halt climate change.

Even though the Movement for Black Lives developed a highly detailed platform, most Black Lives organizers chose to work outside the system, eschewed collaboration with national political leaders, and did not focus on influencing policy. In the words of Alicia Garza, the movement "challenges the notion that only policy change will get us to where we are trying to go."[43] Not all agreed. Black Lives Matter activists DeRay Mckesson and Brittany Packnett worked with the Obama administration on issues of criminal justice reform. Packnett accepted Obama's appointment to serve on the President's Task Force on 21st Century Policing, which convened in December 2014. In 2016 Mckesson ran, unsuccessfully, to become mayor of Baltimore, a city that had exploded in 2015 after Freddie Gray, a twenty-five-year-old black man had died in police custody after being arrested for possession of an illegal knife.

Even though few movement organizers aspired to political influence, the movement had a powerful impact on politics and, to a lesser extent, policy. Many conservatives denounced it for inciting hatred of police. Fox News personality Bill O'Reilly labeled it a hate group. "I have seen them marching down the street essentially calling death to police," Republican presidential candidate Donald Trump told a sympathetic O'Reilly during a July 2016 interview.[44] If Republicans chose to ignore, dismiss, or caricature Black Lives' message, Democrats embraced its demands for criminal justice reforms if not its full agenda. Bernie Sanders developed a platform on racial justice after activists disrupted his 2015 Seattle rally, Hillary Clinton engaged Black Lives' critics in discussion of criminal justice policy and apologized for her support of her husband's crime policy in the 1990s, and the Democratic National Convention endorsed some recommendations for criminal justice reform, including a proposal that police be required to wear body cameras to record interactions with civilians.

Black Lives' most visible impact may have been on President Obama and his attorney general, Eric Holder, both of whom had a strong commitment to criminal justice and law enforcement reform. The Justice Department's Civil

Rights Division intervened when complaints by citizens indicated that police departments systematically violated civil rights. In doing so, it employed authority that had been conferred by Clinton-era criminal justice legislation but had been used sparingly during the Bush administration. The division conducted extensive investigations of twenty police departments—including those in Chicago, Detroit, Los Angeles, and smaller cities like Ferguson and North Charleston, where high-profile cases of police abuse suggested widespread civil rights violations. When investigations revealed a pattern of abuse—which they often did—Justice Department attorneys negotiated consent agreements that required police departments to submit to federal monitoring for an extended period; collect and report data on stops, arrests, and use of force by race and gender; track police encounters with the mentally ill; and initiate cultural competence and implicit bias training programs for officers. Obama also convened a high profile President's Task Force on 21st Century Policing that developed extensive recommendations to improve the quality of policing and especially police interactions with minorities, women, the mentally ill, and youth. Released in March 2015, the task force's report provided guidance for leadership in the nation's police departments and used the president's bully pulpit to call for action.

Although Obama faced a hostile Congress, he also made modest legislative headway. At the end of the Clinton administration, Congress had passed the Death in Custody Reporting Act, requiring law enforcement organizations—including municipal police departments—to report civilian deaths that occurred when the deceased had been detained by officers. When the law expired in 2006, Congress failed to reauthorize it. New legislation, sponsored by Senator Richard Blumenthal, a Connecticut Democrat, and Representative Bobby Scott, a Virginia Democrat and member of the Congressional Black Caucus, passed in December 2014 in the wake of the mass demonstrations in Ferguson and other cities and was signed into law by President Obama. The reporting required by the law was critical to address the problem of police brutality. Without data on the number of deaths in custody, where they occurred, and under what circumstances, the public and policymakers could not understand the extent, nature, and locations of the problem. "Without accurate data, it is nearly impossible to identify variables that lead to an unnecessary and unacceptable risk of people dying," Scott explained, adding that the bill would make information available to allow lawmakers "to enact initiatives that will reduce incidents of avoidable deaths in our criminal justice system."[45]

As Obama neared the end of his second term, he harbored no illusions about the enormity of the challenge and the limits of the changes his administration had effected. "Change has been too slow and we have to have a greater sense of urgency about this," he said in remarks delivered from Poland after two more black men died at the hands of police—Alton Sterling in Baton Rouge, Louisiana, and Philando Castile in a suburb of St. Paul, Minnesota. "This not just a black issue," Obama added. "This is an American issue we should all care about. . . . We are better than this."[46] Making progress in eliminating racism from the criminal justice and law enforcement systems—especially given persistent differences between blacks and whites in employment, income, and educational levels, not to mention whites' attitudes developed over centuries—was like draining a pond with a bucket. The target was much more elusive than "whites only" signs at water fountains and literacy tests. Blacks' and whites' concerns about crime, even at a time when homicide rates were at historic lows, made it difficult to secure sentencing reform for those convicted of violent crimes—the majority of prisoners in state penitentiaries. Reforming police departments, many of them large bureaucracies with unionized employees and deeply rooted cultures, was a daunting challenge. Federal civil rights laws made it difficult to prosecute officers and private citizens who killed African Americans. They required federal attorneys to persuade juries that the accused had acted, beyond a reasonable doubt, with intent to deprive victims of federally protected civil rights—not just to kill them. In most cases, this proved impossible. In the cases of the killers of Trayvon Martin and Michael Brown, the Obama Justice Department decided against bringing civil rights charges because they knew they would fail. Title VI of the Civil Rights Act of 1964 authorized cutting federal funds to states and subdivisions that violated the civil rights of their citizens. But if cities whose police were guilty of civil rights violations were denied federal funds, poor residents would suffer most.

If civil rights advocates were disheartened by Obama's limited accomplishments, they alternated between despondency and rage as they considered his successor. While previous Republican candidates—Richard Nixon, Ronald Reagan, George H. W. Bush—had used code words to appeal to white racism, Donald Trump left nothing to the imagination. When he launched his campaign in June 2015, he singled out Mexican immigrants as a threat. "They're bringing drugs. They're bringing crime. They're rapists," he charged.[47] When a lawsuit against Trump University was assigned to a federal judge who was Mexican American, Trump charged that the judge with bias. "He is a member of a club or society, very strongly pro-Mexican, which all fine," Trump commented. "But I say he's got bias."[48] He was equally disparaging of African Americans, starting with President Obama, whom he charged was a "terrible student, terrible" (even though he had been editor of the *Harvard Law Review*), was lazy because he played too much golf (albeit far less than Trump did as president), and had not been born in the United States (a preposterous claim promoted by conspiracy theorists). At a rally in June 2016, he pointed to a lone African American man in the audience and said, "Oh, look at my black over here. Look at him."[49] He spoke of African Americans as if they were a problem—poor, uneducated, unemployed, and desperate. "You're living in poverty. You're schools are no good. You have no jobs. . . . What the hell do you have to lose," he asked a Detroit audience.[50] Sometimes Trump's flagrant racism even flabbergasted his Republican supporters. Speaker of the House Paul Ryan, the Wisconsin Republican, called one of Trump's most egregious campaign outbursts "the textbook example of a racist comment."[51]

Few were surprised, therefore, that Trump's first two years in office marked him as more hostile to civil rights than any president since Woodrow Wilson. Trump appointed Jeff Sessions, who had long been dogged by charges of racism, as his attorney general. In 1986, the Senate had denied Sessions confirmation as a federal judge after witnesses testified that he used the n-word in conversations with his staff and joked that he thought the Ku Klux Klan was "okay, until he learned they smoked marijuana."[52] As attorney general, Sessions reversed Eric Holder's instructions that directed US attorneys to reduce charges against individuals arrested for low-level drug offenses to avoid steep mandatory minimum sentences. Instead, Sessions ordered prosecutors to pursue the most severe charges with the steepest penalties. He also began a review of consent decrees negotiated with police departments charged with civil rights violations by the Obama administration and signaled that he would not seek new agreements. "Local control and local accountability are necessary for effective policing," Sessions informed US attorneys in March 2017. "It is not the responsibility of the federal government to manage nonfederal law enforcement agencies."[53] Under Sessions's leadership, the FBI created a new category of domestic terrorists—"black identity extremists"—activists whose "grievances about racialized police violence and inequities in the criminal justice system have spurred retaliatory violence against law enforcement officers."[54]

The Trump Justice Department also prepared to accelerate the rollback of other civil rights protections. It quickly reversed course on voting rights. Under Obama, the Department had aggressively challenged state voter ID laws as violations of section 2 of the Voting Rights Act. Sessions directed lawyers in the Voting Rights Section to back off challenges and intervene in support of states' right to protect the integrity of the electoral process. Indeed, in the ongoing challenge to a Texas voter ID law begun by Obama's Justice Department, Sessions reversed the department's position, directing his attorneys to file briefs supporting the state. Affirmative action also became a target. In August 2017, the Justice Department's Civil Rights Division recruited a cadre of attorneys to investigate universities' admissions policies. A year later, the Justice and Education Departments rescinded Obama-era guidelines that allowed universities to consider race in admissions as a way to promote diversity. Instead, they were directed to employ race-neutral policies. The guidelines countered Supreme Court rulings that permitted universities to consider race as one factor in admissions decisions to promote their compelling interest in diversity.

These rulings—going back to the 1978 *Bakke* decision—appeared to many to be vulnerable given the changing composition of the Court. In 2017, Trump placed Neil Gorsuch, a staunch conservative, in the seat of the man for whom he had once clerked, Antonin Scalia, replacing one ideological conservative with another. But when Anthony Kennedy announced his retirement in June 2018, Trump had the opportunity to move the Court further to the right, given that Kennedy had been the swing vote on many critical issues. He leaped at the chance, announcing the nomination of Brett Kavanaugh, a poster child for the Federalist Society, whose confirmation followed explosive hearings reminiscent of the Hill-Thomas inquiry in which a credible witness charged the nominee with sexual assault when they were high school students.

In an unlikely turn of events, however, advocates of criminal justice reform scored their most significant victory in decades with adoption of the First Step Act in 2018. It began as a bipartisan bill to improve conditions in federal prisons, a measure supported by liberals concerned about the plight of prisoners and conservatives who feared that prisons fostered recidivism. When the measure reached the Senate, the Leadership Conference on Civil Rights and a bipartisan group of senators who had backed sentencing reform legislation that died in 2016 forced consideration of sentencing reforms. The result was legislation that mitigated the most draconian elements of the war on drugs by reducing federal mandatory minimum sentences and giving federal judges greater discretion in cases involving non-violent drug offenders. The law also made retroactive the Fair Sentencing Act's reduction in the disparity between crack and powder cocaine, eased the ability of inmates to secure reduced sentences for good behavior while in prison, prohibited shackling of pregnant prisoners, and expanded programs to help prisoners prepare for life outside prison. The bill passed by overwhelming majorities in both houses after President Trump turned heads by announcing his support. *New York Times* Op-Ed writer Michelle Goldberg called it "a real man bites dog story" because a politician infamous for his tough-on-criminals rhetoric supported criminal justice reform.[55] Like many things with the mercurial Trump, his decision was personal, influenced by his son-in-law who had first-hand experience with the devastating consequences of having his father, convicted of tax evasion, incarcerated in a federal prison for sixteen months.

Despite Trump's support for criminal justice reform, civil rights and women's groups looked to the future with trepidation. In the 1970s and 1980s, they had won impressive victories in the face of a conservative political resurgence. These victories built on the triumphs of the 1960s to forge race-conscious tools like affirmative action to challenge the disparities and outright discrimination that survived the demise of Jim Crow. However, the ground shifted in the 1990s and the first two decades of the twenty-first century. The Supreme Court—which had played a critical role in expanding protections for civil rights—continued its rightward drift, which became a stampede during the Trump presidency. Armed with a color-blind approach to constitutional interpretation, the Court reduced or swept away hard-won civil rights protections secured during the previous three decades, even though the effects of slavery and segregation persisted.

The biggest threat, however, may not have been Donald Trump and his racially tinged populism. After all, Trump lost the popular count by almost 3 million votes in 2016, and the nation continued to become more diverse and less white. The Census Bureau forecast that whites would be a minority in the United States by 2043, and some pundits predicted that demographic changes would turn even deep red Texas blue as early as 2020. Many believed that Trump represented the past, not the future. If these predictions were correct, what would come after Trump? Race remained a fault line in American society as the legacy of slavery and segregation continued to affect income, employment opportunities, educational and health outcomes, and so much more. Who would mobilize a deeply divided nation to address these disparities? The policies forged during the civil rights movement and its aftermath brought an end to Jim Crow segregation and disfranchisement and expanded opportunities for many women and minorities. Yet given the wrenching economic transformations of the late twentieth century that slashed jobs in industry and left vast swaths of the nation's cities a wasteland, a criminal justice system that incarcerated tens of thousands of African Americans, and persistent racism, Martin Luther King Jr.'s dream remained elusive. New movements like Black Lives Matter brought a fresh approach to problems that had, for too long, attracted too little attention from mainstream civil rights groups. But could the new crusaders forge a program that would command the moral authority and build the political coalitions that had enabled previous generations of civil rights leaders to topple Jim Crow?

Notes

Chapter 1

1. The phrase comes from Gary B. Nash, *Forging Freedom: The Formation of Philadelphia's Black Community, 1720–1840* (Cambridge, MA: Harvard University Press, 1989), 134.
2. "To the President, Senate, and House of Representatives," 23 January 1797, ed. Herbert Aptheker, *A Documentary History of the Negro People in the United States*, 3 vols. (New York: Citadel Press, 1951–1974), 1:43.
3. Smith quoted in Donald L. Robinson, *Slavery in the Structure of American Politics, 1765–1820* (New York: Harcourt Brace Jovanovich, 1971), 289.
4. First Continental Congress, Declaration and Resolves, 17 October 1774; Second Continental Congress, Declaration of the Causes and Necessities of Taking up Arms, 6 July 1775, in *Great Issues in American History*, ed. Richard Hofstadter, 3 vols. (New York: Vintage, 1958), 2:30, 52.
5. John Phillip Reid, *The Concept of Liberty in the Age of the American Revolution* (Chicago: University of Chicago Press, 1988), 49.
6. Quoted in Winthrop D. Jordan, *White over Black: American Attitudes toward the Negro, 1550–1812* (Chapel Hill, NC, 1968), 293.
7. Ibid., 413.
8. US Constitution, Article I, sec. 2.
9. Max Farrand, ed., *The Records of the Federal Convention of 1787*, rev. ed. in 4 vols. (New Haven: Yale University Press, 1966), 1:593.
10. Ibid., 2:143.
11. Ibid., 2:222.
12. US Constitution, Article I, sec. 9.
13. Farrand, *Records*, 2:364.
14. Ibid., 443.
15. US Constitution, Article IV, sec. 2.
16. Farrand, *Records*, 2:417.
17. Quoted in Don E. Fehrenbacher, *The Dred Scott Case: Its Significance in American Law and Politics* (New York: Oxford University Press, 1978), 86.
18. Paul Finkelman, "*Prigg v. Pennsylvania* and Northern State Courts: Anti-Slavery Uses of a Pro-Slavery Decision," *Civil War History* 25 (March 1979): 5–35.
19. *Barron v. Baltimore*, 7 Peters 243 (1833).
20. *Livingston v. Van Ingen*, 9 Johnson's Reports 507 (NY, 1812), 577.
21. *Corfield v. Coryell*, 6 Fed. Cases 546 (No. 3230) (C.C.E.D. Pa. 1823), 551–52. For a good treatment of judicial interpretation of the privileges and immunities clause, see James H. Kettner, *The Development of American Citizenship, 1608–1870* (Chapel Hill: University of North Carolina Press, 1978), 255–61.

22. Quoted in William M. Wiecek, *The Sources of Antislavery Constitutionalism in America, 1760–1848* (Ithaca, NY: Cornell University Press, 1977), 123–24.

23. Ibid., 123.

24. Wirt did not expressly say that blacks who had full citizenship rights in the state in which they resided were US citizens. He did say, however, that it was clear that "no person is included in the description of citizen of the United States who has not the full rights of a citizen in the State of his residence." Because few states allowed blacks to vote (and the number shrank over time), most free blacks did not possess full citizenship rights in their home state and would not be considered national citizens under Wirt's criterion. *Official Opinions of the Attorneys General of the United States*, 10 vols. (Washington, DC: Government Printing Office, 1852), 1:507.

25. Quoted in Kenneth M. Stampp, *The Peculiar Institution: Slavery in the Antebellum South* (New York: Knopf, 1956), 197.

26. Ibid., 198.

27. Ibid., 208.

28. Ibid., 219.

29. Quoted in Ira Berlin, *Slaves without Masters: The Free Negro in the Antebellum South* (New York: New Press, 1974), 89.

30. Quoted in Theodore Brantner Wilson, *The Black Codes of the South* (Tuscaloosa: University of Alabama Press, 1965), 35.

31. Ibid., 27.

32. Ibid., 35.

Chapter 2

1. Philip S. Foner and George E. Walker, eds., *Proceedings of the Black State Conventions, 1840–1865*, 2 vols. (Philadelphia: Temple University Press, 1979), 1:259–60.

2. Ibid., 261.

3. Ibid., 262–63.

4. [William Lloyd Garrison], "Henry Clay's Colonization Address," *The Genius of Universal Emancipation*, 12 February 1830; Romans 13:9; Elizur Wright Jr., *The Sin of Slavery and Its Remedy* (New York: self-pub., 1836), reprinted in John L. Thomas, ed., *Slavery Attacked* (Englewood Cliffs, NJ: Prentice-Hall, 1965), 11.

5. Garrison quoted in Louis Filler, *The Crusade against Slavery, 1830–1860* (New York: Harper & Row, 1960), 216.

6. Philip S. Foner, ed., *The Life and Writings of Frederick Douglass*, 4 vols. (New York: International Publishers, 1950), 2:415, 420, 423.

7. William Goodell quoted in William M. Wiecek, *The Sources of Antislavery Constitutionalism in America, 1760–1848* (Ithaca, NY: Cornell University Press, 1978), 265.

8. Foner and Walker, *Black State Conventions*, 1:11, 192.

9. Martha S. Jones, *Birthright Citizens: A History of Race and Rights in Antebellum America* (New York: Cambridge University Press, 2018), 1.

10. *Colored American*, 9 May 1840; Hosea Easton, *A Treatise on the Intellectual Character and Civil and Political Condition of the Colored People of the United States* (Boston: n.p., 1837), 47.

11. Foner and Walker, *Black State Conventions*, 1:21.

12. Ibid., 22; Kirk H. Porter and Donald Bruce Johnson, *National Party Platforms, 1840–1956* (Urbana: University of Illinois Press, 1956), 7–8.

13. Tiffany quoted in Jacobus tenBroek, *Equal under Law*, rev. ed. (New York: Collier Books, 1965), 110.

14. Quotes are from Sumner's brief in Leonard Levy and Douglas Jones, eds., *Jim Crow in Boston: The Origin of the Separate but Equal Doctrine* (New York: Da Capo Press, 1974), 181, 210.

15. *Frederick Douglass' Newspaper*, 11 May 1855, 1.

16. *New York Times*, 27 August 1855, 3; 20 December 1856, 2.

17. Roy P. Basler, ed., *The Collected Works of Abraham Lincoln*, 9 vols. (New Brunswick, NJ: Rutgers University Press, 1953–55), 3:16.

18. Comity is the courtesy one nation or state pays another by recognizing and giving effect to its laws. This is done as a matter of respect rather than obligation and recognizes that no nation or state is bound to give effect to "foreign" laws that are contrary to its policy.

19. Fehrenbacher, *The Dred Scott Case*, 333–34.

20. *Dred Scott v. Sandford*, 19 Howard 393 (1857), 407.

21. Ibid., 451–52.

22. Foner, *Writings of Frederick Douglass*, 2:412–14.

Chapter 3

1. *Coger v. The North West Union Packet Co.*, 37 Iowa 145 (1873), 148, 149.

2. Ibid., 153, 155, 156.

3. Ibid., 149, 153–54.

4. Quoted in Harold M. Hyman, *A More Perfect Union: The Impact of the Civil War and Reconstruction on the Constitution* (New York: Houghton Mifflin, 1973), 543.

5. Basler, ed., *The Collected Works of Abraham Lincoln*, 4:263; U.S., Congress, Senate, *Congressional Globe*, 37th Cong., 1st sess., 22 July 1861, 222–23.

6. Foner, ed., *The Life and Writings of Frederick Douglass*, 3:64–65; resolution of New York convention quoted in Ira Berlin et al., eds., *Freedom: A Documentary History of Emancipation. Series II. The Black Military Experience* (Cambridge: Cambridge University Press, 1982), 9.

7. LaWanda Cox, *Lincoln and Black Freedom: A Study in Presidential Leadership* (Columbia: University of South Carolina Press, 1981), 6.

8. One year earlier, in August 1861, Congress had enacted a more limited Confiscation Act, which authorized seizure of property—including slaves—used to support the Confederate war effort.

9. U.S., *Statutes at Large*, 12:592.

10. Richard Hofstadter, *The American Political Tradition and the Men Who Made It* (New York: Knopf, 1948), 131.

11. Eric Foner, *The Fiery Trial: Abraham Lincoln and American Slavery* (New York: W. W. Norton, 2010), 245.

12. Louis P. Masur, *Lincoln's Hundred Days: The Emancipation Proclamation and the War for the Union* (Cambridge, MA: Harvard University Press, 2012), 7–8.

13. Hyman, *A More Perfect Union*, 124–40.

14. Schenck quoted in Herman Belz, *A New Birth of Freedom: The Republican Party and Freedmen's Rights, 1861 to 1866* (Westport, CT: Greenwood Press, 1976), 108.

15. George Rawick, ed., *The American Slave: A Composite Autobiography*, 39 vols. (Westport, CT: Greenwood Press, 1972–79), vol. 2, pt. 1, 328; Supplement, ser. 2, 6:1945, 1947; Leon Litwack, *Been in the Storm So Long: The Aftermath of Slavery* (New York: Knopf, 1979), 224. The language in the text are quotes from transciptions of speeches and interviews, done in the 1930s and 1860s, respectively.

16. Lt. A. Dyer, "Report of Refugees, Freedmen, and Abandoned Lands for the Month Ending June 30, 1866," Records of the Freedmen's Bureau, Assistant Commissioner for Arkansas, Reports, Record Group 105, National Archives, Washington, DC.

17. Eric Foner, *Free Soil, Free Labor, Free Men: The Ideology of the Republican Party before the Civil War* (New York: Oxford University Press, 1970).

18. U.S., *Congressional Globe*, 39th Cong., 1st sess., pt. 1, January 19, 1866, 320 (remarks of Lyman Trumbull).

19. The text of the Freedmen's Bureau bill is reprinted in Edward McPherson, ed., *The Political History of the United States . . . during the Period of Reconstruction . . .* (Washington, DC: Solomons & Chapman, 1875), 72–74.

20. U.S., *Statutes at Large*, 14:27–30.

21. Colfax to Ames, 10 April 1866, Mary Clemmer Ames Papers, Rutherford B. Hayes Library, Fremont, Ohio; U.S., *Congressional Globe*, 39th Cong., 1st sess., pt. 2, 2 March 1866, 1154 (remarks of Charles Eldridge).

22. Michael Les Benedict, *A Compromise of Principle: Congressional Republicans and Reconstruction, 1863–1869* (New York: W. W. Norton, 1974) and "Preserving the Constitution: The Conservative Basis of Radical Reconstruction," *Journal of American History* 61 (June 1974): 65–90.

23. U.S., *Congressional Globe*, 39th Cong., 1st sess., pt. 2, 10 May 1866, 2542 (remarks of John A. Bingham).

24. Capt. H. Sweeney to General J. W. Sprague, 5 January 1867, Freedmen's Bureau Records, Assistant Commissioner for Arkansas, Letters Received, Record Group 105, National Archives, Washington, DC.

25. G. Franklin et al. to General Daniel Sickles, 8 August 1866, Records of the Freedmen's Bureau, Assistant Commissioner for South Carolina, Letters Received, Record Group 105, National Archives, Washington, DC.

26. Lt. George Cook to Capt. R. S. Lacey, 31 October 1866, Records of the Freedmen's Bureau, Assistant Commissioner for Virginia, Reports, Record Group 105, National Archives, Washington, DC.

27. Maj. Fred Thibant to General Absalom Baird, 6 November 1866, Records of the Freedmen's Bureau, Office of the Assistant Commissioner for Louisiana, Letters Received, Record Group 105, National Archives, Washington, DC.
28. James Bailey to Robert K. Scott, 26 February 1870, Governor's Papers, South Carolina Archives.
29. Lawrence Smith to E. B. Seabrook, 17 December 1869; Joseph Sanders to Johnson Hagood, 17 May 1877, Legislative Records, Penal System File, South Carolina Archives.
30. Benjamin Perry quoted in Eric Foner, *Reconstruction: America's Unfinished Revolution, 1863–1877* (New York: Harper & Row, 1988), 294; *Daily Arkansas Gazette*, 8 February 1868, quoted in Allen Trelease, *White Terror: The Ku Klux Klan Conspiracy and Southern Reconstruction* (New York: Harper & Row, 1971), xxxvi; *Montgomery* (Alabama) *Daily Advertiser*, 7 January 1868 and *Natchez* (Mississippi) *Democrat*, 15 January 1875 quoted in Michael Les Benedict, "The Problem of Constitutionalism and Constitutional Liberty in the Reconstruction South," in *An Uncertain Tradition: Constitutionalism and the History of the South*, ed. Kermit L. Hall and James W. Ely Jr. (Athens: University of Georgia Press, 1989), 238, 240.

Chapter 4

1. *Brenham Daily Banner*, 9 December 1886, 1.
2. U.S., Congress, Senate, *Congressional Globe*, 42nd Cong., 1st sess., pt. 1, 3 April 1871, 427 (remarks of George McKee).
3. Rainey quoted in Foner, *Reconstruction*, 456.
4. U.S., *Statutes at Large*, 17:13. The writ of habeas corpus commanded officials to bring persons who were under arrest before a judge for an inquiry into the legality of their arrest and detention. Suspension of habeas corpus would enable federal officials to make mass arrests without having to prepare formal charges and justify them in court immediately. This would enable them to act quickly, reducing the chance that some suspects would be alerted and flee before arrests could be made. Suspension did not mean that persons arrested would be tried in military courts.
5. *United States v. Hall et al.*, 26 Fed. Cases 79 (No. 15,282) (C.C.S.D., Ala., 1871).
6. U.S., *Congressional Globe*, 43rd Cong., 2nd sess., pt. 2, 4 February 1875, 980 (remarks of Ellis Roberts).
7. Quoted in William Gillette, *Retreat from Reconstruction, 1869–1879* (Baton Rouge: Louisiana State University Press, 1979), 199.
8. *Harper's Weekly*, 10 January 1874, 27; U.S., *Congressional Globe*, 43rd Cong., 2nd sess., pt. 2, 3 February 1875, 944 (remarks of John Lynch); Downing quoted in McPherson, "Abolitionists and the Civil Rights Act of 1875," *Journal of American History* 52 (December 1965): 505; U.S., *Congressional Globe*, 43rd Cong., 1st sess., pt. 4, 29 April 1874, 3452 (remarks of Frederick Frelinghuysen).
9. Quoted in Gillette, *Retreat from Reconstruction*, 209.
10. John Y. Simon, ed., *The Papers of Ulysses S. Grant*. Volume 26: 1875 (Carbondale: Southern Illinois University Press, 2003), xii.

11. Quoted in Vernon Lane Wharton, *The Negro in Mississippi, 1865–1900* (Chapel Hill: University of North Carolina Press, 1947), 206.

12. *The Slaughter-House Cases*, 83 U.S. 36 (1873), 78, 129.

13. Ibid., 71.

14. *United States v. Cruikshank*, 92 U.S. 542 (1876), 554.

15. *The Civil Rights Cases*, 109 U.S. 1 (1883), 20–21, 24.

16. Ibid., 25.

17. Ibid., 26.

18. *Strauder v. West Virginia*, 100 U.S. 303 (1880), 307–308.

19. *Ex Parte In the Matter of The Commonwealth of Virginia and J. D. Coles*, 100 U.S. 339 (1880), 345, 347; *Neal v. Delaware*, 103, U.S. 370 (1880).

20. *Yick Wo v. Peter Hopkins*, 118 U.S. 356 (1887), 373–74.

21. *United States v. Hiram Reese and Matthew Foushee*, 92 U.S. 214 (1876), 218; *United States v. Butler*, 25 Fed. Cases 213 (14,700) (C.C.D.S.C., 1877).

22. *Ex Parte: In the Matter of Jasper Yarbrough, et al.*, 110 U.S. 651 (1884).

23. Robert Goldman, *"A Free Ballot and a Fair Count": The Department of Justice and the Enforcement of Voting Rights in the South, 1877–1893* (New York: Fordham University Press, 2001).

24. Lucius Northrup, the United States attorney in South Carolina, quoted in Ibid., 71.

25. *Ferguson v. Gies*, 82 Michigan 358 (1890), 363, 364.

26. J. Morgan Kousser, *The Shaping of Southern Politics: Suffrage Restriction and the Establishment of the One-Party South, 1880–1910* (New Haven: Yale University Press, 1974), 62.

27. The term "Jim Crow" first appeared in the North in the 1830s as the title of a minstrel song-and-dance show. (Minstrel shows were presented by white performers with blackened faces, and contained a series of sketches that portrayed black life, humor, and music in a patronizing and derogatory fashion.) As early as the 1840s the term was applied to cars set aside for blacks on Massachusetts railroads.

28. *Nashville Clarion* and *Jacksonville Florida Times-Union* quoted in August Meier and Elliot Rudwick, "The Boycott Movement against Jim Crow Streetcars in the South, 1900–1906," *Journal of American History* 45 (March 1969): 761.

29. *Plessy v. Ferguson*, 163 U.S. 537 (1896), 544, 551, 559.

30. *Williams v. Mississippi*, 170 U.S. 213 (1898), 222.

31. *Giles v. Harris*, 189 U.S. 476 (1903), 188–89.

Chapter 5

1. Wechsler quoted in Richard Kluger, *Simple Justice* (New York: Knopf, 1975), 160.

2. Ibid., 159.

3. Ibid., 159–60.

4. Restrictive covenants were special provisions added to real estate deeds that limited the owner's freedom to use or sell the property in some specified manner, such as selling it to non-whites.

5. Stephan Thernstrom, *The Other Bostonians: Poverty and Progress in the American Metropolis, 1880–1970* (Cambridge, MA: Harvard University Press, 1973), 197.

6. Villard quoted in Charles Flint Kellogg, *NAACP: A History of the National Association for the Advancement of Colored People, 1890–1920* (Baltimore: Johns Hopkins University Press, 1967), 297–98.

7. Unlike the House of Representatives, the smaller Senate prided itself on being a truly deliberative body, and its rules allowed unlimited debate. In practice, this permitted members to hold the floor indefinitely, enabling a determined minority to bring the business of the Senate to a halt. Once they were recognized by the presiding officer, members bent on obstruction could speak on any topic that came to mind and frequently read from books or newspapers. Moreover, when one filibustering senator became too tired to continue, he could yield the floor to a co-conspirator who could carry on the obstruction. In 1917 the Senate adopted a rule that permitted a majority of two-thirds of senators present to adopt a motion of "cloture," ending debate and requiring a vote on the pending measure. Southern strength in the Senate, however, made obtaining cloture difficult to achieve.

8. 42 U.S. Code 1994 https://www.law.cornell.edu/uscode/text/42/1994 (accessed May 6, 2019).

9. *Clyatt v. United States*, 197 U.S. 207 (1905); *Bailey v. Alabama*, 219 U.S. 219 (1911); *United States v. Reynolds*, 235 U.S. 133 (1914).

10. Pete Daniel, *The Shadow of Slavery: Peonage in the South, 1901–1969* (New York: Oxford University Press, 1972).

11. The phrase means "friend of the court." Groups or individuals who are not parties to a case but who have an interest in its outcome or special expertise on issues raised by it are often allowed to submit briefs on behalf of one of the parties.

12. *Guinn v. United States*, 238 U.S. 347 (1915).

13. *Buchanan v. Warley*, 245 U.S. 60 (1917), 76, 79, 82.

14. The *Corrigan* case arose in the District of Columbia, technically not a state but an area subject to the jurisdiction of the federal government. Therefore, there was doubt as to whether the Fourteenth Amendment, which barred *states* from denying persons due process of law, was applicable. However, the Fifth Amendment, which applied to the federal government, provided that no person "shall be . . . deprived of life, liberty, or property without due process of law" and was therefore relied on by the NAACP.

15. *Corrigan v. Buckley*, 271 U.S. 323 (1926).

16. *Moore v. Dempsey*, 261 U.S. 86 (1923).

17. Harvard Sitkoff, *A New Deal for Blacks. The Emergence of Civil Rights as a National Issue: The Depression Decade* (New York: Oxford University Press, 1978), 66, 69.

18. Leigh Ann Wheeler, *How Sex Became a Civil Liberty* (New York: Oxford University Press, 2013), 180.

19. *Powell v. Alabama*, 287 U.S. 45 (1932).

20. *Twining v. New Jersey*, 211 U.S. 78 (1908), 114.

21. *Brown v. Mississippi*, 297 U.S. 278 (1936), 286.

22. *Chambers v. Florida*, 309 U.S. 227 (1940), 238.

23. *Norris v. Alabama*, 294 U.S. 587 (1935).

24. *Smith v. Texas,* 311 U.S. 128 (1940).

25. *University of Maryland v. Murray,* 169 Maryland 478 (1936).

26. *Missouri ex rel Gaines v. Canada,* 305 U.S. 337 (1938), 346, 349.

27. *Mills v. Board of Education of Ann Arundel County,* 30 F. Supp. 245 (D. Maryland 1939).

28. *Alston v. School Board of City of Norfolk,* 112 F.2d 992 (4th Cir. 1940).

29. Schuyler's *Pittsburgh Courier* editorial of 5 October 1940 and War Department order of 5 September 1940 quoted in Sitkoff, *New Deal for Blacks,* 301, 305.

30. White and Randolph quoted in Sitkoff, *New Deal for Blacks,* 324–25.

31. President's Committee on Civil Rights, *To Secure These Rights* (Washington, DC: Government Printing Office, 1947), 148.

32. *Grovey v. Townsend,* 295 U.S. 45 (1935).

33. In 1939 tax considerations prompted the NAACP board of directors to establish the NAACP Legal Defense and Education Fund to manage the organization's increasingly ambitious program of litigation. Because the NAACP engaged in lobbying, it did not enjoy tax-exempt status. As a separate entity that did not lobby, however, the LDF qualified as a tax-exempt organization and contributors' donations were tax-deductible. During the first twenty years of the LDF's existence, the separation was largely nominal. Members of the NAACP's board served as directors of the LDF, and Thurgood Marshall, who became director of the LDF, remained an NAACP employee. Only in 1958 (when this close relationship threatened its tax-exempt status) did the LDF become a truly independent organization.

34. *Smith v. Allwright,* 321 U.S. 649 (1944), 663, 664.

35. *Shelley v. Kraemer,* 334 U.S. 1 (1948), 19.

36. *Morgan v. Virginia,* 328 U.S. 373 (1946).

37. Clark quoted in Mark Tushnet, *The NAACP's Legal Strategy against Segregated Education, 1925–1950* (Chapel Hill: University of North Carolina Press, 1987), 132; *Sweatt v. Painter,* 339 U.S. 629 (1950), 634.

38. Tushnet, *The NAACP's Legal Strategy,* 132.

39. *Henderson v. United States,* 339 U.S. 816 (1950).

Chapter 6

1. David J. Garrow, *Bearing the Cross: Martin Luther King and the Southern Christian Leadership Conference* (New York: William Morrow, 1986), 23–24; Taylor Branch, *Parting the Waters: America in the King Years, 1954–1963* (New York: Simon & Schuster, 1988), 138–42.

2. Branch, *Parting the Waters,* 168.

3. *Gayle v. Browder,* 352 U.S. 903 (1956).

4. Garrow, *Bearing the Cross,* 24.

5. The state cases turned on whether the Fourteenth Amendment's stipulation that no state shall "deny any person . . . equal protection of the laws" outlawed segregation. Since the District of Columbia was not a state, the Fourteenth Amendment did not apply to it. Segregation there had to be challenged as a violation of the Fifth

Amendment's prohibition against federal action that denied persons due process of law.

6. Kluger, *Simple Justice*, 679.
7. *Brown v. Board of Education of Topeka*, 347 U.S. 483 (1954), 493–95.
8. *Brown v. Board of Education of Topeka*, 349 U.S. 294 (1955), 300, 301.
9. Jack W. Peltason, *Fifty-Eight Lonely Men: Southern Federal Judges and School Desegregation* (New York: Harcourt, Brace & World, 1961), 60.
10. Michael J. Klarman, *From Jim Crow to Civil Rights: The Supreme Court and the Struggle for Racial Equality* (New York: Oxford University Press, 2004), 390–91.
11. Alabama pupil placement law as quoted in Peltason, *Fifty-eight Lonely Men*, 83.
12. Frederick Morrow quoted in Michal R. Belknap, *Federal Law and Southern Order: Racial Violence and Constitutional Conflict in the Post-Brown South* (Athens: University of Georgia Press, 1987), 33–34.
13. Davidson quoted in Peltason, *Fifty-eight Lonely Men*, 119, 121.
14. Eisenhower quoted in Ibid., 49.
15. *Cooper v. Aaron*, 358 U.S. 1 (1958), 17, 19–20.
16. *Mayor of Baltimore v. Dawson*, 350 U.S. 877 (1955); *Holmes v. City of Atlanta*, 350 U.S. 879 (1955); *Gayle v. Browder*, 352 U.S. 903 (1956); *New Orleans Park Improvement Association v. Detige*, 358 U.S. 54 (1958).
17. *Burton v. Wilmington Parking Authority*, 365 U.S. 715 (1961).
18. *NAACP v. Alabama*, 357 U.S. 449 (1958); *Bates v. Little Rock*, 361 U.S. 516 (1960).
19. Quoted in Harvard Sitkoff, *The Struggle for Black Equality, 1954–1980* (New York: Hill and Wang, 1981), 79.
20. Belknap, *Federal Law and Southern Order*, 74.
21. *Boynton v. Virginia*, 364 U.S. 454 (1960).
22. Sitkoff, *Struggle for Black Equality*, 154.
23. Kennedy quoted in Carl M. Brauer, *John F. Kennedy and the Second Reconstruction* (New York: Columbia University Press, 1977), 260.
24. "President Johnson's Special Message to Congress," March 15, 1965 http://www.lbjlibrary.org/lyndon-baines-johnson/speeches-films/president-johnsons-special-message-to-the-congress-the-american-promise (accessed May 5, 2019).
25. *Heart of Atlanta Motel v. United States*, 379 U.S. 241 (1964); *Katzenbach v. McClung*, 379 U.S. 294 (1964).
26. *South Carolina v. Katzenbach*, 383 U.S. 301 (1966).
27. *Harper v. Virginia Board of Elections*, 383 U.S. 667 (1966).
28. *United States v. Williams*, 341 U.S. 70 (1951).
29. *United States v. Price*, 383 U.S. 787 (1966), 805.
30. *United States v. Guest*, 383 U.S. 745 (1966), 782, 784.
31. *Annual Report of the Attorney General of the United States, 1968* (Washington, DC: Government Printing Office, 1969), 67.
32. *United States v. Jefferson County Board of Education*, 372 F.2d 836 (5th Circuit, 1966), 869.
33. *Green v. County School Board*, 391 U.S. 430 (1968), 435, 437–38, 439.

34. Allen Matusow, *The Unraveling of America: A History of Liberalism in the 1960s* (New York: Harper & Row, 1984), 194.

35. Cashin quoted in Steven F. Lawson, *Black Ballots: Voting Rights in the South, 1944–1969* (New York: Columbia University Press, 1976), 339.

36. Premilla Nadasen, *Welfare Warriors: The Welfare Rights Movement in the United States* (New York: Routledge, 2005).

37. "The President's Address to the Nation on Civil Disorders, July 27, 1967," https://quod.lib.umich.edu/p/ppotpus/4731566.1967.002/113?page=root;rgn=full+text;size =100;view=image;q1=Remarks+Upon+Signing+Order+Establishing+the+National +Advisory+Commission+on+Civil+Disorders (accessed December 30, 2018).

38. "Report of the National Advisory Commission on Civil Disorders," https://www.ncjrs.gov/pdffiles1/Digitization/8073NCJRS.pdf, 1 (accessed December 30, 2018).

39. *Jones v. Alfred H. Mayer Co.*, 392 U.S. 409 (1968), 443.

40. The Supreme Court so ruled in *Runyon v. McCrary*, 427 U.S. 160 (1976).

Chapter 7

1. J. Harvie Wilkinson III, *From Brown to Bakke: The Supreme Court and School Integration, 1954–1978* (New York: Oxford University Press, 1979), 210.

2. J. Anthony Lukas, *Common Ground: A Turbulent Decade in the Lives of Three American Families* (New York: Knopf, 1985), 261.

3. Nixon quoted in Gary Orfield, *Must We Bus? Segregated Schools and National Policy* (Washington, DC: Brookings Institution, 1978), 244.

4. *Alexander v. Holmes County Board of Education*, 396 U.S. 19 (1969), 20.

5. *Green v. County School Board*, 391 U.S. 430 (1968), 437.

6. *Swann v. Charlotte-Mecklenburg Board of Education*, 402 U.S. 1 (1971), 25, 28, 30.

7. *Keyes v. School District No. 1, Denver, Colo.*, 413 U.S. 189 (1973), 201.

8. Justin Driver, *The Schoolhouse Gate: Public Education, the Supreme Court, and the Battle for the American Mind* (New York: Pantheon, 2018).

9. *Milliken v. Bradley*, 418 U.S. 717 (1974), 741.

10. Ibid., 772.

11. Ibid., 782, 814–15.

12. *Griggs v. Duke Power*, 401 U.S. 424 (1971), 427.

13. Ibid., 429–30, 431.

14. *Federal Register*, 4 December 1971, sec. 60–2.10, 23, 153.

15. Equal Employment Opportunity Commission, *Affirmative Action and Equal Employment* (Washington, DC: Office of Equal Employment Opportunity, 1974), 1.

16. Alexander Bickel, *The Morality of Consent* (New Haven: Yale University Press, 1975), 133. Bickel's statement was the starting point for one of the most sharply argued challenges to affirmative action, William Van Alstyne, "Rites of Passage: Race, the Supreme Court, and the Constitution," *University of Chicago Law Review* 46 (1979): 775–810.

17. J. Skelly Wright, "Color-Blind Theories and Color-Conscious Remedies," *University of Chicago Law Review* 47 (1980): 213–45.

18. *Regents of the University of California v. Bakke*, 438 U.S. 265 (1978), 407.

19. Ibid., 289–90.

20. *United Steelworkers of America v. Weber*, 443 U.S. 193 (1979), 204.

21. *Fullilove v. Klutznik*, 448 U.S. 448 (1980), 484.

22. *Allen v. State Board of Elections*, 393 U.S. 544 (1969), 565–66, 569.

23. *White v. Regester*, 412 U.S. 756 (1973), 769–70.

24. *City of Mobile v. Bolden*, 446 U.S. 55 (1980), 62.

25. "Transcript of Ronald Reagan's 1980 Neshoba County Fair Speech," http://neshobademocrat.com/Content/NEWS/News/Article/Transcript-of-Ronald-Reagan-s-1980-Neshoba-County-Fair-speech/2/297/15599 (accessed December 28, 2018).

26. Pendleton quoted in "The Rise and Fall of the United States Commission on Civil Rights," *Harvard Civil Rights-Civil Liberties Review* 22 (1987): 484.

27. "Civil Rights Activists Locked Horns with William Bradford Reynolds," UPI Archives, August 9, 1982 https://www.upi.com/Archives/1982/08/09/Civil-rights-activists-locked-horns-with-William-Bradford-Reynolds/1347397713600/ (December 28, 2018).

28. Reagan quoted in Steven F. Lawson, *In Pursuit of Power: Southern Blacks and Electoral Politics, 1965–1982* (New York: Columbia University Press, 1985), 288.

29. Ibid., 288–89.

30. United States Code, Title 42, sec. 1973 https://www.govinfo.gov/content/pkg/USCODE-2012-title42/pdf/USCODE-2012-title42-chap20-subchapI-A-sec1973.pdf (accessed May 8, 2019).

31. Reagan quoted in Lawson, *Pursuit of Power*, 292.

32. *Thornburgh v. Gingles*, 478 U.S. 30 (1986).

33. U.S., Senate Committee on the Judiciary, *Hearing on the Nomination of William Bradford Reynolds to be Associate Attorney General of the United States*, 99th Cong., 1st sess., 390.

34. The quote is from Edwin M. Meese III, who replaced William French Smith as attorney general in 1985. *New York Times*, 7 October 1985, 20.

35. *Firefighters v. Stotts*, 467 U.S. 561 (1984).

36. *Wygant v. Jackson Board of Education*, 476 U.S. 267 (1986), 280–81, 282.

37. *Local 28 of the Sheet Metal Workers' International Association v. Equal Employment Opportunity Commission*, 478 U.S. 421 (1986), 483.

38. *Local Number 93, International Association of Firefighters v. City of Cleveland*, 478 U.S. 501 (1986), 518.

39. *Johnson v. Transportation Agency*, 480 U.S. 616 (1987), 642.

40. National Center for Education Statistics, "Digest of Education Statistics," https://nces.ed.gov/programs/digest/d13/tables/dt13_104.20.asp (February 7, 2019).

41. U.S. Department of Labor, "Labor Force Characteristics by Race and Ethnicity, 2007," https://www.bls.gov/opub/reports/race-and-ethnicity/archive/race_ethnicity_2007.pdf (February 8, 2019).

42. U.S. Department of Commerce, "Detailed Occupation of Employed Persons by Race and Sex for the United States: 1970," https://www2.census.gov/library/publications/decennial/1970/pc-s1-supplementary-reports/pc-s1-32.pdf (February 8, 2019).

43. Black Demographics, "African American Income," http://blackdemographics.com/households/african-american-income/ (February 7, 2019).

44. U.S. Census Bureau, "Poverty in the U.S.: 2000," https://www2.census.gov/programs-surveys/demo/visualizations/p60/214/fig07.jpg (February 7, 2019).

45. Douglas S. Massey and Nancy A. Denton, "Hypersegregation in US Metropolitan Areas: Black and Hispanic Segregation Along Five Dimensions," *Demography* 26 (August 1989): 373–91.

46. *New York Times*, October 3, 1982 https://www.nytimes.com/1982/10/03/us/no-headline-194726.html (February 10, 2019).

47. *Los Angeles Times*, January 9, 1986 http://articles.latimes.com/1986-01-09/news/mn-14186_1_crime-control-act (February 10, 2019).

48. *New York Times*, June 24, 1986.

49. US Sentencing Commission, *Mandatory Minimum Penalties in the Federal Criminal Justice System* (August 1991), 15 https://www.ussc.gov/sites/default/files/pdf/news/congressional-testimony-and-reports/mandatory-minimum-penalties/1991_Mand_Min_Report.pdf (July 2, 2018).

50. Michelle Alexander, *The New Jim Crow: Mass Incarceration in the Age of Colorblindness* (New York: New Press, 2010).

51. http://www.sentencingproject.org/publications/democracy-imprisoned-a-review-of-the-prevalence-and-impact-of-felony-disenfranchisement-laws-in-the-united-states/ (July 8, 2018).

52. *McCleskey v. Kemp* 481 U.S. 270 (1987).

53. *Martin v. Wilks*, 490 US 755 (1989).

54. *Patterson v. McLean Credit Union*, 491 U.S. 164 (1989).

55. *Ward's Cove Packing Co. v. Atonio*, 490 U.S. 642 (1989).

56. *City of Richmond. v. J. A. Crosson*, 488 U.S. 469 (1989).

57. *New York Times*, 18 June 1989.

58. *Ward's Cove Packing Co. v. Atonio*, 490 U.S. 642 (1989), 662.

Chapter 8

1. Jane Mayer and Jill Abrahamson, *Strange Justice: The Selling of Clarence Thomas* (New York: Plume, 1995) 205.

2. *Strange Justice*, 104.

3. *New York Times*, October 13, 1991, 28.

4. *Strange Justice*, 299.

5. *Public Papers of the President of the United States: George Bush, 1990* (Washington, DC: National Archives and Records Administration, 1990), 1438.

6. *New York Times*, October 31, 1991.

7. https://www.youtube.com/watch?v=KIyewCdXMzk (June 1, 2018).

8. "Remarks on Affirmative Action at the National Archives and Records Administration," July 19, 1995 https://www.washingtonpost.com/wp-srv/politics/special/affirm/docs/clintonspeech.htm (June 5, 2018).

9. Pew Research Center, "Public Backs Affirmative Action, Not Minority Preferences," June 2, 2009 http://www.pewresearch.org/2009/06/02/public-backs-affirmative-action-but-not-minority-preferences/ (June 6, 2018).

10. "Losing Its Preference: Affirmative Action Fades as an Issue," *Washington Post*, September 18, 1996.

11. *Adarand Constructors, Inc. v. Peña*, 515 U.S. 200 (1995).

12. *Washington Post*, March 7, 1998 https://www.washingtonpost.com/archive/politics/1998/03/07/minority-set-aside-survives-in-senate/41ad3983-73bb-49a0-aca9-6ce4ad6548e3/?utm_term=.62a62e884821 (June 13, 2018).

13. *Hopwood v. Texas*, 78 F.3d 932 (Fifth Circuit 1996).

14. Barbara A. Perry, *The Michigan Affirmative Action Cases* (Lawrence: University Press of Kansas, 2007), 98, 100–101.

15. *Grutter v. Bollinger*, 539 U.S. 306 (2003).

16. Abigail Thernstrom, *Whose Votes Count: Affirmative Action and Minority Voting Rights* (Cambridge, MA: Harvard University Press, 1987).

17. Ari Berman, *Give Us the Ballot: The Modern Struggle for Voting Rights in America* (New York: Picador, 2015), 192.

18. "Fairness or Racial Gerrymander? Justices Study Serpentine District," *New York Times*, April 16, 1993.

19. *Shaw v. Reno*, 509 U.S. 630 (1993).

20. *Miller v. Johnson*, 515 U.S. 900 (1995).

21. J. Morgan Kousser, *Colorblind Injustice: Minority Voting Rights and the Second Reconstruction* (Chapel Hill: University of North Carolina Press, 1999), 405.

22. *Easley v. Cromartie*, 532 U.S. 234 (2001).

23. "115th Congress Will Be Most Racially Diverse in History," *The Hill*, November 17, 2016   http://thehill.com/homenews/house/306480-115th-congress-will-be-most-racially-diverse-in-history (June 20, 2018).

24. Berman, *Give Us the Ballot*, 260.

25. *New York Times*, July 3, 1992 https://www.nytimes.com/1992/07/03/us/the-1992-campaign-president-vetoes-the-motor-voter-measure.html (June 24, 2018).

26. *Crawford v. Marion County Election Board*, 355 U.S. 181 (2008).

27. *New York Times*, March 23, 2012 https://thecaucus.blogs.nytimes.com/2012/03/23/obama-makes-first-comments-on-trayvon-martin-shooting/ (June 27, 2018)

28. Berman, *Give Us the Ballot*, 264.

29. Jim Rutenberg, "A Dream Undone," *New York Times Magazine*, July 29, 2015.

30. Berman, *Give Us the Ballot*, 150.

31. *Shelby County v. Holder*, 570 U.S. 2 (2013)

32. *Washington Post*, October 31, 1995 https://www.washingtonpost.com/archive/politics/1995/10/31/clinton-retains-tough-law-on-crack-cocaine/0f435210-4bfd-45b5-b1ab-3f95b65a0e68/?utm_term=.29be0614b55e (July 15, 2018).

33. *New York Times*, November 5, 1995 https://www.nytimes.com/1995/11/05/opinion/cocaine-sentencing-still-unjust.html (July 15, 2018).

34. http://www.drugpolicy.org/publications-resources/sign-letters/ungass-public-letter-kofi-annan (July 15, 2018).

35. "Prepared Testimony of Wade Henderson Leadership Conference on Civil Rights before the House Government Reform Committee Subcommittee on Criminal Justice, May 11, 2000," http://lobby.la.psu.edu/049_Criminal_Justice_Reform/Congressional_Hearings/Testimony/H_Government_Reform_CJ_Henderson_051100.htm (July 15, 2018).

36. *Kimbrough v. United States*, 552 U.S. 85 (2007).

37. *Washington Post*, September 25, 2012 https://www.washingtonpost.com/blogs/fact-checker/post/when-did-mcconnell-say-he-wanted-to-make-obama-a-one-term-president/2012/09/24/79fd5cd8-0696-11e2-afff-d6c7f20a83bf_blog.html?utm_term=.e5e1583bea21 (July 21, 2018).

38. Memorandum to the United States Attorneys and Assistant Attorney General for the Criminal Division, August 12, 2013 https://www.justice.gov/sites/default/files/oip/legacy/2014/07/23/ag-memo-department-policypon-charging-mandatory-minimum-sentences-recidivist-enhancements-in-certain-drugcases.pdf (July 21, 2018)

39. *Wall Street Journal*, July 14, 2015

40. Text of Obama's Speech on Trayvon Martin, July 19, 2013 https://www.business-insider.com/obama-trayvon-martin-race-speech-video-text-2013-7 (July 24, 2018)

41. Dewey M. Clayton, "Black Lives Matter and the Civil Rights Movement: A Comparative Analysis of Two Social Movements in the United States," *Journal of Black Studies* 49 (2018): 453.

42. *New York Times*, December 20, 2014 https://www.nytimes.com/2014/12/21/us/chanting-black-lives-matter-protesters-shut-down-part-of-mall-of-america.html (July 20, 2018)

43. Darren Sands, "What Happened to Black Lives Matter?" Buzz Feed News, June 21, 2017 https://www.buzzfeednews.com/article/darrensands/what-happened-to-black-lives-matter (July 25, 2018)

44. https://www.cbsnews.com/news/donald-trump-black-lives-matter-calls-for-killing-police/ (July 25, 2018).

45. https://bobbyscott.house.gov/media-center/press-releases/senate-passes-death-in-custody-act (July 26, 2018)

46. http://time.com/4397611/president-obama/ (July 26, 2018)

47. https://www.nytimes.com/politics/first-draft/2015/06/16/choice-words-from-donald-trump-presidential-candidate/ (July 26, 2018)

48. https://www.politifact.com/wisconsin/article/2016/jun/08/donald-trumps-racial-comments-about-judge-trump-un/ (July 26, 2018)

49. https://www.nytimes.com/interactive/2018/01/15/opinion/leonhardt-trump-racist.html (July, 26, 2018)

50. https://thinkprogress.org/donald-trump-made-an-aggressive-new-pitch-to-black-voters-it-didnt-go-well-657208e15842/#.kzmi3y5qu (July 26, 2018)

51. https://www.politifact.com/wisconsin/article/2016/jun/08/donald-trumps-racial-comments-about-judge-trump-un/ (July 26, 2018)

52. https://www.washingtonpost.com/news/the-fix/wp/2016/11/18/10-things-to-know-about-sen-jeff-sessions-donald-trumps-pick-for-attorney-general/?utm_term=.4e36ace0d721 (July 26, 2018)

53. https://www.washingtonpost.com/news/post-nation/wp/2017/04/04/sessions-wants-a-review-of-consent-decrees-which-have-been-used-for-decades-to-force-reforms/?utm_term=.3dba337dfd76 (July 26, 2018)

54. Vann R. Newkirk II, "The End of Civil Rights," *The Atlantic*, June 18, 2018 https://www.theatlantic.com/politics/archive/2018/06/sessions/563006/ (July 27, 2018).

55. Michelle Goldberg, "Donald Trump Is Doing Something . . . Good?," *New York Times*, December 20, 2018 https://www.nytimes.com/2018/12/20/opinion/first-step-act-trump.html (accessed February 2, 2019).

Bibliographical Essay

Promises to Keep draws on a rich body of scholarship in African American, constitutional and legal, and civil rights history. The civil rights revolution of the 1950s and 1960s sparked interest among a group of scholars—John Hope Franklin, LaWanda Cox, C. Vann Woodward, Kenneth Stamp, and Don Fehrenbacher to name a few—who insisted that race and African Americans have been central to the American experience. They inspired a generation of Ph. D. students who came of age during the 1960s and were deeply influenced by the "Second Reconstruction" to focus their intellectual work on African American history, civil rights, and the relationship among law, race, and social change in the United States. The result was an outpouring of critical, deeply researched scholarly articles and books that emerged during the 1960s and grew in breadth and depth in the following decades. Given the continuing salience of race during the last decades of the twentieth and the first two decades of the twenty-first century, a new generation of scholars has engaged these issues, not only expanding the literature but also contributing exciting new perspectives. Therefore, the literature on African Americans and civil rights is one of the richest in American history. What follows is a brief essay on the sources that I found most useful in writing *Promises to Keep* in 1991 and revising and expanding it a quarter century later.

A number of general works serve as a useful starting pointing for anyone interested in African Americans, law, and social change in US history. Herman Belz and Winfred Harbison, *The American Constitution: Its Origins and Development*, 7th ed. (New York: W. W. Norton, 1991); Melvin Urofsky and Paul Finkelman, *A March of Liberty: A Constitutional History of the United States*, 3rd ed. (New York: Oxford University Press, 2011); and Kermit L. Hall and Peter Karsten, *The Magic Mirror: Law in American History*, 2nd ed. (New York: Oxford University Press, 2008) provide excellent introductions to American constitutional-legal history. John Hope Franklin and Evelyn Brooks Higginbotham, *From Slavery to Freedom: A History of African Americans*, 9th ed. (New York: McGraw Hill, 2010); Henry Louis Gates Jr. , *Life upon these Shores: Looking at African American History, 1513–2008* (New York: Knopf, 2008); and Darlene Clark Hine and William C. Hine, *African Americans: A Concise History*, 5th ed. (New York: Pearson, 2013) are useful surveys of African American history. Herbert Aptheker, ed. , *A Documentary History of the Negro People in the United States*, 3 vols. (Secaucus, NJ: Citadel Press, 1973) is an indispensable collection of sources on the African American experience. Mary Frances Berry, *Black Resistance/White Law: A History of Constitutional Racism in America*, rev. ed. (New York: Penguin Books, 1994); Michael Les Benedict, *Civil Rights and Civil Liberties* (Washington, DC: American Historical Association, 1987); and Stanley N. Katz, "The Strange Birth and Unlikely History of Constitutional Equality," *Journal of American History* 75 (1988) are stimulating overviews of civil rights and the law. Richard Bardolph, *The Civil Rights Record: Black Americans and the Law, 1849–1970* (New York: Thomas Y. Crowell, 1970) and Jonathan Birnbaum and Clarence Taylor, *Civil Rights since 1787: A Reader on the Black Struggle* (New York: New York University Press, 2000) are useful collections of documents on the history of civil rights.

From the Revolution to the Civil War

The literature on slavery and race in the Age of the American Revolution is voluminous. Winthrop Jordan, *White over Black: American Attitudes toward the Negro, 1550–1812* (Chapel Hill: University of North Carolina Press,1968); David Brion Davis, *The Problem of Slavery in the Age of Revolution, 1770–1823* (Ithaca, NY: Cornell University Press, 1975); Bernard Bailyn, *The Ideological Origins of the American Revolution* (Cambridge, MA: Harvard University Press, 1967); John Philip Reid, *The Concept of Liberty in the Age of the American Revolution* (Chicago: University of Chicago Press, 1988); Gerald Horne, *The Counter-Revolution of 1776: Slave Resistance and the Origins of the United States of America* (New York: New York University Press, 2014); Nicholas Guyatt, *Bind Us Apart: How Enlightened Americans Invented Racial Segregation* (New York: Basic Books, 2016); and Robert G. Parkinson, *The Common Cause: Creating Race and Nation in the American Revolution* (Chapel Hill: University of North Carolina Press, 2016) are good starting points. For the antislavery movement that blossomed during the American Revolution, see Arthur Zilversmit, *The First Emancipation: The Abolition of Slavery in the North* (Chicago: University of Chicago Press, 1967); Ira Berlin, *The Long Emancipation: The Demise of Slavery in the United States* (Cambridge, MA: Harvard University Press, 2015); David N. Gellman, *Emancipating New York: The Politics of Slavery and Freedom, 1777–1827* (Baton Rouge: Louisiana State University Press, 2006); JoAnn Pope Melish, *Disowning Slavery: Gradual Emancipation and Race in New England, 1780–1860* (Ithaca, NY: Cornell University Press, 1998); and Manisha Sinha, *The Slave's Cause: A History of Abolition* (New Haven: Yale University Press, 2016). Robert McColley, *Slavery and Jeffersonian Virginia* (Urbana: University of Illinois Press, 1964) examines the limits of antislavery action in the South. Sylvia R. Frey, *Water from the Rock: Black Resistance in a Revolutionary Age* (Princeton, NJ: Princeton University Press, 1991); Benjamin Quarles, *The Negro in the American Revolution* (New York: Da Capo Press, 1961); Gary B. Nash, *Forging Freedom: The Formation of Philadelphia's Black Community, 1720–1840* (Cambridge, MA: Harvard University Press, 1988); and Ira Berlin and Reginald Horsman, eds. , *Slavery and Freedom in the Age of the American Revolution* (Charlottesville: University of Virginia Press, 1983) are important studies of African Americans' quest for freedom.

The role of slavery at the Constitutional Convention has generated considerable controversy. Michael J. Klarman, *The Framer's Coup: The Making of the United States Constitution* (New York: Oxford University Press, 2016) is a recent account of the convention. Max Farrand, ed. , *The Records of the Federal Convention*, 4 vols. (New Haven: Yale University Press, 1937) and James Hutson, ed. , *Supplement to Max Farrand's The Records of the Federal Convention* (New Haven: Yale University Press, 1987) present notes and documents written by members of the convention, including James Madison's notes, the most important source on the proceedings. Mary Sarah Bilder, *Madison's Hand: Revising the Constitutional Convention* (Cambridge, MA: Harvard University Press, 2015) follows changes Madison made in his notes from the weeks following the convention until his death. She concludes that these changes cast doubt on Madison's notes "as a reliable source. "

While agreeing that the framers provided support for slavery in the new Constitution, historians have disagreed about the extent of their proslavery commitment. Paul Finkelman, "Slavery and the Constitutional Convention: Making a Covenant with Death," in *Beyond Confederation: Origins of the Constitution and American National Identity*, ed. Richard Beeman, Stephen Botein, and Edward C. Carter III, (Chapel Hill: University of

North Carolina Press, 1987); William Wiecek, *The Sources of Antislavery Constitutionalism in America, 1760–1848* (Ithaca, NY: Cornell University Press, 1977); David Waldstreicher, *Slavery's Constitution: From Revolution to Ratification* (New York: Oxford University Press, 2009); and George William Van Cleve, *A Slaveholder's Union: Slavery, Politics, and the Constitution in the Early American Republic* (Chicago: University of Chicago Press, 2010) argue that the framers carefully designed a document that would promote slavery and the interests of slaveowners. Other historians disagree, contending that, despite concessions to southerners, the framers drafted a document that was open-ended with respect to slavery and contained provisions that could be turned against the institution. These include Don E. Fehrenbacher, *The Dred Scott Case: Its Significance in American Law and Politics* (New York: Oxford University Press, 1978); William W. Freehling, "The Founding Fathers and Slavery," *American Historical Review* 77 (1972); and Sean Wilentz, *No Property in Man: Slavery and Antislavery at the Nation's Founding* (Cambridge, MA: Harvard University Press, 2018). Other useful treatments of the framers and slavery include Donald L. Robinson, *Slavery in the Structure of American Politics, 1765–1820* (New York: Harcourt, 1971); Howard A. Ohline, "Republicanism and Slavery: Origins of the Three-fifths Clause of the Constitution," *William and Mary Quarterly* 28 (1971); and Calvin Jillson and Thornton Anderson, "Realignments in the Convention of 1787: The Slave Trade Compromise," *Journal of Politics* 39 (1977).

A number of important studies examine the role of slavery in American politics and national policy from the 1790s to the Mexican War. Don E. Fehrenbacher, *The Dred Scott Case* and *The Slaveholding Republic: An Account of the United States Government's Relations to Slavery* (New York: Oxford University Press, 2001) are masterful treatments of these issues. Other worthwhile studies include Donald Robinson's *Slavery in the Structure of American Politics*; Matthew Mason, *Slavery & Politics in the Early American Republic* (Chapel Hill: University of North Carolina Press, 2006) and "Slavery Overshadowed: Congress Debates Prohibiting the Atlantic Slave Trade to the United States, 1806–1807," *Journal of the Early Republic* 20 (2000): 59–81; Richard Brown, "The Missouri Crisis, Slavery, and the Politics of Jacksonianism," *South Atlantic Quarterly* 65 (1966): 55–72; Glover Moore, *The Missouri Controversy* (Lexington: University of Kentucky Press, 1953); Robert Pierce Forbes, *The Missouri Compromise and Its Aftermath: Slavery and the Meaning of America* (Chapel Hill: University of North Carolina Press, 2007); William J. Cooper, *The South and the Politics of Slavery, 1828–1856* (Baton Rouge: Louisiana State University Press, 1978) and *Liberty and Slavery: Southern Politics to 1860* (New York: Knopf, 1983); Leonard Richards, *The Life and Times of Congressman John Quincy Adams* (New York: Oxford University Press, 1986); and William W. Freehling, *Prelude to Civil War: The Nullification Controversy in South Carolina, 1816–1836* (New York: Harper & Row, 1966) and *The Road to Disunion: The Secessionists at Bay, 1776–1854* (New York: Oxford University Press, 1990).

Slavery and race had a profound effect on constitutional developments in the early nineteenth century. Harold M. Hyman and William Wiecek, *Equal Justice under Law: Constitutional Development, 1835–1875* (New York: Harper & Row, 1982) and Don Fehrenbacher, *The Dred Scott Case* and *The Slaveholding Republic* remain the best starting points. James H. Kettner, *The Development of American Citizenship, 1608–1870* (Chapel Hill: University of North Carolina Press, 1978) shows how slavery and race affected Americans' understanding of citizenship. Michael A. Schoeppner, *Moral Contagion: Black Atlantic Sailors, Citizenship, and Diplomacy in Antebellum America* (Cambridge, UK: Cambridge University Press, 2019) is a valuable study of an important flashpoint over

African American citizenship. Paul Finkelman, *An Imperfect Union: Slavery, Federalism, and Comity* (Chapel Hill: University of North Carolina Press, 1981) and*"Prigg v. Pennsylvania* and Northern State Courts: Antislavery Uses of a Proslavery Decision," *Civil War History* 25 (1979); Steven Lubet, *Fugitive Justice: Runaways, Rescuers, and Slavery on Trial* (Cambridge, UK: Cambridge University Press, 2010); Angela F. Murphy, *The Jerry Rescue: The Fugitive Slave Law, Northern Rights, and the American Sectional Controversy* (New York: Oxford University Press, 2016); Andrew Delbanco, *The War before the War: Fugitive Slaves and the Struggle for America's Soul from the Revolution to the Civil War* (New York: Penguin Press, 2018); R. J. M. Blackett, *The Captive's Quest for Freedom: Fugitive Slaves, the 1850 Fugitive Slave Law, and the Politics of Slavery* (Cambridge, UK: Cambridge University Press, 2018); and Thomas D. Morris, *Free Men All: The Personal Liberty Laws of the North, 1780–1861* (Baltimore: Johns Hopkins University Press, 1974) are valuable studies of slavery, interstate relations, and fugitive slaves. For the US Supreme Court and slavery, see Donald M. Roper, "In Quest of Judicial Objectivity: The Marshall Court and the Legitimation of Slavery," *Stanford Law Review* 21 (1969) and William Wiecek, "Slavery and Abolition before the United States Supreme Court, 1820–1860," *Journal of American History* 65 (1978).

The legal position of African Americans before the Civil War has generated a rich literature. On the law of slavery, Kenneth M. Stampp, *The Peculiar Institution: Slavery in the Antebellum South* (New York: Knopf, 1956); Eugene D. Genovese, *Roll, Jordan, Roll: The World the Slaves Made* (New York: Pantheon, 1974); and Daniel J. Flanigan, "Criminal Procedure in Slave Trials in the Antebellum South," *Journal of Southern History* 40 (1974) remain useful starting points. See also Phillip J. Schwartz, *Twice Condemned: Slaves and the Criminal Law of Virginia, 1705–1865* (Baton Rouge: Louisiana State University Press, 1988); Melton McLaurin, *Celia, a Slave* (Athens: University of Georgia Press, 1999); Ariela Gross, *Double Character: Slavery and Mastery in the Antebellum Southern Courtroom* (Princeton, NJ: Princeton University Press, 2000); Mark Tushnet, *Slave Law in the American South: State v. Mann in History and Literature* (Lawrence: University Press of Kansas, 2003); Sally Hadden, *Slave Patrols: Law and Violence in Virginia and the Carolinas* (Cambridge, MA: Harvard University Press, 2003); and Judith Keleher Schafer, *Slavery, the Civil Law, and the Supreme Court of Louisiana* (Baton Rouge: Louisiana State University Press, 1997) for more recent treatments. The anomalous position of free blacks is examined in Theodore Brantner Wilson, *The Black Codes of the South* (Tuscaloosa: University of Alabama Press, 1965); Ira Berlin, *Slaves without Masters: The Free Negro in the Antebellum South* (New York: Pantheon, 1974); Leon Litwack, *North of Slavery: The Free Negro in the Free States, 1790–1860* (Chicago: University of Chicago Press, 1961); and Paul Finkelman, "Prelude to the Fourteenth Amendment: Black Legal Rights in the Antebellum North," *Rutgers Law Journal* 17 (1986).

The Declaration of Independence and the Constitution inspired many Americans to challenge slavery and demand equal rights. Richard D. Brown, *Self-Evident Truths: Contesting Equal Rights from the Revolution to the Civil War* (New Haven: Yale University Press, 2016) examines the legacy of the Declaration. For antislavery readings of the Constitution, see Jacobus tenBroek, *The Antislavery Origins of the Fourteenth Amendment* (Berkeley: University of California Press, 1951); William Wiecek, *The Sources of Antislavery Constitutionalism in America*; and William E. Nelson, "The Impact of the Antislavery Movement on Styles of Judicial Reasoning in Nineteenth-Century America," *Harvard Law Review* 87 (1974). Earl M. Maltz, "Fourteenth Amendment Concepts in the Antebellum Era," *American Journal of Legal History* 32 (1988) examines the debate between antislavery and proslavery advocates over the meaning of due process, equal protection, and privileges and immunities.

There is a rich and growing body of scholarship on African American resistance, protest, and political and constitutional ideas in the decades preceding the Civil War. Philip S. Foner and George E. Walker, ed. , *Proceedings of the Black State Conventions, 1840–1865*, 2 vols. (Philadelphia: Temple University Press, 1979) is an indispensable source. It can be supplemented with Benjamin Quarles, *The Black Abolitionists* (New York: Oxford University Press, 1969); R. J. M. Blackett, *Beating against the Barriers: Biographical Essays on Nineteenth Century Afro-American History* (Baton Rouge: Louisiana State University Press, 1986); Vincent Harding, *There Is a River: The Black Freedom Struggle in America* (New York: Harcourt, 1981); Jane H. Pease and William H. Pease, *They Who Would Be Free: Blacks' Search for Freedom, 1830–1861* (New York: Atheneum, 1974); Patrick Rael, *Black Identity & Black Protest in the Antebellum North* (Chapel Hill: University of North Carolina Press, 2002); Stephen Kantrowitz, *More than Freedom: Citizenship in a White Republic, 1829–1889* (New York: Penguin, 2012); Leslie M. Alexander, *African or American?: Black Identity and Political Activism in New York City, 1784–1861* (Chicago: University of Illinois Press, 2008); and Martha S. Jones, *Birthright Citizens: A History of Race and Rights in Antebellum America* (Baltimore: Johns Hopkins University Press, 2018).

There is a vast literature on political and constitutional conflict over slavery in the 1840s and 1850s. See Arthur Bestor, "State Sovereignty and Slavery: A Reinterpretation of Proslavery Constitutional Doctrine, 1848–1860," *Journal of the Illinois State Historical Society* 54 (1961); Eric Foner, *Free Soil, Free Labor, Free Men: The Ideology of the Republican Party before the Civil War* (New York: Oxford University Press, 1970); Richard Sewell, *Ballots for Freedom: Antislavery Politics in the United States, 1837–1860* (New York: Oxford University Press, 1976); Hans L. Trefousse, *The Radical Republicans: Lincoln's Vanguard for Racial Justice* (New York: Knopf, 1968); William W. Freehling, *The Road to Disunion: The Secessionists Triumphant, 1854–1861* (New York: Oxford University Press, 2008); Leonard L. Richards, *The Slave Power: The Free North and Southern Domination, 1780–1860* (Baton Rouge: Louisiana State University Press, 2000); Shearer Davis Bowman, *At the Precipice: Americans North and South during the Secession Crisis* (Chapel Hill: University of North Carolina Press, 2010); James Oakes, *The Scorpion's Sting: Antislavery and the Coming of the Civil War* (New York: W. W. Norton, 2014); and Steven E. Maizlish, *A Strife of Tongues: The Compromise of 1850 and the Ideological Foundations of the American Civil War* (Charlottesville: University of Virginia Press, 2018).

On the pivotal *Dred Scott* case, see Don Fehrenbacher, *The Dred Scott Case*; Austin Allen, *Origins of the 'Dred Scott' Case: Jacksonian Jurisprudence and the Supreme Court, 1837–1857* (Athens: University of Georgia Press, 2006); and Timothy Huebner, "Roger B. Taney and the Slavery Issue: Looking beyond—and Before—Dred Scott," *Journal of American History* 97 (2010).

The Civil War, Reconstruction, and Its Aftermath

The best treatments of the constitutional issues of the Civil War and Reconstruction are Harold M. Hyman, *A More Perfect Union: The Impact of the Civil War and Reconstruction on the Constitution* (New York: Knopf, 1973); Philip S. Paludan, *A Covenant with Death: The Constitution, Law, and Equality in the Civil War Era* (Urbana: University of Illinois Press, 1975); Harold M. Hyman and William Wiecek, *Equal Justice under Law: Constitutional*

Development, 1835–1875 (New York: Harper & Row, 1982); and Laura Edwards, *A Legal History of the Civil War and Reconstruction* (Cambridge, UK: Cambridge University Press, 2015). Eric Foner's monumental *Reconstruction: America's Unfinished Revolution, 1863–1877*, updated ed. (New York: HarperCollins, 2014) is the best treatment of the struggle for African American freedom and civil rights.

Lincoln's decision to issue the Emancipation Proclamation, stand behind it, and lend critical support to the Thirteenth Amendment has attracted the attention of many scholars. Eric Foner, *The Fiery Trial: Abraham Lincoln and American Slavery* (New York: W. W. Norton, 2010) and LaWanda Cox, *Lincoln and Black Freedom* (Columbia: University of South Carolina Press, 1981) offer the best analyses of the wartime president's approach to emancipation and African American civil rights. Other useful studies include John Hope Franklin, *The Emancipation Proclamation* (Garden City, NY: Doubleday, 1963); Alan C. Guelzo, *The Emancipation Proclamation: The End of Slavery in America* (New York: Simon & Schuster 2004); James Oakes, *The Radical and the Republican: Frederick Douglass, Abraham Lincoln, and the Triumph of Antislavery Politics* (New York: W. W. Norton, 2007); and Louis P. Masur, *Lincoln's Hundred Days: The Emancipation Proclamation and the War for the Union* (Cambridge, MA: Harvard University Press, 2012). The evolution of Republican policy on slavery and race is treated by Herman Belz, *Reconstructing the Union: Theory and Practice during the Civil War* (Ithaca, NY: Cornell University Press, 1969); Mary Frances Berry, *Military Necessity and Civil Rights Policy: Black Citizenship and the Constitution* (Port Washington, NY: Kennikat Press, 1977); Michael Vorenberg, *Final Freedom: The Civil War, the Abolition of Slavery, and the Thirteenth Amendment* (Cambridge, UK: Cambridge University Press, 2001); James Oakes, *Freedom National: The Destruction of Slavery in the United States, 1861–1865* (New York: W. W. Norton, 2012); and Leonard Richards, *Who Freed the Slaves? The Fight over the Thirteenth Amendment* (Chicago: University of Chicago Press, 2015). For the role of abolitionists and African Americans, see James M. McPherson, *The Struggle for Equality: Abolitionists and the Negro in the Civil War and Reconstruction* (Princeton, NJ: Princeton University Press, 1964) and *The Negro's Civil War* (New York: Pantheon, 1965); and Ira Berlin et. al. , *Slaves No More: Three Essays on Emancipation and the Civil War* (Cambridge, UK: Cambridge University Press, 1992) and *Freedom's Soldiers: The Black Military Experience in the Civil War* (Cambridge, UK: Cambridge University Press, 1998). Ira Berlin, et al. , *Freedom: A Documentary History of Emancipation, 1861–1867* (6 vols. to date, 1982, 1985, 1986, 1998, 2012; Cambridge, UK: Cambridge University Press) is a rich documentary collection with illuminating essays by the editors.

Republican civil rights policy during Reconstruction is the subject of many outstanding works. Especially important are LaWanda Cox and John H. Cox, *Politics, Principle, and Prejudice: Dilemma of Reconstruction America, 1865–1866* (New York; Free Press, 1963); Michael Les Benedict, *A Compromise of Principle: Congressional Republicans and Reconstruction, 1863–1869* (New York: W. W. Norton, 1974) and "Preserving the Constitution: The Conservative Basis of Radical Reconstruction," *Journal of American History* 61 (1974); Robert J. Kaczorowski, "Revolutionary Constitutionalism in the Era of the Civil War and Reconstruction," *New York University Law Review* 61 (1986); Christian G. Samito and Michael Vorenberg, *The Greatest and the Grandest: The Civil Rights of 1866 from Reconstruction to Today* (Carbondale: Southern Illinois University Press, 2018); and George Rutherglen, *Civil Rights in the Shadow of Slavery: The Constitution, Common Law, and the Civil Rights Act of 1866* (New York: Oxford University Press, 2013). The Fourteenth Amendment, which has had a transformative effect on the Constitution, has been the subject of a great deal of scholarly attention. See Jacobus tenBroek, *The Antislavery Origins of the Fourteenth Amendment* (Berkeley: University of California Press, 1951); Alfred H. Kelly, "The Fourteenth Amendment Reconsidered: The Segregation Question," *Michigan Law Review* 54 (1956); Howard J. Graham, *Everyman's Constitution: Essays on the Fourteenth Amendment, the 'Conspiracy Theory,' and American Constitutionalism* (1968); Jonathan Lurie, "The Fourteenth Amendment: Uses and Applications in Selected State Court Civil Liberties Cases," *American Journal of Legal History* 28 (1984); William E. Nelson, *The Fourteenth Amendment: From Political Principle to Judicial Doctrine* (Cambridge, MA: Harvard University Press, 1988); and Kurt T. Lash, *The Fourteenth Amendment and the Privileges and Immunities of American Citizenship* (Cambridge, UK: Cambridge University Press, 2014).

The adoption of the Fifteenth Amendment, which prohibited restrictions on the right to vote based on race, has generated scholarly controversy. William Gillette, *The Right to Vote: Politics and the Passage of the Fifteenth Amendment* (Baltimore: Johns Hopkins University Press, 1965) argues that Republican opportunism lay behind the amendment, an interpretation challenged by LaWanda Cox and John H. Cox, "Negro Suffrage and Republican Politics: The Problem of Motivation in Reconstruction Historiography," *Journal of Southern History* 33 (1967). Women's rights advocates—longtime allies of the abolitionists—viewed discussion of a suffrage amendment as the opportunity to win the right to vote for women. Although part of the conversation, they were ultimately unsuccessful, as Ellen Carol DuBois, *Feminism & Suffrage: The Emergence of an Independent Women's Movement in America, 1848–1869* (Ithaca, NY: Cornell University Press, 1978) and Faye E. Dudden, *Fighting Chance: The Fight over Woman Suffrage and Black Suffrage in Reconstruction America* (New York: Oxford University Press, 2011) demonstrate.

The effect of Republican Reconstruction policies at the grass roots is the subject of a number of studies. Steven Hahn, *A Nation under Our Feet: Black Political Struggles in the South from Slavery to the Great Migration* (Cambridge, MA: Harvard University Press, 2003) examines how emancipation and Reconstruction policies encouraged the growth of African American political consciousness and activism. Donald G. Nieman, *To Set the Law in Motion: The Freedmen's Bureau and the Legal Rights of Blacks, 1865–1868* (Millwood, NY: KTO Press, 1979) and Mary J. Farmer-Kaiser, *Freedwomen and the Freedmen's Bureau: Race, Gender, and Public Policy in the Age of Emancipation* (New York: Fordham University Press, 2010) examine the bureau's role in affording rights to former slaves. Allen Trelease, *White Terror: The Ku Klux Klan Conspiracy and Southern Reconstruction* (New York: Harper & Row, 1971); Everett Swinney, "Enforcing the Fifteenth Amendment, 1870–1877," *Journal of Southern History* 28 (1962); Robert J. Kaczorowski, *The Politics of Federal Judicial Interpretation: The Federal Courts, the Department of Justice, and Civil Rights, 1866–1876* (New York: Oceana, 1985); and Lou Falkner Williams, *The Great South Carolina Ku Klux Klan Trials, 1871–1872* (Athens: University of Georgia Press, 1996) explore the federal campaign against the Klan. For the effects of Reconstruction on southern constitutionalism and law, see Jack B. Scroggs, "Carpetbagger Constitutional Reform in the South Atlantic States, 1867–1868," *Journal of Southern History* 27 (1961); Eric Foner, *Nothing but Freedom* (Baton Rouge: Louisiana State University Press, 1983) and *Freedom's Lawmakers: A Directory of Black Lawmakers during Reconstruction* (New York: Oxford University Press, 1996); Thomas Holt, *Black over White: Negro Political Leadership in South Carolina during Reconstruction* (Chicago: University of Chicago Press, 1977); Donald G. Nieman, "Black Political Power and Criminal Justice: Washington County, Texas, 1868–1884," *Journal of Southern History* 55 (1989) and "African Americans and the Meaning of Freedom: Washington County, Texas, as a Case Study, 1865–1868," *Chicago-Kent Law Review* 70 (1994); and Michael Les Benedict, "The Problem of Constitutionalism and Constitutional Liberty in the Reconstruction South," in *An Uncertain Tradition: Constitutionalism and the History of the South*, ed. Kermit L. Hall and James W. Ely Jr. (Athens: University of Georgia Press, 1989).

Historians have developed a more nuanced understanding of law, politics, and race in the decades following Reconstruction, showing that African Americans continued to demand rights and were sometimes successful in defending them. For African Americans' continued participation in the political process, see J. Morgan Kousser, *The Shaping of Southern Politics: Suffrage Restriction and the Establishment of the One-Party South* (New Haven: Yale University Press, 1974), Glenda Elizabeth Gilmore, *Gender and Jim Crow: Women and the Politics of White Supremacy in North Carolina, 1896–1920* (Chapel Hill: University of North Carolina Press, 1996); Jane Dailey, *Before Jim Crow: The Politics of Race in Postemancipation Virginia* (Chapel Hill: University of North Carolina Press, 2000); Stephen Kantrowitz, *Ben Tillman and the Reconstruction of White Supremacy* (Chapel Hill: University of North Carolina Press, 2000); Michael Perman, *The Struggle for Mastery: Disfranchisement in the South, 1888–1908* (Chapel Hill: University of North Carolina Press 2001); James Beeby, *The Revolt of the Tarheels: The North Carolina Populist Movement, 1890–1901* (Jackson: University Press of Mississippi, 2008); and R. Volney Riser, *Defying Disfranchisement: Black Voting Rights Activism in the Jim Crow South, 1890–1908* (Baton Rouge: Louisiana State University Press, 2010).

The classic works on the development of segregation are C. Vann Woodward, *The Strange Career of Jim Crow*, 3rd ed. (New York: Oxford University Press, 1974) and Howard N. Rabinowitz, *Race Relations in the Urban South, 1865–1890* (Urbana: University of Illinois Press, 1978). See also the exchange between Woodward and Rabinowitz in the *Journal of American History* 75 (1988). Leon Litwack, *Trouble in Mind: Black Southerners in the Age of Jim Crow* (New York: Knopf, 1998) and William Chafe, Raymond Gavins, and Robert Korstad, *Remembering Jim Crow: African Americans Tell about Life in the Segregated South* (New York: New Press, 2001) are important treatments of life under segregation. For African American challenges to segregation, see *Dead End: The Development of Nineteenth-Century Litigation on Segregation in the Schools* (Oxford: Clarendon Press, 1986) and "Making Separate Equal: Integration of Black and White School Funds in Kentucky," *Journal of Interdisciplinary History* 10 (1980); Shawn Leigh Alexander, *An Army of Lions: The Civil Rights Struggle before the NAACP* (Philadelphia: University of Pennsylvania Press, 2012); Susan D. Carle, *Defining the Struggle: National Organizations for Racial Justice, 1880–1915* (New York: Oxford University Press, 2013); and Blair L. M. Kelley, *Right to Ride: Streetcar Boycotts and African American Citizenship in the Era of Plessy v. Ferguson* (Chapel Hill: University of North Carolina Press, 2010).

Good evaluations of the Supreme Court and race in the aftermath of Reconstruction include Michael Les Benedict, "Preserving Federalism: The Supreme Court and Reconstruction," *Supreme Court Review 1978* (1979); Robert J. Kaczorowski, *The Politics of Judicial Interpretation: The Federal Courts, the Department of Justice, and Civil Rights, 1866–1876*; Charles Fairman, *Reconstruction and Reunion: 1864–1888*, 2 vols. (New York: Macmillan, 1971, 1987); Robert Goldman, *"A Free Ballot and a Fair Count": The Department of Justice and Voting Rights in the South* (New York: Fordham University Press, 2001) and *Reconstruction and Black Suffrage: Losing the Vote in Reese & Cruikshank* (Lawrence: University Press of Kansas, 2001); Charles Lofgren, *The Plessy Case* (New York: Oxford University Press, 1987); Williamjames Hull-Hoffer, *Plessy v. Ferguson: Race and Inequality in Jim Crow America* (Lawrence: University Press of Kansas, 2012); and J. Morgan Kousser, "Separate but Not Equal: The Supreme Court's First Decision on Racial Discrimination in Schools," *Journal of Southern History* 46 (1980).

The lives and freedom of black southerners were sharply constrained by the criminal justice system, sharecropping, and debt peonage. Important studies of these include Pete Daniel, *The Shadow of Slavery: Peonage in the South* (New York: Oxford University Press, 1969); William Cohen, "Negro Involuntary Servitude in the South, 1865–1940: A Preliminary Inventory," *Journal of Southern History* 42 (1976) and *At Freedom's Edge: Black Mobility and the Southern White Quest for Racial Control, 1861–1915* (Chicago: University of Chicago Press, 1991); Harold D. Woodman, "Post-War Southern Agriculture and the Law," *Agricultural History* 53 (1979); Edward L. Ayers, *Vengeance and Justice: Crime and Punishment in the 19th-Century American South* (New York: Oxford University Press, 1984); David M. Oshinsky, *Worse than Slavery: Parchman Farm and the Ordeal of Jim Crow Justice* (New York: Simon & Schuster, 1996); Douglas A. Blackmon, *Slavery by Another Name: The Re-Enslavement of Black Americans from the Civil War to World War II* (New York: Doubleday, 2008); and Sarah Haley, *No Mercy Here: Gender, Punishment, and the Making of Jim Crow Modernity* (Chapel Hill: University of North Carolina Press, 2016).

The Age of Segregation

Early twentieth-century social scientists and activists produced important studies of segregation and discrimination that remain worthwhile. See W. E . B. Du Bois, *The Philadelphia Negro: A Social Study* (Philadelphia: University of Pennsylvania, 1899); Mary White Ovington, *Half a Man: The Status of the Negro in New York* (New York: Longmans, Green & Co. , 1911); John Dollard, *Caste and Class in a Southern Town* (New Haven: Yale University Press, 1937); Arthur Raper, *Preface to Peasantry* (Chapel Hill: University of North Carolina Press, 1936); and Gunnar Myrdal et al. , *The American Dilemma: The Negro Problem and Modern Democracy*, 2 vols. (New York: Harper & Brothers, 1944).

Historians have produced important studies of how segregation affected the lives of whites and blacks in the South during the first half of the twentieth century. See Grace Elizabeth Hale, *Making Whiteness: The Culture of Segregation in the South, 1890–1940* (New York: Pantheon, 1998); Leslie Brown, *Upbuilding Black Durham: Gender, Class, and Community Development in the Jim Crow South* (Chapel Hill: University of North Carolina Press, 2008); Kristina DuRocher, *Raising Racists: The Socialization of Children in the Jim Crow South* (Lexington: University of Kentucky Press, 2011); Marek D. Steedman, *Jim Crow Citizenship: Liberalism and the Southern Defense of Racial Hierarchy* (New York: Routledge, 2012); Robert Cassanello, *To Render Invisible: Jim Crow and New South Jacksonville* (Gainesville: University Press of Florida, 2013); Stephen A. Berry, *The Jim Crow Routine: Everyday Performance of Race, Civil Rights, and Segregation in Mississippi* (Chapel Hill: University of North Carolina Press, 2015); and LeeAnn G. Reynolds, *Maintaining Segregation: Children and Racial Instruction in the South, 1920–1955* (Baton Rouge: Louisiana State University Press, 2017).

Jim Crow's subordination of African Americans was maintained by violence, including lynching. Valuable studies include Ida B. Wells-Barnett, *Southern Horrors: Lynch Law in All Its Phases* (New York: New York Age Print, 1892); National Association for the Advancement of Colored People, *Thirty Years of Lynching in the United States,*

1889-1918 (New York: National Association for the Advancement of Colored People, 1919); W. Fitzhugh Brundage, *Lynching in the New South: Georgia and Virginia, 1880-1930* (Urbana: University of Illinois Press, 1993); Michael J. Pfeifer, *Rough Justice: Lynching and American Society, 1874-1947* (Urbana: University of Illinois Press, 2004); Christopher Waldrep, *Lynching in America: A History in Documents* (New York: New York University Press, 2006) and *African Americans Confront Lynching: Strategies of Resistance from the Civil War to the Civil Rights Era* (Lanham, MD: Rowman & Littlefield, 2009); Amy Louise Wood, *Lynching and Spectacle: Witnessing Racial Violence in America, 1890-1940* (Chapel Hill: University of North Carolina Press, 2009); Evelyn M. Simien, *Gender and Lynching: The Politics of Memory* (New York: Palgrave Macmillan, 2011); Karlos K. Hill, *Beyond the Rope: The Impact of Lynching on Black Culture and Memory* (New York: Cambridge University Press, 2016); and Donald G. Matthews, *At the Altar of Lynching: Burning Sam Hose in the American South* (Cambridge, UK: Cambridge University Press, 2017).

Millions of southern blacks migrated to northern cities during the first six decades of the twentieth century. Important studies of the Great Migration include Nicholas Lemann, *The Promised Land: The Great Migration and How It Changed America* (New York: Knopf, 1991); James N. Gregory, *The Southern Diaspora: How the Great Migrations of Black and White Southerners Transformed America* (Chapel Hill: University of North Carolina Press, 2005); and Isabel Wilkerson, *The Warmth of Other Suns: The Epic Story of America's Great Migration* (New York: Random House, 2010). African Americans found that the North was no promised land. See Gilbert Osofsky, *Harlem: The Making of a Ghetto* (New York: Harper & Row, 1971); David A. Gerber, *Black Ohio and the Color Line, 1860-1915* (Urbana: University of Illinois Press, 1976); Kenneth Kusmer, *A Ghetto Takes Shape: Black Cleveland, 1870-1930* (Urbana: University of Illinois Press, 1976); Michael W. Homel, *Down from Equality: Black Chicagoans and the Public Schools, 1920-1941* (Urbana: University of Illinois Press, 1984); Vincent P. Franklin, *The Education of Black Philadelphia: The Social and Educational History of a Minority Community, 1900-1950* (Philadelphia: University of Pennsylvania Press, 1979); August Meier and Elliott Rudwick, *Black Detroit and the Rise of the UAW* (New York: Oxford University Press, 1979); Stephan Thernstrom, *The Other Bostonians: Poverty in the American Metropolis, 1900-1970* (Cambridge, MA: Harvard University Press, 1973); and Davison Douglas, *Jim Crow Moves North: The Battle over Northern School Segregation, 1865-1954* (New York: Cambridge University Press, 2015).

Just as they challenged the creation of segregation, African Americans organized and fought hard to end it. August Meier, *Negro Thought in America, 1880-1915* (Ann Arbor: University of Michigan Press, 1963) is a pioneering study of the emergence of black protest thought in the early twentieth century. August Meier, Elliott Rudwick, and Francis Broderick, eds. , *Black Protest Thought in the Twentieth Century*, 2nd ed. (Indianapolis: Bobbs-Merrill, 1971) is a useful documentary collection. David Levering Lewis, *W. E. B. Du Bois: Biography of a Race* (New York: Henry Holt & Co. , 1993) and *W. E. B. Du Bois: The Fight for Equality in the American Century* (New York: Henry Holt & Co. , 2000) not only constitute the definitive biography of the most influential African American leader of the period, but they also illuminate the history of the struggle for black rights. The National Association for the Advancement of Colored People (NAACP), an organization Du Bois was pivotal in founding and leading, played a critical role in the fight. For its origins, see James M. McPherson, *The Abolitionist Legacy: From*

Reconstruction to the NAACP (Princeton, NJ: Princeton University Press, 1975); Charles Kellogg, *NAACP: A History of the National Association for the Advancement of Colored People, 1890–1920* (Baltimore: Johns Hopkins University Press, 1967); and Patricia Sullivan, *Lift Every Voice: The NAACP and the Making of the Civil Rights Movement* (New York: New Press, 2009). Susan D. Carle, *Defining the Struggle: National Organizations for Racial Justice, 1880–1915* (New York: Oxford University Press, 2013) explores the predecessors of the NAACP, the lessons it learned from them, and its formative years. Robert L. Zangrando, *The NAACP Crusade against Lynching, 1909–1950* (Philadelphia: Temple University Press, 1980) examines the organization's early and continuing efforts to raise consciousness about and secure federal legislation against lynching. Kenneth Robert Janken, *Walter White: Mr. NAACP* (Chapel Hill: University of North Carolina Press, 2006) is the biography of a key figure in the organization from the 1910s to the 1950s.

For the NAACP's early efforts to use the Constitution and litigation to challenge discrimination, see William B. Hixon Jr. , "Moorfield Storey and the Struggle for Equality," *Journal of American History* 55 (1968) and *Moorfield Storey and the Abolitionist Tradition* (New York: Oxford University Press, 1972); Alexander M. Bickel and Benno Schmidt Jr. , *The Judiciary and Responsible Government, 1910–1922* (New York: Macmillan, 1984); Richard C. Cortner, *A Mob Intent on Death* (Middeltown, CT: Wesleyan University Press, 1988); Michael J. Klarman, *From Jim Crow to Civil Rights: The Supreme Court and the Struggle for Racial Equality* (New York: Oxford University Press, 2004); and Kevin Boyle, *Arc of Justice: A Saga of Race, Civil Rights, and Murder in the Jazz Age* (New York: Henry Holt, 2004).

While the NAACP's headquarters was in New York and much African American activism was centered in the North, southern blacks also worked against the caste system. See Lee Sartain, *Invisible Activists: Women of the Louisiana NAACP and the Struggle for Civil Rights, 1915–1945* (Baton Rouge: Louisiana State University Press, 2007); Leslie Brown, *Upbuilding Black Durham: Gender, Class, and Community Development in the Jim Crow South* (Chapel Hill: University of North Carolina Press, 2008); Kimberly Johnson, *Reforming Jim Crow: Southern Politics and State in the Age before Brown* (New York: Oxford University Press, 2010); Audrey Thomas McCluskey, *A Forgotten Sisterhood: Pioneering Black Women Educators and Activists in the Jim Crow South* (Lanham, MD: Rowman & Littlefield, 2014); Donald E. Devore, *Defying Jim Crow: African American Community Development and the Struggle for Racial Equality in New Orleans, 1900–1960* (Baton Rouge: Louisiana State University Press, 2015); and Claudrena N. Harold, *New Negro Politics in the Jim Crow South* (Athens: University of Georgia Press, 2016).

The Great Depression and the New Deal were turning points in the history of American politics and civil rights. See Harvard Sitkoff, *A New Deal for Blacks. The Emergence of Civil Rights as a National Issue: The Depression Decade* (New York: Oxford University Press, 1978); Dan T. Carter, *Scottsboro: A Tragedy of the American South* (New York: Oxford University Press, 1966); Robin D. G. Kelley, *Hammer and Hoe: Alabama Communists during the Great Depression* (Chapel Hill: University of North Carolina Press, 1990); James E. Goodman, *Stories of Scottsboro* (New York: Random House, 1994); Charles H. Martin, *The Angelo Herndon Case and Southern Justice* (Baton Rouge: Louisiana State University Press, 1976); Karen Ferguson, *Black Politics in New Deal Atlanta* (Chapel Hill: University of North Carolina Press, 2002); Cheryl Lynn Greenberg, *To Ask for an Equal Chance: African Americans in the Great Depression* (Lanham, MD: Rowman

& Littlefield, 2009) and *"Or Does It Explode?": Black Harlem in the Great Depression* (New York: Oxford University Press, 1991); Lauren Rebecca Sklaroff, *Black Culture and the New Deal: The Quest for Civil Rights in the Roosevelt Era* (Chapel Hill: University of North Carolina Press, 2009); Christopher Robert Reed, *The Depression Comes to the South Side: Protest and Politics in the Black Metropolis, 1930–1933* (Bloomington: Indiana University Press, 2011); and Eric S. Gellman, *Death Blow to Jim Crow: The National Negro Congress and the Rise of Militant Civil Rights* (Chapel Hill: University of North Carolina Press, 2012).

The NAACP's campaign against school segregation, which began in the 1920s and culminated in the Supreme Court's landmark decision in *Brown v. Board of Education*, has been treated in Richard Kluger, *Simple Justice* (New York: Random House, 1975); Genna Rae McNeil, "Justiciable Cause: Howard University Law School and the Struggle for Civil Rights," *Howard Law Journal* 22 (1979) and *Groundwork: Charles Hamilton Houston and the Struggle for Civil Rights* (Philadelphia: University of Pennsylvania Press, 1983); Mark Tushnet, *The NAACP's Campaign against Segregated Education, 1925–1950* (Chapel Hill: University of North Carolina Press, 1983) and *Making Civil Rights Law: Thurgood Marshall and the Supreme Court, 1936–1961* (New York: Oxford University Press, 1996); Jack Greenberg, *Crusaders in the Courts: How a Dedicated Band of Lawyers Fought for the Civil Rights Revolution* (New York: Basic Books, 1994); and Juan Williams, *Thurgood Marshall: American Revolutionary* (New York: Times Books, 1998).

World War II and its aftermath saw change in race relations accelerate. On World War II, see Maureen Honey, *Bitter Fruit: African American Women in World War II* (Columbia: University of Missouri Press, 1999); Daniel Kryder, *Divided Arsenal: Race and the American State during World War II* (New York: Cambridge University Press, 2000); Cheryl Muhlenberg, *Double Victory: How African American Women Broke Race and Gender Barriers to Help Win World War II* (Chicago: Chicago Review Press, 2013); and David Welky, *Marching across the Color Line: A. Philip Randolph and Civil Rights in the World War II Era* (New York: Oxford University Press, 2013). Useful studies of the postwar years include Richard Dalfiume, "The Forgotten Years of the Negro Revolution," *Journal of American History* 55 (1968); Duane Lockard, *Toward Equal Opportunity: A Study of State and Local Antidiscrimination Laws* (New York: Macmillan, 1968); William C. Berman, *The Politics of Civil Rights in the Truman Administration* (Columbus: Ohio State University Press, 1970); Peter J. Kellogg, "Civil Rights Consciousness in the 1940s," *The Historian* 42 (1979); Mary Dudziak, *Cold War Civil Rights: Race and the Image of American Democracy* (Princeton, NJ: Princeton University Press, 2000); Michael Gardner, *Harry Truman and Civil Rights: Moral Courage and Political Risk* (Carbondale: Southern Illinois University Press, 2002); Steven F. Lawson, ed. , *To Secure These Rights: The Report of President Harry S. Truman's Committee on Civil Rights* (Boston: Bedford St. Martins, 2003); Jon E. Taylor, *Freedom to Serve: Truman, Civil Rights, and Executive Order 9981* (New York: Routledge, 2013); and Robert Shogan, *Harry Truman and the Struggle for Racial Justice* (Lawrence: University Press of Kansas, 2013). For the Supreme Court's increasingly bold stand on civil rights, see Clement E. Vose, *Caucasians Only: The Supreme Court, the NAACP, and the Restrictive Covenant Cases* (Berkeley: University of California Press, 1959); Darlene Clark Hine, *Black Victory: The Rise and Fall of the White Primary in Texas* (Millwood, NY: KTO Press, 1979); Catherine A. Barnes, *Journey from Jim Crow: The Desegregation of Southern Transit* (New York: Columbia University Press, 1983); and Melvin I. Urofsky, *Division and Discord: The Supreme Court under Stone and Vinson* (Columbia: University of South Carolina Press, 1997).

The Civil Rights Movement

The literature on the civil rights movement of the 1950s and 1960s is vast and continues to grow. Good general treatments include Charles Eagles, ed. , *The Civil Rights Movement in America* (Jackson: University Press of Mississippi, 1986); Harvard Sitkoff, *The Struggle for Black Equality, 1954–1992*, rev. ed. (New York: Hill & Wang, 1993); Robert Weisbrot, *Freedom Bound: A History of America's Civil Rights Movement* (New York: W. W. Norton, 1989); David Chalmers, *And the Crooked Places Made Straight: The Struggle for Social Change in the 1960s*, 2nd ed. , updated (Baltimore: Johns Hopkins University Press, 2013); Taylor Branch's trilogy on the Civil Rights Era: *Parting the Waters: America in the King Years, 1954–1963* (New York: Simon & Schuster, 1988), *Pillar of Fire: America in the King Years, 1963–1965* (New York: Simon & Schuster, 1998), and *At Canaan's Edge: America in the King Years, 1965–1968* (New York: Simon & Schuster, 2006); Steven F. Lawson, *Running for Freedom: Civil Rights and Black Politics since 1941*, 3rd ed. (New York: John Wiley & Sons, 2014); Jeanne Theoharis, *A More Beautiful and Terrible History: The Uses and Misuses of Civil Rights History* (Boston: Beacon Press, 2018); and Thomas L. Sugrue, *Sweet Land of Liberty: The Forgotten Struggle for Civil Rights in the North* (New York: Random House, 2008). Biographies and autobiographies of movement leaders are plentiful; several that are especially useful include Anne Moody, *Coming of Age in Mississippi* (New York: Bantam Dell, 1968); David J. Garrow, *Bearing the Cross: Martin Luther King Jr. and the Southern Christian Leadership Conference* (New York: HarperCollins, 1986); John Lewis, *Walking with the Wind: A Memoir of the Movement* (New York: Simon & Schuster, 1998); Malcolm X, *The Autobiography of Martin Luther King Jr.* (New York: Grove Press, 1965); Barbara Ransby, *Ella Baker and the Black Freedom Movement: A Radical Democratic Vision* (Chapel Hill: University of North Carolina Press, 2002); Manning Marable, *Malcolm X: A Life of Reinvention* (New York: Viking, 2011); and Jeanne Theoharis, *The Rebellious Life of Mrs. Rosa Parks* (Boston: Beacon Press, 2013). Important studies of major civil rights organizations include August Meier and Elliott Rudwick, *C. O. R. E. : A Study of the Civil Rights Movement* (New York: Oxford University Press, 1973); Clayborn Carson, *In Struggle: SNCC and the Black Awakening of the 1960s*, 2nd ed. (Cambridge, MA: Harvard University Press, 1995); Wesley C. Hogan, *Many Minds, One Heart: SNCC's Dream for a New America* (Chapel Hill: University of North Carolina Press, 2007); Adam Fairclough, *To Redeem the Soul of America: The Southern Christian Leadership Conference and Martin Luther King Jr.* (Athens: University of Georgia Press, 1987); and studies of the NAACP referenced above. Leigh Ann Wheeler, *How Sex Became a Civil Liberty* (New York: Oxford University Press, 2013) is essential to understand the ACLU's role in critical legal issues at the intersection of race, sex, and gender.

The Supreme Court's *Brown* decision was a turning point. Important treatments of the case include Richard Kuger, *Simple Justice* (New York: Random House, 1975); G. Edward White, *Earl Warren: A Biography* (New York: Oxford University Press, 1984); and Robert J. Cottrol, Raymond T. Diamond, and Leland B. Ware, *Brown v. Board of Education: Caste, Culture, and the Constitution* (Lawrence: University Press of Kansas, 2003). Gerald N. Rosenberg, *The Hollow Hope: Can Courts Bring About Social Change?* (Chicago: University of Chicago Press, 1991) and Michael J. Klarman, "How Brown Changed Race Relations: The Backlash Thesis," *Journal of American History* 81 (1994) and *From Jim Crow to Civil Rights: The Supreme Court and the Struggle for Racial Equality* (New York: Oxford University Press, 2004) argue that historians have exaggerated the significance of the Court in effecting change.

White southerners had no doubts about *Brown*'s significance, and they met the threat with a campaign of massive resistance. See Numan V. Bartley, *The Rise of Massive Resistance: Race and Politics in the South during the 1950s* (Baton Rouge: Louisiana State University Press, 1969); Neil McMillen, *The Citizens' Council: Organize Resistance to the Second Reconstruction, 1954–1964* (Urbana: University of Illinois Press, 1971); Dan T. Carter, *The Politics of Rage: George Wallace, the Origins of the New Conservatism, and the Transformation of American Politics* (New York: Simon & Schuster, 1995); Michael J. Klarman, *Brown v. Board of Education and the Civil Rights Movement* (New York: Oxford University Press, 2007); Kermit Hall and Melvin Urofsky, *The New York Times v. Sullivan: Civil Rights, Libel Law, and the Free Press* (Lawrence: University Press of Kansas, 2011); John Kyle Day, *The Southern Manifesto: Massive Resistance and the Fight to Preserve Segregation* (Jackson: University Press of Mississippi, 2014); Elizabeth Gillespie McRae, *Mothers of Massive Resistance: White Women and the Politics of Massive Resistance* (New York: Oxford University Press, 2018); and Stephanie R. Rolph, *Resisting Equality: The Citizens Council, 1954–1989* (Baton Rouge: Louisiana State University Press, 2018).

White resistance effectively blocked school desegregation efforts for almost a decade. See Jack W. Peltason, *Fifty-eight Lonely Men: Southern Federal Judges and School Desegregation* (New York: Harcourt, Brace & World, 1961); Benjamin Muse, *Ten Years of Prelude: The Story of Integration since the Supreme Court's 1954 Decision* (New York: Viking Press, 1964); J. Harvie Wilkinson III, *From Brown to Bakke: The Supreme Court and School Integration, 1954–1978* (New York: Oxford University Press, 1979); Jack Bass, *Unlikely Heroes* (New York: Simon & Schuster, 1981); Tinsley Yarbrough, *Judge Frank Johnson and Human Rights in Alabama* (Tuscaloosa: University of Alabama Press, 1981) and *A Passion for Justice: J. Waties Waring and Civil Rights* (New York: Oxford University Press, 1987); Tony A. Freyer, *Little Rock on Trial: Cooper v. Aaron and School Desegregation* (Lawrence: University Press of Kansas, 2007); Joel William Friedman, *Champion of Civil Rights: John Minor Wisdom* (Baton Rouge: Louisiana State University Press, 2009); Anne Emanuel, *Elbert Parr Tuttle: Chief Jurist of the Civil Rights Revolution* (Athens: University of Georgia Press, 2011); and Brian J. Daugherity, *Keep On Keepin' On: The NAACP and the Implementation of Brown v. Board of Education in Virginia* (Charlottesville: University of Virginia Press, 2016).

Conflict between civil rights activists and southern segregationists put pressure on the federal government—and especially Presidents Eisenhower, Kennedy, and Johnson—to act and ultimately led to adoption of transformative civil rights legislation. Some of the pressure came from national civil rights organizations as Doug McAdam, *Freedom Summer* (New York: Oxford University Press, 1988); Raymond Arsenault, *Freedom Riders: 1961 and the Struggle for Equal Justice* (New York: Oxford University Press, 2006); and Bruce Watson, *Freedom Summer: The Savage Season of 1964 That Made Mississippi Burn and America a Democracy* (New York: Viking, 2010) demonstrate. Grass-roots organizations also played an important role. See William H. Chafe, *Civilities and Civil Rights: Greensboro, North Carolina, and the Black Struggle for Freedom* (New York: Oxford University Press, 1980); Robert J. Norrell, *Reaping the Whirlwind: The Civil Rights Movement in Tuskegee* (New York: Knopf, 1985); John Dittmer, *Local People: The Struggle for Civil Rights in Mississippi* (Urbana: University of Illinois Press, 1994); Glenn T. Eskew, *But for Birmingham: The Local and National Movement in the Civil Rights Struggle* (Chapel Hill: University of North Carolina Press, 1997); Hassan Kwame Jeffries, *Bloody Lowndes: Civil Rights and Black Power in*

Alabama's Black Belt (New York: New York University Press, 2009); Tomiko Brown-Nagin, *Courage to Dissent: Atlanta and the Long History of the Civil Rights Movement* (New York: Oxford University Press, 2011); and Emilye Crosby, ed. , *Civil Rights History from the Ground Up: Local Struggles, A National Movement* (Athens: University of Georgia Press, 2011).

For the federal response to racial conflict and civil rights activists' demands for change see Robert Frederick Buck, *The Eisenhower Administration and Black Civil Rights* (Knoxville: University of Tennessee Press, 1984); David A. Nichols, *A Matter of Justice: Eisenhower and the Beginning of the Civil Rights Revolution* (New York: Simon & Schuster, 2007); James F. Simon, *Eisenhower and Warren: The Battle for Civil Rights and Civil Liberties* (New York: W. W. Norton & Co. , 2018); Carl M. Brauer, *John F. Kennedy and the Second Reconstruction* (Cambridge, MA: Harvard University Press, 1977); Steven Levingston, *Kennedy and King: The President, the Pastor, and the Battle over Civil Rights* (New York: Hachette Book Group, 2017); Nick Kotz, *Judgment Days: Lyndon Baines Johnson, Martin Luther King Jr. , and the Laws That Changed America* (New York: Houghton & Mifflin, 2005); Clay Risen, *The Bill of the Century: The Epic Battle for the Civil Rights Act* (New York: Bloomsbury, 2014); Steven F. Lawson, *Black Ballots: Voting Rights in the South, 1944–1969* (New York: Columbia University Press, 1976); David Garrow, *Protest at Selma: Martin Luther King Jr. and the Voting Rights Act of 1965* (New Haven: Yale University Press, 1978); Gary May, *Bending toward Justice: The Voting Rights Act and the Transformation of American Democracy* (New York: Basic Books, 2013); and Brian K. Landsberg, *Enforcing Civil Rights: Race Discrimination and the Department of Justice* (Lawrence: University Press of Kansas, 1997). Hugh Davis Graham, *The Civil Rights Era: Origins and Development of National Policy, 1960–1972* (New York: Oxford University Press, 1990) is an important interpretation of a decade of change in federal civil rights policy. Denton L. Watson, *The Lion in the Lobby: Clarence Mitchell Jr. 's Struggle for the Passage of Civil Rights Laws* (New York: William Morrow, 2002) is a biography of the NAACP's legendary congressional lobbyist.

Southern whites frequently unleashed violence against civil rights activists. The federal response to racist violence is the subject of Michal Belknap, *Federal Law and Southern Order: Racial Violence and Constitutional Conflict in the Post-Brown South* (Athens: University of Georgia Press, 1987); David Chalmers, *Backfire: How the Ku Klux Klan Helped the Civil Rights Movement* (Lanham, MD: Rowman & Littlefield, 2003); Howard Ball, *Murder in Mississippi: United States v. Price and the Struggle for Civil Rights* (Lawrence: University Press of Kansas, 2004); David Cunningham, *Klansville U. S. A. : The Rise and Fall of the Civil Rights Era Ku Klux Klan* (New York: Oxford University Press, 2013); and Renee C. Romano, *Racial Reckoning: Prosecuting America's Civil Rights Murders* (Cambridge, MA: Harvard University Press, 2014).

From the Civil Rights Movement to the Present

Presidents, champions of civil rights in the 1960s, have been less reliable allies in the past fifty years, as Republican presidents have pursued civil rights policies calculated to appeal to southern whites and blue-collar white men in the North. See Thomas Byrne Edsall and Mary D. Edsall, *Chain Reaction: The Impact of Race, Rights, and Taxes on American Politics* (New York: W. W. Norton, 1992); David T. Courtwright, *No Right Turn: Conservative Politics in a Liberal America* (Cambridge, MA: Harvard University Press, 2010); Donald

T. Critchlow, *The Conservative Ascendancy: How the Republican Right Rose to Power in Modern America*, 2nd ed. (Cambridge, MA: Harvard University Press, 2011); Dean J. Kotlowski, *Nixon's Civil Rights: Politics, Principle, and Policy* (Cambridge, MA: Harvard University Press, 2001); Burton I. Kaufman and Scott Kaufman, *The Presidency of Jimmy Carter*, 2nd ed. (Lawrence: University Press of Kansas, 2016); Raymond Wolters, *Right Turn: William Bradford Reynolds, the Reagan Administration, and Black Civil Rights* (New Brunswick, NJ: Transaction Books, 1996); John Robert Greene, *The Presidency of George H. W. Bush*, 2nd ed. (Lawrence: University Press of Kansas, 2015); and Thomas Sugrue, *Not Even Past: Barack Obama and the Burden of Race* (Princeton, NJ: Princeton University Press, 2010). For the role of the federal bureaucracy, see Charles R. Epp, *Making Rights Real: Activists, Bureaucrats, and the Creation of the Legalistic State* (Chicago: University of Chicago Press, 2009) and Hugh Davis Graham, *The Civil Rights Era* (1990).

Republican presidents have sought to move the Supreme Court—a champion of African American civil rights since the 1930s—to the right. Important studies that illuminate the Court's recent history include Vincent Blasi, ed. , *The Burger Court: The Counter-Revolution That Wasn't* (New Haven: Yale University Press, 1983); Michael J. Graetz and Linda Greehouse, *The Burger Court and the Rise of the Judicial Right* (New York: Simon & Schuster, 2016); Peter Irons, *Brennan vs. Rehnquist: The Battle for the Constitution* (New York: Knopf, 1994); Mark Tushnet, *A Court Divided: The Rehnquist Court and the Future of Constitutional Law* (New York: W. W. Norton, 2005) and *In the Balance: Law and Politics on the Roberts Court* (New York: W. W. Norton, 2013); Eric J. Segall, *Originalism as Faith* (New York: Cambridge University Press, 2018); Joan Biskupic, *Sandra Day O'Connor: How the First Woman on the Supreme Court Became Its Most Influential Justice* (New York: HarperCollins, 2005); Jane Mayer and Jill Abrahamson, *Strange Justice: The Selling of Clarence Thomas* (New York: Penguin Books, 1995); and Jane Sherron De Hart, *Ruth Bader Ginsburg: A Life* (New York: Knopf, 2018).

School desegregation had been a goal of civil rights advocates since the 1920s. *Brown*, reinforced by 1960s civil rights legislation and policies, advanced the cause in significant ways. Although the struggle continued in the 1970s and 1980s, civil rights advocates lost ground. See Gary Orfield, *Must We Bus? Segregated Schools and National Policy* (Washington, DC: Brookings Institution, 1978); Eleanor Wolf, *Trial and Error: The Detroit School Desegregation Case* (Detroit: Wayne State University Press, 1981); Daniel Monti, *A Semblance of Justice: St. Louis School Desegregation and Order in Urban America* (Columbia: University of Missouri Press, 1985); Bernard Schwartz, *Swann's Way: The School Busing Case and the Supreme Court* (New York: Oxford University Press, 1986); Paul Diamond, *Beyond Busing: Inside the Challenge of Urban Segregation* (Ann Arbor: University of Michigan Press, 1985); J. Anthony Lucas, *Common Ground: A Turbulent Deacde in the Lives of Three American Families* (New York: Knopf, 1985); Ronald P. Formisano, *Boston against Busing: Race, Class, and Ethnicity in the 1960s and 1970s* (Chapel Hill: University of North Carolina Press, 1991); Gary Orfield, Susan E. Eaton, and the Harvard Project on School Desegregation, *Dismantling Desegregation: The Quiet Reversal of Brown v. Board of Education* (New York: New Press, 1996); and Gregory S. Jacobs, *Getting around Brown: Desegregation, Development, and the Columbus Public Schools* (Columbus: Ohio State University Press, 1998); Peter Irons, *Jim Crow's Children: The Broken Promise of the Brown Decision* (New York: Viking, 2002); Kevin Kruse, *White Flight: Atlanta and the Making of Modern Conservatism* (Princeton, NJ: Princeton University Press, 2005); Frye P. Gaillard, *The Dream Long Deferred: The Landmark Struggle for Desegregation in North Carolina* (Chapel Hill: University of

North Carolina Press, 2006); Joyce A. Baugh, *The Detroit School Busing Case: Milliken v. Bradley and the Controversy over School Desegregation* (Lawrence: University Press of Kansas, 2011); Erica Frankenberg and Gary Orfield, eds. , *The Resegregation of Suburban Schools: A Hidden Crisis in American Education* (Cambridge, MA: Harvard Education Press, 2013); and Tracy E. K'Meyer, *From Brown to Meredith: The Long Struggle for School Desegregation in Louisville, Kentucky, 1954–2007* (Chapel Hill: University of North Carolina Press, 2013).

Although the 1970s saw important victories in the battle against discrimination in the workplace, affirmative action generated controversy that has persisted and become a political wedge issue. On the struggle for and controversies over workplace equity, see Paul Burstein, *Discrimination, Jobs, and Politics: The Struggle for Equal Employment Opportunity in the United States since the New Deal* (Chicago: University of Chicago Press, 1985); Howard Ball, *The Bakke Case: Race Education and Affirmative Action* (Lawrence: University Press of Kansas, 2000); Terry H. Anderson, *In Pursuit of Fairness: A History of Affirmative Action* (New York: Oxford University Press, 2004); Ira Katznelson, *When Affirmative Action Was White: An Untold History of Racial Inequality in Twentieth-Century America* (New York: W. W. Norton, 2005); Nancy Maclean, *Freedom Is Not Enough: The Opening of the American Workplace* (Cambridge, MA: Harvard University Press, 2006); Kevin Yull, *Richard Nixon and the Rise of Affirmative Action: The Pursuit of Racial Equality in an Era of Limits* (Lanham, MD: Rowman & Littlefield, 2006); Barbara A. Perry, *The Michigan Affirmative Action Cases* (Lawrence: University Press of Kansas, 2007); Robert Samuel Smith, *Race, Labor, and Civil Rights: Griggs versus Duke Power and Struggle for Equal Employment Opportunity* (Baton Rouge: Louisana State University Press, 2008); Randall Kennedy, *For Discrimination: Race, Affirmative Action, and the Law* (New York: Random House, 2013); Nancy DiTomaso, *The American Non-Dilemma: Racial Inequality without Racism* (New York: Russell Sage Foundation, 2013); John D. Skrentny, *After Civil Rights: Racial Realism in the New American Workplace* (Princeton, NJ: Princeton University Press, 2014); Gillian Thomas, *Because of Sex: One Law, Ten Cases, and Fifty Years That Changed American Women's Lives at Work* (New York: St. Martin's Press, 2016); Leigh Ann Wheeler, *How Sex Became a Civil Liberty* (New York: Oxford University Press, 2013); Karen Williamson Pedrick and Sandra Arnold Scham, *Inside Affirmative Action: The Executive Order That Transformed America* (New York: Routledge, 2019).

A powerful barrier to African American economic progress has been deindustrialization and the emergence of a service economy. See William Julius Wilson, *The Declining Significance of Race* (Chicago: University of Chicago Press, 1978), *The Truly Disadvantaged* (Chicago: University of Chicago Press, 1987), and *More than Just Race: Being Black and Poor in the Inner City* (New York: W. W. Norton, 2009); Brendan O'Flaherty, *The Economics of Race in the United States* (Cambridge, MA: Harvard University Press, 2015); Andrea Flynn, Dorian T. Warren, and Felicia J. Wong, *The Hidden Rules of Race: Barriers to an Inclusive Economy* (New York: Cambridge University Press, 2017); Premilla Nadasen, *Welfare Warriors: The Welfare Rights Movement in the United States* (New York: Routledge, 2005); Bart Landry, *The New Black Middle Class in the Twenty-first Century* (Berkeley: University of California Press, 2018).

Ending disfranchisement and expanding black political power was a major accomplishment of the civil rights movement. Civil rights advocates won major victories in the 1970s and 1980s to assure that African Americans not only had access to the ballot box but also had opportunities to elect candidates of their choice. See Chandler Davidson, ed. , *Minority Vote Dilution* (1984); Steven F. Lawson, *In Pursuit of Power: Southern Blacks and Electoral Politics, 1965–1982* (New York: Columbia University Press, 1985); Chandler Davidson and Bernard Grofman, eds. , *Quiet Revolution in the South: The Impact of the Voting Rights Act, 1965–1990* (Princeton, NJ: Princeton University Press, 1994); and Loughlin McDonald, *A Voting Rights Odyssey: Black Enfranchisement in Georgia* (New York: Cambridge University Press, 2003). The 1980s and 1990s saw growing conservative opposition to broad interpretation of the Voting Rights Act. The most influential statement of the conservative position is Abigail Thernstrom, *Whose Votes Counts?: Affirmative Action and Minority Voting Rights* (Cambridge, MA: Harvard University Press, 1987). A conservative Supreme Court limited the Voting Rights Act in the 1990s and 2000s. See J. Morgan Kousser, *Colorblind Injustice: Minority Voting Rights and the Undoing of the Second Reconstruction* (Chapel Hill: University of North Carolina Press 1999); Tinsley Yarbrough, *Race and Redistricting: The Shaw-Cromartie Cases* (Lawrence: University Press of Kansas, 2002); Ari Berman, *Give Us the Ballot: The Modern Struggle for Voting Rights in America* (New York: Macmillan, 2015); Charles Bullock III, Ronald Keith Gaddie, and Justin J. Wert, *The Rise and Fall of the Voting Rights Act* (Norman: University of Oklahoma Press, 2016); and Jesse H. Rhodes, *Ballot Blocked: The Political Erosion of the Voting Rights Act* (Palo Alto, CA: Stanford University Press, 2017). Concerns about voter fraud have been increasingly used to restrict the right to vote. See Lorraine C. Minnite, *The Myth of Voter Fraud* (Ithaca, NY: Cornell University Press, 2010) and Carol Anderson, *One Person, No Vote: How Voter Suppression Is Destroying Democracy* (New York: Bloomsbury, 2018).

The war on crime of the 1970s and the war on drugs of the 1980s and 1990s created a criminal justice system that threatened the liberty of millions of Africans Americans. The most influential study of this phenomenon, Michelle Alexander, *The New Jim Crow: Mass Incarceration in the Age of Colorblindness* (New York: New Press, 2010), likens the consequences to the system the civil rights movement ostensibly toppled. See also Michael W. Flamm, *Law and Order: Street Crime, Civil Unrest, and the Crisis of Liberalism in the 1960s* (New York: Columbia University Press, 2005); Wesley Lowrey, *They Can't Kill Us All: The Story of the Struggle for Black Lives* (New York: Little, Brown, 2016); Paul Butler, *Chokehold: Policing Black Men* (New York: New Press, 2017); James Forman Jr. , *Locking Up Our Own: Crime and Punishment in Black America* (New York: Farrar, Straus & Giroux, 2017); Elizabeth Hinton, *From the War on Poverty to the War on Crime* (Cambridge, MA: Harvard University Press, 2017); US Department of Justice, *Federal Reports on Police Killings: Ferguson, Cleveland, Baltimore, and Chicago* (Brooklyn, NY: Melville House Publishing, 2017); and Clarence Taylor, *Fight the Power: African Americans and Police Brutality in New York City* (New York: New York University Press, 2018).

Index

For the benefit of digital users, indexed terms that span two pages (e.g., 52–53) may, on occasion, appear on only one of those pages.